The Musical Gift

Critical Conjunctures in

Music & Sound

Series Editors Jairo Moreno and Gavin Steingo

Composing the World: Harmony in the Medieval Platonic Cosmos, Andrew Hicks

Music and Belonging Between Revolution and Restoration,
Naomi Waltham-Smith

The Musical Gift: Sonic Generosity in Post-War Sri Lanka, Jim Sykes

The Musical Gift

Sonic Generosity in Post-War Sri Lanka

JIM SYKES

Oxford University Press is a department of the University of Oxford. It furthers
the University's objective of excellence in research, scholarship, and education
by publishing worldwide. Oxford is a registered trade mark of Oxford University
Press in the UK and certain other countries.

Published in the United States of America by Oxford University Press
198 Madison Avenue, New York, NY 10016, United States of America.

© Oxford University Press 2018

First issued as an Oxford University Press paperback, 2020

All rights reserved. No part of this publication may be reproduced, stored in
a retrieval system, or transmitted, in any form or by any means, without the
prior permission in writing of Oxford University Press, or as expressly permitted
by law, by license, or under terms agreed with the appropriate reproduction
rights organization. Inquiries concerning reproduction outside the scope of the
above should be sent to the Rights Department, Oxford University Press, at the
address above.

You must not circulate this work in any other form
and you must impose this same condition on any acquirer.

Library of Congress Cataloging-in-Publication Data
Names: Sykes, Jim, 1976– author.
Title: The musical gift : sonic generosity in post-war Sri Lanka / Jim Sykes.
Description: New York, NY : Oxford University Press, [2018] |
Includes bibliographical references and index.
Identifiers: LCCN 2018008557 | ISBN 9780190912024 (hardcover) |
ISBN 9780190077143 (paperback) | ISBN 9780190912055 (online component)
Subjects: LCSH: Music—Social aspects—Sri Lanka. | Music—Sri Lanka—History and criticism.
Classification: LCC ML3917.S75 S94 2018 | DDC 780.95493—dc23
LC record available at https://lccn.loc.gov/2018008557

This volume is published with the generous support of the AMS 75 PAYS Endowment of the
American Musicological Society, funded in part by the National Endowment for the Humanities and
the Andrew W. Mellon Foundation.

> But when their rhythms
>   mesh
> then though the pain of living
>   never lets up
>
>   the singing begins.
>
> —Denise Levertov (2002: 97)

CONTENTS

Preface ix
Acknowledgments xvii
Note on Transliteration xix
Supplementary Materials xxi

PART I   FINDING MUSICAL GIFTS

Introduction: For a Musicology of Karma and Reincarnation   3

1. Sonic Generosity: Beyond Secularism and Conflict in Music Studies   15

PART II   MUSICAL GIVING AS PROTECTION AND DESTRUCTION

Checkpoint: *Musical Gifts and the Movement of Ghosts*   63

2. Beravā Secrecy and the Hoarding of Musical Gifts   69

3. Sri Lankan Tamil Musical Giving: An Introduction   97

4. The Cartography of Culture Zones: Social Relations and the Conversion of Sonic Money   119

PART III   THE DISCURSIVE ERASURE OF MUSICAL GIVING

5. Beyond the Musicology of Disaster: War, Tsunami, Post-War   165

Checkpoint: *The Malays Who Sing in Six Languages*   195

Checkpoint: *Sound as Commodity (Identity) versus Sound as Gift (Identity + Relations)*   208

6. The Island Space: Music, Buddhism, and the Sinhalas   210

PART IV   REDISCOVERING MUSICAL GIVING

Checkpoint: *Re-Connecting Sinhala and Tamil Musical Cultures*   229

Conclusion: The Regulation of Happiness in Post-War Sri Lanka   236

References   241
Index   255

PREFACE

In this book, I argue that the premier philosophy of nineteenth-century Britain, political liberalism, as well as tendencies internal to Sri Lankan discourses on ethnic and religious identities, combined in postcolonial Sri Lanka to define traditional music as a sphere for the articulation of communal difference. This book is a study of how Sri Lanka's Sinhala Buddhist ethnic majority and Tamil minority became conceived as having thoroughly separate music histories—two communities deemed to be on opposite sides of the island's long-standing civil war (1983–2009).[1] I argue that in Sri Lanka's postcolonial period, traditional music (with its counterpart, dance) became a key mode through which the Sinhala-dominated state and Tamil separatists formulated regional identities and ideologies of territorial separation. However, this book is less a study of music's entanglements with rival nationalisms than it is an attempt to decolonize Sri Lankan music history and dislodge the island's traditional musics from their internal difference-making tendencies. I produce an alternative history of musical connections between Sinhalas, Tamils, and other Sri Lankans—based on what I will argue is a pan–Sri Lankan aesthetic of musical gift-giving that emerges differently in different contexts and traditions—and ask how the recognition of such connections might productively contribute to post-war reconciliation.

My starting point for doing so is a study of sonic efficacy attuned to Buddhist notions of the not-self (*anatta*) and gift, drawing on the sonic offerings (*sabda pujāva*) made to the Buddha and deities by a caste of Sinhala Buddhist ritualists

---

[1] The Sinhalese are Sri Lanka's ethnic majority, 74% of the population. The war was fought by numerous Tamil rebel groups, most notably the Liberation Tigers of Tamil Eelam (LTTE), for an independent Tamil nation (Eelam) in their traditional homelands of the north and east. Demographics in Sri Lanka are highly politicized; for now I'll say the numbers of Tamils are typically estimated as between 12% and 18%. Bear in mind that Sri Lanka is a radically diverse place, with numerous other distinct populations I introduce later on.

called the Beravā.² In ritual contexts, the Beravā give musical and other gifts to the divine sovereign powers to ask them to protect the Sinhala community from calamities like drought, pestilence, and disease. Branching out from the Beravā, I use the notions of sonic generosity and musical giving more broadly to show that Sri Lankan music history is characterized by multi-ethnic, human-divine, human-demon, and human-nonhuman animal interactions, processes that involve giving, borrowing, taking, and hoarding music/sound, which in turn facilitate complex sets of relations demonstrating communal differences, similarities, and connected histories across various levels of being and vast swaths of land. Bringing "the gift" into music studies formally for the first time, I argue that liberalism (and its offshoot, secularism) mandated certain relations between the self, community, sound, and territory that obscured histories of sonic exchange. I contend this positioned music (and dance) as definitive of community and a community's historical attachment to land in a way that laid discursive groundwork for the ideologies of ethnic separation that continue to drive Sri Lanka's myriad communal conflicts in the island's post-war period. This book, then, uses a study of sonic exchange to produce a music history in which music sometimes originates with and is offered to gods, is used against evil spirits or demons, and can travel across vast geographic spaces when given by one population to another, connecting ethnic and religious groups now considered to have separate "cultures."

In doing so, *The Musical Gift* considers the political implications of anthropology's "ontological turn" for discourses on the nation and identity in music studies by asking, how does the recognition of nonhumans as actors, as well as broader geographies of sonic exchanges between humans who belong to different ethnic and religious groups, affect the ways we conceive of a country's music history? While Sinhala Buddhist religious contexts are my initial focus, I argue that traditions of nonhuman musical exchange linked to (and *linking*) Sinhala Buddhism, Tamil Hinduism, and other Sri Lankan religious traditions were adopted in Sri Lankan modernity as approaches to music in secular contexts. Foremost among them is the idea that musical gifts are gestures of respect and ways of caring for Others that are also ways of caring for oneself, because of the pleasant response musical offerings generate. The book is thus less a study of the transformation of an indigenous aesthetic system in modernity than a study of its persistence. It also aims to firmly implant "the gift" in the emerging field of economic ethnomusicology, which has predominantly focused on musical commoditization.

My ethnographic focus in what follows is three elder, male culture-bearers from distinct ethnic groups—one Sinhala, one Tamil, and one from Sri Lanka's

---

² The majority of Sinhalese are Theravada Buddhists, the type of Buddhism that is prevalent throughout Southeast Asia. "Beravā" means "drummer," but the Beravā perform a wide array of Ayurvedic medicinal practices (including astrology and dancing) that I spell out in Chapter 1.

tiny Malay (Muslim) community—who embody histories of sonic exchange and have suffered because of and/or acted out against the idea that music simply is about the expression of ethnic and regional identity.[3] This book, then, is an idealistic attempt to build a less-ethnicized cultural history for Sri Lanka's post-war period by attending to Sri Lankan musicians and their aesthetics. In turn, it is also a critique of the symbiosis between normative approaches to "community" in ethnomusicology—in which scholars typically focus on a single community and how their music expresses belonging in a nation-state—and ethnonationalist discourses that do not recognize communal relations and exchanges as valid for narratives on ethnic and national cultural histories.[4]

All this being said, in what follows I do not romanticize the gift. I find in Sri Lanka's sonic economies the adoption and adaptation of ideas, the occasional rejection of ideas, and respect and competition shown between individuals I call "musical givers." I show that musical gift-giving facilitates social hierarchies and that musical gifts do not always circulate freely: for example, the Beravā are a low caste in Sinhala society, and their musical offerings to the Buddha and gods are their "inalienable possessions," in the terms provided by Annette Weiner (1992). Furthermore, since Beravā rituals shield people from calamity, they have long been used to protect Sinhala Buddhists *from* Others. For instance, during Sri Lanka's war, the state organized Beravā rituals that were both nationalistic "cultural displays" (*sandharsana*) of ethnic pride intended as entertainment and efficacious rituals that protected soldiers fighting in the war (De Silva 2000: 46). I foreground a paradox at the heart of Sri Lankan music history: On the one hand, it is defined by the incorporation of the Other's sonic techniques (e.g., musical instruments and ideas) through acts of musical giving, yet on the other hand, musical giving shields people from Others when they are deemed a threat. This paradox is foundational for Beravā drumming, whose very name is thought to be a Sinhala-ization of the word for the outcaste Tamil drummers called Paraiyars, and who in premodern times protected kings from outside forces, including invading Tamil forces.

Thus I do not build a dialectic between the gift and identity in this book, though I do argue that identity discourses about music hide the evidence available

---

[3] I regret that I do not focus on women enough in this book. However, Sri Lanka is rare in that there have been *more* ethnographic studies in the English-language sources of women musicians and dancers than men, and I encourage readers to put my work in dialogue with these studies, e.g., Reed (2010), De Mel (2006), Sheeran (1997), and Claus-Bachmann (2004).

[4] I find that the eastern Indian Ocean Region differs substantially from the Caribbean in this regard. In Cuba, for instance, Afro-Cuban musics are celebrated as hybrid and as articulating national identity. By contrast, in Sri Lanka and elsewhere in the eastern Indian Ocean Region (e.g., Malaysia), national music histories are articulated according to narratives of ethnic, religious, and regional difference, despite their embodiment of histories of communal interaction. For example, in Malaysia, both Malays and Indians tend to emphasize differences between Malay and Indian traditional cultures (Willford 2006), despite the Indian influences embedded in many Malay musical traditions.

to refute them. Should such histories of inter-ethnic musical interaction and exchange *matter* for post-war Sri Lanka? What *is* reconciliation, and what role might formations of cultural history play in producing it? What are the political impacts *for humans* of recognizing nonhumans as actors in music history? And how does the persistence of musical giving in the modern world force us to reshape the narratives we use to describe musical modernity? These are some of the questions that animate this book. While I do write against Sinhala and Tamil nationalist appropriations of culture in what follows, this is a book that respects them, too: for while I explore histories communal relations through music, in the process I set up Sinhala, Tamil, and other Sri Lankan communities as having distinct music histories. My perspective is one that recognizes that people have differences, but also that they have often gotten along. And it is the memory of this, I suggest, that is critical for building a stable peace in post-war Sri Lanka.

"Sri Lankan Music? Haven't You Traveled a Bit Too Far South?"

When I first began studying Sri Lanka long ago (in 2004) as a drummer with experience living in North India, the island's Sinhala Buddhist majority could not have been more off the beaten path for an ethnomusicologist.[5] To this day, Sri Lanka has received less ethnomusicological attention than virtually any other country in the world. Even Myanmar drew far more ethnomusicologists during its years of military dictatorship. Initially, I could not locate any book that summarized music on the island (save for a few short texts that were already several decades old); nor could I find a book that provided a detailed study of a Sri Lankan musical aesthetic system, let alone a book written in an ethnographic, theoretically-oriented style that considered the politics of music-making on the island. The musics of Sri Lanka's Tamil and Muslim minorities in particular were so unknown in the late 1990s that when Anne Sheeran produced a well-researched (1998) essay on Sri Lanka for the *Garland Encyclopedia of Music*, she had to admit she could not say anything about them. This was during the war years, and Sri Lanka's Tamil-dominated north was more or less off limits to researchers from the early 1980s through the early 2010s. Just to drive home how dire the situation was, I was told at the beginning of this project by a senior Sri Lankanist colleague that the U.S. Fulbright Program did not offer scholarships to study music in Sri Lanka until about the mid-1990s because it was assumed Sri Lankan music doesn't exist! This

---

[5] The question that leads off this section was uttered by a Colombo resident to the anthropologist Anne Sheeran (1997: 1) in the mid-1990s, when Sheeran told the person she was in Sri Lanka to do a research project on Sri Lankan music. The resident was noting, of course, the far greater musical reputation owned by Sri Lanka's giant northern neighbor, India.

was the first time I ran into the belief that Sri Lankan musics are simply derivative of Indian musics—that studying music in Sri Lanka is going a bit too far south—and it wouldn't be the last.[6]

I now know that my initial assumptions were wrong—there are in fact many fine writings on Sri Lankan musics, most by Sri Lankan authors writing in Sinhala, Tamil, and English. These include numerous dissertations on Sri Lankan musicological topics by scholars at universities in Sri Lanka, India, North America, Britain, New Zealand, Germany, and elsewhere. Detailed articles on Sri Lankan musics now routinely appear in Sri Lankan newspapers and well-known blogs like *Groundviews* and Michael Roberts' *Tuppahi* blog, providing nuanced considerations of musicological topics that were absent from the literature a decade ago. Even so, these writings are barely known outside Sri Lankan studies. In fact, even the very basics of Sri Lankanist anthropology and a cursory knowledge of the island's musical genres remain unknown to virtually *all* ethnomusicologists, even those working on South Asia (even those working on South India!). I provide reasons for this absence throughout, but suffice it to say here that ethnomusicology has long foregrounded India and Indonesia, cutting a line down the Bay of Bengal, forgetting the historical importance of the Indian Ocean while separating Theravada Buddhist-majority Sri Lanka (into "South Asia") from the other Theravada-majority countries ("Southeast Asia"). Buddhism gained a reputation in the West as an unmusical or silent religion, while even in Sri Lanka it is commonly assumed that Buddhist prohibitions against music stunted the growth of a Sinhala musical tradition (see Chapter 1). And because of what I describe later as "Beravā secrecy," even in Sri Lankan studies, technical aspects of Beravā drumming remain wildly under-researched. Thus I entered a world that was decades if not a hundred years behind the musicological scholarship of India and Indonesia—though I learned this was not because Sri Lanka is a musically derivative or unmusical place.

I turned to Sri Lanka because I was fascinated by recordings I heard of low-country (Beravā) drumming, the drum usually called *yak beraya* ("demon drum," also known as the "low country drum," *pahata rata beraya*). Consisting of repetitive patterns that generally do not sound as though they are in a time signature or beat cycle, I could tell there was a logic behind the drumming but could not figure out what it was. Given my initial impression that Sri Lanka is a musical backwater from India, I was surprised to hear drumming so unlike Indian traditions, and I was intrigued.[7] By contrast, the Carnatic classical music tradition

---

[6] Sri Lanka is frequently described as a "teardrop off the coast of India." I try to nuance this relationship with India throughout this book, both acknowledging it and broader Indian Ocean influences as relevant for Sri Lankan music history, while identifying Sri Lanka as its own musical sphere with a unique music history all its own.

[7] Again, the issue is nuancing the relationship to India: in what follows, I argue that Beravā drumming developed in dialogue with Indian (and other) traditions but took on a Buddhist shape that has left it utterly different from Indian drumming styles.

of Tamil-majority South India is one of the most studied topics in ethnomusicology, so I was initially less interested in Sri Lankan Tamil musics (nor did I have any clue about the musics of other communities on the island).[8]

Upon "relocating" my academic interests to Sri Lanka, however, I found that the situation in Sri Lankan studies was precisely reversed. The Sinhala Buddhist low-country rituals that contain the drumming I was so intrigued by have long been the most researched anthropological topic on the island—to some peoples' minds, over-researched. What was a hot topic from an ethnomusicological perspective was a dated one from an anthropological perspective. Low country rituals received *so* much attention from the 1950s through the 1990s (e.g., Wirz 1954; Tambiah 1968; Kapferer 1983, 1997; Obeyesekere 1984; Scott 1994; Vogt 1998) that over the past twenty years or so, anthropologists have seemingly turned their attention toward anything *but* what I was studying, focusing particularly on the plight of Tamils and Muslims during the war and after it. I came to learn, as well, that while Sri Lankan Tamil musicians have long contributed to and share a music history with South Indian Tamils, there are unique Sri Lankan Tamil musical techniques, practices, and genres, including regional musical differences *within* Sri Lankan Tamil society. As mentioned above, I also found out that Sri Lankans of various stripes have contributed *together* to the island's music history in ways that belie a strictly ethnic music history, contradicting the widespread notion in the international community that the island is strictly ethnically divided.

While I remain committed to the politics of locality, and I hope this is evident throughout the book, this project developed into the kind of "national" estimation of Sri Lankan musics that I found to be lacking when I started the project. While I intended to write a study of low country Beravā drumming (details of musical techniques, analyses of music in rituals, and a historical study of low-country drummers) set within a broader context of the politics of music-making in Sri Lanka, this book developed into something different. The "big picture" of Sri Lankan musics, I decided, needed first to be better brought into ethnomusicology in order for that smaller-scale study to be properly understood.[9] This is because

---

[8] While Tamils are a minority in Sri Lanka, they are the ethnic majority of South India, where over 60 million live in the South Indian state of Tamil Nadu. Tamils are a large minority in Malaysia, Singapore, Myanmar, Mauritius, and South Africa, places where they migrated as laborers in the British colonial period, particularly for work on rubber and sugar plantations. There is also a small number of Tamils of Indian descent in the Sri Lankan hill country (Malaiyaha or Estate Tamils) who moved there in the colonial period to work on tea plantations.

[9] For that detailed study of low-country Sinhala drum speech, techniques, and accompanying videos of *yak beraya* drumming, see my essays "South Asian Drumming Beyond Tala: The Problem with 'Meter' in Buddhist Sri Lanka" and "On the Sonic Materialization of Buddhist History: Drum Speech in Southern Sri Lanka," as well as my fieldwork videos posted on the *AAWM* journal website: http://www.aawmjournal.com/. This material is intended to complement this book, and I refer readers to those videos should you want to hear the Sinhala Buddhist drumming I am talking about. Periodically

the ways that Sri Lankan musical genres are assigned to different ethnic groups and regions operates through a historical amnesia that obscures their historical relations in favor of narratives of ethnic musical purity that serve Sinhala and Tamil nationalist interests. In what follows, I argue that this has created problems for the low country drummers I worked with, by granting them a low status in Sri Lanka's cultural hierarchy while also misrepresenting their aesthetics of musical giving and history of connection with Others.

In this book, then, my primary research on drum strokes and analyses of ritual has been pushed aside in favor of a comparative study that brings into dialogue the voluminous, yet to date disparately situated, studies of Sri Lankan musics across the island. I hope my anthropologist friends can see that the ways the conceptualization and carving up of the "national" (so far as conceptions of Sri Lankan musics are concerned) has a rather shocking determining affect on how local Sri Lankan musical lives are lived. The intervention I needed to make was at this national level—a reconceptualization of what Sri Lankan musics *are* and how genres, populations, and regions are deemed to relate musically—in order to challenge dynamics that I felt were negatively affecting the low country drummers I was working with. This book can best be thought of as a critical geography of Sri Lankan musics. I respond to Sri Lanka's post-war dynamics in ways that will hopefully be relevant for Sri Lanka-focused readers, while finally bringing the island into ethnomusicology at a more substantial level.

throughout this book, I suggest certain YouTube searches and videos pertaining to other Sri Lankan musical genres.

ACKNOWLEDGMENTS

I need to thank the low-country drummers I worked with, particularly my teacher (*gurunnānse*) Herbert Dayasheela, master drummer, dancer, ritual specialist (*kattadirala*), and healer of the Bentara Korale in low-country Sri Lanka. I owe a debt of gratitude to low-country ritual master W. Edin and master Kandyan drummers Piyasara Shilpadhipathi and Ravibandu Vidyapathi. Thanks to Tamil *kooththu* master Sinniah Maunaguru and the late Kartigesu Sivathamby, who were supportive of this project. So many Sri Lankans made me feel welcome: Adhil Aziz and Aftab Aziz are guitar legends. The Perera family (Sarani's guitar solos, Uvindu's bassist humor, Kakuli's drumming, and Mr. and Mrs. Perera's violin playing and singing) provided an extraordinary home base. Pabalu provided drum skills and metalhead wizardry. Rohana Wasantha read the stars (literally). Dharmasiri Bandaranayake provided guidance and courage. Thanks to: Eshantha Peiris, Sumudi Suraweera, and the Musicmatters crew; Praveen Vijayakumar; Dany Dilshon; Natasha Senanayake; Sathyan; the University of Jaffna; late Professor Tissa Kariyawasam, who provided initial guidance; Social Scientists' Association; American Institute for Sri Lankan Studies; Eastern University (Batticaloa); Jeyasankar Sivagnanam; and John Rogers, John Holt, and Dennis McGilvray for not laughing me out the door. Vivian Choi, Alessandra Radicati, and Peter Slomanson provided lifelines.

This book would surely not have been possible without another ritual specialist and healer (of a different sort), Philip V. Bohlman. Thanks to the rest of my committee who read this work in its initial guise as a dissertation at the University of Chicago: Martin Stokes, Kaley Mason, Steven Collins, and Berthold Hoeckner. At Chicago, numerous *shisyas* turned into *gurunnānses* when I needed an ear: Jamie Jones, Melissa Reilly, Majel Connery, Shayna Silverstein, Rumya Putcha, Suzi Wint, Rehanna Keshgi, Adrienne Alton-Gust, Josh Pilzer, Jeffers Engelhardt, Byron Dueck, and Rich Jankowsky. Thanks to my cohort at King's College London where I was a postdoctoral fellow: Katherine Schofield remains an inspiration, as does the rest of the "transitions" crew—Julia Byl, David Irving,

Jim Kippen, Meg Walker, Larry Hilarian, Jenny McCallum, and Adil Johan. At my new home at the University of Pennsylvania, numerous individuals deserve thanks, particularly Timothy Rommen, Carol Muller, Jairo Moreno, Naomi Waltham-Smith, Guthrie Ramsey, Glenda Goodman, Mary Caldwell, Justin McDaniel, Lisa Mitchell, Teren Sevea, and Davesh Soneji, and an amazing array of graduate students (who truly deserve a collective thanks). Thanks especially to Lee Veeraraghavan for her hard work on the index. Thanks to the Yale Institute of Sacred Music, which handled me as I hoarded my musical gifts in this project's final stages. And special thanks to Suzanne Ryan, Gavin Steingo, Jamie Kim, and the three anonymous peer-reviewers, all of whom thoroughly whacked this project into shape in its final stages. The journey was made possible by nonmusical gifts from the Mellon Foundation, Fulbright-Hays DDRA, Wenner-Gren Foundation, and the Department of Music and Committee for South Asian Studies at the University of Chicago. Lindsay Aveilhe deserves special mention for her support at the beginning of this project. The Coffee Bean provided Internet, James C. Scott and Elizabeth Povinelli provided inspiration. My partner Lauren Flood deserves more credit than I can possibly muster for her patient ear and thorough consideration of every idea in this book, even the bad ones. Thanks to the Sykes family: I dedicate this book to my father, George Sykes Sr.—what follows may not be a biography of Lincoln, but it is somehow about a civil war. Lastly, how can I forget Cassiere and Tony Hassan: thanks for demonstrating that tolerance and love will continue to thrive despite those motivated by guns and bombs. Cassiere, you are deeply missed. As one says on the low-country drum at the end of a *magul bera* (auspicious drumming for the Buddha): *tat tat gum*!

NOTE ON TRANSLITERATION

In this book, I adopt a stripped down approach to Sinhala transliteration that is largely devoid of diacritics (for a similar approach, see Reed 2010 and Kapferer 1997). I italicize Sinhala words and adopt the standard convention of adding *s* to plural nouns (*pada* becomes *padas*), with one significant exception: I use *beraya* (drum) in the singular and *bera* (drums) in the plural. Besides this, I use *ā* to signify a long "ah" sound (like the vowel in "father"); Sinhala words with the letter *a* without this marking are pronounced like the vowel in the word "cup." The letter *ä* (e.g., *horanäva*) is pronounced like the vowel in "bat."

In contrast to the stripped down Sinhala transliteration, for Tamil words I adopt the standard convention of using the University of Madras Tamil Lexicon (1982) system of transliteration, except for words of Sanskrit origin. Tamil words that have a common English appearance (names of famous composers like Tyagaraja, instruments like the *mridangam*, place names, and already-transliterated place names like Yazhpanam—a common way to spell the Tamil name for the city of Jaffna) I write without diacritics. Also, I do not use diacritics for words that have an accepted English transliteration in the Sri Lankan (rather than South Indian) Tamil context (*kooththu* rather than *kūttu*).

Finally, I leave the spellings of Sinhala and Tamil words in quotations the way they appear in the original sources.

SUPPLEMENTARY MATERIALS

The core musical instrument at the heart of this book is the "low-country drum" (*pahata rata beraya*), associated with Sinhala Buddhists (Sri Lanka's ethnic majority) who live in the island's southern coastal region. Readers are encouraged to visit the website for the journal *Analytical Approaches to World Music* (http://www.aawmjournal.com/), where one will find two articles written by the author of this book: "South Asian Drumming Beyond Tala: The Problem with 'Meter' in Buddhist Sri Lanka" and "On the Sonic Materialization of Buddhist History: Drum Speech in Southern Sri Lanka." These articles are accompanied by numerous instructional videos of my *gurunnānse* (teacher) demonstrating how to play the low-country drum, as well as footage of low-country rituals I recorded. This material can be considered an extension of Chapter 2.

For readers interested in other musical genres described in this book, I recommend simple YouTube searches. One can search for the following terms: Kandyan Dance; Kohomba Kankariya; Jaffna kooththu; Batticaloa kooththu; Jaffna parai; Batticaloa parai; Sri Lanka Malaiyaha kooththu; Sinhala nadagam; Sri Lanka baila; Sri Lanka Burghers music; Sri Lanka Kaffir music; Sri Lanka rifai ratib. Specific links are provided in the text, and readers are encouraged to search for the name of any artist mentioned in the book.

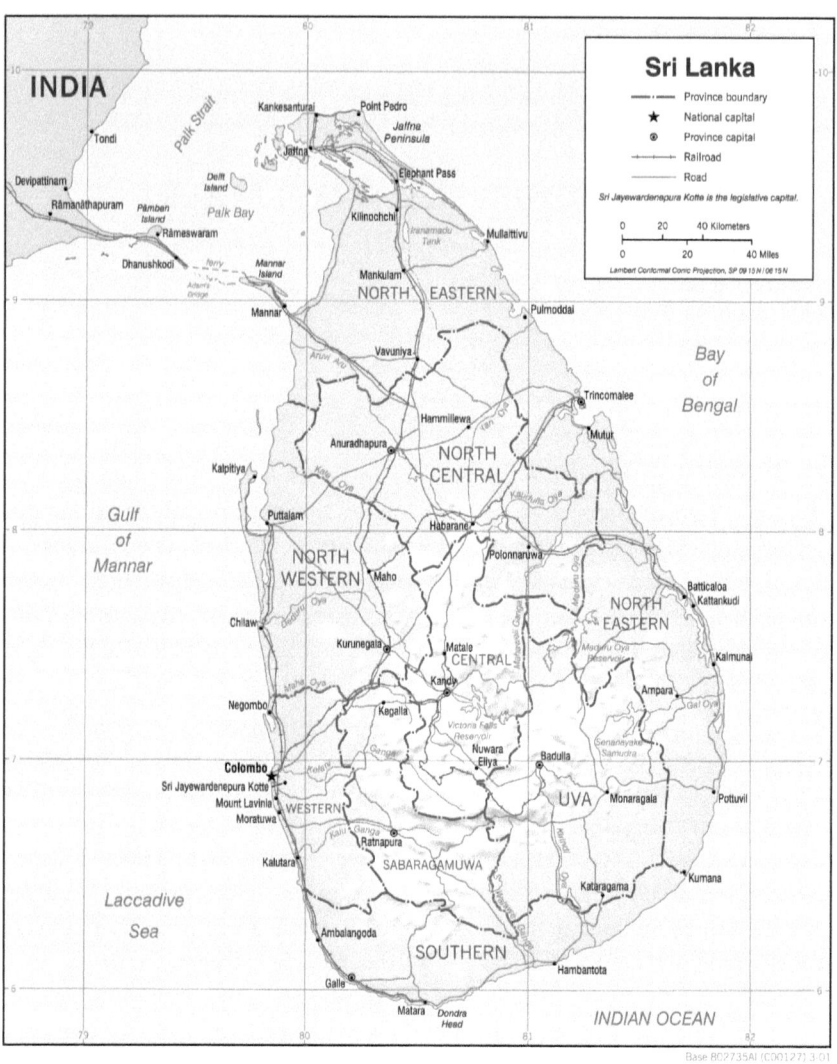

Map of Sri Lanka.

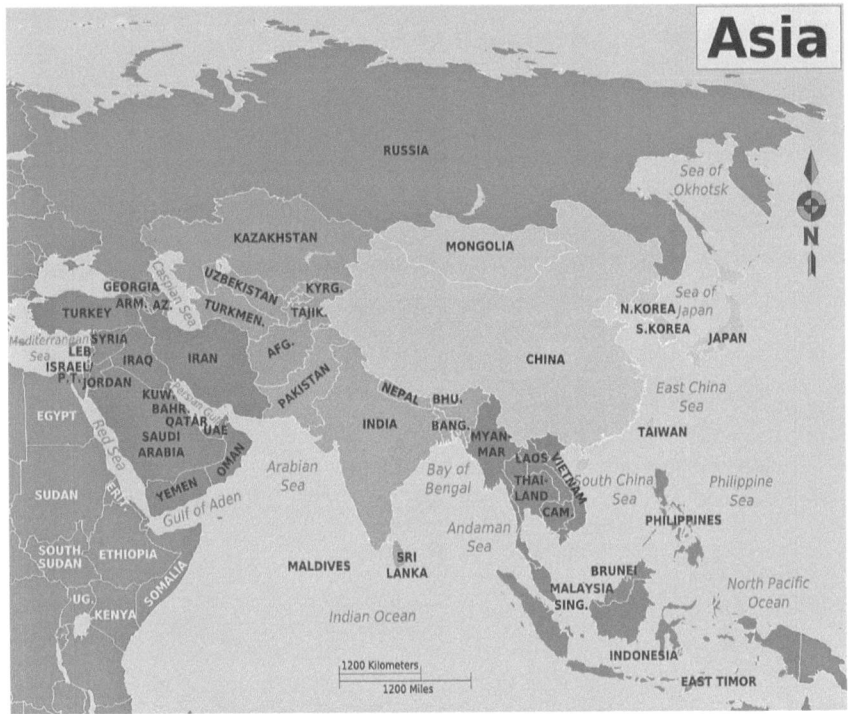

Sri Lanka and the Indian Ocean.

Map by Cacahuate with amendments by Peter Fitzgerald, Globe-trotter, Joelf, and Texugo [CC BY-SA 4.0-3.0-2.5-2.0-1.0], Wikimedia Commons.

The gate to the Sri Lanka Broadcasting Corporation, the oldest radio station in Asia, contains a retro-futuristic image of lightning bolts intersecting an image of the island.

The Musical Gift

PART I

FINDING MUSICAL GIFTS

Introduction

For a Musicology of Karma and Reincarnation

> Mistakes about race were at the heart of the Rwandan genocide; the invasion of Iraq in 2003 was shaped by American nationalism and chauvinism about Muslims; nationality is clearly stopping us doing our part in dealing with things such as the refugee crisis, because we feel like it will threaten our own identity.... This crisis that we are facing now is rooted in these moral and intellectual confusions about identity. And it is very costly to keep making these mistakes.
>
> —Kwame Anthony Appiah[1]

Imagine that you travel to a foreign country. A musically curious person, you decide to explore the country's musical traditions. You discover that each ethnic and religious group "has" its own music, and you learn where to place these on a map. While in the capital, you attend a performance of the national music tradition (flamenco in Spain, tango in Argentina). If your politics shade to the left, you delve into the music of a disenfranchised minority (in Burma and Thailand, you visit the hill country "tribal" populations). If you gravitate toward pop music, you attend a concert of a singer who mixes traditional (read: ethnic and/or religious) musics with global pop sounds. You feel that you are now up to date, in style, and educated: you think you now know something about *who these people are*.

In this classic example of a Foucauldian episteme, people from across the political spectrum in our era share a belief that music is intimately associated with what it means to be a person, with the cultural history of that person's community, and with that community's placement on the map of a nation. This is a way of thinking we are all aware of, even if we by now take it for granted. Scholars have long traced it to the writings of Johann Gottfried Herder (1744–1803) and to eighteenth- and nineteenth-century Orientalist scholarship on music in the

---

[1] Appiah in Hannah Ellis-Petersen, "Racial identity is a biological nonsense, says Reith lecturer," *The Guardian*, October 18, 2016.

colonies, but it is a mode of thought that blossomed fully only in the twentieth century, with the growth of the recording industry, the emergence of the discipline of ethnomusicology and the phenomenon of "world music," the spread of air travel and the tourism industry, and the efforts of culture brokers and government officials to invest in traditional culture in newly postcolonial countries.[2] By the twenty-first century, the notion that there is an inherent link between music, community, and the history of territory has achieved such global prominence it may scarcely seem in need of being questioned.

Yet I suggest that while we continue to live in "the music and identity episteme," for many of us who study music professionally, the link between music and identity has become a trap from which we want to escape. Many of us got sick of writing about identity, and who can blame us, for the concept emerged as central to music studies in the 1980s and became fully hegemonic in the 1990s. While I remain committed to the progressive work done by many scholars writing about identity in music, I often feel the ubiquity of studies showing how "music x" produces a feeling of "community y" fail in their objective: by showing how music plays a role in constructing (rather than simply expressing) identity, we still reinforce the idea that music history simply *is* about how music produces identity and place. A study that explores how music produces nationalist sentiments, for example, is not outside the identity episteme even if it critiques nationalist appropriations of music.

Perhaps a tacit awareness of this is why, from the early 2000s, music scholars started turning toward new and seemingly more exciting vistas—topics that on the surface seem to have little to do with identity, in emerging fields like sound studies and ecomusicology.[3] Yet I suggest the astounding plurality of these approaches has been less about avoiding "identity" as a structuring concept than about dismantling the music and identity episteme altogether, due to what is now viewed by many as its destructive and politically regressive tendencies. To take a few examples, one critique leveled at our episteme is that it facilitates a focus on identities as though they arise in isolation—hence Piekut's (2014) advocation for the use of Actor-Network Theory to tell music history and Born's (2010) call for a "relational musicology." Another is that it facilitates a narrow focus on works, composers, and genres set apart from senses and events; hence the adoption of a sound studies approach to explore how people experienced sounds in the

---

[2] See Bohlman (1988, 2002); Herder and Bohlman (2017).

[3] What I have in mind here is how many scholars of music have recently situated themselves in intellectual currents whose popularity has surged across the academy in the past decade and a half: the writings of Latour (2005) and the Actor-Network theorists; histories of sound reproduction technologies and listening in the West that culminated in the birth of sound studies (e.g., Sterne 2003, 2012; Corbin 1998; White and White 2006; Ochoa Gautier 2014); Object-Oriented Ontology (e.g., Bryant 2011; Bryant, Harman, and Srnicek 2011); the ontological turn in anthropology (e.g., Viveiros de Castro 2004, 2016; Holbraad and Pederson 2017); and writings on the relationship between nature and culture (e.g., Chakrabarty 2009; Morton 2010), among others.

European past (Dillon 2012; Fisher 2014). Another critique is that it fails to engage how non-human factors shape musical developments: hence Roda's (2014) adoption of a "flat ontology" in his study of how weather affects the construction of *tabla* drums in India. The adoption of methods from outside music studies, in other words, has been channeled to combat the unsavory biases of the identity episteme.

Yet even as we celebrate a newfound freedom from "identity" in music studies, we need to remember that even liberatory moments have limitations. And topics that are crucial for dismantling some of the more unjust aspects of the identity episteme—such as for better representing non-Judeo-Christian ontologies of sound—have been dealt with unevenly. Some that I consider in this book are: sonic causality (as different from, though sometimes related to, human agency); the secularism inherent in the identity episteme (and our critiques of it), that is, the ways we still subordinate non-Western cosmologies and sonic efficacies to Western-derived, disenchanted notions of personhood, territory, and music; the lingering idea that music is *always* an expression of an interior state, which though rooted in the identity episteme is routinely invoked in newer theorizations of networks and relations; the ways our episteme drives wedges between populations, rooting the Other out of an ethnic group's music history; and the issue of how our acknowledgment of fluid definitions of personhood and premodern notions of territory and sovereignty should affect how music is deemed to relate to bodies, personhood, and territory in a historical narrative.[4] The current trend of moving to a "posthuman" approach, for instance, does not mean its construction of sound, humans, nonhumans, and how these relate are not couched in Eurocentric terms.

Consider that in many times and places, such as Afro-Cuban Lucumi rituals (e.g., Schweitzer 2013), Tamil Hindu processions (e.g., Sykes 2015), imperial sacrifices at the Qing court (e.g., Rawski and Rawlins 2005: 126–127), the praising of spirits and/or saints in Sufi rituals in Tunisia (e.g., Jankowsky 2010), Pakistan, and India (e.g., Qureshi 2006), and apparently throughout much of premodern Europe (e.g., Attali 1985)—practically everywhere—certain sounds were in their first instance offerings to god(s): isn't it insulting to tell people that, sure, you say your sounds are gifts to god(s), but what they're really *about* is who you are, how you're feeling, and where you come from? The centrality to music history of the subordination of human-divine relations to a story just of the persons or community involved should not be ignored; it was Johann Sebastian Bach, after all, who

---

[4] To take one example, classic scholarship on Southeast Asia posits *mandala* or "galactic" polities in the Southeast Asian past (e.g., Tambiah 1976), in which sovereignty emanated out from a center in concentric circles, decreasing in power the further one goes. Small-scale polities at the edge of one circle may have also been at the edge of another and paid tribute to two states whose centers of power lay elsewhere. I am concerned that such regionally specific ways of constituting belonging are routinely ignored in the identity episteme by applying modern notions of territory to the musical past.

reportedly said, "I play the notes as they are written, but it is God who makes the music."⁵ As I show later on, in the Sri Lankan (Sinhala Buddhist) context I foreground in this book, some sounds were created by gods, given to people, given to other people, and are now given back to gods in a ritual context; such sounds are best thought of not as an "expression" of the musician's inner "devotion"—a Judeo-Christian concept if there ever was one—but as objects separate from the body, gifts that *must* be given as gestures of respect to the divine powers, since the gods are by nature not benign but judicial. What *can* we do with such cases, historiographically speaking, than situate them in a discourse linking music, community, and the history of land?⁶ I want to digress for a moment and discuss some of the ways our music and identity episteme takes a hold of us and determines *for us* our perspectives on sound/music, even when we recognize that it fails to respect many engagements with sound throughout the world: for this book is (1) a study of the negative effects of the identity episteme on musicians, particularly how it drives wedges between populations and lays discursive groundwork for the perception of communal differences and conflict; and (2) it is a work that wriggles music studies more fully away from "identity" by using Sri Lankan aesthetics to develop new ways to think about the relations between music/sound, self, community, territory, sonic causality, human-divine and human-nonhuman relations, and time. I do so (3) by naming a particular Sri Lankan arrangement of those elements that, while unique and not itself homogenous, I contend can be considered broadly, outside Sri Lanka, as a global phenomenon that has gone largely unrecognized in (or is typically presumed to have died out via) the identity paradigm. I call this arrangement "the musical gift" or (in a less static manner) "musical giving," a term that recognizes myriad assemblages of sonic efficacy, generosity, and bodily and social relations to sound that, I will argue, call for a definition of music history as stories of entanglement between acts of musical giving and the terms of the identity paradigm.

Consider the Iñupiaq of Barrow, Alaska, who sing to call whales, and when the whales arrive, they hunt them; the songs are believed to be songs *given* to them by previous whales they've hunted (Sakakibara 2009; Fox 2014).⁷ Whose music history does the whale/Iñupiaq songs belong to—is this a history in the sea, whales,

---

⁵ I have been unable to verify that Bach said this, but its attribution demonstrates a belief in the divine origins of the Western canon in some quarters.

⁶ I do not pretend I am the first to strive to avoid the reduction of a study of "music" to "identity"; rather, I am pointing out that *despite* the existence of studies that demonstrate how the Judeo-Christian language about music, self, and place fails in certain contexts (e.g., Feld 2012; Seeger 2004), music studies and our teaching methodologies are still driven by that language, *even as* we recognize its limitations.

⁷ "All our songs and drum beats were originally inherited from animals. That's why all rituals exist: to retain animal spirits in the drums. Songs are [the] agent, [the] mother of all animals, and they can be demanding because [drums] need good care and respect like animals. We have to sing animals' songs. If we do, they will come near" (consultant Frankson in Sakakibara 2009: 292).

the Iñupiaq, drums, Alaska, the United States, indigenous conceptions of territory, or some combination of these? Not only are Iñupiaq drums made of whale parts, but the Iñupiaq consider themselves to be part whale; and since you are what you eat (and the Iñupiaq eat whales), this view cannot be easily dismissed. So is this a single music history (a whale/person music history) or a "connected history" (Subrahmanyam 1997) between humans and whales forged through a sonic gift economy? If the latter, how can we locate a sonic gift economy in a historical narrative without reducing it to the history of just one of the communities/places involved, as happens routinely in our "identity episteme"?[8] Is there a way for music history to be "about" relations without producing hierarchy?[9]

Anya Bernstein's (2013) study of Buryat Buddhists (the majority of whom live in the Buryat Republic in Siberia, today a part of Russia) allows us to grasp how the neglect of sonic gift economies arose in some contexts not (or not just) through Judeo-Christian notions of the soul but through the biopolitics of secularizing regimes. Writing about the Soviet influence on Buryat Buddhists, she writes, "Soviet secularization attempted to expel religion not only from the public space, but also from the body . . . a serious and sustained attempt to create what I call 'closed' bodies, whose sovereignty would be based on physical and moral strength, autonomy, and their impenetrability to religious influences" (Bernstein 2013: 10). In the postsocialist world, bodies are "powerful tools for the contemporary political imagination" through reincarnation, as some Tibetan lamas are reincarnations of Buryat lamas from previous eras and "incorporated into the Buryat body politic" (Bernstein 2013: 70).[10] Leaving aside that Buddhist monks would not normally perform "music," we can ask: do their engagements with sound (say, in ritual contexts) belong in this case to Tibetan or Buryatian history? How do we write a history of sound/music for a single being that lived multiple lives, decades if not hundreds of years apart?[11] In other words, what

---

[8] Sakakibara acknowledges a sonic gift economy among the Iñupiaq/whales: "Songs are the *gifts* from the animals, and hunters and their families are responsible for entertaining their animal spirit guests" (ibid.; my italics).

[9] In a book with an agenda similar to my own, Gary Tomlinson (1993: 10) writes that "the voices of the occult past" in medieval Europe tend to be silenced "almost before dialogue with them can begin"; writers do this by failing "to perceive either '*difference* without its degenerating into superiority/inferiority' or '*equality* without its compelling us to accept identity'" (his italics).

[10] Lest we think this esoteric, Bernstein (2013: 72) emphasizes belief in reincarnation is common "in many cultures, [where] past lives constitute a vital part of one's identity, with newborns conceptualized as complex beings, far from being a simple tabula rasa."

[11] Writing about the *Traiphum* cosmology in the Theravada Buddhist context of Thailand, Rosalind Morris (2000: 158) describes the significance of duration and merit for situating beings in a place: "The *Traiphum* consists in a descriptive account of all the realms in the universe, from the lowliest hell to the most ethereal heaven. But these are not locations so much as moral spaces, the domains in which particular kinds of beings reside by virtue of their store of merit. Accordingly, the traversal of these spaces is made possible by merit-producing or diminishing acts; merit itself works only in and through time. The *Traiphum* cosmology has thus been likened by many to a kind of temporal map in which an

would a musicology of karma and reincarnation look like constructed according to Buddhist terms and values rather than the "hygienic" inoculating discourse of a Eurocentric musicological approach? Isn't our identity episteme defined by this process of inoculation?

Indeed, the presumption that a stable, closed self is the natural way humans exist colors many attempts to understand music in non-Western contexts where scholars have shown the self to be understood as fluid, composite, and/or ultimately a fiction. For example, studies of music and trance often fixate on the loss of a sense of self that occurs, a preoccupation that surely stems from Western notions of experience and an anxiety rooted in Christian attachments to the soul. The focus on *devotion* and *praise*, while relevant for some religions (e.g., Sufism), nevertheless construes the devotee's *experience* as more essential than, say, the importance of sound as an offering to gods or spirits. This is surely a part of what Jankowsky (2007: 190–191) calls the "inherited epistemological assumptions that shape the parameters of scholarly discourse on music and trance." More to my point is that for the Theravada Buddhists who are the protagonists of this book, talk about "the self" (*atta*) and "person" (*purisa/puggala*) is accepted in specific contexts by religious experts and everyday discourse by the laity, but belief in "the doctrine of self" (*attavada*) "is one of the four forms of 'grasping' (the others are sense-pleasures, (mere) rule-and-ritual, and 'views')" (Collins 1982: 76). Doctrinal Buddhism stipulates a "not-self" (*anatta*).

How should ethno/musicology think about not-selves? It is one thing to say sound/music expresses the feelings of a not-self at a particular moment on its journey up or down the karmic ladder, and another to say music captures the essential quality of a person or community as demonstrative of the "soul" of a territory. From such a perspective, so much of music studies—indeed, so many uses of music around the world—narrates and produces stories of people grasping through music for something that is not there. I suggest music studies needs to better recognize that "concern with identity as an attribute of the individual person is a Western phenomenon" (Strathern 1988: 59).[12]

---

overarching principle of duration provides the frame. In this context, the relationships between places are to be comprehended in the idiom of time-bound movement."

[12] It is the ubiquity of fluid notions of the person that surprises. In Melanesia, Strathern famously argued, people are "frequently construed as the plural and composite site of the relationships that produce them" (1988: 13). McIntosh (2009: 17) discusses comparable notions on the self that emerge in ethnographic studies from Sub-Saharan Africa. In South India, Daniel (1984) claims there is ontological consubstantiality between persons and "the communities, places, and objects with which the person interacts"; the shape of the village is assumed to affect bodily substance, as "manifest in significant events as varied as the ups and downs of personal fortune, happiness, state of health, or anxiety about the afterlife." Note that these do not preclude a link between music, identity, and place; rather, it should inspire us to explore how this construction may happen differently than via the Judeo-Christian idea that music is an outer expression of an interior state of an individual and/or community.

Let me sum up by showing how the link between music and identity inevitably returns to take hold of music scholarship even when scholars notice it is a historical construction. Consider a review of Ana Maria Ochoa Gautier's masterful book *Aurality* (2014), where the reviewer first lauds her for unearthing "varying understandings of the term voice and how it relates (*or does not relate*) to human identity, but more so with the relationship between the human and the non-human," only to end the review by saying, "A challenging and rewarding read, I recommend her work to persons who are seriously interested in new approaches to *retelling the history of any nation*" (Ledford 2015; my italics). Wasn't it Ochoa Gautier's goal, as the author of the review notes, to show that the voice did *not* previously relate to identity, at least not in the ways it does now? Don't we do an injustice to the indigenous boat rowers on the Magdalena River in nineteenth-century Columbia that Ochoa Gautier describes if we consider the value of their vocal utterances merely to be that they allow us to better grasp a national context as it currently exists, thus making the ultimate protagonists of her book the contemporary state's ideologies of personhood, its borders, and its definitions of sound that she just spent several hundred pages demonstrating to have done physical harm to the boat rowers precisely *through* the forging of a link between the voice and identity? This sort of mistake is rampant in ethnomusicology, a discipline whose focus on ethnography forces a presentist view of the past rather than a view of the past from within its own concepts and values.[13]

I made a similar point to a colleague once and he laughed, saying I was merely repeating the famous statement by Dipesh Chakrabarty (2000) in his *Provincializing Europe* about the difference between "History 1" and "History 2": the latter are the "local" perspectives the world over in which (to take Chakrabarty's example) gods are a significant causal player in local understandings of history (as when Hindu workers perform rituals to bless their machinery) but these factors are expunged in History 1—the abstract, secular language of the social sciences—which defines causality as disenchanted. "Isn't that point played out by now?" he asked. Isn't the right question whether it is played out for reincarnated lamas, Afro-Cuban Lucumi ritual specialists, Bach, whales/Iñupiaq, and those many others who continue to construe the relations between sound, personhood, community, and territory in ways that contradict the terms of the identity episteme? It's as though we acknowledge the point, shrug, and go on misrepresenting the people/gods/whales/sounds/terrains we are invested in adequately representing.[14]

---

[13] The idea that music is inherently linked to identity is a kind of ghost that migrated into bodies across the world: "Once ideas or thoughts (Gedanke) are detached from their substratum, one engenders some ghost by giving them a body. Not by returning to the living body from which ideas and thoughts have been torn loose, but by incarnating the latter in another artifactual body, a prosthetic body, a ghost of spirit" (Derrida quoted in Cheah 2003: 190). "These prostheses," Pheng Cheah (2003: 188) writes, "turn out to be necessary supplements to the living national body."

[14] The term "music" is of course deeply implicated in the historical *pressures* I register in this book (of the conceptual transformation of sonic gift economies into metonyms for disenchanted, geographically

The problem emerges more subtly through our tendency to study sounds that have been *transformed* in the identity episteme—for example, through nationalism into staged exhibitions of traditional culture—rather than sounds that have *resisted* the link with identity altogether. The tendency to use "identity" as a method to focus on the historical transformation of genres for whom that link was not originally important reminds me of James C. Scott's (1998) advice that when we use state-driven, European-derived concepts for describing populations and indigenous knowledge systems we are "seeing like a state," playing a role in governmentalization. No offense to North American ethnomusicologists (I am one), but it makes sense that we are sometimes mistaken for CIA agents in the field, because the use of culture to identify who people are and where they rightfully belong is useful for those in charge of putting them and keeping them there. Don't we always tell people we're studying a music, a genre, a people, who live *there*? Isn't that what it means to hear like a state? Music became the "stuff" of personhood, or as Pheng Cheah (2003: 7) writes, "culture is the ontological paradigm of the political." But it wasn't always this way—and have we recognized the *methodological* importance of this for music studies?

In this book I explore a key feature of the identity episteme: multiethnic, human-divine, human-demon, and human-animal interactions through the giving of sound from one to the other become inoculated, the body and community closed off, as relations *between* beings are erased in the drive to define the cultures of distinct communities in national cultural histories. We tend to acknowledge hybrid cultures and diasporic groups (e.g., Indian musicians in Trinidad; Manuel 2015), but those of us working in music studies have been less good at recognizing that musicians who maintain distinct ethnic and religious identities create music history together. Thus we too easily forget, say, the Armenian contribution to Turkish music, the Jewish contribution to the Iraqi maqam, and the Tamil and Muslim contribution to Sinhala music in Sri Lanka; we forget the Arab contribution to Western music, the African contribution to American country music, and

---

placed musical identities), which it is nominally meant to describe in phrases like "music history" (for a similar argument, see Wong 2014). Throughout this book, I use the terms "sound" and "music" judiciously and not interchangeably. "Music" is a term that has historically drawn distinctions between the sounds of nature and culture (Ochoa Gautier 2014, 2016); it is a historically developed term, translated not unproblematically into South Asian languages (like the Sinhala word *sangita* and Tamil word *icai*). While I take "music" to mean "humanly organized sound that has been self-consciously articulated, if not by performers then by observers, as 'music'" it is not my intention to define "sound" as a pristine "Other" (or as a historically prior formation); rather, "sound" is a useful way to think about sonic practices outside the confines of historically emergent definitions of "music." As we will see, this is essential for considering Buddhist engagements with sound that they do not consider "music" but which have been situated in a discourse on music in contemporary Sri Lanka. Embedded in my phrase "the musical gift," then, is the idea that sounds are still *given* to non-humans in today's world, even though discourses on "music" tend to obscure their function as sonic gift economies.

the European contribution to Indian classical music.[15] In this book, I argue that normative formations of music history legitimize histories of communal separation that, besides being historically inaccurate, drive the perception of essential differences between communities that lay the groundwork for the idea that a "clash of civilizations" is inevitable.

The backbone of the identity episteme is that the promotion of communal culture generates freedom through recognition; but I show in this book that the conceptual chopping up of land and peoples does not generate freedom but the physical and conceptual enclosures that force people into ethnicized regions and neighborhoods. In what follows, I argue we need to develop a notion of culture-as-freedom that does not rely on territory, cosmopolitanism, nationalism, communal recognition, or self-expression but on a comfortableness in oneself achieved through the ability to *give* to Others without fear of reprisal and without fear of losing one's identity (having *territorial* control does not necessarily make one free). At its heart, the notion of sonic generosity I build in this book is based on the idea that sound/music is a technology of care, offered as a gesture of respect (to gods and to humans) that protects and heals people, and that such offerings not only help Others but are ways of caring for oneself. This is an idea traceable to Foucault's notion of care for the self: as Robert Nichols puts it, "'Freedom' [for Foucault] does not denote a property or capacity of the subject. Rather, it is a feature of the *relationship to which one is subject*" (Nichols 2014: 151; his italics).

Consider the following question: do the Rohingya Muslims in Rakhine State in Myanmar (a Buddhist-majority country), who (at the time of writing) are being driven out of the country, play "Burmese" music? To answer "no" seems to justify their ethnic cleansing; but to say "yes" is to forge a link between music, identity, and territory in a region that not long ago did not have borders, let alone the idea that "music" is something everybody "has." It would also assume an equivalency between Muslim and Buddhist ontologies of sound, personhood, and history. And yet, to argue that a disenfranchised minority should *not* promote a link between music, identity, and place seems to do an injustice to them and reinforce narratives that they don't belong. Likewise, to argue that an ethnic majority or state should not promote a link between music, identity, and place seems to legitimize rebel groups and breakaway territories. In the identity episteme, such links must be made. And so the left and right essentialize communities, obscuring histories of connection, including histories of musical exchanges between peoples who nevertheless maintain different definitions of sound, personhood, and territory. It is this problem that I try to find a way out of in this book, in the Sri Lankan context.

---

[15] A rare exception are studies of Israeli-Palestinian musical relations (e.g., Brinner 2009; Belkind 2014).

Chapter Summaries

Gavin Steingo (2016: 14) writes that, "equality is not an 'ontological principle' that people simply harness and then press into the service of politics. It is merely an assumption that is determined *experimentally* through practice" (his italics). This book is such an experiment at forging equality, by using a study of Sri Lankan styles of sonic generosity to recognize histories of communal respect for Others and histories of communal interaction through Sri Lankan practices now believed to mark geographically bounded, ethnically distinct communities. As "a methodological project that poses ontological questions to solve epistemological problems" (Holbraad and Pedersen 2017: 5), the book brings insights from anthropology's recent "ontological turn" into music studies.[16] As we will see in Chapter One, my dominant concern is to locate sonic efficacy, enchantment, and exchange in the modern world, granting agency to the "art object" (Gell 1998) and asking us to question how such a recognition allows us to rethink how communities relate in a national cultural narrative, and what the persistence of sonic efficacy means for ethno/musicology's normative "disenchantment tale" (e.g., Attali 1985; see Chapter 1). In turn, the book is a study of the processes through which the historic importance and persistence of sonic generosity is forgotten in the identity episteme.

Chapter 1 argues that the obscuring of sonic generosity in Sri Lanka was fostered by a distinction between "the monetary economy" and "the arts" reinforced by British colonial liberalism and postcolonial ethnonationalism; it introduces forms of Sri Lankan sonic generosity and considers how "the gift" might allow us to rethink how "identities" relate through music. Chapter 2 explores the musical giving of a group of Sinhala Buddhist ritualists called the Beravā, whose music and dance were promoted by the state after the island's independence from Britain (in 1948) as the premier traditional culture of the island's Sinhala Buddhist ethnic

---

[16] In the 1990s, "ontology" in music studies was defined via a multiculturalist language in which each society is deemed to have its own "ontology of music" (Bohlman 1999). I owe much to Bohlman's classic formulation; however, a problem I face in the Sri Lankan context is that such a conception reinforces narratives of ethnic separation while running ramshod over indigenous Sri Lankan aesthetics of sound/music in which it had little to do with identity or belonging. The "ontological turn" is useful not just because it allows me a way out of these problems inherent to Sri Lanka; by positioning "ontologies of the otherwise" (Povinelli 2015) as means to generate new analytical concepts (Holbraad and Pedersen 2017), the approach asks us to locate the phenomena I demarcate in this book (e.g., musical gifts, the historical *newness* of the link between music and identity) elsewhere in the world, giving us new conceptual tools for thinking about the world's music history more generally. Perhaps music, *ontologically*, is typically a gift before or in addition to it being "about" identity? See Chapter 1 for a utilization of this approach via a discussion of the relations between musical gifts and commodities. For a discussion of how the ontological turn differs from object-oriented ontology while intersecting with (yet differing from) a few related "turns" (ecological, material), see Holbraad and Pedersen (ibid. 30–68).

majority. Chapter 3 is a cartography of Sri Lankan Tamil musics (the island's main minority group), whose "musical giving" I identify as sonic exchanges across geographic and human/divine boundaries. Chapter 4 breaks this binary between Sinhala and Tamil musics down by identifying musics of other Sri Lankan communities and considering contexts where they have interacted musically with one another.[17]

I alert ethnomusicologists to Chapter 5, which is the ethnographic heart of the book. The chapter explores how musicians were affected by (and responded to) the 2004 tsunami and war (1983–2009); I also consider how NGOs and musicians have tried to suture communal relations through musical workshops, concerts, and festivals in the post-war period. I argue that uses of music to promote reconciliation tend to succeed if they can let go of the idea that music simply "is" about how it expresses communal identity. In this penultimate chapter, I argue that a core component of post-war reconciliation should be the public recognition that Sri Lankans from distinct ethnic and religious groups have a shared cultural history based on encounters and exchange.

Chapter 6 provides a historical backdrop for how the identity episteme emerged in Sri Lanka. I argue that the bounding of the island as a political unit separate from India (the "islanding" of Sri Lanka; Sivasundaram 2013) brought about a reevaluation of the island's musical practices and their relations to India and the Indian Ocean Region. I argue that this drove notions of difference between communities, while defining the island's minorities as playing music that is not really Sri Lankan. While Sinhala musicians in the early- to mid-twentieth century saw Sinhala musics as connected to North Indian musics (on account of the Sinhalas' origin story, which places their mythical ancestor, Prince Vijaya, in

---

[17] Because Sri Lanka is underrepresented in music studies, I can be forgiven for providing basic demographic information here. Sri Lanka is an island nation of 25,332 square miles (roughly the size of the U.S. state of West Virginia) off the southeastern coast of India that at the time of writing has a population of about 21 million. The 2012 census put the Sinhalese at 74.9%, Sri Lankan Tamils at 11.1%, Indian Tamils (also known as Estate, Up Country, or Malaiyaha Tamils) at 4.1%, and Muslims (an ethnic as well as religious category) at 9.3%. Smaller populations include the Väddas (the indigenous population), Burghers (Eurasians), and Malays, who together total around 1%. The vast majority of Sinhalas are Theravada Buddhist and speak Sinhala (classified as an Indo-Aryan language), while Tamils are mostly Saivite Hindus and speak Tamil (part of the Dravidian language family widespread throughout South India). The island has a significant Christian population (7.6%) split between Sinhalas, Tamils, and Burghers (the latter are often native English speakers). Most Muslims speak Tamil as their native tongue, but they are not considered ethnically Tamil (and many Sri Lankans are multilingual, with Sinhala, Tamil, and English listed as national languages). Any demographic account of Sri Lanka is highly politicized; the official census numbers just provided, for example, split Tamils into two categories (Sri Lankan and Indian Tamils—the latter's ancestors were brought to the island from India in the late colonial period to work on tea estates; Peebles 2001), downplaying their presence on the island. It is also true that the number of Tamils has diminished due to their fleeing the war. McGilvray (2008: 7–8) puts the number of Sri Lankan Tamils as 12% and Malaiyaha Tamils at 6%, thus totaling 18%.

North India), in the decades after independence from Britain in 1948, Sinhala musicians rejected connections to North India. They developed a "pure" Sinhala music, and later on, they rooted Sinhala musical identity in the prehistoric period by developing the figure of Ravana (the "evil king of Lanka" in the Hindu epic the *Ramayana*) as their musical progenitor.

At a few points in the book, I include interludes called "Checkpoints." During the war, checkpoints were ubiquitous at certain times in the capital Colombo and many places throughout the island. They were sites that brought on stress, fear, harassment, and detainment (Jeganathan 2004). Rather than checking one's "identity card" (as soldiers do at checkpoints), my Checkpoints use ethnographic vignettes to dismantle hegemonic notions of ethnic identity in Sri Lanka. The first Checkpoint considers the travails of my Sinhala drum teacher in the identity episteme, a time when a discourse that celebrates his ritual music and dance as ethnic culture has delegitimized the use of it as medicine to help individuals and families. I put his story into dialogue with a discussion of Tamil musical giving at Point Pedro (in the north) during and after the war, and I consider the use of Buddhist chant by government soldiers in Mullaitivu (in the northeast) to drive ghosts away from a rebel graveyard after it was bulldozed to make way for a military camp. Collectively, these stories mark sonic efficacy and giving as integral to Sri Lankan music history and civilians' protection from violence during and after the war. The middle Checkpoint considers Malay singers who sing in six languages and provides a brief history of musical giving in Sri Lankan popular musics. Finally, a Checkpoint before the book's conclusion focuses on two well-known cultural activists, one Sinhala and one Tamil, who acted during the war to use the historic relations between the music drama traditions of each group to demonstrate to villagers in the Tamil-dominated north and Sinhala-dominated south that Tamils and Sinhalas have a shared history of music, dance, and drama. I interpret their efforts as a use of the link between culture, identity, and freedom to fold the identity episteme in on itself by arguing that *if* one believes culture is about identity, what Sri Lankan cultural history shows is that Sri Lankans are not that different from one another.

The book's conclusion argues that the jettisoning of liberalism's definition of the arts—in which the arts are an outer expression of self and community rather than an economy through which people develop their identities through exchanges with or in front of one another—is critical for building peace in post-war Sri Lanka. Recognizing the efforts of Sri Lankan activists who risked their lives during the war by making similar claims, I argue that happiness and "freedom" can be better achieved by publicly promoting histories of communal interaction through the arts rather than adopting a liberal multiculturalist or ethnonationalist mindset in which each group's culture is presumed to have arisen in isolation.

1

Sonic Generosity

Beyond Secularism and Conflict in Music Studies

> What a strange scene you describe
> and what strange prisoners,
> They are just like us.
>
> —Plato, *The Republic*, Book VII[1]

This book is a study of an aesthetic system in Sri Lanka that I find emerging across the island, among people of different ethnicities, religions, castes, classes, genders, and geographical locations. I call this system "the musical gift." In this way of thinking, some sounds are meant to be given; musical gifts can be thought of as things like aspirin or coffee, in that they can be shipped and tracked as they move, given or bought and re-gifted by one person to another, and enjoyed, but which should not be construed as inherently expressive of the soul of the person or community who offers it. Musical gifts are *not* like a fancy car obtained in a midlife crisis, which says a lot about the car-buyer and can be linked to national preferences for certain automobiles. Rather, musical giving is an act that, like aspirin, is a technology of care—in Sri Lanka, musical gifts are ways of helping others with sound. They are also ways of helping oneself, because the respect shown through the musical offering tends to generate a pleasant response. Musical gifts are like the small present a fieldworker gives to her consultant—they are the gesture of recognition that opens doors.

Sri Lankans maintain communal affiliations that often determine who is allowed to give which musical gift; some gifts are the inalienable possessions of castes, who alone are traditionally allowed to offer them in ritual contexts. For them, musical giving may be their job. While musical gifts differ from musical commodities, sonic generosity does exist in capitalism (as shown by the "free download"). In this book, I argue that Sri Lankan musical giving is more about *protecting* people with sound than about using sound to produce definitions of

---

[1] In this translation, the quote is the epigraph of Jose Saramago's (2003) novel *The Cave*.

people and places. Musical gifts are in their first instance techniques rather than symbols (Asad 1993). A Sri Lankan musical gift is less an expression of identity and place than it is a persuasive speech, a firewall on your computer, a hammer, a philosophy of action, a cup of tea, a token of appreciation to God(s) and to you, medicine, something that can be held and thrown, sipped and shared, and a method of communicating between this-worldly and that-worldly Others. Musical giving is like the practice of *qat*-chewing (a plant stimulant) in Yemen: it enables ways to enjoy the company of others while commenting on the issues of the day. But as with *qat*-chewing (Wedeen 2008), this does not mean it is frivolous. In Sri Lanka, some musical gifts *must* be offered to gods if they are to protect the community from drought, pestilence, and disease; to *not* give musical gifts might be interpreted as a sign of disrespect, and would be asking for divine retribution. Thus musical giving can be a matter of life and death.

As for music history, some musical gifts can be re-gifted and re-gifted, again and again, creating broad chains of social relations and histories of musical giving across communities, generating aesthetic similarities and shared origins for different traditions of musical giving that cut across political, ethnic, and religious lines. To consider this merely "circulation" (a word that appears to deny human and nonhuman agency) or "appropriation" (which implies taking in a negative sense) ignores the profound fact that beings may be *generous* with sound even when they give it to further their interests. Sure, a musical gift could be someone's stolen property; as I show later on, some musical gifts are guarded as well-kept secrets. There is also a tradition in Sri Lanka of borrowing, taking, or stealing sounds from a community that is different from one's own and then giving them back to a person from that community as a sign of respect. Nevertheless, I suggest musical gifts need to be recognized *as gifts*.

Musical giving is perhaps *the* major missing actor from music studies. Given that ethnomusicology remains indebted to its ancestor discipline anthropology, we might wonder why there is a lack of discussion of the gift in ethnomusicology when the gift is literally Anthropology 101. In the general public, people say they received "the gift of music," but any scan of the ethnomusicological literature will find both the global ubiquity of musical giving and a tendency to fail to identify it as such.[2] In ethnomusicology's sister discipline historical musicology, one

---

[2] Significant touchstones for my work here include writings on music and capitalism (e.g., Beaster-Jones 2016; Morcom 2015; Taylor 2012; Qureshi 2002), while Nettl (1989), Muller (1999: 58–63). Seeger (2004), Steingo (2016), Stirr (2017), Sakakibara (2009), and Ladzekpo (n.d.)—to name a few—demonstrate the presence of music/sound as gifts and/or as an element of exchange in their regions of study without foregrounding "the gift" per se in their writings. "The gift" occasionally surfaces in classic writings on appropriation in ethnomusicology (e.g., Feld 1996), and it can be read into certain parts of the classic ethnographies of Feld (2012), Seeger (2004), and Viveiros de Castro (1992: 124, 224). My efforts here are probably most similar to Du Bois's (1903) famous discussion of music, the gift, and race in the United States (see Radano 2003). I probe the historical relations between musical gifts and commodities later in this chapter, and address Radano's study in Chapter 5.

finds writings on the giving of a composition in a book to a patron or friend (e.g., Wegman 2005; Davies 2006), but the gift in that case is the object or composition rather than the *act* of giving sound, and besides, a discourse on the gift is virtually absent in historical musicology, anyway.[3] Thus in both musicological subfields, music is rarely if ever described *ontologically* as a gift. Why is this?

In this book, I argue that musical giving is ignored because of the centrality to the modern global imagination of the idea that music is a form of personal and communal expression. *The economy* became the domain defined by the money form, where exchange, transaction, and circulation were understood as valid; *the arts* became the site for the imaginative presentation of self (Poovey 2008). While "economy" seems to imply all sorts of arrows moving to and fro, involving the circulation of commodities, "the arts" came to imply a linear arrow from the self and community out into the world, from which it stands as a (re)presentation of the interior state, history, and culture of whomever produced it.[4] The arts exist *in* economies but are not typically considered to *be* economies. Rather, they are conceived as the public presentation of already-formed selves or communities who emerge into shared public spaces in moments of presentation or performance. This makes it difficult to understand how the arts might be formed *initially* through encounters *between* people who belong to different communities.

I call this way of thinking *liberal aesthetics* because I believe it is part of a broader discourse on the relations between the self, community, politics, ethics, freedom, territory, and public and private space that came to fruition in the British colonies through the premier philosophy of nineteenth-century Britain, political liberalism (Sartori 2008, 2014). David Scott (1999: 179) writes that political liberalism marks a distinction between "a political community of citizens

---

[3] As we will see, Wegman's (2005) argument that there was a "paradigm shift" in Europe circa 1500 where music, previously inscribed in books given as gifts, was conceptually transformed into a marketable commodity, lays critical background for the more global argument I provide in this book, in which I assert that musical giving—the gift as sound rather than simply in book form—did not die out in global modernity but became firmly entangled with discourses of identity and capitalism that feed off each other and in large part *require* the erasure of a discourse on music-as-gift.

[4] Mary Poovey (2008: 4–5) provides a history of the emergence of this division, which laid significant groundwork for political liberalism in the eighteenth and nineteenth centuries. She argues that the discipline of economics came to seem more credible "when its writing appeared to be *transparent*—that is, when texts seemed simply to describe or refer to economic and financial matters rather than calling attention to themselves as writing or books." By contrast, literature was assumed to be successful "precisely to the degree to which its writing was *not* transparent and, sometimes, primarily because of its material embodiment in a beautiful or rare book" (her italics). This distinction is important because it "constitutes one of the earliest, and most important, forms of representation in relation to which it seemed crucial to make and reinforce a distinction between fact and fiction." With regard to music, as the mechanics of capitalism came to seem natural, music came to appear less a "factual" exchange with gods and more an artistic production that, through its link to the self, could be sold through performance and sheet music (and later, a recording). I pursue this idea in more detail later in this chapter.

and a cultural community of culture-bearers": the culture of the community is not supposed to intrude into the political sphere, for to do so would corrupt "reasonable political ends" (Scott 1999: 179). Ritu Birla (2009: 6) writes about colonial India (a point that can be extended to colonial Ceylon)[5] that, "a defining feature of Indian modernity and its capitalist genealogy" was "the staging of a distinction between public and private as a distinction between economy and culture":

> Colonial law sought to restrict what I call the *extensive negotiability* that characterized vernacular practices: an extensive negotiability between the symbolic capital of kinship, caste, and lineage, and the capital flows of market exchange and production. New forms of contractual association and exchange—the company, the trust, the pension fund, the futures trade—all produced a bifurcation between the material logics governing the public and the cultural logics governing the private (Birla 2009: 21; her italics).[6]

As Birla puts it elsewhere, "For Marx, we will remember, sovereignty in the name of the public sustains capitalist subjects and the subjects of capitalism, for it monopolizes the terrain of the political and renders its effect—the private, the acquisitive individual—as a natural, a priori origin of the social" (Birla 2009: 25). This is why it seems that music must be situated in or contribute *to* politics rather than already *being* politics.[7]

Elizabeth Povinelli (2011: 61) writes about Aboriginal Australians that "native title, land rights, and cultural heritage and property laws demanded of Indigenous people a genealogical reckoning, not within their own language of obligation and belonging, caring and being cared for, but with a liberal imaginary of individual determination." She suggests that because of the *care* embedded in liberal projects of cultural recognition, "to assess care in late liberalism is to assess the capacity

---

[5] Sri Lanka was called "Ceylon" until 1972. It is a corruption of the word "Sinhala," the name for the island's dominant ethnic group and their language.

[6] Partha Chatterjee (1986) famously explored the importance of this distinction for anticolonial nationalism, which Birla summarizes thusly: "Performing difference, anticolonial nationalism thus operates through the distinction between an "outer" realm of statecraft and economy, where the *nation-state* is embedded *inside* capital's social logic; and an "inner" realm of national culture and unconquered sovereignty, where the *nation* asserts itself as *outside* this logic" (Birla 2009: 27; her italics). Amanda Weidman (2006) has shown that this distinction was mapped onto the female voice in colonial South India: in virtue of the female voice's presumed association with the "private" sphere of the household, it appeared to channel an ancient and authentic Indian identity that seemed free from colonial influence.

[7] Of course, ethnomusicology's area studies paradigm and its ethos of cultural recognition are offshoots of liberalism because they isolate discreet communities in nations (and nations in culture areas), making it difficult to study interactions between peoples and across regions. Ethnomusicologists have tended to explore such connections through colonialism (e.g., Irving 2010) but have less commonly explored connections between non-Western communities, e.g., between Sinhalas and Tamils.

of culture as an agent of care" (Povinelli 2011: 26). I propose that the conceptual transformation of musical gifts as technologies of care into music as an expression of geographically determined communal identities is part of this liberal imaginary of individual determination. What was originally a mechanism of caring for people *with* music and dance was interpreted as being about identity and the history of land by those who believed they were wielding care by recognizing the cultural identities of musical givers. The historical narrative that unfolds in this book is that the idea that culture forms in private, communally sheltered places was imported to a Sri Lankan context where many sounds in their first instance were conceived as separate from the body and given as public offerings to encourage deities to protect people.[8]

The Beravā

The main protagonists of this book are the Beravā ("drummer"), a caste of Sinhala Buddhist ritualists with an array of talents, from magic spells (*mantras*) and sung poetry to dancing, drumming, astrology, flame throwing, mask-making and altar-making (Simpson, 1984; Kapferer 1983; Reed 2010). Beravā subcastes and their ritual repertoire differ depending on their location; in what follows, I foreground the tradition from the southern low country (*pahata rata*), particularly those in the Bentara Korale, a region that includes my teacher (*gurunnānse*) Herbert Dayasheela's hometown of Aluthgama (south of the capital Colombo and north of Galle, on the southwest coast).[9] The focus of my studies was the *yak beraya*, the major musical instrument of southern Sri Lanka.[10] In Chapter 2, I explore how

---

[8] Colonial discourse has a "practical agency" in that it has held "explanatory primacy" (Sartori 2008: 16). In South Asianist ethnomusicology, for example, the emphasis has long been on South Asian classical musics and their transformation via nationalist discourses since the late nineteenth century (Schultz 2013: 13). Consequently, little attention has been paid to what was transformed (Pollock 2011; Schofield 2014) or to the persistence of indigenous aesthetics despite modernization pressures.

[9] The Bentara Korale is one of three major divisions of the low country ritual arts (see Chapter 2 for a map). Since the Beravā are a historically low caste, the word "Beravā" is stigmatized in Sri Lanka; my *gurunnānse* says he is *nāketi* ("astrologer"), which Reed (2010: 79) describes as an equivalent term for "Beravā." I stick with "Beravā" throughout this book to encourage respect for the caste and because (as I show in a moment) their contemporary history is a story of the appropriation of their practices by others.

[10] Technically speaking, the low country drum is called *"yak beraya"* only when it is performed in rituals called *yak tovil*. In the ritual for the god Devol Deviyo, for example, it is called *Devol beraya*; three other names are *mihingu beraya* ("straight drum"), *pahata rata beraya* ("low country drum"), and *ruhunu beraya* (referring to Ruhunu, an ancient name for the low country). According to my *yak beraya* teacher, the drum has fourteen different names. In what follows, I refer to it as *yak beraya* because that is the name it is commonly called in Sri Lanka. Bear in mind, though, that *yak beraya* translates into English as "demon drum," and the drum's association with "demons" (*yakku*) in *yak tovil* rituals

the Beravā give efficacious drum speech on the low-country drum to the Buddha, deities, and beings of low karmic standing, called *yakku*. I show as well that the *yak beraya* and the two other regionally based Beravā drums (the up-country or Kandyan drum called *gäta beraya*, and the *davula* drum associated with the region of Sabaragamuwa) embody unique music theories that draw upon, while not exactly emulating, key aesthetic values and practices in Sinhala Buddhist society. These include: Theravada Buddhist notions of karma, merit-making, and the gift (the paradigmatic example is *dāna*, the giving of alms to monks); the use of righteous sounds as a form of protection, as is also found, for instance, in Buddhist chant (*pirit*) and the magic spells (*mantras*) used in Beravā rituals; the intentionally "unmusical" and metrically "uneven" arrangements of poetry written in Pali (the language of Theravada Buddhist scripture; Kulatillake 1976: 2); and meters of classical poetry in the Sinhala language, namely *gī* ("song"), *sivpada* (quatrains), and *ganachandas* (clusters of beats or *mātras*; Kulatillake 1976: 3).

Put simply, I argue that because Buddhist monks (and serious, practicing laity on certain occasions) must accept a precept that states they cannot enjoy "frivolous entertainments" (including music and dance), the Beravā construct their drumming as poetic speech rather than music so that it may be offered to the Buddha and deities in rituals (the deities are *bodhisatta*, or Buddhas-to-be).[11] Drummers are told to "speak" the drum (*bera kiyenne*) not to "play" it (*gahanne*; the latter term is used for musical instruments, like guitar). In what follows, I show that Beravā drumming developed through interactions with numerous non-Sinhala communities over the centuries; however, I contend the stipulation that drummers must give appropriate drum-speech rather than "music" spurred the Beravā to create a system of acceptably "Buddhist" sonic generosity. Beravā drumming consists of various musical gifts—some of which they received, in a roundabout fashion, from the gods themselves—which are re-gifted to the gods in Beravā rituals.[12]

Beravā rituals are *santi karma*s (peace-bringing rituals), and in Sinhala traditional thought they are part of Ayurvedic medicine (Obeyesekere 1969). While all large-scale Beravā rituals include offerings to the Buddha, he has achieved nirvana (Pali: *nibbana*) and is not usually believed to intervene on behalf of humans

---

(which colonists and missionaries denigrated as exorcisms and "devil-dancing") has reinforced the belief, widespread in Sri Lanka, that low country rituals are not "Buddhist," a claim I contest.

[11] Drumming acts somewhat differently in *yak tovils*, which eradicate illnesses brought on by demons (*yakku*; Chapter 2). Buddhism's Five Precepts require the laity to refrain from violence, stealing, sexual misconduct, false speech, and intoxicating substances. However, for monks and the laity on full moon days (*pōya*), the list is extended to ten and includes the stipulation that one should refrain from "dancing, singing, music and watching grotesque mime" (Niyamatolika, 1971: xii).

[12] In this book, I have space to provide only a taste of the Beravā's use of "metric irregularity," their lack of a time signature or beat cycle (*tāla*), used for the purpose of making their music acceptable in a Buddhist context (for a full technical analysis of Beravā drumming, see the articles and videos at Sykes, 2018a and 2018b).

in return for the Beravā's offerings. Rather, the focus of one set of rituals (*deva tovils*) in the low country is deities, while another (*yak tovils*) eradicates illnesses brought on by beings of low karmic standing (*yakku*, a word usually translated as "demons").[13] The *bali* ritual propitiates deities of the planets (*graha deviyo*) and counteracts planetary misalignment; it makes up a third category.[14]

The Beravā perform smaller acts of healing for individuals, including the use of herbal medicine. One of the first skills my *gurunnānse* demonstrated for me is how to trap a ghost in a bottle.[15] Except for one other ritual (the Bera Pōya Hēvisi, explained below), all large-scale Beravā rituals involve drumming, dancing, and sung poetry. *Yak tovils* feature *yakku* in the form of masked dancers. The Devol Maduva (a *deva tovil*) contains a sequence where a ritual specialist dresses as the goddess Pattini. Beravā rituals I attended in the low country lasted all night (about twelve to fourteen hours each), but in the past they could be combined so that a single event might last days. The *yak beraya* is one of the most physically demanding drums in the world; it involves standing all night, holding a heavy drum and hitting one's hands forcefully against the rim and drum skin (a "rim shot"). Drummers get *enormous* permanent callouses on their upper palms.[16] The Beravā used to split work between paddy fields and rituals—some still do—but many now hold 9-to-5 jobs; some stay up all night performing a demanding ritual only to leave straight for work in the morning. Beravā rituals contain the largest and most historically important repertoire of traditional music and dance in Sinhala-speaking Sri Lanka. Despite their ubiquity in the anthropology of ritual, where they form a cornerstone,[17] and their growing recognition in dance studies,[18] the music of Beravā rituals is largely unknown outside Sri Lanka.[19] This book aims to

---

[13] Kapferer 1983; Scott 1994. Most Sri Lankans do not use the term "*deva tovils*" but refer to this set of rituals by their individual names (e.g., the Gam Maduva for the goddess Pattini). My *gurunnānse* (esteemed teacher) was clear, though, that when classifying the rituals, the name *deva tovils* should be used to describe this set of rituals (for deities) in contrast to *yak tovils* (for *yakku*).

[14] While *bali* is revered in the south, I did not witness it and do not discuss it here (see Suraweera 2009). The drumming in *bali* is softer (rituals sometimes occur inside peoples' homes) and ritualists use bells as they sing.

[15] A ritual specialist of the "demon" cults is a *yak ädurā* (an honorific title meaning "master"), typically a Beravā, while a ritual officiant of shrines to deities (*devales*) is a *kapurala*, often a high caste Govigama. The Oli (potter) caste plays a significant role in *bali* (Sheeran 1998: 962).

[16] When I first performed in a ritual, my hand got ridiculously swollen after about fifteen minutes.

[17] See e.g., Wirz 1954; Obeyesekere 1958, 1969, 1984, 1990; Tambiah 1968; Kapferer 1983, 1997; and Scott 1994.

[18] Nurnberger 1998a; Reed 2010.

[19] For considerations of Sri Lankan music in English that mention Beravā drumming, see Kulatillake 1974, 1976, 1980, 1991; A. Seneviratna 1975, 1979; H. L. Seneviratne 1978; Walcott 1978; Sheeran 1998. For discussions of Beravā drum languages, see Sykes 2011, 2018; Suraweera 2009. Sinhala sources with technical specifics include Fernando 1987; Malalgoda 1998; Bandara 2000, 2004; Rajapakse 2002; Kottegoda 2003, 2004; Kumarathunge 2004. Some of this latter literature is marred by authors' tendencies to analyze Beravā drumming through Indian music theories.

better establish Beravā drumming—and the history and politics of musical giving in Sri Lanka more broadly—in ethnomusicology.

Musical Giving and the Tribulations of Modernity

One ritual deserves special mention and falls into a different category. The Bera Pōya Hēvisi ("Auspicious Drumming on a Full Moon Night") involves only drummers and no dancers or other ritual specialists. It is an all-night competition in which drummers display the breadth of their knowledge. The ritual is a repository of drum-speech (some recited verbally, some played on the drum) that connects drummers to the Buddha, gods, and the history of Buddhism in Sri Lanka. The word *hēvisi* usually refers to a subset of Beravā who do not perform in the above-mentioned rituals but on drums (called *davula* and *thammāttama*) and a reed instrument (*horanāva*) in temple services (*tevāva*) and at funerals (for photos of Sinhala drums, see Chapter 2). The Bera Pōya Hēvisi, though, is an offering of sound (*sabda pujāva*) by the main Beravā ritualists on the premier Beravā drums (depending on where the ritual is performed, the *yak beraya*, *gäta beraya*, or *davula*) on a grander scale than those made by the *hēvisi* ensemble.

The Bera Pōya Hēvisi embodies several histories of musical giving. The drum stanzas (*padas*) revealed in the ritual are what the gods played (e.g., Sakka, king of the gods; Vishnu, the protector of the island; lower rung deities, called Gandharvas; and others) on the day the Buddha achieved Enlightenment. After this, the god Pulastya (the grandfather of Ravana, the evil king of Lanka in the Hindu epic *The Ramayana*) gave the lines of drum poetry (*padas*) to the island's indigenous peoples (the Väddas), who gave them to the Beravā.[20] In the Bera Pōya Hēvisi, the Beravā give the gods' musical gifts back to the gods, reliving the moment of Enlightenment and asking the gods to protect their community in return for the respectful offerings (Figure 1.1).

> The Buddha's Enlightenment → the gods make music to celebrate the Enlightenment → the music is given by god Pulastya to the indigenous Väddas → the Väddas give it to the Beravā → the Beravā give it to the gods in the *Bera Pōya Hēvisi* → the gods protect the Sinhala Buddhist community.

Figure 1.1 A history of Beravā musical giving in the Bera Pōya Hēvisi.

Bear in mind that this is just the story my *gurunnānse* told me: every lineage (*paramparavā*) of ritualists vigorously guards their knowledge, and one might hear a different story up the road. This book is not a study of the Bera Pōya Hēvisi—its

---

[20] There are an estimated 10,000 Väddas living in Sri Lanka today (De Silva 2011). They now live in rural areas east of Kandy up to the northeastern coast near Trincomalee, but were once widespread throughout the island (see Chapters 4 and 5).

texts are long enough that it deserves its own study—but it *is* an attempt to situate the history of musical giving encapsulated by my *gurunnānse's* cherished Bera Pōya Hēvisi (which crosses human/divine and ethnic boundaries) in a narrative that doesn't secularize it by reducing it to a narrative just on Sinhala Buddhist ethnic identity. For while the Beravā *own* the drum patterns they play in the Bera Pōya Hēvisi, they do not conceive of the music as *theirs* (it is the gods' music), nor does it belong to all Sinhala Buddhists (it protects them).

In the years surrounding independence from Britain in 1948, elite culture-brokers decided to put dance in the school curriculum. The Beravā—a historically low and stigmatized caste—initially lauded this development (Reed 2010: 12). Teaching in schools is civil service, a highly regarded mode of employment above their status as a service caste (Reed 2010: 156). The Beravā (particularly those from the Kandyan up country) dominated traditional music and dance for the next few decades. Along the way, they learned to be concerned with cleanliness and dressing "respectably" (Reed 2010). One reported to Reed (2010: 157–158) that while it was commonplace in the past for people on a bus to look at a drum "like you are carrying a rotten piece of fish," nowadays "the drum is covered neatly with a clean cloth. The new generation [of performers] is responsible for that. . . . Now the performers are clean, they have changed." Through their conceptual transformation from ritualists into "artists" (*kalakarayo*), the stigma against the Beravā seems to have lessened (though I suggest it has not been eliminated).

Nevertheless, many Beravā came to loathe certain aspects of their postcolonial celebration as artists. First, it facilitated the stealing of their musical gifts by the higher castes. Schools want teachers who have the proper diploma; even though the dance and drumming syllabi are based on Beravā ritual knowledge, Beravā who do not have the required degree find themselves shut out of teaching jobs, even though they often know more than the teachers do. While the domain of ritual is still occupied largely by Beravā, since the 1990s, they have been increasingly replaced in schools by dance teachers from the upper castes (Reed 2010: 12).[21] Thus, some Beravā feel the main outcome of the state's patronage is that the efficacious traditions they spent centuries guarding are now being performed by others. Thus they feel exploited. Furthermore, the stealing of their musical gifts by non-Beravā foments risk, since an improper offering by novices could render the music inauspicious and anger the gods, bringing calamity on the population. Imagine the Beravā's anxiety when, concurrently with their music and dance being appropriated by the upper castes, Sri Lanka spiraled into decades of political turmoil, civil war, and natural disaster (the 2004 tsunami).

---

[21] Non-Beravā sometimes perform in *santi karmas* in the low country, but these practitioners are usually looked down upon by Beravā. There are also some institutional contexts where musicians from traditional performer families have had roles as teachers, such as at the University of the Visual and Performing Arts in Colombo.

There was also a similar transformation in Beravā dance as what went on in South India, where the dances (*sadir*) performed by female dancers (*devadasis*) wedded to gods in Hindu temples were appropriated by Brahmin (high caste) women in the mid-twentieth century and transformed into South Indian classical dance, Bharata Natyam (Allen 1997; Soneji 2012). Unlike in Carnatic (South Indian) music, though, where the instruments used in Bharata Natyam are also played as solo instruments and classified as classical music, a tradition of solo instrumental performance did not develop from Beravā drumming.[22] Unlike Bharata Natyam, whose ancestor performers were female temple dancers (*devadasis*), once dance moved from male Beravā ritualists into institutions, dance (but not drumming) became a predominantly female activity in Sinhala society.[23] While it is possible for a woman to specialize in drumming (outside the ritual context), not many do. While visiting the University for the Visual and Performing Arts in Colombo, one may see young women practicing drumming, but they are typically doing so because learning drumming is necessary for learning dance. While the newfound prevalence of women dancers is to be lauded, it shifted the spotlight from male Beravā ritualists to middle class Sinhala women. And it is arguable whether drumming developed into a comparable middle class activity. In performances at the University for the Visual and Performing Arts, for example, dozens of female dance students perform in concerts for their parents, while the drummers for such events are often male Beravā.[24]

Finally, the institutionalization process has exacerbated the rivalry between up-country (Kandyan) and low-country Beravā, leaving the latter disadvantaged. Because the up-country Kandyan Kingdom (1469–1815) was the last independent Sinhala kingdom before it was captured by the British in 1815, "Kandyan things" achieved a veneer of authenticity in the early postcolonial period that the southern low country lacked (Wickramasinghe 2002). By contrast, parts of the low country were colonized for over four hundred years by the Portuguese (circa 1505–1658), Dutch (1640–1796), and British (1796–1948).[25] Kandy is home to the country's most famous Buddhist temple, the Dalada Maligawa (Temple of the Tooth), which holds the Buddha's tooth relic; it is also the site of the Äsala Perahera (an annual procession featuring hundreds of Kandyan drummers and dancers), in which the tooth is taken out of the temple and paraded through the streets on the back of an

---

[22] I suspect this is because the drumming is shaped as sacred speech rather than "music."

[23] Sinhala Buddhist society had a tradition of women temple dancers (*digge nätum*), but this had largely died out by the early twentieth century (Reed 2010: 37).

[24] In student concerts I witnessed, excerpts of Beravā rituals are performed for parents and onlookers until about midnight; most of the audience then leaves, and the ritual is continued until morning by Beravā ritualists.

[25] European control of Sri Lanka was partial and shifting until most of the island was eaten up in the Dutch period, leaving the interior Kandyan Kingdom isolated; the British conquered it (gaining sovereignty over the whole island) in 1815.

elephant. While *peraheras* (parades associated with Buddhist temples) and rituals for deities (*deva tovils*) do occur in the low country, ritualists in the south are associated in the public imagination with *yak tovils* (sometimes called "exorcisms"), which are often devalued by orthodox Buddhists. Even though there is evidence that *yak tovils* do occur in Kandy (Vogt 1998), Kandy is associated in the popular imagination with a single auspicious Beravā ritual (the Kohomba Kankariya) and a set of dances on Buddhist themes (the Vannams) that emerged at the court of the Kandyan kings (Reed 2010).[26] For these reasons, the state greatly favored Kandyan over low-country traditions in the postcolonial years. Kandyan dancers and drummers are metonymic for "Buddhism" and the Kandyan Kingdom, while low-country dancers and drummers retain a lesser status as "devil-dancers."[27] Today's Kandyan Dance (Sri Lanka's national dance tradition) consists of excerpts from the Kohomba Kankariya ritual and Vannams.

These days, low-country ritualists feel denigrated by the Kandyans at practically every turn. In state-sponsored performances abroad and for tourists, the three regional Beravā traditions are usually represented but Kandyans always seem to go first, and sometimes Kandyans not trained in low-country drumming pick up the *yak beraya* and play it while wearing Kandyan dress, or switch into low-country dress to perform it. Kandyan drumming (*gäta beraya*) is now routinely played in Sinhala weddings in the south. Images of Kandyan dancers and drummers are featured on billboards, tourist websites, key chains, and postcards. While low country and Sabaragamuwa dancers and drummers are sometimes honored in this way (Sabaragamuwa is a region in between Kandy and the low country), they are not nearly as ubiquitous. Consequently there is much animosity between up-country and low-country Beravā.[28] For example, Reed (2010: 81) notes that her Kandyan Beravā consultants felt more affinity for their upper-caste Kandyan patrons than low country Beravā.

As I argue throughout this book, the hegemony of Kandyan Dance is a postcolonial position that is the result of its usefulness to the Sinhala Buddhist nationalist movement (as Reed herself argues). The current situation not only harms the visibility and potentially the continuity of low country and Sabaragamuwa traditions, it also obscures the fact that both are just as historically important, technically sophisticated, and "Buddhist." In Chapter 2, I show that low-country drummers place themselves at key moments in Buddhist history in Sri Lanka;

---

[26] According to popular belief, the Vannams were initially songs composed with the help of a Buddhist monk and a musician from Kerala (South India) at the Kandyan court. Dance steps were added later, and the Vannams are now a set of eighteen dances on Buddhist themes (see Chapters 2 and 4).

[27] For example, Reed (2010: 81) notes that "one Kandyan Beravā ritualist . . . told me that the Kandyan Beravā were superior to the low-country Beravā because, unlike the low-country ritualists, whose rituals focused on appeasing the lowly, malevolent yakas, their rituals were for the gods."

[28] Sabaragamuwa is understudied, and I do not have much to say about it in what follows.

that their ritual repertoire is based on core Buddhist concepts and values; and that they perform in preeminently "Buddhist" contexts. It is not my aim, though, to argue that they are more authentic than the Kandyans; rather, I seek to build bridges between these traditions by outlining a Buddhist system of sonic generosity that they share. Also, by redefining Beravā drumming and dancing as *gifts* that foster protection and healing rather than as expressions of a generic Sinhala Buddhist ethnic identity, I strive to disrupt the state's appropriation of Beravā rituals via the link between music and identity, which I show (in Chapter 2) disenfranchises minorities from a sense of belonging to the state and the cultural history of the nation.

"Buddhist Music": The Tribulations of an Idea

Much ink has been spilled in Buddhist Studies on the relationship between deity worship and "esoteric" practices that on the surface may seem to have little to do with Buddhism—a division Max Weber made between "Buddhism as a cultural institution and an ethical system" (Swearer 1995: 1).[29] Justin McDaniel (2011: 8), writing about Thai Buddhism, states that, "Ghosts, various deities, magicians, astrologies, healers, amulet dealers, [and] fortune-tellers are normative in Thai 'Theravada' Buddhism, but they are depicted as marginal or as simply an 'unfortunate' leftover of the past or unforeseen side effect of modernity by even the most progressive scholars." This, of course, is the Thai version of the world the Beravā inhabit in Sri Lanka.

The musicology of Theravada Buddhism is still in its infancy (Wong 2001; Greene 2004).[30] The reason, I propose, is that this idea of a division between

---

[29] Donald Swearer (1995: 1) writes that, "All too often a textbook picture of Theravada Buddhism bears little resemblance to the actual practice of Buddhism in Southeast Asia. . . . The observer enters a Theravada Buddhist culture to discover that ordination into the monastic order (sangha) may be motivated more by cultural convention or a young man's sense of social obligation to his parents rather than the pursuit of transforming wisdom; that the peace and quiet sought by a meditating monk may be overwhelmed by the amplified rock music of a temple festival; that somewhat unkempt village temples outnumber tidy, well-organized monasteries; and that the Buddha, austerely imaged in the posture of meditation (*samadhi*) or dispelling Mara's powerful army (*maravijaya*) is venerated more in the hope of gaining privilege and prestige, material gain, and protection on journeys than in the hope of nibbana."

[30] Scholars have recently argued against the broad application of "Theravada Buddhism" as an ascriptive social identity (Skilling et al. 2012). The term appears only once in the canonical texts, and is used narrowly to refer to an elder monk or monks in the commentaries. It achieved its current definition only in the twentieth century (Gethin in ibid.), and Buddhists in South/east Asia rarely self-identify with the term. Nevertheless, I suggest "Theravada Buddhism" has some usefulness in music studies for its ability to conjure up a history of sonic relations and similarities between practices and attitudes toward sound in Sri Lanka and mainland Southeast Asia, so long as these are situated via locally specific concerns.

Buddhism as a cultural institution and ethical system has long made "Theravada Buddhist music" appear equivalent to Buddhist chant (which Buddhists do not consider music), while drumming in rituals (also not traditionally considered "music") propitiating gods and demons struck observers as not authentically Buddhist.[31] The division between doctrinal Buddhism and the "spirit religion" was long ago bridged by scholars of Sinhala Buddhism, who argued it should be treated as having two complementary systems: one an ethical system (doctrinal Buddhism) centered on karma, meditation, and ultimately achieving *nibbana*, the other (e.g., Beravā rituals) aimed at helping devotees in *this* life through offerings to deities (e.g., Gombrich and Obeyesekere 1988; Kapferer 1983). The view remains widespread in Sri Lanka, though, that Buddhism stunted the growth of an indigenous musical tradition because it supposedly favored the visual arts, particularly "the narrative arts" (e.g., storytelling and paintings depicting the Buddha's former lives), rather than "performing arts" like music and dance (Sarachchandra 1952).[32] The view remains widespread amongst Sri Lankans that Sinhalas are invested in history (e.g., Buddhist ruins and paintings) while Tamils are invested in heritage (e.g., music and dance; Daniel 1996).[33] Sinhalas are often viewed as "unmusical"; but while outsiders often fail to appreciate the complexity of Beravā drum-speech, Sinhalese may have appreciated the complexity of Beravā drum-speech but did not classify it as music.[34] The state's redefinition of Beravā

---

[31] Consider Mabbett's (1993) claim that "In Theravada countries . . . Music has no liturgical function where the mainstream urban or 'Great Tradition' culture is strong."

[32] In Sri Lankan scholarship, earlier waves of Mahayana Buddhist influences have been defined as having facilitated a space for the development of music and ritual in Theravada Buddhism, with the latter defined as though it was shielded to remain austere ("scholars have tended to characterize Theravada as antimusic, the locus of no significant music theory or styles"; Sheeran 1998: 965). One example is Kulatillake's (1991: 39) claim that, "Had it not been for [the] accommodation of Mahayanic elements, Buddhism in its pure Theravada ideals could not have stood the intrigues of Hinduism in particular."

[33] Controversies over the worship of deities and the appropriateness of music and dance for Buddhists have erupted sporadically throughout Sri Lankan history. Three examples include: (1) during the reign of Parakramabahu II (1236–1270), the king issued an injunction that monks should refrain from poetry and drama, describing them as "despicable arts" (Sarachchandra 1952: 23); (2) in the fifteenth century, the monk Vīdāgama Maitreya was critical of the influence of what he perceived as the excessive ritualism of members of the Sangha (Seneviratne 2000: 298); and (3) during the reign of King Narendrasinha of Kandy (1707–1739), the higher ordination (*upisampada*) of monks (which had disappeared in favor of a group called the *gaṇinnānse*, who wore white robes and could marry and have children) was reestablished by the monk Weliwita Sri Saraṇankara Thero (Blackburn 2001, 2010). The *gaṇinnānse* were known to have practiced astrology. Such injunctions, though, to a certain extent are rhetorical rather than historically descriptive statements. It is the importance of *the idea* of a Buddhist prohibition on music that cannot be underestimated—it is encountered in virtually all discussions of Sinhala Buddhist music. While I contend it influenced the construction of Beravā drumming as sacred speech, it is not a common topic of conversation among drummers.

[34] For an analysis of the low-country Sinhala drum language, see Sykes forthcoming, 2018a and 2018b.

drumming as "traditional music" placed it in a comparative lens with (say) Indian classical drumming traditions, and the Beravā have had to learn how to make themselves look and sound "musical." This has led to Beravā rituals becoming flashier, the drumming more repetitive and less speech-like, and my *gurunnānse* decries this because it risks making it unacceptable as an offering.

There is also a stereotype in the West that Buddhism is more or less equated with the individual's solitary (and presumed silent) quest for nirvana. From this perspective, Beravā drumming seems un-Buddhist, for how could something be "Buddhist" when it is so loud and (to some ears) disruptive? There is also the fact that Beravā rituals involve offerings to some deities of Hindu origin. For these reasons, it was commonplace from the nineteenth century through about the 1960s for foreign observers and some Sinhala elites to assert that Sinhala Buddhist traditional music, dance, and ritual simply "came from" India, and/or that it contains elements that are of "pre-Buddhist" origin that never properly assimilated with Buddhism, and/or that medieval Sinhala music was at various times "Hindu" or "Indian" in character (see Chapters 4 and 6).[35]

This overemphasis on Sinhala cultural relations with India and Hinduism generated a backlash in writings on Sinhala traditional music from the 1970s, as scholars searched for what makes Sinhala music unique. Musicologist C. de S. Kulatillake (1974, 1976a, 1976b, 1991) published a number of studies on Sinhala approaches to meter, rhythm, and folk song. Sri Lankan popular musics were distinguished as different from Indian musics because they embody an Indian Ocean history of Portuguese colonists and African slaves (Ariyaratne 1985; De Silva and Angenot 2008; De Mel 2006; Sheeran 1997).[36] Scholars documented Kandyan (*gäta beraya*) drumming in the Temple of the Tooth (Seneviratna 1975), though low-country drumming was left largely out of the English-language literature on Sinhala traditional musics. All of these writings emerged *after* a nationalist movement to "purify" Sinhala music from North Indian influence that developed at Radio Ceylon in the 1950s, the oldest radio station in Asia, which started broadcasting in 1923 (Field 2017; I consider these developments in Chapter 6).[37]

As I show in Chapter 6, postcolonial scholarly attempts to root Sinhala music in the soil and connected to the Indian Ocean region rather than just to India were

---

[35] This is what initially made me think about Beravā drumming through a comparative lens: Is it "Buddhist" or not? Are parts of it *actually* of "Indian" origin? What do those terms mean (where in India would the tradition have come from)? Where are the more geographically close Sri Lankan Tamil Hindus in this narrative?

[36] These writings center on Baila, a genre that emerged as the island's most popular music genre in the twentieth century through its drawing on global pop forms like disco and calypso (see the Checkpoint after Chapter 5).

[37] The discussion on the history of precolonial Sinhala poetic genres and folk musics was greatly updated by Michael Roberts (2004).

intended to counter the colonial era's scholarly obsessions with the question of the historical relations between Ceylonese and Indian cultures;[38] but they developed alongside the rise of Sinhala Buddhist nationalism and an extreme hostility toward minorities (particularly Tamils) that developed during the build up to war and the war itself. A path was paved for a Sri Lankan public sphere that today more or less routinely ignores recognizing *any* historical connections between the Sinhala traditional arts, Sri Lankan Tamils, and India. Today, Beravā drumming and dancing are frequently portrayed *just* as Sinhala Buddhist and Sri Lankan. As I show in Chapter 2, nowadays Beravā dancers and drummers are sometimes physically positioned to make minorities feel like they don't belong.

In sum, while one goal of this book is to suggest that we need to acknowledge all forms of Beravā drumming as "Buddhist," another is to suggest it is time to reevaluate how Beravā drumming encapsulates histories of relations (musical giving) between Sinhala and non-Sinhala populations, especially Sri Lankan Tamils (the vast majority of whom are Hindu). Ironically, I find very little about Sinhala drumming that is "Indian," but in what follows, I acknowledge and question the historical relations between Sinhala drumming and comparable traditions from Kerala, Tamil Nadu, and Southeast Asia. In this book, I argue that the ethnic purification of Beravā culture through the link between music and identity has contributed to the alienation of Sri Lankan minorities, a move that was made possible by Beravā practices that embody histories of relations to minorities and non-Sri Lankans. The resuscitation of such histories of cultural relations, I suggest, has a critical role to play in post-war reconciliation.[39]

Literal and Conceptual Checkpoints

I consider the effects of Sri Lanka's war on musicians in Chapter 5, but a short introduction to the conflict is necessary here. As McGilvray (2008: 4) succinctly puts it, "Some argue the antipathy [between Sinhalas and Tamils] dates back to Tamil invasions from South India one or two millennia ago, while others see it as a modern postcolonial rivalry resulting from British colonial divide-and-rule policies that set up invidious communal distinctions and a system of inequitable

---

[38] According to the Sinhala chronicle the *Mahavamsa* (first compiled in the fifth century CE by Buddhist monks and updated over the centuries; Kemper 1991), the Sinhalas are descended from Prince Vijaya and his retinue of seven hundred followers who migrated from North India in the sixth century BCE (see Chapter 6). The *Dipavamsa* (an early chronicle whose material was worked into the *Mahavamsa*) reports that Mahinda Bhikkhu, son of the Indian Buddhist King Ashoka, brought Buddhism to Sri Lanka in the third century BCE.

[39] "Despite my best efforts to steer clear of the civil war and ensure that violence was not my primary focus, the ethnic conflict kept intruding into my research, just as it kept placing limits on my research subjects. The problem with violence is that it cannot be contained. It remains a fact of life on the island" (Bass 2013: 8).

rewards between the Tamils and Sinhalese."[40] With the election of S.W.R.D. Bandaranaike in 1956 on a Sinhala Buddhist nationalist platform (coinciding with the Buddha Jayanti, the 2500th anniversary of the Buddha's birth), the infamous "Sinhala Only" language law was enacted, making Sinhala the official language of government. This had a disenfranchising effect on Tamils and is now considered a major steppingstone toward the war (1983–2009). The decades in between saw policies enacted ostensibly to help the Sinhala masses, who were disenfranchised under the British. These included quotas for Sinhala students at universities, resettlement schemes placing Sinhala settlers in the Tamil- and Muslim-dominated east, and the repatriation of some Estate (Malaiyaha) Tamils to India (Winslow and Woost 2004: 6–7). The Liberation Tigers of Tamil Eelam (LTTE), initially one of several Tamil rebel groups, formed in 1976.

The official start of war was "Black July," the anti-Tamil pogrom that erupted in July 1983 when rampaging mobs (provoked by government officials and police) killed several thousand Tamils (estimates range up to three thousand) and burned down Tamil businesses in response to the killing of twelve government soldiers by Tamil separatists in the north. The war for an independent Tamil country (Eelam) in the north and east proceeded through four phases (Eelam I–IV), killing an estimated 100,000 to 140,000 people (Vimalarajah and Cheran 2010: 5). In the late 1980s, the second JVP (Janata Vimukti Peramuna, People's Liberation Front) insurrection—a Sinhala nationalist (and nominally Marxist) uprising of Sinhala youths in the south (1987–1990; the first, led by an ethnically mixed JVP, was in 1971)—terrorized that region with bombings and assassinations. The terrorism waged by the JVP and their brutal suppression by the United National Party (UNP) in power at the time marked this period as "the Terror" (*Bheeshanaya*), during which an estimated 60,000 to 100,000 people died, mostly at the hands of state forces (Walker 2013: 7; Chandraprema 1991). The JVP Insurrection was a Sinhala nationalist response to the 1987 Indo-Sri Lankan Accord, which promised Tamil autonomy in the north and brought in an Indian Peacekeeping Force (IPKF), which launched its own campaign of rape, killing, and disappearances, well-documented in Batticaloa, in the north at Point Pedro, at a teaching hospital in Jaffna, and elsewhere.[41]

Amid such terror, fighting between Tamils and Muslims escalated, as the Tamil-speaking Muslim population refused to join the LTTE. One hundred and forty-seven Muslim men and boys were killed by the LTTE in a mosque in Kattankudy in July 1990, followed by the ethnic cleansing of Muslims from Jaffna that October (NRC 2010; Thiranagama 2011). The situation only worsened in parts of the island in the 1990s, such as during the "Battle for Jaffna" in 1995, which drove

---

[40] For recent studies of the war and its aftermath, see Thiranagama 2011, Goodhand, Spencer, and Korf 2011, Durges 2013, and Rasaratnam 2016.

[41] Rita Sebastian, "Massacre at Point Pedro," *The Indian Express*, August 24, 1989, pp. 8–9; McDowell 1996; Walker 2013.

many Tamils from their homes to the LTTE-controlled northeast. The LTTE's forced-recruitment strategy turned children into combatants; they pioneered suicide bombing, attacked civilians (e.g., at Colombo's World Trade Center in 1997, the Temple of the Tooth in 1998, and Bandaranaike International Airport in 2001), and assassinated those who stood in their way. Meanwhile, government forces terrorized Tamil civilians through their system of checkpoints and raids on Hindu temple festivals, leading to abduction, torture, and the disappearance of Tamil youths suspected of being militants.

A Norwegian-brokered ceasefire in 2002 brought hopes for a lasting peace. Then in late 2004, a tsunami killed over 35,000 people. The official tally put the number of displaced at 558,287 (3% of the population), and those who suffered a loss of a home or business between one and two million (10% of the population; Walker 2013: 9). By January 2005, one and a half billion dollars had been offered in international aid (a "second tsunami"; Gamburd 2013) that brought with it numerous International Nongovernmental Organizations (INGOs), local aid organizations, and foreign volunteers. While this provided much needed help, some saw the relief effort as poorly coordinated and at worst, as demonstrating "competitive humanitarianism" (Walker 2013: 9; Stirrat 2006: 11). With the LTTE hunkered down in the rural Vanni area, cutting off Jaffna (which was ruled by the government after its defeat of the LTTE there in 1995), aid workers clustered in the east (2005–2008), mixing with conflict-related and development organizations already there. While in Aceh, Indonesia (the area most affected by the tsunami), the disaster brought about peace talks and an eventual end to that region's thirty-year conflict, this did not happen in Sri Lanka. Rather, political factions, such as the conservative party of Buddhist monks the Jathika Hela Urumaya (JHU) and Muslim political parties, remained skeptical of how the tsunami funds were being distributed. The government accused INGOs of (intentionally or not) helping the LTTE, while the enactment of a buffer zone along the southern coast was viewed cynically by many as a way to move poor Sinhalas back in an effort to build new hotels catering to Western tourists (Gamburd 2013). Thus the war and "disaster capitalism" interacted to shape the aftermath of this "natural" disaster.

Also in the mid-2000s, the growth of Islamic reform movements ("known locally under the umbrella term Tawhid Jamaat," also called Wahhabism; Spencer et al. 2015: 92–95) in Sri Lanka spawned violence with the island's Sufi Muslims, adding another dimension to the island's fragmentation. In March, 2004, commander of the eastern faction of the LTTE, Vinayagamoorthy Muralitharan (known as Colonel Karuna), defected to the government. While Karuna "initially made a show of releasing around 2,000 children and young adults to distinguish himself from the northern LTTE, he quickly began his own campaign of child-recruitment and abductions, political killings, assaults, and extortion" (Walker 2013: 8). Karuna's political party, the Tamil Makhal Viduthalai Pulikal (Tamil People's Liberation Tigers, or TMVP), collaborated with the government, gained control of Batticaloa and some other parts of the east, erasing "many of the more positive developments that had followed the 2002 ceasefire" (Walker 2013: 8). In 2006–2007, the government sought to drive the remaining LTTE cadres out of the east, a region that, on account of its status as an area divided between Sinhalas, Tamils, and Muslims, had become the "crucible" of the conflict (McGilvray 2008). This isolated the remaining LTTE cadres in the northeast, setting the stage for the final Eelam war. In January 2008, the government announced its official withdrawal from the ceasefire (Walker 2013: 12). On May 19, 2009, the war ended with the "total military defeat" (Vimalarajah and Cheran 2010: 5) of the LTTE, as remaining cadres were slaughtered (with an estimated 40,000 Tamil civilians) in an area that had been marked a "safe zone."[42]

Sri Lanka's war was "fragmented" (Thiranagama 2011: 8; Lubkemann 2005). How one experienced it was determined by one's identity, where one lived and traveled, when one did so, and one's gender, age, caste, and class. For many Sri Lankans, the war was something that occurred mostly elsewhere. Colombo was certainly overridden with fear and checkpoints during the earlier parts of my research, and the city experienced periodic bus bombs and some major attacks, but after the breakout of war in 1983, Colombo has largely been a safe place to live. As Thiranagama (2011: 229; her italics) notes, Colombo "has historically always been a place *of* minority life. The question remains to what extent it can become a place *for* minority life." Tamil and Muslim residents and visitors know where the Tamil and Muslim districts are, such as the vibrant Pettah market area and Wellawatte neighborhood. They learn the safest places to wait for buses and how to find appropriate three-wheelers (Thiranagama 2011: 229). While the south was traumatized during the JVP years of the late 1980s, the north was affected most drastically during the IPKF years in the late 1980s, the Battle for Jaffna in 1995, and the renewed fight for the region in 2006. The east suffered gravely during the 1990s (the height of war there), but had largely calmed down by the mid-2000s. But one should not underestimate the fear that a single event can generate, such as the high-profile murder of Tamil MP Joseph Pararajasingham at Mass in Batticaloa on Christmas Eve, 2005, at 1:10 a.m. (Spencer et al. 2015: 116), or the possibility of one's child being abducted to be a child soldier (which was an acute possibility in the north and east during the war). Thiranagama (2011: 12) urges us to consider how "new kinds of Tamil and Muslim identities were produced that cannot just be resolved or cast away because the war ended, but now have to be negotiated anew." At the end of the war, there were 250,000 non-combatants detained in camps (Vimalarajah and Cheran 2010: 5) and 89,000 widows living in the north and east (Louis and Deenadayalan 2011: ix). It will take many researchers to

---

[42] Details of the carnage that accompanied the end of the war were documented by the BBC in their Channel 4 documentaries *Sri Lanka's Killing Fields* (2011) and *Sri Lanka's Killing Fields: War Crimes Unpunished* (2012), as well as reports by human rights organizations (e.g., UTHR) and *The Cage*, a publication by UN spokesperson Gordon Weiss (Walker 2013: 13).

understand how these events have influenced and reshaped Sri Lankan musical practices—my work here is just a start.

While justice advocates sought reconciliation and accountability from the government for the way it concluded the war, then-president Mahinda Rajapaksa (in power from 2005 to 2014) cozied up to the Chinese. Sri Lanka was named "dialogue partner" in the Shanghai Cooperation Organization (SCO), an intergovernmental security association that includes China, Russia, and Central Asian nations (Samaranayake 2011: 119). China funded a widely publicized and controversial port project in the president's hometown of Hambantota, which opened in 2010, seen by many as extravagant because of the rural nature of the area. Rajapaksa used a language of pan-Asian brotherhood, particularly Buddhism, to justify his turn toward China, but some saw him as wanting to avoid criticism from the West for how the government ended the war. At one point the Rajapaksa family controlled 70% of Sri Lanka's national budget.[43] Rajapaksa "seized this opportune moment to consolidate the unitary state, entrench a new political dynasty . . . and neutralize the threat of Tamil nationalism and secessionism"; thus there were "strong continuities between the 'war for peace' and the 'post-war' periods" (Goodhand 2012: 130).

In 2014, the Committee to Protect Journalists ranked Sri Lanka fourth worst in its Impunity Index, which documents how easily murderers of journalists go free. The committee placed the country sixth on a list of journalists killed "without a single perpetrator being convicted," after Somalia, Iraq, Syria, the Philippines, and South Sudan.[44] From 2012 to 2014, a rise in xenophobic rhetoric by a faction of Buddhist monks (the Bodu Bala Sena, or Buddhist Defense Force) led to attacks against Muslims and Christians in the south, leading to the destruction of Muslim homes and businesses in my drum teacher's hometown of Aluthgama, generating fear among Muslims that with the end of the Tamil conflict, extremist Sinhala factions were now targeting them (Holt 2016). Rajapaksa's government was widely viewed as covertly supporting these monks. In an especially galling incident, a Buddhist monk who defied the BBS was stripped naked, beaten, and left by the side of the road for dead, after which he was thrown in jail by the government on "charges of self-inflicted violence" (the BBS denied involvement).[45] The government displaced Muslims in Colombo and elsewhere for development projects at this time (Amarasuriya and Spencer 2015).

Since the election of Maithripala Sirisena in early 2015, the island has turned a corner—though at the time of writing, to where remains to be seen. One of the first acts Sirisena made, about which I have more to say later on, was to proclaim that Tamils could once again sing Sri Lanka's national anthem in Tamil.

---

[43] The president's brother was secretary of the Ministry of Defense, another brother was Minister of Economic Development, another Speaker of Parliament.

[44] "Getting Away With Murder." Committee to Protect Journalists, Impunity List, October 8, 2015.

[45] Rohini Mohan, "Sri Lanka's Violent Buddhists," *New York Times*, January 3, 2015.

promised to devolve power and disperse the cult of personality that grew around the presidency in the Rajapaksa years. Jaffna, Trincomalee, and Batticaloa are now open to tourists and have seen enormous development—though many feel that Sinhala contractors are benefiting more from this than the local Tamil and Muslim populations.[46] Violence against Muslims returned full-force in March, 2018, in the form of rioting in Ampara and Kandy District, after Muslim youths killed a Sinhala truck driver following a traffic accident. This event led to two fatalities, numerous injuries, and damage to Muslim houses, businesses, and mosques.[47]

Here I want to consider briefly how my experience of the war's conclusion influenced the conceptual framework of this book. During the bulk of my early fieldwork (from fall 2006 to summer 2008), Colombo was dominated by stress, paranoia, and fear, embodied in countless checkpoints littering the streets. I was living in Wellawatte, a Tamil-majority neighborhood, and there was a palpable sense of impending doom as the ceasefire was officially abandoned. At one point, there were reports of a bomb going off outside a shopping center a few blocks from my apartment; a few weeks later, one went off down the street in the other direction. A bomb in a shopping district in Nugegoda during this period killed sixteen and injured thirty-seven (Satkumaratnam 2009: 191). I was in Sri Lanka on a Fulbright-Hays fellowship, and we were told to stop taking buses because of the possibility of bus bombs. More benignly, my band's gig was canceled on Independence Day in 2008 because there was a fear of violence and shops were closed.

By summer 2008, I had started broadening my research into the comparative project it became. I lived in the Tamil- and Muslim-majority region of Ampara for four months at this time (the north was still off limits), and I conducted interviews with Tamil musicians in Batticaloa and Colombo (then in 2013 and summer 2015, I conducted fieldwork in Jaffna and Mullaitivu, former warzones in the far north). I encountered musicians who had seen their children shot or abducted, who spoke of torture, fear, and harassment at checkpoints, of being trapped in their house for years, who said the north and east had become like a "camp," their movements severely restricted. I met a musician who had been trapped in his home for almost ten years (see Chapter 5). Once I drove through the all-Muslim town of Kattankudy after violence between rival Muslim factions; burning tires lined the streets and tanks were driving in my direction. Potholed streets and detours in

---

[46] At the time of writing, Sinhala extremism has arisen in a new guise, through the Sinhale movement ("Sinha" = "lion," "le" = "blood"), with graffiti and stickers emerging with the word "Sinhale" on it, as a proclamation that the island rightfully belongs just to Sinhalas. Luckily, the move has generated a fiercely negative response across social media, out of fears of a return to chauvinism and violence. Easwaran Rutnam, "Sinhale Campaign Raises Alarms," *Sunday Leader*, December 16, 2016.

[47] Mujib Mashal and Dharisha Bastians, "Sri Lanka Declares State of Emergency After Mob Attacks on Muslims," *New York Times*, March 6, 2018.

the east meant it could take hours down barely functioning roads to get anywhere in the region at that time. An older research assistant in Batticaloa said he had his home confiscated by the military in the early 1980s to be used by soldiers and got it back in 2008, void of furniture and smothered in graffiti. It bears emphasizing that the situation has improved in the north and east, and I consider a Tamil musical revival that has been brewing in Jaffna in Chapter 5.

One might think I had started a different project, one on Tamil musicians that is utterly removed from my initial study of Beravā drumming. But a key argument I want to make is that the problems I encountered in the north and east are related to the state's appropriation of the Beravā ritual arts and the subordination of low country ritualists to the Kandyans. This is because these processes posit an ideal Sinhala traditional identity—in the form of an ethnically purified Kandyan culture—and position other groups in a descending hierarchy based on how much they corrupt this ideal. Ironically, this demonstrates an awareness of the *actual* heterogeneity of Sinhala cultures through the issuing of a proclamation that such differences should be papered over and ultimately superseded. A similar process—positing an ideal Tamil figure based on cultural characteristics from Jaffna (in the north) and rejecting the diversity of Sri Lankan Tamil cultures (particularly in the east)—has been produced by some Sri Lankan Tamils, a parallel theme I trace in what follows. The positing of ethnic homogeneity and the presumed essential differences between ethnic groups and distinct parcels of land are perhaps the key legitimating discourses that drove the war, on each side.

It is not that I decided to "use" the genre I am studying, in a knee-jerk reaction, to respond to the island's political problems; rather, I had some choices in front of me: I could contribute to the discourses of separation that drove the Sinhala-Tamil conflict by simply avoiding Beravā drumming's historic relations to non-Sinhala cultures, particularly Tamils; I could "throw the baby out with the bathwater" by regurgitating colonial era claims that Beravā drumming "is" Hindu; or I could find a more balanced perspective that emphasizes *both* the Buddhist-ness of Beravā drumming *and* how it embodies a history of relations to Tamils (and other Sri Lankans and non-Sri Lankans). I chose the latter option.[48]

---

[48] Saying so should not be taken to mean I supported violence by the LTTE, whose brutality I also acknowledge. Nor does it mean I support Western imperialism (U.S. or otherwise), a common charge leveled at virtually anybody from the West who claims minorities have a legitimate right to live in Sri Lanka. Careful readers will note that I am critical of the U.S. government throughout this book—of late the U.S. has been looking a lot like Sri Lanka did during the war, with police forces armed with tanks and sound canons aimed at peaceful protestors, the shooting of innocent black civilians with impunity, and the sycophantic, nepotistic, and autocratic regime of Donald Trump. Careful Sri Lankan readers will note that I *do* trace an authentic Sinhala musical system back over a thousand years and note it is not Tamil or Indian. Critics who think I am out to bastardize Sinhala music need to read the book. I say like a mantra over and over that I am not arguing that Sinhala culture is a hybrid or modern invention. But I *also* say it is a deeply heterogenous tradition that shows countless interactions with non-Sinhalas over the centuries.

The Politics of Sri Lankan Musical Giving

In talking to musicians in the north and east, I encountered the types of stories that fill books about Sri Lanka's war, with titles like *This Divided Island* (Subramaniam 2015), *The Seasons of Trouble* (Mohan 2015), *Still Counting the Dead* (Harrison 2013), *Paradise Poisoned* (Richardson 2005), and *Not Quite Paradise* (Barker 2011). While much of my fieldwork occurred as the war was ongoing, by now the war has ended a long time ago and the island is in a different place—one I try to feel out, culturally, in what follows. Thus I didn't want to write a book called *Divided Sounds on a Fractured Island*, nor did the data I was collecting propel me toward that narrative. The challenge was to acknowledge the recent history of disaster without getting swallowed up by it.

I decided to position the Beravā in an island-wide narrative on the plight of Sri Lankan musical givers in modernity.[49] As my studies progressed, I realized that the link between music and identity has transformed many syncretic Sri Lankan musical practices into "genres" understood as naturally demonstrative of the history of ethnic and religious communities. I learned that in the recent past, Tamil musicians from the north would learn Sinhala language pop songs when they toured the south; Sinhala musicians would collaborate with Tamil and Muslim musicians on film scores; some of the most important musicians contributing to "Sinhala" music in the mid-twentieth century were Tamils and Muslims; and I met musicians who sing in six languages.

My secondary protagonists—my other main example of musical givers—are Sri Lankan Tamils who practice a music, dance, and theater genre called *kooththu*. Just as Beravā rituals are associated with Sinhala-dominated places in the south and hill country, so are particular *kooththus* associated with Tamil-majority areas in the north and east (Maunaguru 1992, 1993, 1998; Shanmugalingam 2012). The *kooththu* is a musical gift: it is not a gift to the gods per se (though it may, at times, be that)[50] but it embodies what I consider a geographically broad history of musical giving from Tamil Christians to Tamil Hindus, from Tamil Christians to Sinhala Christians, and from Sinhala Christians to Sinhala Buddhists and secularists. I heard two versions of the story. Everyone agrees the genre emerged from the South Indian "street theater" (*terukkuttu*) that was adopted by Jesuit priests in Jaffna for their Portuguese-derived Passion Plays, and by Tamil Hindus

---

[49] Doing so attends to the structural conditions that drive violence because it challenges the difference-making that happens when a syncretic cultural genre is situated in a narrative only on the history of a single ethnic community. While studies of the uses of music in wartime to generate violence or produce peace drive ethnomusicology's "conflict studies" paradigm (e.g., O'Connell et al. 2010; Pettan 1998; Pieslak 2009; Ritter and Daughtry 2007; Daughtry 2015), I suggest an attention to the structural conditions that drive violence is also important.

[50] For example, consultants stated that the Vasanthan Kooththu used to be performed to pray for rain.

for performances of Hindu epics the *Mahabharata* and *Ramayana* (and other stories) on the grounds of Hindu temples. From there the genre traveled down the west coast to the small island of Mannar and west coast town of Chilaw, where Sinhala Christians turned it into a genre called *nadagam*, with stories on saints and Catholic themes. The *nadagam* was then popularized as a secular genre—it is now widely hailed as the first "secular" Sinhala theater—by Phillippo Singho (b. 1770), whose well-known play *Ehelapola Nadagama* was produced in 1824 (though he also produced Catholic *nadagams*). While Singho's name is synonymous with the Sinhala *nadagam*, Dr. Edmund Peiris (former bishop of Chilaw) discovered that the Sinhala *nadagam* dates back at least to M. S. Gabriel Fernando's staging of *Raja Tunkattuwa* in Chilaw in 1761, a *nadagam* modeled on the Tamil *naṭakam* (i.e., *kooththu*) *Muvrasikai Naṭakam* about the Birth of Christ.[51] *Nadagam*'s popularity declined in the late nineteenth century in the wake of visiting Parsi theater troupes from Bombay, who bequeathed a local genre (called *nurthi*) that would become an important site for a "renewed Sinhala identity encompassing Sinhalese music, dress, social etiquette and language" (Wickramasinghe 2006: 81), which met its own demise with the advent of film. Nevertheless, Christian-themed Sinhala *nadagams* (including the use of puppets) continued after *nadagam*'s popularity declined. The music in Sinhala *nadagams* was heavily Tamil in flavor, drawing on South Indian Carnatic music and the *kooththu*, and it used the same drum as the *kooththu*, which Tamils call *maththalam* and Sinhalese call *maddalaya* or *Demala bera* ("Tamil drum").[52]

A few Tamil *kooththu* performers in Jaffna told me a different story that, while less publicized, is interesting to ponder. They said the Vanni region south of Jaffna is rural and would have been hard to traverse in the eighteenth century (though this does not account for travel by boat). They said the *kooththu* spread east from Jaffna through Tamil-speaking Trincomalee and Batticaloa. During the Kandyan Kingdom (1469–1815), the east was ruled by feudal Tamil warlords who held allegiances to Sinhala-dominated Kandy. My interlocutors suggested the genre then moved west, through Kandy to the west coast—though this narrative is not

---

[51] Leslie Fernando, "Did Sinhala Drama Originate in Christmas?" http://www.lankalibrary.com/rit/drama.htm. Earlier than this, Oratorian priest and missionary Joseph Vaz (canonized by Pope Francis in 2015) introduced the Pasku genre, modeled on Passion Plays he witnessed in Goa. Passion Plays were held in Kandy and the Vanni in 1706 and some years later in Trincomalee. The tradition of performing Passion Plays in Sri Lanka dates to the Portuguese, with the most famous still held annually at Pesalai in Mannar and Duwa (islands off the west coast). These used life-sized statues instead of actors; the one at Pesalai still does, while the Duwa Passion Play now uses actors and was significantly transformed in the twentieth century.

[52] Weerakkody (2011) states the traditional accompanying instruments for Sinhala *nadagams* included two drums (*maddala*), *horanāva* (a reed instrument played in Sinhala Buddhist temples), and cymbals (*talam*), though in my experience it is more common to see one *maddalaya*, a harmonium, and violin. The latter combination probably comes from the revitalization of the *nadagam* in the 1950s by Ediriweera Sarachchandra (see below).

> **Version 1 (mainstream theory).** South India → Tamil Jesuits and Saivite Hindus in Jaffna → West Coast (Mannar, Chilaw) → Sinhala Catholic and secular *nadagams*.
>
> **Version 2 (alternative theory).** South India → Tamil Jesuits and Saivite Hindus in Jaffna → Tamil Catholics and Hindus in Batticaloa → Sinhalas in Kandy → Sinhala Buddhists and Christians in Colombo.

Figure 1.2 Two versions of a history of musical giving embodied by the Tamil *kooththu*, which generated the Sinhala *nadagam*.

typically accounted for in histories of the Sinhala *nadagam* (the fact it circulates in Jaffna, though, demonstrates the remembrance of Sinhala-Tamil artistic relations from a different angle than is typically acknowledged; Figure 1.2).

The Sinhala *nadagam* had a resurgence in the 1950s when Sinhala playwright, Ediriweera Sarachchandra (1914–1996) adapted it to the stage for plays based on canonic stories about the origins of Sinhala Buddhist society. Born to a Buddhist father and Christian mother, Sarachchandra was "perhaps the foremost intellectual, scholar, teacher, and creative artist of twentieth-century Sri Lanka."[53] His 1956 play *Maname* retells a Buddhist Jataka tale (a story about a former life of the Buddha), though it is set in Sri Lanka. The story was traditionally part of *Kōlam* performances (a masked theater genre associated with the south accompanied by *yak bera* drummers). Sarachchandra's other most famous *nadagam* is *Sinhabahu* (1961), about the father of the progenital ancestor of the Sinhalas, who was half-lion ("Sinha" = "Lion"). These plays emerged in tandem with the cresting of Sinhala Buddhist nationalism, though Sarachchandra was an innovator who drew on global theater forms, from Japanese Noh to Western and Indian traditions (Dissanayake 2006). *Nadagam* formed the foundation for his plays, which Sarachchandra acknowledged as based on the Tamil *kooththu*.[54] Because

---

[53] Rajini Obeyesekere, "Ediriweera Sarachchandra: A Renaissance Man," *Colombo Telegraph*, June 10, 2014.

[54] Sarachchandra's *nadagams* are almost Wagnerian in style, in that they are through-composed and the lines of the play are sung or recited. The music is heavy on harmonium and flute, which usually mirrors the melodies of the lead singers (who are sometimes overtaken by a chorus). Sarachchandra studied at Rabindranath Tagore's school in Shantiniketan (Bengal) for two years, and *Maname* frequently features a drone note played on a *tambura*, a common feature of North Indian classical music. The music often uses *talampota* (finger cymbals) to keep time, a characteristic of South Indian and Kandyan music and dance. I suspect the drums used for his plays may change these days depending on where a performance is staged, but in the classic audio recordings, I hear what sounds like drum rolls and high-pitched accents one typically hears on the *gäta beraya*, but I suspect this is a Sinhala drummer playing *gäta beraya*-style drums on a *maddalaya* (*Demala beraya*). There are moments where drum solos emerge that to my ears sound like they are played in a Sinhala style but not in the drum-speech characteristic of Beravā drumming: they are fit into a beat cycle. Thus Sarachchandra's plays involve a

Sarachchandra knew about the relations between the *kooththu* and *nadagam*, he traveled to the Tamil-majority regions to learn about the *kooththu* for his plays. At the end of this book, I consider how the memory of Sarachchandra's drawing on the *kooththu* resurfaced in the work of Sinhala and Tamil cultural activists during the war (see "Reconnecting Sinhala and Tamil Musical Cultures").

In its traditional setting, though, the *kooththu* is best understood in relation to other Tamil artistic and religious traditions in the regions in which they exist (see Chapter 3). The genre's connections with the Sinhala *nadagam* are undoubtedly less important to Tamils today than the genre's status as their premier traditional music, dance, and drama genre. During the war, the LTTE invested in *kooththus* to spread its messages (Thompson 2005), though it was halted during the war in some Tamil-majority areas under government control because of curfews and violence.

While Beravā rituals and *kooththus* have separate histories and emerged in different periods, the genres have had parallel postcolonial histories. Each has been turned into the most hallowed traditional culture associated with Sinhalas and Tamils, respectively, through their historic attachment to regions of the island. Through this process (and despite the efforts of individuals I consider later), their historical movements around the island and interactions with Others have been neglected in favor of narratives that place them in distinct villages as projecting an ethnic and regional community's attachments to those villages back in time. I fully lay out this cultural geography of ethnic separation, with maps, in Chapter 4. Just as Kandy became the premier culture zone for Sinhalas and the site of authentic Buddhist culture, so Jaffna became the premier culture zone for Tamils and authentic Hindu culture, with other Tamil-dominated regions (particularly Batticaloa) developing a secondary status, much as the low country did for Sinhalas. The result is an ethnic bifurcation of the island's traditional music, dance, and drama traditions that mirrors the divisions inherent in the Sinhala-Tamil conflict—a geographical bifurcation into a "Tamil" northeast and "Sinhala" southwest and hill country that ignores the histories of musical giving across ethnic, regional, religious, and human-deity boundaries embodied by (Sinhala) Beravā rituals and (Tamil) *kooththus*.

Furthermore, as I show in Chapter 4, there are historic links between Sinhala and Tamil drumming that are relevant for thinking about Beravā drumming—which after all was the starting point of my research. It is commonly believed "Beravā" is a Sinhalization of the Tamil word "Paraiyar," the stigmatized Tamil Hindu drummers (known in India, though not so widely in Sri Lanka, as Dalits) who play at Hindu festivals (at non-Agamic temples) and at funerals.[55] *Beraya* (the

combination of Sinhala, North Indian, and South Indian rhythmic sensibilities played by Sinhalese on a South Indian/Sri Lankan Tamil drum.

[55] The Agamas are canonic Hindu texts in Sanskrit and South Indian languages (including Tamil). In Sri Lanka, criticisms have periodically been lodged against certain temples because they are not built according to Agamic principles, and toward some practices because they are not sanctioned by the Agamas.

Sinhala word for drum; *bera* is the plural) is probably a Sinhalization of the Tamil word *parai* (the drum played by Paraiyars).[56] While I do not think the Beravā are actually descended from Paraiyars, Chapter 4 explores possible connections between Beravā and *kooththu* drumming, and between Beravā temple musicians (the *hēvisi* ensemble) and Paraiyar Hindu temple drumming. Tracing such connections—and placing them not in a discussion of hybridity but a history of largely harmonious cultural exchange that I consider a kind of musical giving—is my contribution to post-war reconciliation.

Musical Giving as a Pre-War Utopia

To be clear, I do not think musical giving in the past was totally incapable of marking ethnic difference, a pre-war musical utopia that can be mobilized in the present day to create a "kumbaya" moment of communal harmony—a post-war multiethnic drum circle. Rather, as my studies persisted, I had to admit that to frame my project solely in the manner of recovering a communally connected past would overly romanticize musical giving, treating it as though it always ends in a transcendent moment of communal harmony.[57]

Liberal aesthetics is the modern version of what is an array of alienating ideologies embedded in forms of Sri Lankan musical giving. For example, while the European zoopolitics uses a discourse on culture, the lettered city, and the arts to demarcate who falls on the side of culture and who falls on the side of a less-than-human animal nature (Ochoa Gautier 2014),[58] for Buddhists, being an animal is an "'unfortunate destiny' (*durgati*) won through negative karma" (Ohnuma 2017) but animals have always been conceived as past and future humans and future Buddhas,[59] and their "passively listening to dharma preaching" may yield "spiritually productive consequences" (Stewart 2017: 40). To put this bluntly (and I don't wish to exaggerate the point), this indigenous zoopolitics is one where animals have the potential to move towards "culture" if they hear the words of the Buddha, while Others veer towards "nature" when they willfully do not. In some

---

[56] Thomas Borchert, "The Role of Beravā Exorcists in Sorcery," *Sunday Observer*, September 5, 2004.

[57] I recognize Janet McIntosh's (2009: 7) point that, "the current anthropological fashion for valorizing boundary crossing can too easily lead to a fetishization of it that is misplaced, given that ethnic fluidity is not a universal experience."

[58] One's "zoopolitics"—a term stemming from Derrida's (2009) discussion of logos in Aristotle's *Politics*—is "the place of an analysis and an interpretation of our political modernity in its links with the animality of the human and that of the animal, or more precisely still in its links with the proper of the human [*le propre de l'homme*] as it thinks of itself as a political and rational animal, in opposition to the animal that would be neither political nor rational" (Llored 2014: 115).

[59] For example, numerous Jataka tales include the Buddha (as a *bodhisatta*) talking to or reborn as an animal, preaching or living his Dhamma as an example for other animals, and animals may be reborn as humans and vice versa.

contexts, Beravā musical giving can be interpreted as a way to safeguard the whole island for Buddhism, an idea that goes back to the *Mahavamsa*: in common Sinhala parlance, the Buddha deemed the island a place for the protection of Buddhism, as *Dhammadipa* (the island of the Buddha's Dharma), and thus "to fight for Sri Lanka is to fight for Buddhism, and vice versa" (Bass 2013: 47; Bartholomeusz 2002).

Gift-giving generated ethnic solidarity and difference in precolonial Sinhala society (Roberts 2004). In the Kandyan Kingdom, peripheral rulers acknowledged the Kandyan king as *cakkavatti* (world ruler) through gift-giving, forming "a sense of collective identity against the threat of foreign others" (Sivasundaram 2007: 117). In postcolonial Sri Lanka, Buddhist parades (*peraheras*) featuring Beravā drummers and dancers have nationalist overtones, and thus some Beravā musical gifts today mobilize ethnonationalist sentiment *through* sonic generosity to gods or VIPs. Eventually, I realized that to recognize Beravā musical giving-as-protection according to its own values is to recognize that it has long played a role in producing the notions of difference I was trying to undermine through examples of musical giving across Sri Lankan communities. Premodern Beravā musical giving however, was not *about* difference but was rather a form of *exchange* that exacerbated differences, because it was used on certain occasions to protect against Others.

Similar to Sinhala society, Tamil music and dance was (and to certain extents, still is) an efficacious offering to gods that must be made to ward off calamity. Consider Carnatic classical dance (Bharata Natyam), which is derived from the dance (*sadir*) of female temple dancers (*devadasis*): "The most important task of the devadasi," writes Saskia Kersenboom (1987: 119), ". . . was to remove evil influences from the deity," a task the dancer qualified for on account of her "being ever-auspicious" (Kersenboom 1987: 119). Besides their offerings of songs and dances for the gods' comfort (Kersenboom 1987: 119), they were required to safeguard "the generation of Cosmic Energy in the *linga*," which if not "safeguarded . . . cooled off (by various offerings) and reabsorbed into an undifferentiated unity . . . would "burn up the entire kingdom and *bhutaloka* [a period where bad spirits and evil demons hold sway] would come into existence" (Kersenboom 1987: 120). Music is one of the sixteen "rites of adoration" (*upacāram*) offered to deities in South Indian temples (Appadurai 1981: 22, 26), including the *nadaswaram* (a reed instrument) and *thavil* (a barrel-shaped drum) played for gods in Hindu temples. One might also consider the devotional songs of the medieval Tamil Saivite saints (*Thevaram*) and the later "Trinity" of Carnatic composers as gifts to gods. A full study of how these traditions are and are not "gifts" would require vastly more space than I am allotted here.[60] Jacob Copeman (2011: 1055) notes that the gift (*dana*) in South

---

[60] I am not claiming music in all Hindu contexts is a gift; Paraiyar drumming at funerals, which ensures safe passage of the soul of the deceased, may be based more on sonic efficacy than gift (and it would be hard to consider it a gift to upper caste patrons, who pay Dalits for the service, and to whom they traditionally felt degraded).

Asia (a term that operates in Hinduism, Buddhism, and Jainism) has appeared to some scholars as "a kind of special access route to Indian cultural logics," i.e., "a deeper structure that is simply South Asian" (Babb 1996: 94).[61] I suggest we eschew this homogenizing notion of the "Indian" or "Hindu" (or "Buddhist") gift, though I do suggest in what follows that Tamil discourses on music and dance tend to ignore the role of music in the redistribution of rights and honors in Hindu contexts (Appadurai 1981: 33–50) and focus instead on using an ancient Indian treatise on the arts, the *Natya Shastra,* to argue that South Indian music and dance (the "Carnatic" classical tradition) developed in ancient times and grew up unaffected by the traditions of outsiders.[62] The *Natya Shastra* narrative, I suggest in Chapter 4, was generated by (or dovetailed with) liberal aesthetics to allow for a forgetting of the efficacious power of sound as a Hindu offering when it comes to historical narratives on music and dance in Tamil society.[63]

Returning to the Beravā, I believe we have a responsibility to recognize their musical giving as protection from Others *and* as embodying an openness and respect for gods and all beings—they're both there and neither should be ignored, but we *can* decide one is more productive to emphasize as a framework for thinking about phenomena now dubbed "Sri Lankan culture." It will be useful here to briefly ruminate on Bruce Kapferer's classic writings on low country *yak tovils* and Sinhala Buddhist nationalism, since I am adopting a somewhat similar strategy of looking internally in Sinhala Buddhist culture to think about nationalism and formations of difference. In his *A Celebration of Demons* (1983), Kapferer states that "exorcists call upon the power of the Buddha and invoke the gods—who symbolize the power in hierarchy and whose power is dependent [on the hierarchical potential of the Buddha]—to restore the cosmic order, an order threatened by demonic malevolence and the illusion of demonic power" (the interpolation here is from Wijeyeratne in his appendix to Kapferer 2011: 292). As Wijeyeratne puts it in his summary of Kapferer's work, "The demonic constitutes an intrinsic, intimate aspect of the cosmic order of Sinhalese Buddhism as that

---

[61] This notion emerged largely through non-South Asianists' reading classic ethnographies of the 1980s that showed *dana* acts as a "mechanism of caste-ranking through 'impurity' transfers," connecting "kingship and kinship models" across the subcontinent (Copeman 2011: 1055). Preeminent among these was Gloria Raheja's (1988) notion of the "poisonous gift," adopted by Derrida to sustain his famous argument in *Given Time* that the gift in its pure form must lie outside the cycle of obligation and reciprocation and therefore also outside recognition: "For there to be gift, it is necessary that the gift not even appear, that it not be perceived or received as gift" (Derrida 1991: 16). Subsequent South Asianists have argued about whether Hindu and Buddhist gifts exemplify Derrida's notion of unreciprocated giving (ibid.; Hibbets 1999; Laidlaw 2000; Heim 2004; Bernstein 2013).

[62] "Redistribution" is a "*within* relation, the collective action of a group. Reciprocity is a *between* relation, the action and reaction of two parties" (Sahlins 1972: 188; in Appadurai 1981: 33). Both may create hieearchy and difference, the former within a community, the latter between communities.

[63] For a discussion of how some Sinhala observers have used the *Natya Shastra* to articulate essential differences between Kandyan Dance and South Indian traditions, also see Chapter 4.

which threatens its hierarchical telos and as an agent who, once transformed into a force of benevolence, is integral to the re-hierarchilizing logic of the cosmic order" (in Kapferer 2011: 292). This re-hierarchilizing in low-country Sri Lankan rituals, it is worth emphasizing, is performed in large part by *yak beraya* drummers. He continues that, "as an ontology of the everyday, the Buddhist cosmic order not only generates the force of transformation intrinsic to healing rituals [*yak tovils*] but also conditions the transformative logic of modern Sinhalese nationalism."[64]

Unlike Kapferer, my goal is not to *explain* nationalism via Beravā rituals but to *find a way out* of reproducing nationalism and its demonization of the Other via Beravā rituals. However, Kapferer's (2011: viii) thesis is similar to mine in that he argues that "nationalist ideology can distort and skew what are otherwise diverse sociocultural possibilities in potentially disastrous directions for human populations." There is, obviously, a symbiosis between the Othering mechanisms of Sinhala Buddhist nationalism, Beravā rituals, and discourses on community in the music and identity episteme, and such "Othering" mechanisms are integral to the reproduction and stability of a sense of safety for Sinhala Buddhists: these are key functions of Beravā drumming. But there is *also* within Beravā drumming an emphasis on respect for the divine, care for people, and commitment to generosity that stems from the prevalence of gift-giving in Buddhism. These factors may be integral to the Othering mechanisms when aimed inward, but in this book, I choose to use them to build a cultural history of Sri Lankan musics that projects *out* from Sinhala society, as a way to break the Othering mechanism, by noticing various kinds of sonic generosity and giving of musical gifts across Sri Lanka. This is an idealistic perspective, but one that I argue is grounded in the historical record.

The Post-Orientalist Debate

Thus I situate this book gingerly in a debate in Sri Lankan studies on the birth of ethnic consciousness on the island that, I suggest, has broad relevance for scholars in music studies. Much writing in Sri Lankan studies has queried the historic fluidity of ethnic categories, arguing that people have long married into ethnic groups to become "Sinhala," "Tamil," or "Muslim," or done so after moving from different regions or from off-island. Studies have demarcated

---

[64] Writing about musical nationalism in Maharashtra in India, Anna Schultz (2013: 12) notes that "nationalism is a cosmopolitan concept, but not all nationalists are cosmopolitan." She suggests that we stay attuned to how "noncosmopolitans actively contribute to nationalism in ways that subvert and reject form" (13). As my work here (and Kapferer's voluminous writings—see also Kapferer 1997) makes clear, Sinhala Buddhist elites and non-elites alike draw on Buddhist concepts of sound and sovereignty in their production of nationalism rather than simply adopt a secularized nationalism taken wholesale from the West in modular fashion.

hybrid villages, hybrid regions, hybrid populations, and some have suggested the whole island is hybrid.[65] Such scholars emphasize that colonial categorizational schemes (e.g., the colonial census) rigidified communal binaries: "Buddhist and Hindu, Sinhalese and Dravidian, Sri Lankan and south Indian, native and invader" (Meegama 2010: 31; Rogers 1994).[66] This emphasis on ethnic fluidity was a rejoinder to colonial era scholarship that, John Rogers (1990: 87) notes, was guided by two background assumptions: "that in ancient times there was a great Sinhala civilization, which later went into decline; and that distinct and often antagonistic ethnic groups existed throughout the island's long history." Colonial era scholarship, for example, tended to situate the ruins of Hindu temples at the ancient city of Polonnaruwa as "intrusions upon a preexisting, 'purely Sinhala civilization'" even though some Sinhalas would have worshipped such deities, and Sri Lanka and India have been in continuous contact since the Mesolithic period (Meegama 2010: 31).

Recent scholarship, though, has issued a rejoinder to this "post-Orientalist" idea that ethnic consciousness in Sri Lanka is traceable to the colonial period. In the Kandyan Kingdom, Michael Roberts (2004) asserts, Sinhala oral modes of communication (e.g., folk songs) channeled popular sentiment and crystallized Sinhala-ness in the wake of foreign threats. Precolonial oral modes of communication "reinforced [the] image of the King and the unitary nature of his kingdom," since visiting chiefs and dignitaries had to partake in *däkum* ("having seen"), a practice of ritually recognizing the king's sovereignty to obtain trading rights.[67] "Each ruler of the principal *Sinhala* state," Roberts (2004: 71) writes, "considered himself to be *Trisinhalesvara* or *Chakravarti* covering the whole island of Trisinhale" (his italics—the latter word refers to an old Sinhala division of the country into three parts). This practice changed, though, once Vanniyars (petty rulers) recognized the sovereignty of the Kandyan king—a situation that was made possible, Roberts suggests, because of the Nayakkar (Tamil) ancestry

---

[65] See, e.g., Yalman 1967; Rajasingham-Senanayake 2002; Jayawardena 2007; and Silva 2002.

[66] It is worth pausing to stress that South India was predominantly Buddhist for much of the first millennia CE. The founder of Zen Buddhism, Bodhidharma, was born in the South Indian city of Kanchipuram, while Nagapattinam was known to be a prominent Buddhist center in the fourth and fifth centuries CE. During the Kandyan Kingdom (1469–1815), King Vira Narendra Sinha (ruled 1707–1739) was married to a Tamil princess from the Madurai Nayak Dynasty of South India, and since they had no children, the royal line passed to her brother, Sri Vijaya Rajasinha (1739–1747). While these later Kandyan Kings identified as Buddhist, and perhaps became zealous in their patronage of Buddhism in order to gain the trust of the people (Holt 1996), they were ethnically Tamil. Thus we should not assume that, from a *longue durée* perspective, being "Tamil" meant being "Hindu" and being "Buddhist" meant being "Sinhala."

[67] Siri Gamage, "Concept of Unitary State and its Roots in the Sinhala Consciousness," *Asian Tribune*, February 15, 2007. *Däkum* is found in Beravā rituals; for example, a section I learned of the Bera Pōya Hēvisi involves playing the words "having seen" the Buddha, one's guru, and various deities on the drum.

of the Kandyan kings at that time (Roberts 2004: 75). In a subtle twist on the post-Orientalist scholars' focus on the fluidity of ethnic identity, Roberts notes that "migrants were able to change their identity to be included in the mainstream Sinhala-Buddhist identity" (Gamage 2007). In other words, there was ethnic fluidity *and* a sense of ethnic boundaries.[68]

Here is why this debate has broader relevance for music studies and this book. The idea that we have to choose between, on the one hand, picking a time when a community's ethnic identity arose and stabilized in a region, or on the other, emphasize that identities are always in flux and ultimately a fiction, has long characterized debates about nationalism, ethnicity, and culture the world over. The debate is particularly important in the world today, from the reemergence of white nationalism in the United States and nativist movements in Europe to burgeoning ethnonationalist movements in South and Southeast Asia, of which Sri Lanka is just one (e.g., Hindutva in India; the Buddhist 969 movement in Myanmar; Islamic revivalism in Bangladesh and Malaysia). All these movements to varying degrees champion violence against and/or strive to displace minorities, often with official sanction from governments. I suggest we're going to get nowhere with them by simply arguing that identities are constructed. Nor do we gain in the long run by promoting a multiculturalism that aims simply for minority cultural recognition—for isolating and delimiting the historical importance of minorities is what ethnonationalism is all about. Rather, I contend a better route is to invest in the public promotion of histories of interaction between communities that ethnonationalists define by sheer difference. Rather than just saying Muslims also have rights in India and Burma, and Hindus also have rights in Bangladesh, and Muslims also have rights in the United States, we need broader recognition of the connected histories between populations in these countries.[69]

Here's how I find my way out of this issue. In what follows, I contend that Sri Lankan musical instruments and styles over the centuries did not have such a rigid

---

[68] Another retort to the post-Orientalist perspective is Anne Blackburn's (2001, 2010) contention that previous scholarship, emphasizing "Protestant Buddhism" (a term famously coined by Gananath Obeyesekere for a nineteenth-century Buddhist revival that utilized Protestant modes of worship and dissemination) neglected to recognize the broad persistence of traditional Buddhist modes of worship and dissemination of texts and ideas. I suggest we do not have to choose between these viewpoints: certain aspects of Buddhism were transformed, others persisted.

[69] As for Sri Lanka, we need to be careful about moving from a claim that a community (e.g., the Sinhalas) had ethnic consciousness quite early on and the fact that they conceptualized a whole territory as united under a sovereign to the idea that the entire place always did belong to that sovereign and therefore the place's cultural history today truly belongs just to the ethnic group that sovereign belonged to. As I show in what follows, the Sri Lankan past is characterized by regional kingdoms and peoples with tenuous connections to sovereign powers that laid elsewhere. Falsely projecting historic ethnic unity over territories is a core component of ethnic nationalism. Much of Texas did belong to Mexico, after all.

"ethnic" demarcation as they do now; however, I identify Sinhala instruments and approaches to drumming, meter, and folk song that have maintained a continuity for centuries, as far back as the thirteenth century and perhaps earlier. What I argue is that despite communal lines being drawn throughout history, musical instruments and ideas often crossed those lines, and when they did so, they were resignified and transformed—and in this book, I focus mainly on the Sinhala side of that line. Furthermore, I suggest the only way to dislodge culture from such violent movements is to dislodge it from the link with identity. I am not suggesting identities or cultural practices are not ancient, but that the latter were not typically about "identity" in the past in they way that they are now. Sri Lankan musics in the past were more like aspirin, glasses, sunblock, or a gun. One can use a gun to protect oneself, but one would not normally think that a gun is the same thing as your identity. That such a situation has developed in the United States, where people fetishize guns to such an extent that they use them to forge a link with territory—such as the invention in Texas of a state flag with a rifle on it—should demonstrate the ridiculousness of making the same assumption about music, that this connection with identity is *in nature*, that it has always been there.

A Musicology of the Secular

To sum up, my broader thesis is that "modern secular governance has contributed to the exacerbation of religious tensions . . . hardening interfaith boundaries and polarizing religious differences" (Mahmood 2015: 1)—and I argue the music and identity episteme needs to be located in this project and its communally divisive results. As Saba Mahmood writes about Egypt (a point that can be extended to Sri Lanka), "the modern state and its political rationality have played a . . . decisive role in transforming preexisting religious differences, producing new forms of communal polarization, and making religion more rather than less salient to minority and majority identities alike" (Mahmood 2015: 2).[70] However, we should not be goaded into thinking that "the ideological discourse of modern disciplinary power . . . [is] its actual modes of operation" (Mazzarrella 2013: 24): a secularizing discourse on the traditional arts and culture may be *utilized* by the state even while government officials *fund* the efficacious sounds of a religious ritual.[71] My point,

---

[70] "This process has resulted in the intensification of interreligious inequality and conflict, the valuation of certain aspects of religious life over others, and the increasingly precarious position of religious minorities in the polity" (Mahmood 2015: 15).

[71] Examples abound in South and Southeast Asia. For example, Jeffrey Dyer (2017: 42) argues that the conceptualization of the *wai khruu/thvāy grū* ritual in Thailand and Cambodia contributes "to the ongoing antagonism" between both countries, since the ritual's "public displays of Thai-ness reduces the chance that Thailand might acknowledge any overlap this ritual shares with Cambodia," while "Cambodia's national anthem gathers ancestors and deities to protect the nation."

then, is not the banal one that modern languages of the arts have secularizing tendencies but that wielders of efficacious sonic practices are put in positions of reluctance, despair, and exploitation when the state defines them as disenchanted representations of communal traditions yet still makes use of their efficacious powers. It is this ethnographic context—the exploitation of the powers of musical givers even as their music is discursively disenchanted—that I foreground in this book.

The Gift

In what follows, though, I do more than just describe musical giving in religious contexts; using the Beravā as a foundation from which I think broadly about various Sri Lankan aesthetic systems that utilize sonic generosity, I locate sonic generosity in Sri Lankan "music history" and ask, in turn, whether thinking of music ontologically first and foremost as a gift might productively contribute to reconciliation in post-war Sri Lanka by surfacing histories of communal exchange and recognition.

Mauss draws out this relationship between gifts and peacemaking in his famous *Essai sur la donne*: "it is by opposing reason to feeling, by pitting the will to peace against sudden outbursts of insanity ... that peoples succeed in substituting alliance, gifts, and trade for war, isolation and stagnation" (2010: 105). Mauss also reasons the obverse is true: "To refuse to give, just as to refuse to accept is tantamount to declaring war; it is to reject the bond of alliance and commonality" (1990: 13).[72] Marshall Sahlins writes that Mauss corrected the "simplified progression from chaos to commonwealth, savagery to civilization, that had been the work of classical contract theory" (1972: 180). For while he argued "from an original condition of disorder" (Sahlins 1972: 169) much like Hobbes did from the state of nature, for Mauss society emerges not through government but prestations that are "total social phenomena," and which later developed into legal contracts. Mauss thus defines the gift as "Reason ... the triumph of human rationality over the folly of war" (Sahlins 1972: 175).

In this book, I argue that discourses on artistic history *as stories about gifts* have a role to play in promoting peace in the world; but I suggest we should avoid positioning them as Reason. Rather, my argument is that once we jettison the idea that music necessarily emanates from a self or community and points back to it as a story about itself, we are left with stories about the arts that do not accord well with state-driven, civil society-driven, corporate, and other top-down narratives of community. Lewis Hyde (2007: 110) describes gifts, rather romantically, "as anarchist property." An anarchist (ethno)musicology, I contend, should

---

[72] Lévi-Strauss (1969: 67) later made the same point more succinctly: "exchanges are peacefully resolved wars and wars are the result of unsuccessful transactions."

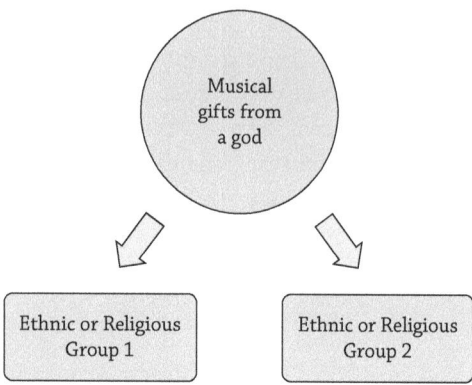

Figure 1.3 The same sounds from a god may protect people from different ethnic and religious groups.

be driven by sonic exchanges across communal, geographic, and human/nonhuman boundaries. This should not only be a story of peace; but it *does* have the ability to avoid producing the boundaries posited by the identity paradigm.

Consider Mauss's famous assertion that "one must give back to another person what is really part and parcel of his nature and substance, because to accept something from somebody is to accept some part of his spiritual essence, of his soul." A significant challenge of the gift to normative conceptions of music history is that musical gifts may not have human origins and thus may not "seek to return" to humans but to the nonhumans that created them. The Beravā's musical gifts in the Bera Pōya Hēvisi, for example, are the drum-speech the gods played to celebrate the Buddha's Enlightenment, and they are headed back to the gods.[73] Once we define some music as things that originated with and can (or must) be exchanged with nonhumans, and once we accept sonic efficacy as ontologically valid, certain musical traditions that the identity paradigm construes as belonging only to one ethnic or religious group emerge as having a multi-ethnic or multi-religious history.

Figure 1.3 argues that because of sonic efficacy, "listeners" help constitute a genre's history so long as they benefit from its sounds, though they may also give such sounds back to the god or gods.[74] One may reverse these arrows and consider,

---

[73] I urge readers to search for examples of return-gifts in the ethnomusicological literature. A great example is Sakakibara's (2009) aforementioned case of Iñupiaq songs given to the whales who initially gave them to humans. The incorporation of nonhumans as "composers" challenges Blacking's (2000: 10) classic definition of music as "humanly organized sound."

[74] One benefit of Actor-Network Theory is that it forces us to account for the *material* effects of immaterial actors: Latour asks, "Why not say that in religion what counts are the beings that make people act, just as every believer has always insisted" (Latour 2005: 119, 235)? Consider as well Arjun Appadurai's (1986: 5) statement that "even though from a *theoretical* point of view human actors

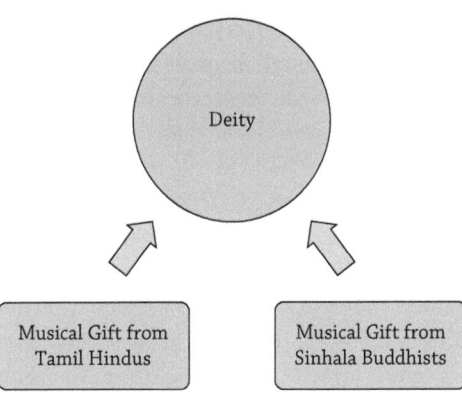

Figure 1.4 Two different religious groups giving musical gifts to the same god.

as well, sonic offerings from people to a god or deified saint who facilitates protection regardless of the person's "religion," such as for Hindus who visit Sufi saints' shrines in India. This model (Figure 1.4) works also for a few cases I found in Sri Lanka of Sinhala Buddhist drummers playing at a "Hindu" temple, their musical offerings going to the same deity as those offered by Tamil Hindu musicians (see Chapter 4). Recognizing the validity of human-nonhuman sonic gift exchanges in music studies requires adhering to the principle that, "as long as they make a difference in what people do, the gods are real actors with relative existence" (Day 2010: 280–281).[75]

Contra Hyde, however, these examples should be enough to demonstrate that musical gifts are not necessarily anarchic—they do not necessarily leap free from or escape the "nation," in the way that some ethnomusicological studies positioned cosmopolitanism and globalization in the 1990s.[76] In a recent essay, Marshall Sahlins (2017) points out that so-called "egalitarian" or "acephalous" societies ("the original political order") "are in structure and practice cosmic polities, ordered and governed by divinities, the dead, species-masters, and other such metapersons endowed with life-and-death powers over the human population." Recognizing that "the state of nature is already something of a political state" (Sahlins 2017) requires, for our purposes, attending to how musical gifts to gods have long materialized state and proto-state structures, and to question whether

encode things with significance, from a *methodological* point of view it is the things-in-motion that illuminate their human and social context" (his italics).

[75] Latour (2011) uses the term "factish." Finch (2012: 628) describes it this way: "Divine beings . . . act on human bodies and are acted upon; they demand, propel, justify, and respond to particular somatic activities and experiences, whether moral, destructive, ecstatic, medical, or otherwise. Gods and humans together, along with all sorts of other things, continuously create the material world."

[76] "Ontologies of the otherwise" need to be recognized as firmly entangled with political developments in the modern world if we are to avoid a return to "the anthropological primitive" (Bessire and Bond 2014).

and how they still do so according to the gift paradigm even when such practices are conceptually transformed through discourses on identity and expression.

I hope the above is enough to demonstrate that noticing that music may be a gift handled and offered by humans rather than "expressed" by them does not require eliminating the emotions or body in music studies. "Power is a thing of the senses," Kathleen Stewart reminds us (2007: 84). Starting with the body as "a sort of phenomenological zero point," Donovan Schaefer (2015: 14) notes that the body appears as a "prisoner in solitary confinement"; however, "contra Descartes, solitary confinement shows that starving bodies of their affective points of contact with their worlds does not liberate them, but drowns them in profound suffering, leaving sustained traumatic effects." To highlight that bodies have "compulsions" is to depict "bodies as animal—as radically dependent on their affective relationship with the world. Affectivity is not optional, but compulsory."[77] In this book, what all of my examples share is that they are compulsory acts that break out of this solitariness to intentionally produce a more harmonious being-in-the-world: the Beravā *have* to give their musical gifts to ensure Others are protected from disaster; a Malay singer feels compelled to sing me "Hotel California" as a gesture of respect that acknowledges my American background; a hip hop artist bravely offers a song demanding human rights for all Sri Lankans despite facing threats from shady groups of thugs; two activists bring Sinhala musical theater to the Tamil-dominated north and Tamil musical theater to the Sinhala-dominated south.[78] While a discourse on expression may make sense for these and some other examples I provide in the book, to *not* call them gifts is a *choice* that obscures the manner through which they act, and which would situate the emotions they elicit in the realm of artificially closed-off performers, listeners, and audiences.

So far as the Beravā are concerned, their musical gifts are their inalienable possessions. "Some things, like most commodities," Annette Weiner (1992: 6) writes, "are easy to give. But there are other possessions . . . imbued with the intrinsic and ineffable identities of their owners which are not easy to give away":

> Ideally, these inalienable possessions are kept by their owners from one generation to the next within the closed context of family, descent group, or dynasty. The loss of such an inalienable possession diminishes the self and by extension, the group to which the person belongs. . . . Connections to ancestors, gods, sacred sites, the legitimating force of divine rulers, or ideologies . . . authenticate the authority that

---

[77] "A body is not a given, but 'acquired,' through ongoing exchanges with things-as-they-are that produce not only the body as a 'sensory medium' but also a 'sensitive world'" (Finch 2012: 628). The perspective on communally entangled, affective listening I build here shares a kinship with Stokes's (2010: 189) notion of "*distribution* in an economy of affect" (his italics).

[78] As a process of reckoning, musical giving is one way to make traumatic experiences sensible (Pilzer 2010: x).

an inalienable possession attains. Through this legitimating force a possession becomes unique, rising above the flux of other things that can easily be exchanged (Weiner 1992: 6).

Inalienable possessions must to some extent circulate publicly, for they must be *known* to maintain the power they hold. However, they must not *actually* be given away, for then their owners lose the authority gained by their possession. Weiner (1992: 6) calls this "keeping-while-giving." She writes, "The inherent tension in keeping-while-giving follows from two fundamental contradictions: one, the challenge to give is at the same time a challenge of the ability to keep, and two, the challenge to surrender the documentation of difference between exchange participants is, at the same time, a challenge to the guardianship of autonomy" (Weiner 1992: 150; Godelier 1999).[79] I suggest it is the need for the Beravā to *show* their musical gifts in public without having them get stolen that greatly influences the structure of Beravā drumming as disguised sacred speech.[80]

While not all music everywhere should be identified as a gift, I suggest an understanding of music as ontologically first and foremost a gift that is then incorporated into and only partly transformed by commoditization will generate insight on the ambiguous relations between music and the commodity form.[81] I contend the language of "musical exceptionalism" that treats music as a "doing" and personal experience at odds with capitalism (often dubbed, erroneously in my view [see below] as "performativity") is the same language that defines music's place in the market economy, including as a resource (Ochoa Gautier 2013; Beaster-Jones 2014). This language obscures the persistence of musical giving in capitalism. My broader idea, which I hope will be applicable to many places beyond Sri Lanka, is that thinking of music history as a game of keeping-while-giving can allow for a new way to understand how musics accrue value in and outside capitalism. For even musical commodities tend to be affiliated with the *names* of those featured on recordings, and thus in a sense are given by musicians without actually being

---

[79] Criticizing Mauss and much classic work on reciprocity, Weiner says that, "it is not the hoary idea of a return gift that generates the thrust of exchange, but the radiating power of keeping inalienable possessions out of exchange" (Weiner 1992: 150). See Muller (1999: 58–63) and Steingo (2016: 116) for discussions of keeping-while-giving in relation to Zulu cosmology and music in South Africa.

[80] In Beravā rituals, this works via what Cimini and Moreno (2016) call "fiduciary aurality": "a quasi realism that links aurality with a given but unexamined and nonnegotiable object [the drum-speech], and second, a relationality wherein aurality harnesses that object to procure a particular good for the listener," in the Beravā's case, protection of the community from disaster.

[81] In what follows, I do not focus on gifts that surround music (e.g., lending an amp, gifting a performance venue for an event); in Maussian total prestations, music often accompanies gifts (I suspect it has often *been* a gift in such situations but not recognized as such by outsiders)—for example, Bataille (1988: 51) notes that among the Aztecs, sacrificial victims were often "well aware of their fate and were forced to stay up the final night, singing and dancing" (see also Tomlinson 2007: 103).

given away. I propose we consider musical giving and gifts as actions that *are* and that produce subjects/objects, and that musical gifts move through different "stages," even becoming commodities, as they move through "tournaments of value" (Appadurai 1986; Beaster-Jones 2016: 62–63).

Thus I do not posit that musical gift-giving is necessarily anathema to musical commoditization (e.g., Hyde 2007). It will be wise to mark a difference between *a music* that functions as a gift, and *musical giving* as an action (with each able to occur in capitalism). For even popular music—the paradigmatic "commercial" music—may be more of a gift than a commodity (Baym 2011; Anderson 2014), or "something produced for subsistence rather than surplus" (Morcom 2015). I do recognize a tension between musical giving and capitalism, since in the digital age "the potential for corporate exploitation of 'user-generated' gift economies is ever present" (Baym 2011: 25). I do *not* presume a song's meanings and values are necessarily lost when it is bought or sold, nor that the gift loses its ability to foster community once it is commoditized. While musical gifts outside capitalism can be alienable—a folk song can be given from one person to another, its composer forgotten—in capitalism, music becomes *less* alienable.[82] It also becomes *less* compulsory. Consider how, in the digital age, "aligning the care of the self to performative efficacy is slowly changing in the midst of the transformation of the music industry itself" (Ochoa 2013: 14). Musicians often have little chance to make money off music and so many turn to styles "regardless of [their] political, cultural, or economic translatability" (Ochoa 2013: 14). This involves less concern with the star system, favoring a niche audience that is seen to be more nurturing.[83]

Hyde describes gift exchange "as an 'erotic' commerce" that opposes "eros (the principle of attraction, union, involvement which binds together) to logos (reason and logic in general, the principle of differentiation in particular)" (Hyde 2007: xx).[84] Of course, gifts do set up hierarchies in and between communities,

---

[82] There are songs that are valuable because of their link to identity outside of capitalism (e.g., national anthems), while some songs that have been commodified (e.g., Christmas songs) find their value more because of sentiment than "identity." But I believe these are exceptions to the rule: the musical commodity circulates and accrues value because of its attachment to a name. In cases of appropriation, I suggest, what happens is that one identity is erased by another (this is not to say that recordings fail to accrue new and take on different values as they circulate; see Beaster-Jones 2016: 62).

[83] In concerts, I suggest, the act of giving is more easily recognized than in a recording (and in more intimate settings, more so), even though both may function as gifts and commodities.

[84] Hyde believes that "a gift, when it moves across the boundary, either stops being a gift or else abolishes the boundary. A commodity can cross the line without any change in its nature; moreover, its exchange will often establish a boundary where none previously existed (as, for example, in the sale of a necessity to a friend). Logos: trade draws the boundary—eros: trade erases it" (Hyde 2007: 78). This articulation, though, neglects the "feedback" that occurs when gifts and commodities circulate, which "defers and distorts communication, even as it enables new possibilities for connection" (Novak 2013: 19). Moreover, the talent of star performers who connect with an audience in a huge arena, e.g., Bruce Springsteen, is their ability to mix this erotic commerce with the principle of differentiation.

but thinking about the gift as eros and commodity as logos can help us further nuance the relations between musical giving and capitalism. Consider Genevieve Vaughan's work from the 1970's. Reflecting on Marx's footnote that "the human being does not come into the world bringing a mirror with him.... The man Peter grasps his relation to himself as a human being through becoming aware of his relation to the man Paul as a being of like kind with himself" (2004), Vaughan had the following thought:

> Well ... he may not come into the world with a mirror, but he does come with a mother! The child identifies with the mother first. It is only later that Peter has to see himself as a male through his relation to Paul, in the same way that a commodity has to find its value reflected in money. It was then that I first began to think of the market as a derivative of an artificially non nurturing male gender construction. I developed this idea extensively later (1997), and coined the term "masculation" for the process in which the boy child is alienated from his identification with his nurturing mother, and has to create an identity based on categorization itself, with the father or other significant male as exemplar of the category. The boy then has to compete to become the exemplar, and the female model is eclipsed. The daughter continues her identification with the mother but also has to accept the mother's eclipse and therefore her own. The mother then preferentially and contradictorily nurtures the males more than the females, including herself, because the males have given up nurturing.

Vaughan (2004) concluded that in contrast to "the market as alienated material communication," gift-giving is best thought of as mothering, which she theorizes at the level of language (where communication is thought of as a kind of gift-giving). Monetized exchange is altered material gift-giving/communication that has been "alienated by incarnating a process similar to naming," while "(male) gender [is] the artificial construction of biological males as not mothering, not nurturing." Thus the market is a projection "of the non nurturing role onto (so-called 'developed') societies' modes of production and distribution of goods," as "housework and surplus labor [become] unpaid gifts that are given to the capitalist and the market as a whole, to create profit."

While we can criticize Vaughan's theory as simplistic (I only have space to summarize it here) and the recovery of nurturing as utopic (contradicted by Weiner's theory of how inalienable possessions formulate social hierarchy), I believe it is important to recognize the role of naming in the transforming of musical gifts into commodized expressions of identity in the identity episteme, an obscuring of sonic generosity that is necessary for musical commodities to be bought and sold. The drive to represent identity in music studies appears to have had a non-nurturing role (made through the nominally nurturing act of representing!) that helps support the foundations of capitalist uses of music that are based on the suppression and eradication of the nurturing act of sonic generosity.[85] Though this book is by and large about male musicians, I hope it can open the door to a feminist theory of sonic value as action (e.g., Graeber 2001) that will emerge through a better recognition of the patriarchical nature of musical commodities and the intersection between the emergence of the "music and identity episteme" and the growth of capitalist uses of music that, founded on the appropriation and exploitation of musical givers, subordinates sonic nurturing to the promotion of naming ostensibly for the benefit of those so named.[86]

The failure of capitalist societies to name music as a gift explains the disconnect between, on the one hand, musicians who are not making a living off music, and on the other, their parents and friends in finance who say what they are doing is narcissistic. From the Goldman Sachs perspective, such music is a failed commodity. From your parents' perspective, music that doesn't sell not only fails to financially support yourself, it is narcissistic because since music is an expression of your emotions, you are whiling away the years thinking about yourself rather than helping others. From this perspective, being a musician is the opposite of being a doctor. But from a musician's perspective, playing to an empty bar is sad not for the lack of income but because there is no one to receive the musical gift (being out of gas money just adds insult to injury). There are many drummer jokes that capture this disconnect: "What is the difference between a drummer and a savings bond? One will mature and make money." "How do you get a drummer off of your porch? Pay him ten bucks for the pizza." "What do you call a drummer that breaks up with his girlfriend? Homeless."[87] That music can become commercially successful shows that music's value as a technology of care can accord with capitalism; but the failure of the drummer to get out of the pizza delivery business is a failure of capitalism, not the other way around.[88]

---

[85] "As Mauss knew well," both credit and debt are "transferring resources across the spectrum of time, but the gift 'contract' is silent and invisible (or 'misrecognized'), whereas the commodity contract is enunciated and visible" (Peebles 2010: 229).

[86] There is a kinship between this thought and Ochoa Gautier's (2014: 20) argument that "anthropotechnologies" (such as the use of orthography in music notation) "generated an 'immunization' of the voice in the name of the formation of the political community of 'the people' and in the name of an aesthetics of a proper mode of the voice."

[87] http://www.musicradar.com/news/drums/the-23-best-drummer-jokes-ever-169967

[88] Bohemia "turns the artist into a stereotype" (Craven in Bradshaw 2015), defining "the artist as starving and dying; the artist as a deviant and a suicide; the artist as insane and alcoholic; the artist as undiscovered genius whose greatness is not recognized until after his death" (Griff in ibid.). Consider Hyde's (2007: xix) thought that "the mythology of a market society reverses the picture: getting rather than giving is the mark of a substantial person, and the hero is 'self-possessed,' 'self-made.' So long as these assumptions rule, a disquieting sense of triviality, of worthlessness even, will nag the man or woman who labors in the service of a gift and whose products are not adequately described as commodities. Where we reckon our substance by our acquisitions, the gifts of the gifted man are powerless to make him substantial."

This leads directly to the issue of taste. The capitalist/identity paradigm hinges on the denial of sonic efficacy: playing music incorrectly is not going to destroy the world; you can just ignore it. But this is not the same as saying that in the modern world, the art object has become autonomous: quite the opposite. The hegemony of class and economic considerations in shaping the sustainability of music facilitates government actions to support traditions who are left behind by the evolving tastes of the market, some of which thrived in prior generations because of sonic efficacy (if you believe incorrect drum patterns will destroy the world, you will economically support the drummers who know how to play them correctly). This is not to say taste was never a factor, it was just not the driving force: for the Beravā, their drum patterns are "autonomous from society" because they are magical, outside time, and historically unchanging.[89] It is placing them in the marketplace and its hegemony of taste that harms *the perception of* autonomy and sonic efficacy (sound *is* still efficacious, just perhaps not in the same ways and is not recognized as such). The decline in recognizing the existence of sonic efficacy is thus tied to the rise of musicians in non-musical menial labor (Figure 1.5 describes the entire historical process).[90]

What has been lacking in capitalist modernity, then, is a mechanism that treats sonic efficacy as real, that rewards musicians monetarily for their ability to care for others (outside of the discourse on culture-as-representation), in which they are no longer denigrated for work that they do (as Bohemians or in traditional caste systems), including for its seeming irrelevance to commodity exchange. The only system I can think of like this in capitalist modernity is music therapy: musicians *as* doctors. I think this is what William Cheng (2016: 36) is getting at when he makes a similar case that music and musicology are fundamentally acts of care:

> Without painting an exceptionalist portrait of musicianship, is it possible that people who work with music for a living can lead by example in agendas of interpersonal care and communication? Could we go beyond modest understandings of empathy as a complement to musicality, and venture empathy as a resonant form of musicality?

[89] Writing about the giving of free MP3s in Internet culture, Baym notes that classic theories of gift economies don't account for "this evaluative component of gift giving," i.e., taste (Baym 2011: 30).

[90] In her influential book "The Imaginary Museum of Musical Works," Lydia Goehr (1992: 1) describes how the nineteenth-century music critic E. T. A. Hoffman wished musicians could erase social commitments to concentrate on the production of "the work"; against musicians who faced the humiliation of being "in service," Hoffman believed that "'the genuine artist'

> lives only for the work, which he understands as the composer understood it and which he now performs. He does not make his personality count in any way. All his thoughts and actions are directed towards bringing into being all the wonderful, enchanting pictures and impressions the composer sealed in his work with magical power.

> So it was that musicians' magic refrained from being aimed at the world and began to be aimed only at the "work." And how ironic it is that the word "work," which refers to the labor process, refrains here from signifying the social responsibility of musicians to engage in labor for the good of society, and comes to refer just to the product of that labor—the commodity—which is conceptually removed from direct social purpose.

> Delegitimization and conceptual erasure of pre-capitalist forms of musical giving as labor →
>
> Conceptual attachment of "the work" to the soul (identity) →
>
> The sale, giving, and stealing of musical commodities →
>
> Commodity fetishism (the hiding, in stories about the work, of the processes of labor that involved Others in the production of the work) →
>
> The perception of music's worthlessness as labor except as an expression of the self (artist/community or consumer)

Figure 1.5 The conceptual erasure of musical giving in capitalism.

If part of musicianship can involve listening for better worlds, then musicology has the potential to initiate various progressive currents in ethics and critical thinking. To be clear, this isn't saying that music makes us good people. It's saying that certain aural positions may hold profound uses outside the music classroom, and that as much as anyone else, musicians and music scholars already recognize the immense challenges and rewards of listening creatively and caringly.

I have two proposals for recovering and promoting this notion of sonic efficacy-as-care in music studies and the world at large. The first step is to redraw a line between the self and sounds that are offered, reconstituting sound as having an independent existence—as an agent of care—whose efficacy emerges through its being given.[91] In an early (1968) adoption of performativity theory from J. L. Austin (1962), Sri Lankan anthropologist Stanley Tambiah's essay "On the Power

---

[91] A precedent for this approach is Alfred Gell's (1998) discussion of artworks mediating social agency in his *Art and Agency* ("the technology of enchantment is founded on the enchantment of technology"). Born (2005: 16) describes Gell's theory of agency in art as centering "on the idea that the objects that result from creative agency condense or embody social relations, and that they do so by spinning forms of connectedness across time and space. Through the art object, these social relations are distributed and dispersed both temporally and spatially. But in the process the social relations are also relayed and transformed, as are the objects themselves." However, I find a theory of *sonic causality* to be missing from Born's adoption of Gell's approach in her influential account of musical mediation and her (2010) call for a relational musicology. I suggest attuning to sonic efficacy can allow us to understand how sound/music connects various assemblages (in Deleuze and Guattari's terms), such that we can speak of "the relations between culture, economy, and the social . . . not as a matter of enfolding culture within the economy or the social, or, on the contrary, of attributing it to the power to construct these, but as historically contingent divisions between different sectors of activity each of which is composed of the same heterogenous 'mangle of practices' and is situated on the same plane (Bennett and Joyce 2010: 7).

of Words" (a study of Beravā rituals) notes that the Beravā use "a variety of verbal forms in a particular sequence and that the very logic of the ritual depends on this order and distinction" (Tambiah 1968: 176). Comparing these to the rituals of the Trobriand islanders studied by Malinowski and uses of language in Buddhism and Christianity, Tambiah argues what these systems share is a belief that "deities or first ancestors or their equivalents instituted speech and the classifying activity; man himself is the creator and user of this propensity; finally, language as such has an independent existence and has the power to influence reality." The use of performativity theory in ethnomusicology has tended to jettison this emphasis on the magical ability of the ordering of language to change reality due to its independent existence in favor of an understanding of "the performative" through the terms of the identity episteme: this means that a turn toward "performance studies" is not *ipso facto* liberating but may reinforce problems it seeks to dismantle.

Historian Ritu Birla (2009) shows us a second path: to legally sanction the validity of sonic offerings. In her study of "Indian vernacular capitalism" in the colonial period, Birla describes economic contracts written for Hindu temples that legally defined a god as having a stake in the gifts given to a temple: "The deity, to which Hindu endowments were consecrated, was rendered a legal subject and thus the beneficiary in the trusts' tripartite contract" (Birla 2009: 72). From the perspective of colonial capitalism, the important legal component of merchant families' gifts to Hindu temples was the question of the "intention of the gift":

> By asking the question of public or private intent, colonial authorities sought to identify charitable projects from those tied to family benefit, and thus to the family firm's profitable ventures. This juridical process privileged the a priori intentionality of contract and so recognized the purpose of customary gifts by reading their ritual dedications as contracts and interpreting them literally (Birla 2009: 77–78).[92]

But this contract system did not safeguard sonic efficacy, for in the liberal paradigm, music is conceptually taken out of exchange and reformulated as identity, a position from which it re-enters exchange via capitalism.

What I'm longing for, then, is the opposite of the utopia imagined by Jacques Attali in his classic book *Noise*. Attali predicted that after our current era (he wrote in the 1970s), a period will emerge in which music will be "beyond exchange," performed solely for its worth to the musician as a source of enjoyment, "as *self-communication*, with no other goal than *his own pleasure*, as something

---

[92] The Beravā did have a contract system called *rajakariya* ("work for the king") during the Kandyan Kingdom, but this is now viewed negatively as having been a kind of bonded servitude. I am not arguing for bringing this back, but for a contract system that would legally safeguard sonic efficacy on terms beneficial for those invested in it, allowing for economic support.

fundamentally outside all communication, as *self-transcendence*, a solitary egotistical, noncommercial act" (Attali 1985: 32; my italics). But is a lack of musical engagement with others—a solipsistic musicality—really a situation any of us want? Attali is right to place blame on capitalism, but we should be skeptical of his hanging onto the link between music and expression as the core component of a musical utopia outside of or in spite of capitalism. In the digital age, musicians may more easily obtain control over their sounds since they are less beholden to record companies, but they are not any more likely to make a living. The newfound inability of musicians to make money from recordings, without a concomitant increase in local performance opportunities in which the *name* of performers does not matter, requires musicians to live on the road like never before, reliant on others' taste for their continued success, and many cannot make enough money from touring to ever stop touring. While the Internet has made it easier to hold odd jobs that may make it easier to eke it out as a musician, our current era has not achieved what Attali was calling for—and that is a good thing. What is missing from our current reality and Attali's utopia is a discourse on the gift that validates musical labor on a local level, outside the star system, where musicians are *required* for sustaining the world.[93]

To sum up, the world-sustaining capacity of musical giving (I argue throughout this book) is akin to *reconciliation* and emerges through the intention of the gift: "What matters is the presence of a *relation* that invests an object/scene with the prospect of the world's continuity" (Berlant 2011: 52; my italics). This book conjures up a framework to suture relations through an investment in sonic efficacy as labor required to protect and heal.

Conclusion: Musicology/Ethnomusicology, or, The Politics of Naming

The same process of linking music and identity that divides populations in Sri Lanka is the same that divides the music of the West from the Rest. Hybridization, "the experimental mixing of elements that, in the current order of things, it is important not to conjoin" is in Bennett's view, "a modern form of magic and a potential site of enchantment" (Bennett 2001: 98). Since this book is about a tradition that some might call "magical," and since it is in part about the damage Western aesthetics has wrought to the sonic efficacies of the non-West, it makes sense to construe this book as a conjoining of musicology and ethnomusicology. However, I do not mean to position ethnomusicology as a Trojan Horse that can be opened up inside musicology to destroy it. Rather, I envision both fields as firm equals

---

[93] Indeed, such a view is diametrically opposed to the Romantic notion of musicians as self-destructive (Bradshaw 2015).

in a global story of sound/music in which the legacy of Western philosophies of music on the non-West are a part of the West's history of itself.[94] The danger of the turn toward a supposedly post-disciplinary "music studies" is that it may re-subordinate the non-West to the vocabulary of an older Eurocentric musicology. A music studies of revenge, meanwhile, would include projects that tell the history of European music from the perspective of reincarnated lamas, whales, and not-selves, because the subordination of the latter to European definitions of closed bodies, purified sounds, and bounded territories is what Western philosophies of music did to such perspectives. Now *that* would be a musicology of karma, if you get what I mean. But what I am after here is not revenge but a future in which we are removed from our present time in which we hang on to twentieth-century acts of sonic purification that were achieved, via an admittedly noble anti-imperial impulse during the dawn of postcolonial independence, but which subsequently helped generate the notions of difference that drove ethnic tensions and tragedies in postcolonial states. What follows has much in common with James C. Scott's (2010) anarchist anthropology, but ironically, it remains tethered to a national lens: it is perhaps best thought of as an attempt to save the form of the nation for music studies by retelling its past through components of indigenous aesthetic systems that contradict ethnonationalist ideologies.

---

[94] "The idea of modernity as a radical break is a function not only of conceit but also of guilt. We are proud of our power but also dimly aware of the extraordinary crimes against nature and other cultures that make it possible" (Bennett 2001: 98).

PART II

MUSICAL GIVING AS PROTECTION AND DESTRUCTION

Checkpoint

Musical Gifts and the Movement of Ghosts

> Enter the chamber of God Skanda
> And pay homage to him
> Whose majesty and fame are beyond words
> And where music of various forms is played
> In offerings to protect the people and the king.[1]

In the mid-1990s, as Sri Lanka's government made its push to drive the LTTE out of the Northern Province, some residents in the town of Point Pedro (Paruthithurai) ran for shelter inside their local Hindu temple. The villagers were facing an onslaught of shelling that was leveling homes, killing families and neighbors. The temple was their last resort. Once inside, they prayed to Sandika Parameswari Amman for help. They hoped that the goddess, who had protected them their whole lives, would come through for them now in their moment of need. Miraculously, she did. Suddenly the shelling stopped, and those who hid in the temple survived. The goddess had protected them from disaster.

When I visited in 2015, Point Pedro had emerged from the ashes of war and seemed to be thriving. There was a new playground on the beach that was filled with schoolchildren. The jetty at Vadamarachchi reopened to fishermen in 2012 after being closed for fourteen years. But the residents of Point Pedro have not forgotten what the goddess did for them during the war. One told a local musician from Jaffna how the goddess protected them from falling shells. The musician, Sathyan, composed an album of songs for her with lyrics recounting her act of protection during the war. The album was finished at his home recording studio, after which he burned the songs onto a CD. On a day chosen in consultation with an astrologer, Sathyan went to the temple at Point Pedro and had the goddess bless the CD in a formal *puja* ceremony. He told me this act channeled her protective power into the CD. From then on, whenever songs from the CD were played

---

[1] *Hamsa Sandesa* (author unknown), translated by Edmund Jayasuriya (Colombo: Central Cultural Fund, 2005), 39, verse 47 (cited in Meegama 2011: 96).

on the temple's loudspeakers (which face out towards the village), Point Pedro's residents received the goddess's protection in the form of songs with lyrics that recalled how she protected them during the war. The musical gift to the goddess had become a musical gift to the people, one that documents for posterity of her protective powers while ensuring the villagers' safety from future calamity.

Today, one can easily visit the temple at Point Pedro. The area is no longer cordoned off, though there is a military camp nearby. You can even take an eight-hour, air-conditioned train from Colombo to Jaffna, and (after a bus or car ride) find yourself in Point Pedro without going through a single checkpoint. This kind of speed, luxury, and access was scarcely imaginable only a few years ago, when military checkpoints littered the whole island and the Northern Province was blocked off to visitors—a situation that had been in place since just after the start of war in 1983. When I visited Point Pedro, in what seemed like a curious bid to enter Western music history, an ice cream truck was driving around in circles, blasting a distorted version of Beethoven's "Für Elise."

* * * * * * * * *

Dani, a friend of mine from Jaffna, begged me to focus my research on topics other than the war. "The war ended so long ago," he said, "but it's the only topic any foreigner wants to ask us about." A twenty-one-year-old NGO worker when I met him in 2015, Dani was fifteen when the war ended in 2009. He told me that people of his age know the war years were terrible, but they can't help but reminisce about the good old days of their youths. They discuss how bad things were, but also how people bonded, how they took care of one another. Now, he said, people seem to care only about making money. Like others in Jaffna over the past few decades, Dani's family had no electricity for years during his youth. When they finally did get electricity, it was in the form of a single light bulb that hung, dangling, by a string. Dani laughed when he told me that for years, he thought "electricity" meant a single, swinging light bulb.

Dani told me this as we sat in the headquarters of the NGO he works for in Mullaitivu, a town that was once a critical component of the LTTE's landholdings (according to Dani, the town received electricity and paved roads just two years before I arrived—places in the north had their electricity cut by the government when the LTTE took them over). The house sits across from a military camp with a Buddhist temple run by the government. The camp sits on top of a former LTTE graveyard, and was erected right after the war. "Did they move the bodies?" I asked macabrely, and half-jokingly, for I remembered *Poltergeist*, the classic 1980s movie where a house built on top of a graveyard causes all sorts of ghostly visitations. Much to my surprise, Dani answered "No." He said the first few weeks after the tombstones were leveled and the military camp set up, people all across town heard wailing sounds through the night. The soldiers, sleeping on top of where the bodies are buried, were terrified. They called Buddhist monks to come in from Colombo to chant *pirit* (the Buddha's Dhamma, his teachings) at the site, to drive the ghosts away. This Sinhala Buddhist belief in righteous sound as a form of purification and protection was described in detail for me in 2008 by a former Buddhist monk who, though he had disrobed and worked for a socialist nonprofit, continues to identify as a Buddhist and performs rituals at *devales* (shrines for deities). He told me that, much like a single, swinging light bulb, the chanting of the Buddha's Dhamma by people trained in right speech and right action (i.e., monks) creates a focused electric charge. The sounds, he said, are "like a firewall on your computer that protects you from viruses."

The chanting must have worked, for Dani says the wailing sounds were not heard again. At the time I visited, I was surprised by the town's serenity, not what one might expect from a former war zone. With the piercing sunlight, casual breeze, and only the occasional car or bus going by, the region embodied a stillness Sri Lankans from urban areas expect when they have to work "out station": every day I was there, I saw soldiers in tracksuits, jogging casually around the camp's periphery, on top of where the bodies are buried.

* * * * * * * * *

A few weeks before meeting Dani, I arrived in Sri Lanka and called my Sinhala drum teacher (*gurunnānse*), Herbert Dayasheela, to tell him I was in town and ask if he wanted to meet. Herbert replied that he was fine (*hondai*), that he had retired since we last met (he worked at the Sri Lanka Broadcasting Corporation for decades), but that his retirement was far from boring. He had been preoccupied lately with driving a ghost (*pretayo*) out of the basement of a building in Colombo that houses a major Sri Lankan corporation. The CEO's recently deceased grandfather was the culprit, and while Herbert had successfully driven the ghost outside, it was now haunting the street in front of the building. Herbert had to return to recite the appropriate mantras, facing in the right direction, to drive the ghost away for good. (By coincidence, I had just watched the 1980s film *Ghostbusters* on the plane to Sri Lanka, and I couldn't believe that after all these years of working with Herbert, I had never imagined him with Bill Murray's backpack, wandering through the hallways of a giant building, blasting ghosts into oblivion.)

Herbert defines himself as an astrologer (*näketi*). But he is also one of Sri Lanka's most revered low-country dancers and drummers. He specializes in the Sanni Yakuma, a *yak tovil* that cures eighteen illnesses brought on by the *dishti* (malignant eyesight) of eighteen *sanni* demons (Wirz 1954: 47–63). Herbert knows how to perform other rituals large and small, but the Sanni Yakuma is his specialty; he learned it from his father, and he traces his lineage (*paramparavā*) back fourteen generations. According to Herbert's own reckoning, as recently as the late 1980s, he performed several Sanni Yakumas a month for patients; by the time I began my research with him, he said he was performing just three or four *a year* for patients—and bear in mind that he is one of Sri Lanka's most esteemed ritualists, and the Sanni Yakuma is one of the island's most hallowed traditions. He remains busy, but what he performs nowadays falls basically into two categories: (1) the use of Ayurvedic medicine, including mantras, to drive away ghosts or heal individuals in personal, private sessions (with no music and dance); and (2) the performance of large-scale Beravā rituals (e.g., Sanni Yakumas) with music and dance as *patient-less* versions of healing rituals with students.

Herbert blames this situation not just on the failure to recognize music and dance as Ayurvedic medicine but on the drive to publicize Western medicine that occurred after the liberalization of the economy in 1977. At that time, billboards were erected on the main thoroughfare (Galle Road) instructing villagers to turn from Ayurveda to doctors trained in Western medicine. Some villagers became embarrassed to hold *yak tovils* in public, and the economic changes wrought by liberalization meant that many who would wish to hold a *yak tovil* could not afford to do so. While *yak tovils* help a sick individual and are usually sponsored by the individual's family, *deva tovils* protect an entire village and are held on the grounds of a Buddhist temple (or a family's house if they have a shrine to the deities). Donors display their wealth and generosity by funding the deity rituals, which benefit everyone, but these days they seldom sponsor a *yak tovil*. To be clear, the public's belief in *yak tovils* was not eliminated; rather, the rituals were effectively driven underground, at just the moment (perhaps *because*) music and dance was redefined as art rather than medicine. De Silva (2000: 15) explains it this way:

> On the one hand, collectively organized larger exorcist and healing rituals of the traditional Sinhala communities are shifting away from the public arena to a much narrower focus, namely, the family or individual level. This process can be identified as the personalization of the once village-based public rituals. One remarkable feature of this family or private level ritual is the removal of the public display aspects of the ritual, such as dancing, drumming and comic drama. *Now it only concentrates on its healing aspect*. On the other hand, its performative and displaying aspects (drumming, singing, dancing, and comic drama, etc.) are reappearing in an entirely new context, encompassing public (or national) ritual performances. [my italics][2]

Now, some scholars (e.g., Scott 1994) argue that Beravā music and dance has always only been entertainment, acting as a foil to lure audiences, and that the efficacy of Beravā rituals is achieved just through magic spells (*mantras*). For Herbert, though, this argument misses a key point. The music and dance are necessary for the rituals to work because they are gestures of respect made to the deities, who protect the population in return for their offerings. Music and dance must be offered in "the right way" (Engelhardt 2014) or it could anger the gods. The recitation of *mantras* is necessary—and perhaps sufficient—for the rituals to work,

---

[2] These nationalistic displays (*sandharsana*) should not be construed as mere disenchanted displays of traditional culture, since they were also held to protect soldiers fighting the war.

but it alone is not *appropriate*. Ignoring the musical gift is like the child who takes without saying please and thanks, if failing to say please and thanks could lead to the destruction of your town.

The result of this is that *deva tovils* are now favored over the *yak tovils* Herbert specializes in, and this decline has shaped much of his adult life. The ritualists who live just up the coast from his ancestral Bentara Korale, in Raigam Korale, specialize in the deity rituals, and at the time of my research, their business was thriving. While *deva tovils* used to be held just once a year at Buddhist temples, nowadays (it seems to me) they are ubiquitous and held whenever there is a donor to fund them.[3] By contrast, Herbert finds himself clinging to musical gifts he rarely gets to give. Thus there has been an enormous rupture in the ritual repertoire of low-country Sri Lanka.[4]

Anthropologist Bob Simpson (1997) notes that during his research with low-country Beravā in 1978–1980 he found a "community rich in knowledge and skills and active in their ritual applications," but during his return trip in 1995 he found "considerable ambivalence among the Beravā towards their particular heritage and the link which this heritage engenders with caste identity and oppression.... [T]here is a progressive backing away from hereditary, stigmatized occupations among the low castes." Simpson found that

> [By 1995] many activities previously "owned" by the Beravā were seen to be appearing in different social settings (for example, as public entertainments or as private, domestic healing rites), performed by different social actors (for example, for members of higher castes and cultural elites) for different ends (for example, the articulation of nationalist sentiments). (1997: 44–45)

Simpson says that during his 1995 trip he asked *gurunnānses*, "*Golayo hadanavada?*" ("Are you making pupils?") and that the answer "was invariably negative" (Simpson 1997: 48). Sadly, one of his interlocutors described his village as "the village that danced" (*nätapu gama*). For my as well as Simpson's interlocutors, there seems to be a sense of "fatalistic acceptance":

> Better standards of living, freedom from the humiliating strictures of caste, and opportunities to participate in the wider economy were considered alongside a more pessimistic and characteristically Buddhist image of entropy; an image of a gradual and inexorable move away from a golden age towards chaos in which words and actions become increasingly corrupt and meaningless (Simpson 1997: 48).

---

[3] This surely has also to do with the aforementioned promotion of Kandyan dance as authentically "Buddhist" and the need for low-country ritualists to prove their auspiciousness.

[4] In interviews, several low country interlocutors agreed I was correct in this presumption.

What might be perceived as liberation from caste stigma, then, is not viewed as freedom but as a necessary move in a disruptive capitalist modernity that appears to lack meaning.

In sum, Beravā music and dance are now treated like curry that flavors food but is not essential for nutrition. This has led some ritualists making due better than others if they can play up the spiciness of their act, for those who want its particular flavor. The stigma against *yak tovils* and the drive towards Western medicine generates a belief that the celebration of Herbert's Sanni Yakuma as heritage is the only way to save it, but Herbert sees it is the celebration of it as heritage rather than medicine that is killing it. Meanwhile, ritualists have ambiguous feelings about leaving a life that, while stigmatized as low caste, was their hereditary occupation. Herbert remains in demand to help people with health problems through herbal medicine, astrology, and the recitation of mantras, but his musical gifts are like Post-It Notes stuck to his chest saying, "This [Herbert] is who we [Sinhalas] *were*." While his daughter continues the family tradition of being a dance teacher, women are not allowed to perform in the rituals, and Herbert worries that the amount of people who know the mantras and *slokas* (ritual stanzas) has dwindled, threatening the continuance of the rituals. I get the sense he feels he is living at the end of times.

* * * * * * * * *

If these stories signify anything, it is that Sri Lankans still need a firewall—not just the protection afforded (to some) by the state and military, but the sounds that dispel the ghosts of the past to prevent disasters in the future. We still need Herbert's musical gifts. Ethnographers of post-war Sri Lanka are left with a dual gaze: a backward glance of remembrance—the horrendous memories, the surprising bonding moments they initiated, the ways traditions were conceived before postcolonial modernity took hold and changed things forever—and the future-oriented gaze of wanting to move on. Postwar Sri Lanka is a state of transition, a state of peace that is also a state of emergency (to use Zizek's [2002] memorable phrase; see Choi 2012: 113) and a "melancholic" freedom (to use Thomas Blom Hansen's (2012) phrase about South Asian communities in post-apartheid South Africa), though one that, for those living in Sri Lanka's Tamil-majority northern and eastern provinces at least, is a freedom from violence that is not political freedom. As Vivian Choi (2012: 47) puts it, "disasters manage to operate and live on in different ways and forms, persisting, despite attempts made to contain, manage, settle, or foreclose them." The post-disaster present *is* that fearful anticipation and trying-to-forget remembrance of disaster, a past that might return, a past with traditions some wish to survive unchanged, and a future already conditioned on the reframing of that past through the strategic movement of ghosts.

2

Beravā Secrecy and the Hoarding of Musical Gifts

Tat takata Muni daking / dit takata Devi daking / ton takata Raja daking / nang takata Guru daking / daking! daking! daking! / Raja daruwan daking. (Tat takata seeing the Buddha[1] / dit takata seeing the Gods / ton takata seeing the King / nang takata seeing the Guru / Regard! Regard! Regard! / Come see us honor the King).
—Drum rhythm from the *Bera Pōya Hēvisi.*

This chapter describes how the Beravā's hoarding of their musical gifts is the result of the efficacy of lines of drum poetry (*padas*), and it explores how the Beravā's account of their history tells a story of sonic gift exchange between the gods, demons, the indigenous Väddas, and a giant crab. I then consider how the representation of the Beravā on the 500-rupee bill embodies an erasure of this sonic gift economy through the confluence of the money form, discourses on culture, and nationalism, and I show that this enables uses of Beravā drumming to alienate minorities.

When speaking about Beravā music and dance today, the caste name "Beravā" is jettisoned for a regional terminology: the three Beravā traditions are from the low country (*pahata rata*), the central hill country region of Kandy (called the "up country"; *uda rata*), and Sabaragmuwa, a rural area that lies in between (Figure 2.1).[2]

Each tradition has its own dress, dancing, drumming, singing, and ritual repertoire. The low country drum is the *yak beraya*, a straight drum with a booming, low tone; the Kandyan or up country drum is the *gäta beraya*, which has tapered ends and a high tone. Both are played with the hands, while the Sabaragamuwa drum, the *davula*, is a short, fat, cylindrical drum played with one hand and a stick.

---

[1] *Muni*, "one who has attained perfection in self-restrain and insight" (*Digha Nikaya* 1984: 233), is another name for the Buddha (Obeyesekere 2002a: 167).

[2] Sabaragamuwa is said to be the oldest, but it surely is the least known; I refer to it only occasionally in this book.

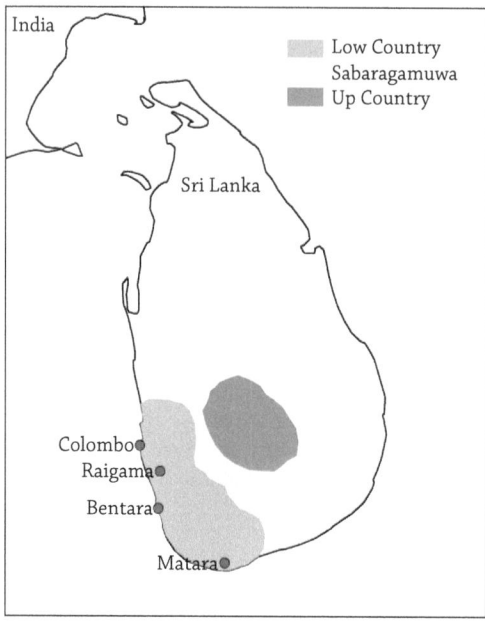

Figure 2.1 Regional traditions of Sinhala Buddhist traditional music and dance. Low-country sub-traditions (Korales) are given grey dots (with another showing Colombo, the capital city). Map by Girmaye Misgna (modeled on Suraweera 2009: 2). Used with permission.

The *hēvisi* ensemble plays at Buddhist temples, funerals, and processions (*peraheras*): this ensemble uses the *davula*, the reed instrument *horanāva*, and two drums played with sticks, called *thammāttama* (either this or the Tamil word *tappāṭṭam*—a related drum I consider in Chapter Four—appears to be the origin of the English word "tom-toms"). *Hēvisi* drummers are usually poorer, less educated, and looked down upon by other ritualists; they play in Buddhist temples before major rituals are held on temple grounds. They also alternate with a *gäta beraya* drummer at the Temple of the Tooth (Dalada Maligawa) in Kandy, Sri Lanka's most famous Buddhist temple. There is a physical closeness and alternation happening between drummers of the three regional drums traditions and *hēvsi* drummers in the all-night rituals: for example, at the start of the Bera Pōya Hēvisi that I played in, I offered *magul bera* (auspicious drumming for the Buddha) on a *yak beraya* facing a Buddha statue inside a temple, while *hēvisi* drummers stood behind and alternated with me as I proceeded through the three sections of the composition. While each regional drum tradition has its own drum language (*bera basāva*), the *hēvisi* ensemble is found all over Sinhala-speaking parts of the island. Bear in mind that the regionally associated drums are not traditionally performed at the same time (one will never see a *gäta beraya* and *yak beraya* performed at the same time in a ritual—they use different drum languages), nor are those drums played *with* the hēvisi ensemble. All three major Beravā drums are performed in hallowed Buddhist contexts in their respective regions, such as Buddhist chant

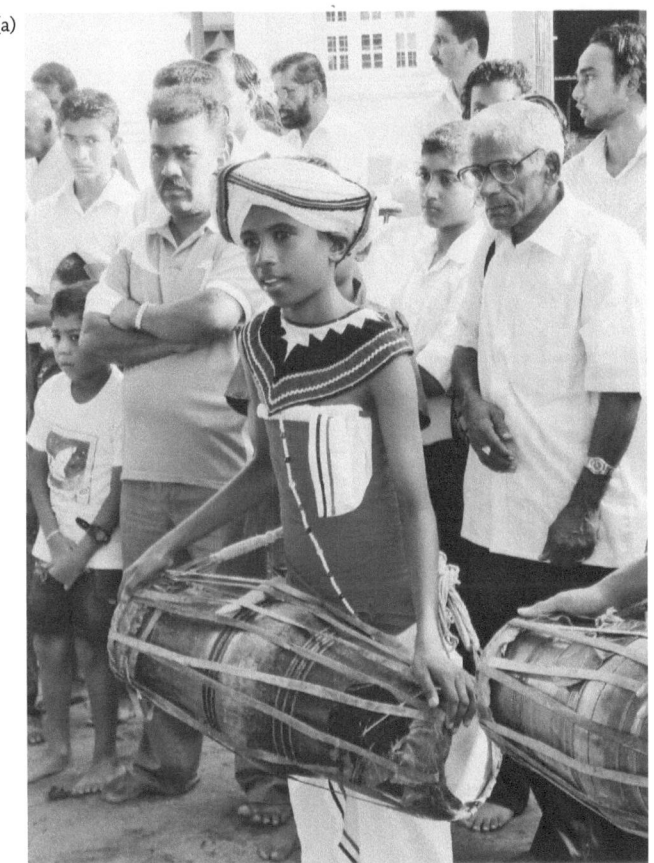

Figure 2.2a Gäta beraya.

ceremonies (*pirit*), *peraheras* (large-scale processions of music and dance associated with Buddhist temples held on the full moon or *pōya*), and rituals for deities (*deva tovils*) held at shrines (*devales*), which may be located in someone's backyard but are commonly found at Buddhist temples.

A class difference is mapped onto the *gäta beraya* and *yak beraya*—surely the result of the former's reputation as an auspicious drum synonymous with Sinhala Buddhist nationalism and the latter's association with rituals eliminating diseases brought on by demonic illness (see Chapter 1). One time I was walking in Colombo with my *yak beraya* not in a case, and some young, male, business types (wearing expensive-looking suits) saw me walking with the drum. Mistaking it for a *gäta beraya*, they recited bits of the up-country drum language for me. Farther down the road, I passed a disheveled-looking homeless man who had witnessed my encounter with the businessmen. With a gleam in his eye, he recited bits of the low-country drum language as I walked by (correcting the businessmen), and we both burst out laughing. While I do not wish to read too much into the incident,

Figure 2.2b Yak beraya.

it shows the extent to which the Kandyan drum has achieved a higher status and greater visibility among middle and upper class Sinhalas. It also demonstrates that such individuals might have some knowledge of the Kandyan drum language and yet not be able to distinguish a *yak beraya* from a *gäta beraya*.

Sinhala organology classifies instruments according to five types (*panchaturyanāda*, "five-fold sounds"; Kartomi 1990: 68): *atata* (single-headed drums); *vitata* (double-headed drums); *atatavitata* (stringed instruments or stringed drums); *susira* (aerophones); and *ghana* (idiophones). This definition has come under attack from Sedaraman (1968) and Suraweera (2009: 44), who give the following reinterpretation: *atata* (instruments played by hand); *vitata* (instruments played with a stick); and *atatavitata* (instruments played by hand on one side, and by stick on the other). Sinhala categories tend to define things according to function rather than physical constitution, and the latter definition better accords with how the drums are played: the *yak beraya* and *gäta beraya* are played with two hands (*atata*); the *thammättama* with two sticks (*vitata*); and the

Figure 2.3 A *hēvisi* ensemble featuring a *davula* (left), *thammättama* (right), and *horanäva* (reed instrument in back).

davula with one hand and one stick (*atatavitata*). Aerophones include the *horanäva* and conch (*häk gediya*), and idiophones include bells (*mini gediya*) used in the *bali* ritual and finger cymbals (*talampota*; these are played in Kandy but not in the low country). Many Sinhala instruments are reported in medieval treatises but are no longer played, including a Sinhala *veena* (stringed instrument; Chapter 4).

Trainor (2007: 160–161) classifies music in temples as "material" offerings (*āmisa-pūjā*) to the Buddha, akin to flowers, betel, and light in the form of oil lamps and candles. He reminds us the Buddha did not make the resolution to become a Buddha "for the sake of garlands, scents, music, and song. The Buddha is said to have objected to this form of worship out of concern for the longevity of the *sāsana* and for the benefit of the Assembly" (51). However, Trainor notes this does not have to be interpreted as a full rejection of material offerings (52). One interpretation is that the prohibition applies just to the monastic community; another is that material offerings are acceptable so long as they turn one's mind to the Triple Gem.[3] I suggest Beravā drumming is best thought of as sacred speech rather than music, but this does not preclude it being classified as a material offering. In Buddhist temple services (*tevāva*) and *peraheras*, music is considered *sabda pujāva*, a "sound offering" (Kariyawasam 1995: 15). Egge (2013: 5) describes

---

[3] See Ross Carter (1993: 133) for a similar argument.

karma as "a category that embraces acts of meritorious giving as well as acts of mental purification. . . . [M]eritorious and purificatory acts are both understood as forms of good karma." *Sabda pujāva*, I suggest, is a meritorious and purificatory act that produces and/or accompanies the creation of good karma.[4] The function of drumming in all-night rituals (particularly *yak tovils*) is a different matter, however, which I turn to below.

The Low Country: Korales and the Ritual Repertoire

The low country includes the western and southern provinces, stretching from Colombo south along the coast through the cities of Galle and Matara, halting past the southeastern town of Hambantota at Yala National Park. The latter acts as a barrier between the Sinhala-dominated low country and the Tamil- and Muslim-dominated east. In premodern times, the area was part of Ruhuna (or Ruhunu), an enormous territory that stretched from Kalu Ganga (a river south of Colombo) along the southern coast up through and including today's eastern provinces (all the way to the start of the Mahaveli river, just south of Trincomalee). Despite the known presence of an ancient kingdom in Ruhuna, the low country was largely uninhabited jungle throughout the premodern period, and the ancient kingdom remains largely a mystery to historians.[5]

In ancient times, Ruhuna was one of three sections of the island (*Thun Sinhale*), the others being Rajarata in the north and Malaya Rata in the central hill country. The Malvathu River connected the ancient Sinhala kingdom of Anuradhapura (377 BCE–1017 CE) in the interior to the northwest coast, near the island of Mannar. Rajaraja Chola I, a South Indian Tamil King, invaded Anuradhapura around 993 CE, conquering the northern region. His son, Rajendra Chola I, completed the conquest of Anuradhapura around 1017 CE and captured Ruhuna as well. The Cholas moved their capital to Polonnaruwa (about 100 kilometers southeast from Anuradhapura), where they ruled for fifty-two years until they were expelled in 1070 by the forces of Sinhala king Vijayabahu I (who was of royal blood but born in Ruhuna). Polonnaruwa was later conquered by the Orissan (east Indian) king Kalinga Magha, who ruled for two decades and founded the (Tamil) Jaffna Kingdom (1215–1624) in the north. Little is known about music in these kingdoms, though I discuss possibilities in Chapter 4.

The low country was greatly transformed after the decline of Polonnaruwa (from the fourteenth century), as the center of Sinhala power "drifted to the southwest," where it fractured into competing regional kingdoms. The most famous was Kotte (1412–1597) on the west coast, which was captured by the Portuguese

---

[4] The issue of whether drumming actively *creates* merit is ambiguous and considered later.

[5] In the *Mahavamsa*, it is depicted as the place kings from Anuradhapura and Polonnaruwa would flee to when avoiding foreign invaders.

(whose presence on the island lasted between 1505–1658). The Portuguese founded Colombo and took over the western coastal region, and they built forts at Trincomalee and Batticaloa (in the east). The Portuguese presence on the coast is a reason for the ascendance of the Kingdom of Kandy (1469–1815) in the interior in this period. The Dutch (1640–1796) wrested control of the Portuguese territories (involving cleverly crafted treatises with Kandy), gaining more control of the coasts, leaving the Kandyan Kingdom sequestered in the middle. The British arrived in 1796, signing a treatise with the Dutch in 1802 that made the island a crown colony; they attacked Kandy in 1803 but were repelled, finally conquering it in 1815, whereupon the whole island fell under colonial rule for the first time.

As one can tell from this briefest of surveys of Sri Lankan history, regional kingdoms and outside powers held frequent sway in Sri Lankan history; parts of the low country were colonized for roughly four hundred years. But low country, up country, and Sabaragamuwa remain divided today into Korales, a precolonial word that describes smaller regional traditions of Beravā music and dance. The low country has three main Korales: Raigam Korale (from Horana to Kalutara), Bentara Korale (south of Kalutara through Ambalangoda), and Matara Korale (south of Ambalangoda through Matara).[6] The main Korales from the up country include Nuvara (Kandy), Hat Korale (Seven Korales), and Hatara Korale (Four Korales)—the latter two are adjacent to Kandy. There are differences in drumming and ritual repertoire in each Korale, though at an even more local level, there are differences between each school (kalayatanaya) headed by a Beravā teacher or gurunnānse.

The Portuguese used the Korale division for census and taxation, information that from the early seventeenth century was kept in books called tombos (De Queiroz 1992; Strathern 2007); the Dutch adopted the practice. It seems likely the colonial use of the Korale structure played a role in allowing it to persist for centuries, lending stability to the regional traditions of Beravā music and dance. I suggest the word "Korale" to describe regional styles of dance and drumming reflects a medieval crystallization of Beravā traditions (thirteenth through the sixteenth centuries), since that is the period when the low country became vastly more populated, and the regional kingdoms thrived.[7]

---

[6] Other low-country Korales are not prominent in discourse on the low-country arts, but they exist. Hevan Korale, for example, includes Colombo and runs from Homagama to Kelaniya, including Kiribathgoda. Raigam, Bentara, and Matara are the three major styles, though, and even in Colombo (the supposed home of the Hevan Korale), I am told the arts of Raigam are most prominent (Raigam was the name of a medieval regional kingdom, but the boundaries of today's Raigam Korale do not match up with it).

[7] Low-country drummers say their tradition goes back farther, and it surely did in some form or another. They say they were present in Anuradhapura when the Bō tree (under which the Buddha found Enlightenment) was brought to the island. The thirteenth-century *Thupavamsa* mentions *mihingu beraya* (name for the low country drum) as being played when the first stone was placed for the Buddha's Relic Shrine at Anuradhapura (Berkwitz 2007: 201), though it is arguable whether this is the same drum as today's low-country drum (see Chapter 4).

Each of the three Korales is distinguished by repertoire. Raigam Korale is famous for its Gam Maduva for the Goddess Pattini and Devol Maduva for Devol Deviyo, both *deva tovils*; these are agricultural rites held for the sake of a good harvest and to ward off drought and pestilence.[8] By contrast, Bentara and Matara are known for *yak tovils*: in Bentara, the Sanni Yakuma is the most important, while in Matara, it is the Mahasona and Suniyama.[9] While the repertoire as a whole is performed more or less throughout the low country, each Korale has its own specialization, though its performance differs according to region and *kalayatanaya*. For example, while Raigam Korale is known for the Gam Maduva, that ritual is also found in Sabaragamuwa province[10] and Bentara Korale (and for all I know in Matara), and one can find *yak tovils* in Raigam Korale. Raigam is famous for the Gam Maduva because it is a fertility ritual, and the region is known for agriculture.[11]

Because of the large differences in geography, soteriological justification, and aims of performance between *deva tovils* and *yak tovils*, the anthropological literature is right to discuss them separately.[12] But musicologically, we cannot easily pick out one or the other set of rituals to study, because the low country drum is used throughout the ritual repertoire. The rituals are a form of medicine, and specialists know how to perform many in order to help people the best they can. Low country rituals exist on a continuum that mirrors the hierarchy of the Sinhala pantheon, from deities to demons, with the *yak beraya* and various types of singing forming the music of this religious tradition.

The Sanni Yakuma

The mythological tales and structures of *deva tovils* and *yak tovils* have been covered extensively in the literature (e.g., Wirz 1954; Obeyesekere 1984; Kapferer 1983). Here I summarize the main functions and structure of my *gurunnānse's* specialty, the Sanni Yakuma, an all-night healing ritual centered on the removal

---

[8] Pattini brings luck to newborns; it is common to see mothers with babies at these rituals. "Gam" means "village" and "maduva" means "shed": the term refers to the "village shed" set up for the ritual (Obeyesekere 1984).

[9] Suniyama is a "counter-sorcery" ritual classified as in between a *yak tovil* and a *deva tovil* (Kapferer 1997).

[10] The Gam Maduvas of Sabaragamuwa (the area between the low country and hill country) are arguably more famous than that from the low country, and Obeyesekere (1984) states this is where the ritual originated. The up country ritual Kohomba Kankariya (discussed farther below), as I see it, is more or less the equivalent of the Gam Maduva in the up country.

[11] *Yak tovil* practitioners are sometimes hired to work in other parts of the island. For example, my *gurunnānse* told me about a Sanni Yakuma he performed in Nuvara Eliya, in the hill country.

[12] Kapferer's (1983, 1997) writings on *yak tovils* are based on fieldwork in Matara, and they do not go into detail about the Gam Maduva; Obeyesekere's (1984) *Cult of the Goddess Pattini*, based on fieldwork throughout the southwest and east of the island, is about the Gam Maduva and does not discuss *yak tovils* in detail.

of demonic influences from a patient (*aturaya*). The ritual propitiates the *daha ata sanni* ("eighteen *sannis*"), eighteen demons responsible for eighteen illnesses (one attributed to each demon).[13] In Sinhala Ayurvedic thought (which closely follows the Sanskritic tradition), illness is caused by the disturbance of one or more of the body's core constituents or "humours": *vata* (wind), *pitta* (bile), and *sleshma* (phlegm), the *tun-dosa* or "three troubles" (Obeyeskere 1969: 175). When a person falls ill, he or she may visit an Ayurvedic practitioner (*vedarala*) who, if the disturbance of the *tun-dosa* is found to be due to natural causes (*svabhavika dosa*), may prescribe a natural remedy. If supernatural forces (*amanusya dosa*) are the cause, a ritual will be needed (Obeyesekere 1984: 44).[14] Smaller rites or protective charms (*araksava*) are tried first, but if these fail, a larger ritual (*tovil*), such as a Sanni Yakuma, will be held.[15]

Supernatural causes of illness include *deviyanne dosa* (caused by a deity), *yaksha dosa* (a demon), *preta dosa* (ghost), *graha dosa* (negative planetary influence), and *vas dosa* (ritual danger; Obeyesekere 1984: 44).[16] These supernatural troubles "form a class wider than illness—for example, family discontent, drought, or famine. Their causes may include the wrath of a *deva* (god), envy or assault by a demon, bad planetary constellations, fright from evil spirits, and so on" (Obeyesekere 1984: 44). However, all *dos* are the result of planetary misalignment (*graha dosa*), which is an indication of one's bad karma (*karma dosa*; Obeyesekere 1984: 175). For this reason, to find the cause of an illness or problem, a Sinhala

---

[13] Much has been written about the Sanni Yakuma, and I keep repetition to a minimum here. For those familiar with the standard texts (e.g. Wirz 1954; Obeyesekere 1968, 1969), bear in mind they are based on fieldwork conducted farther south than my *gurunnānse*'s ancestral village, Aluthgama; my work here closely accords to a lesser-known article by Halverson (1971), who studied with my *gurunnānse*'s father, K. S. Fernando. The differences between versions are found mainly in the second half of the ritual (see also Amarasekara 2002).

[14] It is possible for both natural and supernatural factors to be determined the cause. For example, Obeyesekere (1969: 175) writes that, "*lē māle* (menorraghia) can be caused by a natural excitement of heat or bile (*pitta*) in the body, or by the demon Sanni Yaka, or Riri Yaka (blood demon). If Ayurvedic medicine doesn't work for this condition, one assumes that it is caused by a demonic agency and ritual curing is in order."

[15] Although the overall structure of the Sanni Yakuma is rigid, the ritual can be expanded to include smaller sequences if needed. It depends on what illness the patient has. For example, Obeyesekere (ibid. 177) remarks that, "if a woman is afflicted by the sensual demon Kalu Kumaraya (Black Prince), one may perform a *sanni* ritual, but in addition one may have an image (*bali*) of Kalu Kumaraya and special invocations and oblations to him." Likewise, if the illness is a spirit of an ancestor (*preta*), one may hold a Sanni Yakuma but add offerings to the *preta* (ibid.).

[16] Obeyesekere (1984: 46) describes *vas dosa* (pl. *vas dos*) as "an impersonal magic force that is unleashed as a result of certain actions." The effects happen instantly, caused by violating a taboo, incorrectly performing or omitting part of a ritual, witchcraft, or the failure to perform a vow. A common concluding section of rituals is *gara nātuma* (dance of Gara), where Gara Yaka, a demon immune to ritual pollution, cleans up *vas dos* acquired by ritualists during the ritual. "Gara's manifest ritual role is clear; he is like the washerman in secular life whose caste duty is to dispose of polluted objects" (Obeyesekere 1984: 184).

person consults an astrologer (*näketi*), who may also be an Ayurvedic practitioner (*vedarala*), priest (*kapurala*) at deity shrines (*devales*), or ritual specialist of the demon cults (*kattadirala*). The latter is responsible for organizing and performing a Sanni Yakuma.[17]

According to legend, the Buddha banished *yakku* from Lanka to the island of Yak Giri. However, he gave them a warrant (*varam*) to look on a person or object, an action that infuses the person or object with the demon's "malign energy" (*disti*; Scott 1994: 280). According to their *varam*, demons must accept the offerings given to them and remove the *disti*; whether they do so is due largely to the skill of the ritualist. Demons are stubborn, and sometimes a cure is impossible or partly effective. If successful, the *yak tovil* "binds" the *yakkha*, usually for a few years, until another is necessary. A large part of the skill of the ritualist is his ability to take the *disti* of the *yakkha* and "tie" it to another object or ritualist (such as the ritualist himself), after which it is "cut" through the recitation of mantras and undertaking certain actions, like cutting limes.

Deities have malevolent and benevolent aspects, and they, too, can look unfavorably at individuals, which is one reason offerings are made to them. There is a relativity between the divine and demonic that plays itself out in the ritual space. Kapferer (1983: 163) notes "this ambiguity is founded in the fact that deities and demons are constituted in a process whereby the forces of relative purity, of goodness, of fortune, of life, to mention but a few, are inextricably linked with the forces of pollution, of evil, of misfortune and of death." While the purpose of *deva tovils* is to call deities to look favorably on a ritual and accept the requests made to them on behalf of the offerings they are given, the purpose of *yak tovils* is to give offerings to a demon or demons who are *already* looking at an individual and afflicting illness by doing so. *Yakku* embody values anathema to Buddhism, such as desire, craving, greed, and jealousy. This means individuals experiencing success have a reason to fear them, as *yakku* want what they have. *Yakku* are prone to look at individuals in solitary places (e.g., long walks in a forest) at inauspicious times. They are bloodthirsty tricksters who harm, but also laughable buffoons: when *yakku* emerge in the ritual space as masked dancers in *yak tovils*, they are mocked by the ritualist and audience (Kapferer 1983). All *tovils* rely on the recitation of myths as sung poetry (*kavi*) backed by drumming, or as plaintives (*kannilav*). These instruct the audience about the history of the rite and the biographies of deities and/or demons who look upon the ritual.

---

[17] For a list of the eighteen sannis and the diseases they cause, see Obeyesekere (1969: 189). In the Matara Korale where Obeyesekere and Wirz studied, six or seven *yakku* commonly made an appearance as masked dancers in a Sanni Yakuma. In the Bentara Korale that I studied (as also reported by Halverson 1971), only *one* of the eighteen *sanni* commonly emerges in the ritual space. However, offerings to all *sanni yakku* are made on the belief that they become jealous when others receive offerings (Wirz 1954: 49). Major deities of the Sinhala pantheon are asked to look favorably on the event, so they, too, are given offerings, including music and dance.

The small amount of writing on music in *yak tovils* has tended to adopt a Western notion of musical "experience" that is divorced from the Beravā's conception of their drumming. Such writings tend to consider only *yak tovils* and not *deva tovils* and *bali*, and thus they neglect the musical ontology the three kinds of ritual share; this influences authors to be overly concerned with the relationship between drumming and the "demonic." For example, Becker (n.d.) assumes the structure of rhythms in *yak tovils* has an intimate relationship to the manifestation of the demonic: she suggests the drumming sounds more "metered" at the start of the ritual and more language-like and unmetered when *yakku* make their appearance in the ritual space. Thus she posits that a lack of meter (i.e., lack of a beat cycle or time signature) for the drumming mirrors the patient's experiential progression through the emergence of the demonic to its dissipation—a return to normalcy mirrored by the return of "metered" drumming at the end of the ritual. Similarly, Kapferer (1983) contends music in *yak tovils* enhances the patient's psychological transformations he/she undergoes through the ritual. In my view, both neglect the fact that, while ritualists are concerned with the patient's health, music in each ritual is an *offering* to deities and/or demons and is not "for" the patient.[18] In *deva tovils* and *bali*, musical offerings are respectful gestures that entice deities to look upon the ritual; in *yak tovils*, drumming entices *yakku* to be present, whereupon the ritualist manipulates their *disti* as they are forced to accept the *varam* of the Buddha and leave the patient alone. Thus in *yak tovils*, music helps to trick *yakku* into being present, by making them think they are being treated like gods. The point of drumming in *yak tovils* is not to make the patient confront his or her *inner demons*: such a view promotes a Western notion of an inherent connection between music and the self.

My aim in this book is to explore the social worlds, politics, and history of Sri Lankan musics; sadly I do not have space for detailed musical analysis. For a study of low country drumming that centers on how it is and is not "metered," see Sykes (2018a and 2018b). I consider those essays an extension of this book: they walk readers through low-country drumming (with accompanying videos) as it is performed in the Sanni Yakuma and Bera Poya Hēvīsi.[19] There, I argue that when Beravā drumming sounds *less* metered, it is for the Buddha and gods; this is because it is not appropriate to give them "music" (the *magul bera* for the Buddha is through-composed and—while it has a pulse—completely lacks meter). By contrast, *yakku* receive short passages of more metered-sounding drumming. However, in both cases, *yak beraya* rhythms are formed by the structure of drum sentences or *padas* (a bit like repeating a sentence over and over) rather than by a system of numbered beats that the drum syllables are slotted into.

---

[18] I do not deny that music entertains, supports singers, and calms patients in these rituals—such activities are just not the soteriological purpose of the drumming.

[19] For analyses of drumming in the Devol Maduva and Bali, see Suraweera 2009.

The Structure of the Sanni Yakuma

The Sanni Yakuma is split into three periods or "watches"—the evening watch (*sända samayama*), midnight watch (*māda yama*), and morning watch (*alu yama*) (Halverson 1971; Kapferer 1983). The following is drawn from my *gurunnānse*'s father's book (Fernando 1987):

> 1. Offerings to the Triple Gem and the Gods/Cleansing of the Ritual Space (*puja vidi raTāva, mal yahan kavi*)
> 2. Summoning the Demons (*bhuta karna vidi*)
> 3. Screen Poem (*kaDaturā kavi*)
> 4. Dance of the Evening Watch (*Sända Samayama*)
> 5. The Masked Demons: Kalu Yaka, Riri Yaka, Huniyam Yaka, Abhimaana Yaka
> 6. The dance of Maru Yaka, one of the eighteen Sanni Yakku
> 7. Liccevi Dance (*kumara pelapāliya*)
> 8. The Twelve Pelapaaliyas (*delos pāli nätum*)
> 9. Mahasona Samayama, also called avatara balima
> 10. Dance of the Sanni Demons (*sanni nätum*)
> 11. Closing songs for the Gods (*deviyanTa ping dime kavi*)

Figure 2.4 Structure of the Sanni Yakuma in Bentara Korale.

The Myth of the Sanni Demons

A myth explains the birth of the *sanni yakku*, their reasons for causing illness, and the Buddha's sanctioning of giving them offerings.[20] By retelling the events that led to the first Sanni Yakuma, the story demonstrates the efficacy of the ritual and marks current performances as reenactments of its first performance.[21]

> A princess had a sun ray hit her, and she became pregnant; when she gave birth, however, she did not give birth to a child, but to a piece of meat, since it was conceived by a ray of sun. Because the "fetus" was not a child, the princess put it on a golden plate and let it go in the Ganga River. But the plate, instead of going downstream, went upstream, so people started to wonder about it. A Brahmin saw the plate floating in the river; he took it and protected it for two weeks. During this time, the meat turned into children: a boy and a girl. They were named "Liccevi prince" and "Liccevi princess," and given to the ruler of the

[20] For alternate versions, see Obeyesekere 1969 and Kapferer 1983.
[21] The version here is from my *gurunnānse*'s father's book (Fernando 1987; translation my own). See Suraweera (2009) for a similar story about *bali*.

village to be brought up. Eventually, they each were married,[22] made a castle, and their generation became known as the "Liccevi Generation."

The king of the town was named Sanka Palla. He married Asu Palla (a princess). The king had to go to war in a different region. While gone, the queen noticed she was pregnant. She was craving mangoes. At the time, there was a maid in the palace who also had a craving for mangoes. The maid asked for mangoes from the queen but the queen didn't have any, so the maid became angry. The maid made up a story and spread it around the palace, that the queen got pregnant from a cabinet minister when the king was away. The palace people informed the king, who was off fighting; he became so angry that he ordered the queen to be killed. She was taken to a cemetery and hung on a tree, and cut into two pieces by the executioner. As she was pregnant, the fetus fell out of her onto the ground, in two pieces. Because of the power of the fetus, the pieces came together and a prince was born. Since there was nothing for the newborn to eat, he ate the remains of his dead mother. Because of this, he became a demon (*yakkha*). He was determined to take revenge on his father, who had ordered his mother to be killed. He went from place to place in the forest and found eighteen poisonous plants. The god Sakka poured honey on them, and they turned into the eighteen Sanni demons (*sanni yakku*).

The eighteen *sannis* became followers of Sanni Yakka and treated him as their leader. One day, they came to him and asked for a new place to play; Sanni Yakka told them to wreak havoc in the town of the Liccevis. He and the eighteen *sanni* demons went to Liccevi town and turned the place upside down. The situation became grave, as people were getting sick, dying, and were afraid to move anywhere. The king, not knowing what to do, asked the Lord Buddha for help. He wished for the Buddha to come to town and recite *pirit* [protective incantations, "Buddhist chant"]. The Buddha did so, and part of his chanting advised the villagers to give offerings to the demons, for this would make them go away. The Buddha then chanted the *Ratana Sutta*, and he described the three fears—disease (*rogabhaya*), demons (*amanushahbaya*, "fear of non-humans"), and starvation (*durbikshabhaya*). This was the birth of the Sanni Yakuma ritual. The ritual is used to cure ill people. It is done not only for Sanni Yakka and the eighteen *sanni yakku*, but for all the prominent and lesser demons (*mahe shakya* and *elpe shakya*). Before the ritual starts, they tie a string (*epa noola*).

---

[22] In this version they were not married to each other, but in Obeyesekere's (1969) version they are, on the reasoning that because they had no family lineage, no one wanted to marry them. In the version Obeyesekere heard, it is the Buddha and not a Brahman who raises and marries them.

With this story, ritualists adopt and transform the canonic Buddhist story the *Ratana Sutta*.²³ In that story, the city of Vesali was suffering from plague, hunger, and demons; to save the city, the Buddha instructs his disciple Ananda to visit the city and recite his the Dhamma. The use of music and dance in the Sanni Yakuma, then, is assumed to gain sanction from the Buddha, although it is placed under the ritually superior *pirit* (Buddhist chant). While *pirit* alleviates all three fears, *yak tovils* counteract fears of demons and illness, while *deva tovils* alleviate fears of starvation and drought.

Birth of the Drum: A Giant Crab Makes Music History

Wirz (1954: 20–21) provides a myth about the invention of the drum (*beraya*) that it is worth citing at length. I did not hear this story from my *gurunnānse*, but it provides a pre-history for the musical giving embodied by the Bera Pōya Hēvisi, since it explains where the gods got their drum rhythms (*padas*) from before they gave them to the Väddas (who gave them to the Beravā). It also shows Beravā music history embeds human-animal relations:

> [One legend] relates that a *bhikshu* [*bhikkhu*] (Buddhist priest or monk), who was born again as an elephant, put himself at the head of a large herd of elephants who inhabited a swampy district. In the same swamp there lived a gigantic crab (*kakuluvā*).... Every day the elephants crossed the swamp and every time the crab grabbed one of the hind feet of the last elephant, dragged it into the water, and devoured it. The bhikshu-elephant became aware that the herd was growing smaller everyday and at length he said to the others, "Let me go last so that I can look after the other ones better." So when they were going through the swamp the next day, the crab wanted to seize the last elephant as was its custom, but the bhikshu-elephant saw it in time and smashed it under his feet. The dead crab floated to the mouth of a river but it was so big that it damned up the water causing a flood. The people who lived by the river did not know what happened and began wailing and lamenting. [The god] Sakra heard their wailings, came down to the earth and dragged the dead crab to heaven, and so allowed the waters to flow again. He charged the ... *Gāndharuvo-dēviyo* with the making of two drums out of the huge claws of the crab and when he began to beat them his children danced to their accompaniment. So was the drum (beraya) invented;

---

²³ The *Ratana Sutta* is in the *Khuddakapatha*, a collection of discourses in the *Khuddaka Nikāya*, the last of the five *Nikāyas* that make up the *Sutta Pitaka* (the second of three divisions of the *Tipitaka*, the "three baskets" of Theravada Buddhist scripture, written in Pali). "Ratana" means "jewel" and refers to the Triple Gem (the Buddha, his teaching or Dhamma, and the community of monks or Sangha).

they measured one yodum [Wirz says this is sixteen miles] in length. The Gāndharuva taught the gods how to beat the drums and instructed them in the various rhythms and ways of playing the drums. They also taught the twenty-one *"sural"* [this is a section of the Bera Pōya Hēvisi, see Sykes 2018b], i.e., the ways of stamping with the foot and jumping to the different tāla, how the body must be turned and whirled, and the positions of the body, arms, and legs must take up. . . . Moreover, they composed the sixty-four *"sandahan"* [I am assuming this should be *"saudam,"* also in the Bera Pōya Hēvisi], or verses, which are recited along with the dances and the music of the drums, and also the two hundred and sixteen *"vandamanang"* [sic; *vandamānam*; also in the Bera Pōya Hēvisi], or hymns, which are delivered in praise of the Buddha.

Secrecy, Text, and Transmission

The ritual knowledge of low-country Sri Lanka is owned and guarded by *gurunnānses*, embodied by their lineage (*paramparavā*), and "housed" in their school for the ritual arts (*kalayatanaya*), typically held out of a *gurunnānse's* home. It is passed on through the apprenticeship of a student to a *gurunnānse* (*guru-shisya*; Figure 2.5), though as in India, the terms of this relationship have loosened over the past century. Competition and jealousy among teacher lineages are legendary, and their hoarding of musical knowledge is surely a reason for the lack of circulating music theoretical treatises in Sri Lankan history. Nowadays, there *are* publicly available books in Sinhala on the ritual arts that include songs and drum rhythms, but *gurunnānses* like to discredit these, saying they are little more than abstract theses written by professors with no intimate knowledge of ritual (some will criticize my attempt here the same way!). While such criticisms are due in part to the need for *gurunnānses* to remain the primary owners of ritual knowledge, such books *do* often contain misleading information, because Beravā sometimes intentionally mislead researchers, while some "misinformation" reflects an author's access to one *gurukula* over another.

The lack of publicly accessible written material does not mean the Beravā do not write things down. My *gurunnānse* has a whole library of texts in his house written by his father, K. S. Fernando (Figure 2.6).[24] These writings contain instructions

---

[24] Fernando was a well-known dance master who also worked at Radio Ceylon; in the 2008 Grade 9 syllabus for dancing (by the Department of Aesthetic Education), he is listed as the one low-country dancer students are encouraged to appreciate as a "developer" of dance (the others are the up country dancer Pani Bharata, and Galukagama Heennilame from Sabaragamuwa). Kulatillake (1976: 26) describes him as "a famous dancer of the Amarasé school in Tundawā of Bentara." According to Amarasinghe and Kariyakarawana (n.d.), Amarasa Gurunnānse was originally from Galle but settled in Suddagoda, which (along with Tundawa) is a Beravā hamlet in Bentara Korale, near the more well-known towns of Aluthgama and Bentota. However, they incorrectly report that Dayaseela's father was Amarasa himself.

Figure 2.5 My *gurunnānse*, Herbert Dayaseela, changing the skins on a *yak beraya*.

for rituals (*tovils*) and the *slokas* (Sanskrit couplets), *mantras* (spells), *kavi* (poetry), and *padas* (drum and dance rhythms) used in them. The texts are written by hand (on palm leaf) in pages that number in the thousands. My *gurunnānse* claims to consult these periodically to jog his memory, since his father (who was his *gurunnānse*) passed away over two decades ago.

Each Sinhala ritual has its own texts. Obeyesekere (1984) found thirty-two variations of texts owned by officiants (*adura*) performing the Gam Maduva for the Goddess Pattini; while they contained a wide array of material, each had the same core content (i.e., the story of the goddess's rage at the death of her husband and her burning of the city of Madurai, South India).[25] Sometimes ritual texts themselves are part of a rite's origin story: Kapferer (1997: 31) relates how the Suniyama ritual follows the "procedures laid down in the Kabala (or Vadiga)

---

[25] This is the same story told in the famous Tamil epic the *Cilappatikāram*; Pattini is the Sinhala version of the Tamil goddess Kannagi (Shulman 2016).

Figure 2.6 K. S. Fernando, my *gurunnānse's* father.

Patuna, the book of the rite said to have been created by Oddissa (the "first sorcerer") to cure the first victim of sorcery attack." The text serves as evidence of the rite's history and proof of its authenticity, and by extension, legitimizes the authority of the *gurunnānse* who owns it. The performance of a ritual, then, is a reenactment of its first performance, as recounted in the ritual texts.

The Bera Pōya Hēvisi and the Poem on Its Repertoire

The Bera Pōya Hēvisi ("Auspicious Drumming on a Full Moon Night") is an all-night drum competition with no dancers or other ritual specialists, in which drummers challenge one another to display the breadth of their drum knowledge. The music they play, though, is *not* the same as that found in the other Beravā rituals. Rather, the Bera Pōya Hēvisi recounts the gods' celebration of the Buddha's Enlightenment through the performance of the music the gods played that day.

As such, the ritual consists of drum-speech and poems (recited by drummers in the ritual) that are found nowhere else in the repertoire. There are versions of this ritual for each Korale, but I witnessed only the Bentara version.²⁶

The contents of the *Bera Pōya Hēvisi* are recited in miniature in a poem that is taught to all beginning *yak beraya* students by their *gurunnānse*:

> *tisdekak tālam—susäTak pamana saudam*
> *visiekak suralin—gäsū pasalos vandamānam*
> *solosak däkum at—satvisi poDi sural at*
> *hatalis aDa padat—gäsuwē melesin desiyasolosak*

The poem states "what there is" in the Bera Pōya Hēvisi: "twenty-one *tālam*, thirty-one *sural*, forty "half-*pada*," and so on.²⁷ It was recited to me countless times, typically in my first meeting with a drummer, and I found it to be common knowledge for drummers and printed in most Sinhala-language books on drumming. My *gurunnānse* owns a Bera Pōya Hēvisi text that contains the rite's stanzas and poems that locate drummers at key moments in the history of Buddhism in Sri Lanka, as well as instructions on how to build the drum, and rites of offerings to spirits (*bhuta*) who inhabit the tree chopped down to make the drum. Thus the text is not just "music theory" but a how-to manual for drum-building and a work of "music history" (that shades into mythological stories about the drum's associations with gods, kings, and the Buddha).

A performance of the Bera Pōya Hēvisi *is* the presentation of the thirty-two *saudam*, twenty-one *tālam* (and so on) listed in the poem. While the poem is known to all *yak beraya* drummers, most drummers do not know all of the ritual's contents described in the poem. The ritual's performance requires drummers to dust off music and poetry they have rarely if ever performed publicly, in a context where they are supposed to show it off to their peers. This is surely one reason why the ritual is rarely performed, which reinforces drummers' lack of experience performing the ritual. The point of having drummers memorize the Bera Pōya Hēvisi poem, I suggest, is not that it functions as a mnemonic device for remembering

---

[26] Suraweera (2009: 16) describes a Raigam Korale Bera Pōya Hēvisi that he saw at the Bellanwilla temple grounds (on the outskirts of Colombo) that was radically different from the version I saw. Instead of the poem on the repertoire, the ritual Suraweera witnessed involved playing short extensions (*hatara vaṭṭam* and *hat vaṭṭam*) of the *magul bera* (a short, auspicious drum composition for the Lord Buddha, unique to each *gurukula*, that every drummer learns), alternating an hour at a time with a *hēvisi* ensemble. The ritual occurred during the day, from 8 a.m. to 5 p.m., while the ritual I witnessed went all night. Overall, the ritual I saw was far more elaborate (see Sykes 2018b).

[27] Anuradha Seneviratna (1979: 52) describes these in the following fashion: "Thirty-two *Tālams* or rhythmic time measures, sixty-four *Saudam* or varieties of drum beats in salutation to Gods, twenty-one *Sural* or elaborations, twenty-seven *Poḍi Sural* or rhythmic subdivisions, fifteen *Vandamānam* or narratives to be played and sung as offering(s) to Buddha, sixteen *Däkum At* or drum beat pieces played in the presence of a God or the King in the form of salutation, forty *Aḍapada* or forty half beats."

the contents of the ritual, but that the poem mystifies the ritual, according it foundational status in the repertoire. The poem functions like the "Library of Babel" described in the story by Jorge Louis Borges (1998): it provides the "boundaries" of the Bera Pōya Hēvisi (the walls of its library), thus demonstrating that the knowledge contained in this musical library is finite, yet it also demonstrates the musical library's vast size. This "infinite boundedness" mystifies the repertoire, allowing drummers to appear (as if by magic) with knowledge presumed to be part of the repertoire no one else knows. It gives the impression that when a greater amount of drummers perform a Bera Pōya Hēvisi, more of its contents will be revealed. And these processes enhance the belief that today's drummers are less knowledgeable than those of the past (who were less knowledgeable than those before them, and so on, back to the gods). The delineation of the content of a repertoire *no one* knows in its entirety romanticizes the tradition, while acting as "proof" that it exists and was known in its entirety in the past. This grants high status to those who know more of it, and it is one reason drummers are not forthcoming about sharing these musical gifts. The status accorded to ritual knowledge leads to jealousies between drummers, which are often based on knowledge claims. Disputes over knowledge of repertoire are legendary: for example, a close drummer friend told me a drummer he knows murdered his first *gurunnānse* because he was jealous of how much his teacher knew. Whether this actually happened is beside the point: the fact that murder over musical knowledge is considered a possibility demonstrates the vast importance accorded to owning and hoarding the ritual knowledge.

Guru Musti: The Poetics of Musical Deception

Anyone asking around in Sri Lanka will learn that drumming is such a specialized activity that the more advanced techniques and rhythms of the *yak beraya* and *gäta beraya* are largely unknown even to the Sinhala public, despite the importance of drumming to Sinhala culture. While it is easy enough for anyone to take lessons in Kandyan and low country drumming, learning the rhythms used in rituals is another matter, and it takes dedication. For instance, it was only midway through my third trip to Sri Lanka (about a year in the field) that I was allowed to learn some of the music used in standard rituals. By then, I had learned exercises (*harambes*), auspicious drumming (*magul bera*) for the Buddha, and basic patterns used in rituals (such as "walking rhythms" or *gaman matra*), but I had yet to learn any of the more valued *padas*. This problem was undoubtedly due to my being a foreigner and inexperienced *yak beraya* drummer, though Sinhala researchers have also expressed difficulties gaining access to certain rhythms (Suraweera 2009).

Midway through fieldwork, I came across a dissertation written in the 1970s by an American ethnomusicologist, Ronald Walcott. A student of Mantle Hood's at UCLA, Walcott lived in a village outside Kandy for a year, where he studied *gäta beraya*. His dissertation explains at great length his trouble learning the rhythms (*padas*) used in the up country Kohomba Kankariya ritual.[28] He would ask his *gurunnānse* time and again to learn drum patterns from the ritual, only to be told to be patient (he was not denied, but told information was forthcoming). But what began as a promise of rigorous daily training sessions turned into hour-long lessons twice a week. Eventually, Walcott discovered a term for what he and I were experiencing: *guru musti*, the tendency for *gurunnānses* to intentionally hide information from their students. *Guru musti* had an enormous effect on Walcott's (and my own) research. Because of *guru musti*, Walcott shifted focus from a study of Kandyan drumming to a study of *singing* in the up country Kohomba Kankariya: this was a more doable project since people were willing to translate his recordings. Thus his dissertation provides an excellent overview of singing in the Kohomba Kankariya, but is virtually silent on drum rhythms.

My Sanni Yakuma Debacle

One day, long after my initiation into the Bera Pōya Hēvisi, Dayasheela informed me out of the blue that I would soon have the opportunity to perform in a Sanni Yakuma. I was thrilled, for I would finally have the opportunity to learn the music of the ritual Dayasheela specializes in. I would also get a chance to test my skills by performing in a live setting with other drummers. As the days progressed and the time for the ritual drew near, however, it became clear that Dayasheela still had no intention of teaching me the music I was about to perform in public! Which is to say, he expected me to sit in, watch the other musicians, and follow along. I am told that this is how musicians learned in the past, but in my experience it is not the case today for drummers with *no* knowledge of a ritual to sit in and follow along (this may be acceptable for dancers, though: on many occasions I have seen young dancers, even small children, perform haphazard dance routines). I can think of just one instance where I saw a young beginner sit in on *yak beraya* in a ritual: he followed along with the opening sequence (*yahan däkma*) before he was run out of the ritual space due to his lack of skills. Besides that, all rituals I saw involved performers who clearly had learned rhythms (*padas*) beforehand.

Before the ritual, Dayasheela announced to the audience that I was his student and was greatly advanced on the *yak beraya* (he was way too kind) and had studied tabla for seven years (this is not true, though I imagine he had misunderstood my background). This led to the inevitable and embarrassing situation where I had to follow this introduction by sitting in with six advanced drummers, as they hammered out complex *padas* that were a complete mystery to me!

---

[28] Walcott completed his dissertation at the University of Sri Lanka, Vidyodaya Campus.

During the *Māha Tē* (the "great tea" break that occurs after midnight), the response of the drummers was cold. Some were kind but distant (surely embarrassed for me), but two were openly hostile. One was drunk and rowdy, and openly mocked me. He asked to look at my palms, and seeing that my calluses were not developed enough to make me an experienced drummer, threw them down in disgust. A second drummer, who had been banned from the ritual because he was playing too much like a Kandyan, was also drunk and on the verge of violence. I couldn't make out all of his Sinhala, but he was clearly mad that I, as a foreigner, was allowed to play in the ritual, while he was not (and who could blame him?). I refrained from "performing" for the rest of the ritual, which proceeded until daybreak. Looking back, I believe Dayasheela invited me to play in the ritual because there was no patient, and its status as an "efficacious ritual" was in doubt (the ritual was a debut performance for a young dancer, whose parents paid to sponsor the event). Still, I believe my performing in the ritual was offensive to some drummers because it signified I was not treating the drum language as though it must be performed correctly at all times.

Despite all the secrecy surrounding the tradition, I did have an ethnographic breakthrough. One dramatic afternoon, as rain poured down heavily on Dayasheela's house and against the trees in his yard, the electricity was out and we sat in darkness with my mp3 recorder on (which he was aware of). Dayasheela chose that moment to offer me a gift: the major drum rhythms in the Sanni Yakuma.[29] It took about two years of living in Sri Lanka to learn what could be said in less than an hour.

While his hesitancy to share *padas* was surely due in part to my status as a foreigner (and is reminiscent of Berliner's classic story of learning *mbira* in Zimbabwe; 1978), I have argued here that the hoarding of musical gifts also affects locals (encapsulated by the term *guru musti*) and arises not only because of their status as inalienable possessions but because of the inauspiciousness of incorrectly offered *padas*.

Kandyan Dance

Today's national dance of Sri Lanka, Kandyan Dance, is based on excerpts from an up country ritual, the Kohomba Kankariya, and eighteen dances on Buddhist themes called Vannams. By the 1980s, the Kohomba Kankariya had virtually died out, but it has since been revived (largely as a state-sponsored event; Reed 2010). A possible reason for this decline is a decline in patronage by the *radala*, an "aristocratic subcaste" (Reed 2010: 79) of the high caste govigama who long supported Kandyan dancers and drummers. Up country ritualists used to perform at the

---

[29] I later found these rhythms had been printed in Fernando (1987); see Sykes (2018b).

radala's homes and sometimes taught music and dance to their children, even performing at their weddings.[30] Legend has it that the Vannams originated as songs during the reign of King Narendrasinghe (1707–1739), composed by a South Indian musician (possibly from Kerala, though living for a time in Jaffna) named Ganāthilankāra in collaboration with a Buddhist monk from the Malwatte chapter in Kandy (Reed 2010: 87; Sarachchandra 1952: 12).[31] The Vannams are named after poetic meters that appear to be derived from Tamil methods of versification (Kulatillake 1976b: 73). According to popular belief, dance steps were added during the time of King Rajadhi Rajasinghe (1782–1798; Reed 2010: 87).

Perhaps the most famous place for Kandyan Dance and the *gäta beraya* is the *Äsala Perahera*, the annual parade that emanates from the Temple of the Tooth every July/August (in the Sinhala month of *Äsala*). In the *Äsala Perahera*, the Buddha's tooth relic is taken out of the temple and paraded through Kandy on the back of an elephant, accompanied by many elephants and hundreds of Kandyan dancers and drummers.[32] It is well known that this *perahera* originally honored the four "guardian deities" (Four Warrant Gods) and that the tooth relic was added to the procession during the reign of Kirti Sri Rajasimha (1747–1782; Seneviratne 1978; Holt 1991). The Vannams, as dances, appear to have been added to the *perahera* in the late nineteenth- or early twentieth-centuries. Similarly, the Ves headdress, once worn only when an up-country dancer had completed a rigorous apprenticeship for seven years, is now commonly worn by children in the Kandy Perahera, much to the consternation of purists (Reed 2010).

As of 2016, O. P. Karunadasa from the Uduwela family leads drummers in the Maha Perahera and guards the Karanduwa (the structure that holds the tooth relic on top of an elephant).[33] Along with him in the procession is G. A. Molagoda from the Molagoda family. Peter Surasena and his sons lead the Kandyan dancers and drummers that introduce the Diyawadana Nilame (the lay custodian of the Temple of the Tooth) to the audience. These dancers are placed in between the

---

[30] During the Kandyan Kingdom (1592–1815), up country drummers contributed to a system of land tenure and taxation called *rajakāriya* ("work for the king"), which specified which duties each caste and family had to perform to help the kingdom. The term *rajakāriyo* used to refer to all service castes (e.g., washermen and smiths) but now refers almost exclusively to drummers providing hereditary ritual services (as opposed to drummers hired by temples on a "freelance" basis; Gombrich 1971: 300). *Rajakāriya* was formally abolished after the 1833 Colebrook-Cameron Commission, which set up a modern form of central government. The service drummers say they perform today is not for kings but the Buddha, who is treated like a king.

[31] Narendrasinghe was married to a Tamil princess from the Madurai Nayak Dynasty of South India; because they had no children, the royal line passed to her brother, Sri Vijaya Rajasinha (1739–1747). South Indian musicians and dancers were brought to the Kandyan court from Madurai during this time, known as the Nayak Dynasty of Kandy (1739–1815).

[32] Traditionally, drummers play different beats for each street of the procession.

[33] The information in this paragraph is culled from the article, "Kandy's Glorious Drummers and Dancers Fight Poverty and Caste Stigma," by Isuri Yasasmin Kaviratne, *Sunday Observer*, August 14, 2016.

Karanduwa and the Nilame. One of Surasena's sons now works for Nestle in Sri Lanka and the other lives in Japan and returns to take part in the annual festivities. Drummers who are teachers apply for leave to perform in the *perahera*. The main occupation of some of the performers during the off-season is to sell flowers near the temple; the temple reportedly pays them 1,000 to 1,200 rupees a day during the *perahera*, with accommodation close to the temple. As for the many other drummers and dancers, the leader of each team of performers gets money to distribute to their group. The major positions in the *perahera* used to be paid for by the Ninda Gam, certain villages (mainly in Kurunegala and Matale districts) that were required during the Kandyan Kingdom to fund the families that work in and organize the *perahera*. Nowadays, money is short for these performers because the Ninda Gam money no longer comes.

Here I want to introduce what I call the "standard narrative," reported in most discussions of Sri Lankan music and dance (I consider this more and challenge it somewhat in Chapter 4). The narrative states that (1) Kandyan Dance began as an ancient (*pre-Buddhist*) ritual, the Kohomba Kankariya, that more or less stayed intact in Kandy over the centuries; (2) elements from Tamil court culture seeped into the tradition through the Vannams in the eighteenth century; (3) Kandyan dance and drumming "became Buddhist" through the incorporation of drummers and dancers in the Temple of the Tooth in Kandy and the Äsala Perahera; and (4) all this developed into staged performances of excerpts from the Kohomba Kankariya and the Vannams in the twentieth century (as "Kandyan Dance"). Here I want to ask *why* such a connection between Kandyan Dance and South Indian Tamil Nayakkar court culture is emphasized in the standard narrative. After all, it would seem to contradict what I argued in my introduction, that Kandyan Dance has been ethnically purified in the Sri Lankan public sphere: how could the premier Sinhala Buddhist nationalist genre be accepted as having been shaped through South Indian Tamil influence?

The reason, I suggest, is that because Sinhala Buddhist kings have traditionally not been allowed to patronize music and dance, Sinhala historiography has emphasized Tamil Nayakkar influence because it helps sediment Kandyan Dance's royal origins without having to emphasize that any other Buddhist kings patronized music and dance, thus threatening their "Buddhist-ness." It is well known that the Nayakkar kings were great patrons of Buddhism, perhaps in order to win the trust of the people (Holt 1996), but in the case of music and dance, I suggest their somewhat foreign status has allowed for a narrative on the generation of "Buddhist" music that puts *Sinhala* Buddhist kings off the hook. The description of the Beravā as "pre-Buddhist" in origin maintains both the indigenousness of Sinhala music and dance and the separateness of the Beravā and Buddhism. Even though the low caste Beravā are the progenitors of Kandyan courtly music and dance, their influence is downplayed in favor of the court influence.

I suggest that in the twentieth century, the Berava became celebrated as "properly Buddhist" because of their connections with the Kandyan court and Äsala Perahera, without adequately celebrated as the originators of up-country music and dance. Meanwhile, the esteem granted the Kandyan Kingdom and Kohomba Kankariya situates low-country Beravā in a space of lack: a lack of Buddhist-ness (on account of their performance of *yak tovils*) and a lack of kingly associations (despite their historic association with medieval Sinhala kingdoms and, perhaps, ancient Ruhuna). By contrast, I contend that Sinhala traditional music and dance originated with the Beravā, not through Tamil Nayakkar influence; that the Beravā were periodically patronized by Sinhala Buddhist kings over the centuries; and that both up-country and low-country traditions are equally "Buddhist" because they draw on Buddhist concepts and values and grew up in Buddhist contexts (temples, *peraheras*). It is to these concepts and values that I now turn.

The Cosmic Hierarchy, Karma, and Merit-Making

Sinhala Buddhist cosmology is covered in detail in many other sources, but a short survey is necessary here. The king of the gods is Sakra (the Buddhist version of the Hindu god Indra) who reigns over the "Gods of the Four Quarters" (the cardinal directions): Dhritarashtra (the guardian of the East), Virudha (the guardian of the south), Virupaksha (the guardian of the west), and Vaisravana (the guardian of the north; Scott 1994: 19).[34] The Sinhala Buddhist pantheon is a hierarchy that mirrors political representation (Winslow 1984); the Buddha sits in a "presidential" position (Obeyesekere 1963), for although he has achieved liberation (*nibbana*) from the wheel of rebirth (*samsara*), he has delegated authority through his warrants (*varam*). These are given to the Four Warrant Gods (*hatara varam deviyo*) in the form of regional sovereignty: Vishnu is protector of the entire island, Natha's main shrine is in Kandy (in the central hill country), Pattini's main shrine is at Navagamuva in the Western Province, and Kataragama's main shrine is in the town that shares his name, in the southeast.[35] Natha is the next Buddha (also known as Maitteya), while Vishnu, Pattini, and Kataragama follow him in succession. The Four Warrant Gods, Holt (2004: 34) notes, "represent the major currents (Vaisnava, Saiva, Sakta, and Mahayana) of South Indian religion that have been contemporary in India for most of this history of the Theravada Buddhist tradition in Sri Lanka, at least since the later centuries of the first millennium CE."

---

[34] Each rules over other beings: Dhritarashtra is chief of the Ghandarvas, a class of minor deities who according to Buddhist mythology are "celestial musicians"; Virudha rules over the Kumbhandas, Virupaksha the Nagas; and Vaisravana the Yakkhas (Scott 1994: 19).

[35] In other regions, such as in Matara, Pattini is replaced in this list by the god Saman; elsewhere Vibhisana, the brother of Ravana of *Ramayana* fame, is added to the list. Obeyesekere (1966) suggests the tradition of the *hatara varam deviyo* derives from that of the Gods of the Four Quarters, which preceded it.

Following the Four Warrant Gods are other deities, such as Ganesha or Gana Deviyo (Kataragama's brother), Valli Amma (mistress of Kataragama), Dadimunda (Alutnuvara Deviyo), and deities called *bandaras*, who have mere local sway.[36] Beneath these are kings (an important category in premodern Sri Lanka), followed by humans, ghosts (*bhutas*), demons (*yakku*), and the ghosts of ancestors who had a poor death (*pretayo*). Finally, an ambiguous place in the hierarchy is allotted for "demon-deities" (Kapferer 1997: 32–33), thought to have been human or the offspring of a divine-human union. These are *devatava*, a word that also refers to the tree deities that are prayed to before chopping down a tree to make a drum. The god of sorcery, Suniyam, is particularly susceptible to his malevolent aspect, and is considered both a *devatava* and a *yakkha*. At the bottom of the hierarchy are demons (*yakku*).[37]

The center of the physical, metaphysical, and spiritual universes is Mt. Sineru (Sanskrit: Mt. Meru), which is surrounded by four continents (we live on Jambadipa, in the south). Gods live in *divya lokaya*, including the *Tusita* and *Tavatimsa* heavens. This spatial cosmology interacts with a Theravada notion of time as linear but eternally recurring, for individuals are reborn in a world where we have knowledge of the names of many of the Buddhas who come before and after us, unfolding in succession in both directions. Offerings of drumming must occur at auspicious times determined by an astrologer (who may also be a drummer) and sometimes in a specified direction. For example, buyers of a new house may hire a drummer to purify the house; this requires the drummer to play in certain parts of the house drumming away from wherever the god of death, Mara, is residing.

The cosmic hierarchy is "ethicized" (Obeyesekere 1966): each being, including ourselves, is ranked according to beneficence and viewed as progressing toward *nibbana* (Sanskrit: *nirvana*), the cessation of suffering and the leaving of the cycle of rebirth (*samsara*). Our ranking is determined by our *kamma* (karma); by performing benevolent actions, we acquire merit or *pin* (*puñña*) and move up the *kammic* ladder, inching closer to *nibbana*.[38] The paradigmatic example of merit-making is *dāna,* the giving of alms to monks; a related term is *pinkama*, public occasions for merit-making that includes *dāna*, preaching *(bāna)*, and chanting of the Buddha's teachings (Dhamma) by monks ("protection" or *pirit*). *Pinkama* also sometimes refers to private merit-making activities such as meditation, following the Buddhist precepts, showing respect, and listening to preaching (Gombrich 1971: 74). The major difference between deities and humans is that deities have accumulated more

---

[36] For a discussion of the minor deities, see Scott (1994: 19), from whom this list is culled.

[37] The whole system is referred to as the "three worlds," i.e., the abodes of deities, humans, and *yakku* (Obeyesekere 1984: 53; Reed 2010: 28).

[38] Achieving *nibbana* is considered a far-off possibility for Sinhala Buddhists that may not be achieved in this lifetime. Thus, Sinhala Buddhists tend to look instead for ways to make small-scale progressions up the *kammic* ladder, in order to have better future lives.

merit and are so high up the *kammic* ladder they have left the human world altogether, to be reborn in the heavens.[39] The higher a deity gets in the pantheon, the less investment he or she has in the this-worldly affairs of humans.[40] This explains why, although the Buddha, Natha, and Vishnu receive offerings in Beravā rituals, it is Pattini, Kataragama, and occasionally other deities farther down the list (like Devol Deviyo) who are more commonly the rituals' center of focus.

While drumming is not typically considered a merit-making activity, it is deeply integrated into some merit-making activities, like *pirit* and *peraheras*. The purpose of Beravā rituals, though, is not to gain merit but to protect the population (in *deva tovils* and *bali*) and eradicate illnesses (in *yak tovils*). While canonic acts of giving in Buddhism (e.g., *dāna*) increase one's store of karma and further one's path toward *nibbana*, Beravā rituals help people in *this* life. According to post-canonical commentaries (the *Atthakatha*) on the canonical text the *Digha Nikaya*, the laity makes merit through honoring others (*apacayana-maya*); offering service (*veyyavacca-maya*); involving others in good deeds (*pattidana-maya*); being thankful for others' good deeds (*pattanumodana-maya*); listening to teachings (*dhammassavana-maya*); instructing others in the teachings (*dhammadesana-maya*); and straightening one's own views in accordance with the teachings (*ditthujukamma*) (Payutto 1997). It is the job of drummers to honor and offer service to serious, practicing Buddhists (the Buddha and deities), and to help involve others in good deeds (e.g., *dāna, pirit*). Thus, I do not think drumming should be *ipso facto* ruled out from the list of merit-making activities (though drummers did not describe it to me as such).[41]

I want to conclude by suggesting the Buddhist notion of the "not-self" (*anatta*) is foundational for the emergence of Beravā drumming as a gift, for it means there is no permanent "self" there for whom music serves as a direct outward expression of an inward identity. I suggest this allows Beravā drumming to be easily conceived as an object (or rather, an objectified language) that can be hoarded and exchanged, which gains power when it is offered. Its power lies in the sounded offering of the phrases (*padas*) of the drum language, not in the drummer per se: as Kapferer (1983: xiii) puts it about low-country *yak tovils*, "exorcists do not themselves embody transformational powers; rather this is the property of the specific rites they perform."

---

[39] However, the deities must be reborn in the human world in order to achieve *nibbana*.

[40] "Buddhists do not so much worship gods as make use of them, and Buddhism says that men are superior to gods in as much as they have greater potentialities for working out their salvation from the cycle of births and deaths" (Sarachchandra 1952: 12).

[41] Gombrich (1971: 126) describes a person who organized a *tun masa dāna* (the feeding of monks by a householder to honor the three-month anniversary of a relative's passing) where drummers stood outside a shrine and played for a few minutes; the donor acquired merit by giving (*dānava*) food to the monks, which he then passed on to his deceased relative. Drumming in such instances appears to accompany, rather than directly facilitate, the creation of merit.

Conclusion: The Discursive Transformation of Beravā Musical Giving

In the music and identity episteme, Beravā drumming has become tethered to a "self," the flow of power in their sonic gift economy inverted. While it used to be that the Beravā's role in society was to honor kingly and divine sovereign powers through musical offerings and thereby facilitate protection for the king and community, now it is the state that honors the Beravā by "protecting" their music and dance by funding rituals, training programs, and staged performances (Figure 2.7).

This transformation can be grasped visually by looking at Sri Lankan bank notes, which frequently picture dancers and drummers (for example, Kandyan dancers and drummers have appeared on the 500- and 20-rupee bill,; Sabaragamuwa ritualists on the 50 and 1000, and low-country ritualists on the 500 and 5000). Such bills point toward two economies: the modern capitalist economy in which they function, and the premodern economy of musical gifts. In the music and identity episteme, it is now the *personhood* of drummers and dancers that matter more than the *content* they perform.

In July 2016, a riot broke out when some Sinhala students at the Tamil-majority University of Jaffna agitated to have Kandyan dancers lead a procession at a graduation ceremony that had already been scheduled to be led by Tamil *thavil* (drum) and *nadaswaram* (reed) players. Reports surfaced that these students did not act alone but were encouraged by Sinhala Buddhist nationalists, some of whom seem to have had connections to the regime of President Mahinda Rajapaksa (in power from 2005–2015). According to journalist DBS Jeyaraj, a Tamil student said,

> "They (Sinhala Students) could have made the suggestion when we were planning the program and making preparations together. Instead they came at the last minute and started arguing." According to Kannan [not his real name] the Sinhala students had said that Sinhala Buddhists were the majority in the country as well as the science faculty and demanded that Kandyan dancing be included in the procession also. Explaining further Kannan said that this "we are the majority" attitude irritated the Tamil students. So we told them this is Jaffna where Tamils are in the majority and that the Tamil custom was to have a procession with Nadaswaram and Thavil and not Kandyan dancing. This

---

(1) Drummers → Musical Offerings → Protect the King (the State) and Community
(2) The State → Monetary Offerings → Protect Drummers (as "Heritage")

Figure 2.7 Drumming in the Old Sonic Gift Economy (1) and the Music and Identity Episteme (2).

then seemed to be the reason for Tamil students remaining obstinate in refusing to comply with the Sinhala request and adjust the program in an accommodative manner.[42]

These two genres have come to symbolize Sinhalas and Tamils, respectively, and in this case, the agitating for Kandyan Dance was clearly more a virulent display of ethnic pride and dominance than it was an efficacious gift to the gods or celebration of graduation. Thankfully, the situation was defused, and several Sinhalas and Tamils worked together to thwart the spread of more violence.[43] It is precisely this kind of abuse of the connection between music and identity that I wish to challenge. Not only does the use of Kandyan Dance in this way make minority groups resent the tradition, it also bastardizes Beravā aesthetics by using sonic generosity as a form of aggression rather than protection—and such acts (it is worth stressing) make all communities *less protected* by making them more susceptible to violence. In what follows, I argue that Kandyan Dance, the Tamil *nadaswaram* and *thavil* tradition, and indeed all Sri Lankan traditional music genres, are not that different from one another because they share a pan-Sri Lankan aesthetic of sonic generosity that originally had little to do with the expression of ethnic identity.

---

[42] D. B. S. Jeyaraj, "Jaffna Varsity Violence: What Really Happened and Why," *Daily Mirror*, July 23, 2016.

[43] Jayaraj (ibid.) reports that those agitating were a small faction; the Kandyan dancers were students but the drummers "were outsiders from among soldiers stationed in Jaffna." He notes that some of these soldiers maintain close relationships with Sinhala students at the University of Jaffna, cooking meals for them.

3

Sri Lankan Tamil Musical Giving

An Introduction

Northern Sri Lanka was home to the Jaffna kingdom (1215–1624) and its Aryacakravarti Dynasty, whose founding is generally attributed to the eastern Indian king Kalinga Magha (Pathmanathan 1978). Devastating the Sinhala-dominated northern region of Rajarata and forcing a "drift to the southwest" for Sinhala society, Magha ruled Polonnaruwa for twenty years, after which he retreated to Jaffna, where he ruled until 1255 CE.[1] Magha "conducted a pro-Saiva, anti-Vaisnava, anti-Buddhist campaign everywhere he went" (McGilvray 2008: 58).[2] He rewarded his troops with land in the east, where they may have displaced descendants of Vanniyar caste warriors who migrated in earlier times from South Arcot in Tamil Nadu, spreading Draupadi worship and giving the name (and possibly political traditions) to the "Vanniyar" chieftains who defined the east's medieval period (McGilvray 2008: 59).[3] Magha's soldiers brought their matrilineal inheritance patterns to the east, facilitating a division between the

---

[1] Political gravity in the north shifted throughout the medieval period, as the region veered between independence, quasi-independence, and tributary or vassal status to South Indian kingdoms (e.g., the Pandyans and Vijayanagara). The period right after Magha's rule witnessed a brief incursion from a Malay king of the Tambralinga dynasty (in present-day Thailand), and the Sinhala-dominated kingdom of Kotte briefly conquered the region in the fifteenth century. The kingdom eventually fell to the Portuguese (Indrapala 2005).

[2] Sri Lankan Tamil Hindus are known for their Saivism (worship of Shiva), a devotional (*bhakti*) tradition associated with poet-saints (*Nāyaṉār*) who lived during the sixth to eighth century CE, and whose sung poetry (*Tēvāram*) was canonized in the Tamil Chola Dynasty. Vaisnavism, which is more prevalent in Tamil Nadu than Sri Lanka, is centered on the worship of Vishnu.

[3] Little is known about the east before Magha, though settlements have been found in the region dating to the second or third century BCE (Indrapala 2005). The major source for the region's past is the eighteenth-century *Mattakkalappu Māṉmiyam*, which includes a list of undated early dynasties (Pathmanathan 1978; McGilvray 2008).

matrilineal (*kudi*) kinship system of eastern Tamils (and Muslims) and the patrilineal kinship patterns of Jaffna Tamils, which continues to this day (McGilvray 2008: 59).[4]

Are these social divisions between northern and eastern Tamils relevant for music history? Or is there a uniquely "Eelam" musical tradition that cuts equally across both regions, marking them as culturally distinct from South India and the Sinhala-dominated parts of the island? Alternatively, should we view the north and east as a mere extension of South Indian Tamil music history? Or is it possible to build a connected music history between the north and east, South India, and Sinhala (and Muslim, Burgher, and other) populations in Sri Lanka? In what follows, I answer "yes" to *all* of these questions. First, in this chapter, I emphasize regional differences, while building a unique Sri Lankan Tamil music history. Then in the next chapter, I consider connected histories. My ultimate question, which I confront in the next chapter, is the following: in light of the modern link between music and identity, what effect might our framing of Sri Lankan Tamil music history have on the political status of Sri Lankan Tamils?

Jaffna has long been a center for Tamil Hinduism, music, and dance. After being largely closed off from the world for nearly three decades because of war, the region is undergoing an artistic revival (Chapter 5). However, its relations to Colombo remain tenuous. Jaffna is famous for its nineteenth-century Hindu revivalist Ārumuka Nāvalar (1822–1879), who promoted a conservative, caste-conscious view of the religion in the wake of Protestant Christian missionization. The Tamil name for Jaffna is *yazhpanam* ("land of the harp"; the word *yazh* refers to an ancient Tamil harp); legend has it the city was founded when a *yazh* player was given a land grant. The *yazh* is no longer in use by Tamil musicians, but its importance in ancient Tamil society is attested by the Sangam sources (the canon of ancient Tamil literature, circa 300 BCE–200 CE) and a later text, the *Cilappatikāram*, which describes four kinds of *yazh*. While the instrument is seldom mentioned in English-language studies of South Indian Carnatic music—that tradition is typically dated to Puraṅdara Dāsa (1484–1564) and the "trinity" of composers he influenced, who lived in South India at the turn of the nineteenth century—the *yazh* and its melodic system of *pans* form the foundation of an ancient Tamil musical system that has much significance for Tamils but has not yet been adequately

---

[4] The dominant northern Tamil caste is the Vēḷāḷar (cultivators), though the Karaiyar (fisherman and merchants, the Tamil equivalent of the Sinhala Karāvā) have "since about the mid-1980s . . . come to rank very high, socially, as patriots and warriors in the forefront of the war of Tamil independence" (Wilson 2000: 19). These are followed by the Chetti (merchant), artisan, and service castes, the latter including Paraiyars (drummers). By contrast, eastern Tamil society is characterized by a "high caste alliance" of Mukkuvars, Vēḷāḷars, and Virasaiva Kurukkal ritualists, followed by five specialist castes in descending order: *taṭṭār* smiths, *sandar* climbers, and three "household servant castes" (*kuṭimai*), the Vaṇṇar washerman, Nāvitaṇ barbers, and Paraiyars (McGilvray 2008: 149–168). Traditionally, high castes reserved the right to enjoy the services of the *kuṭimai*, which included drumming at funerals and weddings (ibid. 247–265).

Figure 3.1 Statue Holding a *yazh* (harp), Jaffna (*Yazhpanam*).

accounted for in ethnomusicology. For example, the masterpiece of the renowned Tamil musicologist from Batticaloa, Swami Vipulanandar (1892–1947), *Yazh Nool*, is a celebrated treatise on the instrument that has yet to be translated into English.[5] The next phase of Carnatic music studies needs to better reach across the 33 to 50 miles that constitutes the Palk Strait (the water in between India and Sri Lanka) to include Sri Lankan Tamils in its narrative. This chapter is just a start.

Jaffna maintains a similar hegemony over Trincomalee and Batticaloa as Kandy does for the Sinhala culture zones. To some, the Jaffna dialect is the purest form of Tamil, while for others, such an assertion reeks of snobbery.[6] Batticaloa

---

[5] See T. M. Krishna, "Celebrating Unheard Melodies," *The Hindu*, October 15, 2016.

[6] The Jaffna-centric mindset had political ramifications during the war. The LTTE's leadership was from the north (the organization's leader, Velupillai Prabhakaran, was from Valvettithurai on the Jaffna Peninsula), and as the war developed, there were feelings among some eastern Tamils that their children were often dying on the front lines for northern interests.

itself is "the land of singing fish," a nickname that refers to sounds that supposedly emanate from fish in the Batticaloa lagoon. The sound has been likened to a Jew's harp or cello string; nineteenth-century naturalist James Emerson Tennent likened it to "the gentle thrills of a musical chord . . . the sweetest treble mingling with the lowest bass" (cited in McGilvray 2008: 25). In the 1960s, a priest named Father Lang recorded the fish on a full moon night and played the recording on the Sri Lanka broadcasting station. During the war, the sounds seem to have disappeared.[7] When I visited Batticaloa a few years after the tsunami, in 2006, a local told me the tsunami killed the singing fish. The legend has given birth to a statue of the fish at a traffic junction; "Singing Fish" is the name of Batticaloa's cricket team, and a few decades ago, a local musical group was named after them.[8] The emblem of the singing fish—a curved tail shaped like a harp, and sometimes drawn as one—is the emblem of Batticaloa. Thus two of the largest and most historically important Tamil-majority cities in Sri Lanka have music built into their mythologies of being.

Starting from Jaffna east through traditionally-minded Mullaitivu, south through Trincomalee (with its gorgeous cliffs and famous harbor), down along the coast through Batticaloa and Akkaraipattu to Panama (the last settlement before Yala National Park) is an interconnected set of Tamil villages interspersed with Muslim ones (Muslims maintain a slight majority in the southeast; some towns, like Akkaraipattu, are split almost evenly between Tamil and Muslim neighborhoods [McGilvray 2008: 32–37]). The Tamil heartlands continue in the other direction, from Jaffna south through Kilinochchi (once the headquarters of the LTTE) through Vavuniya, west towards the island of Mannar (with its large Muslim and majority Tamil Catholic population) and south to the ethnically diverse Puttalam district (with Sinhala Buddhists, Christians, Muslims, and a Tamil Hindu fishing village called Udappu), just north of Colombo. This entire region, referred to by Tamils as "Eelam," was claimed by the LTTE in their war for independence. Tamils live in many other parts of the island besides, such as tea plantations and towns in the hill country (associated with "Indian" or Malaiyaha Tamils), and the Wellawatte neighborhood of Colombo.

Overlapping with the above is a religious cartography. The Pancha Ishwarams (five abodes of Shiva) are temples dedicated to Shiva on or near the coast, which devotees believe go back to the time of Ravana. These were looted and destroyed by the Portuguese, and some suffered mightily during the war (all but one has

---

[7] An old blog entry, no longer active, put forth the following explanation: "It might possibly be the special effect of water tides on a full moon flowing over shells on the lagoon bed and the echoing of it by the bridge overhead. No-one goes over the bridge at night these days [the blogger was writing during the war] and if they do, they wouldn't linger to listen out for the music so maybe, that's why no one's heard it since the conflict started."

[8] Nowadays, one only needs to go on YouTube to find recordings of the singing fish, though videographers can't seem to agree on which fish (or crustaceans) are making the sounds.

since been restored). They include Keerimai Naguleswaram Kovil (in Jaffna), Ketheeswaram Kovil in Mannar (whose restoration was halted for decades because of a military presence on the site), Munneswaram Kovil (in Puttalam District), Koneswaram Kovil (located on an enormous rock overlooking the sea in Trincomalee), and Tondeswaram Kovil (in the south, near Matara), the latter a temple destroyed by the Portuguese and rebuilt as a Sinhala Buddhist *devalaya* for Vishnu.

There is a division between musicians who play in "Brahmanical" temples (built according to the Agamas, canonic Hindu scripture) and non-Agamic temples (e.g., *amman* or mother goddess temples), a tradition famously associated with the east. The former are *Icai Vēḷāḷars* (formerly known as *Mēḷakkāraṉs*), a mid-level caste of musical givers who offer music to deities on *nadaswaram* (reed instrument) and *thavil* (drum) in Hindu temples and festivals. Non-Agamic temples are the abode of Paraiyars (known in India, though not so frequently in Sri Lanka, as Dalits), whose traditional occupations include scavenging dead cattle for drum skins and drumming at funerals, tasks deemed polluting and stigmatizing (Sherinian 2013).[9] It is commonly assumed Paraiyars once held a more respected status in Tamil society. Ethnomusicologists working in South India have noticed the *parai* and another stigmatized drum, the *urumi*, played in auspicious contexts, including Shivaratri (Paige 2008). According to my consultants, Parai drumming was once widespread in Sri Lankan Hindu temples, including those for Shiva. In Batticaloa, the *parai* continues to be associated with the Parai Mela Kooththu, a tradition of dancing with the drum (accompanied by a double-reed instrument called *sornali*) to celebrate the new year and in the courtyards of local VIPs on special occasions (Shanmugalingam 2012). As one consultant in Jaffna put it, with the coming of caste strictures, Paraiyars were forced to work for the high caste Vēḷāḷar in Jaffna, and for the high caste Mukkuvar in Batticaloa. Caste-conscious Hindus generally look down on the *parai* and Paraiyar community, overlooking their roles in auspicious religious contexts and as town criers who made announcements to the community (an original meaning of *parai* is "announcing drum"). While no one knows precisely when these changes happened, all agree caste strictures were more enforced during the time of Nāvalar (Ambalavanar 2006; Bate 2005). One consultant said "it was from the fourteenth century only that the Carnatic music came here. . . . from the seventeenth century, people knew about *nadaswaram* and *thavil*. . . . so the *parai* went down during this time."[10] This statement demonstrates a belief that the Carnatic music system (now synonymous with South Indian

---

[9] "Dalit" ("broken down" or "oppressed") refers to "untouchable" communities, including Paraiyars. Dr. Ambedkar, who worked toward the emancipation of "untouchable" peoples in India and oversaw the drafting of the Indian Constitution, introduced the term in 1928. It was not widely adopted until the latter half of the twentieth century after Mahatma Gandhi's term, *harijan* (children of God), was deemed too paternalistic (Sherinian 2013: 14).

[10] The earliest evidence of the *nadaswaram* in Tamil Nadu is the fifteenth century (Terada 2008).

classical music and Tamils around the world) was first associated with South India and only later spread to Sri Lanka, rather than having always been synonymous with Sri Lankan Tamils (as is often assumed).[11] More to my point, there appears to be a connected history between northern and eastern Tamil Paraiyars that was altered somewhat by the coming of caste strictures and "Carnatic music" first to the north, since it led to the growth of a strong *nadaswaram* and *thavil* tradition there more so than in the east.

It must be stressed that the *parai* in Sri Lanka looks nothing like the *parai* in South India: the former is fat, stocky, and double-sided (resembling the drums called *dhol* or *dollu* in India and *davula* among the Sinhalese); the latter is a skinny frame drum. In South India, a synonym for the *parai* frame drum is *thappu*, though in Sri Lanka, that word is used just for the South Indian frame drum, which maintains a presence on the island because it is used by up-country (Malaiyaha) Tamils, whose ancestors brought it from South India. Despite the shared name, then, the *parai* marks an organological difference between South Indian and Sri Lankan Tamils, and a similarity between the latter and Sinhala Buddhists, a significant issue I explore in the next chapter.

McGilvray did fieldwork in 1975 with the Paraiyar community in Tivukkudi (near Kokkadichcholi) on the western shore of Batticaloa lagoon (at his time of writing, the community had been in LTTE hands for twenty years, so his research could not be updated [McGilvray 1983, 2008: 264]).[12] The traditional headman of the Paraiyars was the *Muppan* (an elected official), who was notified when Mukkuvar families needed drumming.[13] The *Muppan* kept an honorific drum (*rāca mēḷam*) that was given to Paraiyars by Mukkuvars on the founding of the settlement, which was treated deferentially and brought to high caste funerals (McGilvray 2008: 262). Besides life cycle rituals, a few jobs were available for Paraiyars as town criers.[14]

As waves of anti-caste agitation and a Dalit rights movement grew in India in the twentieth century, anti-caste agitation grew in Sri Lanka. Jeyasankar Sivagnanam recounts a story before the war in which some eastern Pariayars burned their drums (the main source of their income) to protest their oppression by the higher castes (Thompson 2005: 103–110). Recordings have sometimes been used to fill

---

[11] The statement is slightly anachronistic, though, for what is known today as Carnatic music is associated mainly with the canonization of the trinity of composers who lived at the turn of the nineteenth century (Tyagaraja [1767–1847], Muthuswami Dikshitar [1775–1835], and Syama Sastri [1762–1827], with Purandara Dasa [1484–1564] as the grandfather of the system.

[12] According to McGilvray (2008: 261), the hamlet "goes back about 150 years, to a time when four major (higher caste) Mukkuvar Podiyars donated a total of 7.3 hectares of paddy land on perpetual service-tenure to a group of Paraiyar families recruited from already established Paraiyar villages elsewhere in the Batticaloa region."

[13] The *Muppan* knew how to play the shawm (*sornāli*) but "his basic function was symbolic" (ibid. 263).

[14] One current exponent of the *parai* drum in the east is Parasuraman of Kaluthavalai.

in for absent drummers (McGilvray 2008), though there has been a long-term trend to replace the *parai* in the east with the auspicious *nadaswaram* and *thavil*. Interlocutors said that because of the modernization of Jaffna before the war, the rural islands of Nagadipa and Delft (off the coast of the Jaffna Peninsula) had become known for retaining the older *parai* tradition. Sadly, Paraiyar hamlets were decimated during the war, and it will take further research to determine their continued presence throughout the north and east. A few years after the tsunami, I met some non-Paraiyar youths who had picked up the drum since no one in their village (near Kalmunai) wanted to play or was still alive to play it.

During the war, the death of the *parai* was challenged from at least two directions. The LTTE was anti-caste, and they championed the *parai* as cultural heritage; consultants told me the LTTE sponsored an all-female *parai* troupe. But they stipulated the Pariayars should drum for *all* castes, and in Jaffna I heard some Paraiyars stopped drumming for that reason—if they drummed for the low castes their high caste patrons would refuse to hire them, so it was easier to stop drumming altogether. The second challenge came from activists like Jeyasankar (a respected professor at the Eastern University), whose "Third Eye Local Knowledge and Skill Activists Group" promotes the *parai* in its original contexts.

In July 2015, I met a man named Inbam who my interlocutors claimed is the last active, hereditary *parai* drummer in Jaffna. While I remain skeptical that he is the last, he has that reputation, as I met drummers as far away as Mullaitivu who claimed, indeed, Inbam is the last one. We pulled up to his funeral home, where coffins were visible through glass windows; the worker directed us to Inbam's house, and my research assistant and I talked to him for quite some time. Inbam said his traditional territory was about eleven kilometers; he plays one beat in the house during funerals, one in a funeral procession, and one when the body is cremated. In the old days, he used to hire up to five *parai* drummers and two *tappāṭṭam* drummers to play in temples (the latter is a single, pot-shaped drum held with a strap that resembles the Sinhala *thammättama*; see the next chapter); nowadays, he uses two each of these drums at funerals, and in temple festivals he uses a larger ensemble (he used the English word "band") that includes a bass drum, snare drum, cymbals, and "trumpet."[15] Inbam is in demand for such events and was just about to leave for a Hindu festival in Wellawatte, Colombo. He owns all the band instruments—they were visible inside and a large bass drum sat on his veranda. For festivals he hires a van to drive him and additional musicians to the gig.[16] Another interlocutor said that in earlier days, parai drummers knew eighteen

---

[15] He used the English word "trumpet" but in retrospect I do not know if he meant the Western instrument of that name or the smaller double-reed (*sornāli*) that often accompanies the *parai*. Inbam insists his group (which includes his son, who he is training to take over his profession) does not play *parai* beats on band instruments.

[16] In a manner reminiscent of Sinhala drumming in the Bera Pōya Hēvisi, where the Gods of the Four Quarters receive offerings of drumming while in their *yahans* ("seats of the gods" placed in the

beats: six for the *kovil* (temple), six for funerals, and six for announcements, but this does not seem to be widespread today.[17] By contrast, a *parai* drummer in Mullaitivu said Paraiyars in funeral processions play a beat for Śūrapadmā, the demon (*asura*) slayed by Murugan, whose killing is celebrated in Murugan temples in the festival of *Sūra-saṃhāraṃ*.

The past few decades in South India has witnessed a resurgence of *parai* drumming. The frame drum is now promoted as cultural heritage and an emblem of the Dalit struggle for equality and justice (Sherinian 2013). These days, a similar revival is underway in Sri Lanka. While I rail against the link between music and identity in this book, the *parai* is a case where, as Zoe Sherinian (2013) has shown, the link with identity is beneficial: by celebrating the drum as a symbol of Dalits' historically oppressed state, heritagization seems to be reducing the stigma against the drum and community. A simple YouTube search will show that *parai* drummers (playing the Sri Lankan version of the drum) are still active at Sri Lankan Tamil Hindu festivals. A full sociological study of the *parai*, including consideration of what happened to Sri Lanka's Paraiyars during the war and how they are faring after the war, needs to be a book in itself—and it is one I would write if I didn't have enough going on in this one. I do, however, consider some of the post-war dynamics affecting Paraiyars in Chapter 5, and I consider the possible historical relations between Paraiyars and the Sinhala *hēvisi* ensemble in the next chapter.

Sri Lankan Tamil Music, Dance, and Theater

Balasugumar (2009) notes that when Vipulananda wrote his magnum opus *Yazh Nool*, he was under "the influence of the tradition of music of the Eelam Tamils which in turn is based on their tradition and culture. The sweet lyrics of Kannagi that he used to hear when he was young, the songs of Vasanthan (Vasanthan Pādalgal), the Music of Koothu (street-play) formed the basis for his research on music."[18] In other words, "Eelam music" forms a coherent system, one deeply integrated with religion and ritual, and (as with Sinhala music) bound up with dance, drama, and temples. Because travel to parts of the north and east was difficult during the war, Tamils from rural areas like

---

four cardinal directions), Inbam demonstrated how he plays different drum beats for different gods located at the four cardinal directions.

[17] Vimal Shankar, personal communication.

[18] I have corrected some grammatical errors in Balasugumar's words to make them more comprehensible to English speakers.

Figure 3.2 A photograph of a *kooththu* actor/dancer.

Mannar and Mullaitivu may not know what is going on in the other place, though I suspect this is changing because of the Internet and newfound mobility brought about by the end of the war.[19] This section provides an overview of music, dance, and ritual in Tamil Hindu contexts in the north and east; then I provide a detailed focus on *kooththus* (dance dramas) associated with Batticaloa. The information I present here is necessarily tentative; it is meant just to put Sri Lankan Tamil musics on the musicological map and pave the way for my comparative discussion of Sinhala and Tamil drums in the next chapter.

---

[19] An interlocutor in Mullaitivu, however, told me he has long performed up to 100 *kooththus* a year throughout the north, east, and in places far afield like Mannar. I have no way to verify if this is true or how this mobility shifted during the war, but it does point to the north and east as an interconnected sphere traversed by *kooththu* artists. Yet, see Thompson 2005 for a discussion of the *lack* of interaction between Batticaloa and Jaffna *kooththu* artists during the war, an issue I return to below.

Batticaloa and Ampara[20]

Shanmugalingam (2012) breaks up the arts of the Batticaloa and Ampara regions into eight categories. At one end are Hindu trance possession rituals that appease gods and heal and protect worshippers; at the other end are dramas featuring music and dance (*kooththus*), often held at Hindu temples and more entertainment than ritual (though the line may be blurred). I suggest the *parai* and *uṭukkai* (a handheld drum associated with trance) are typically used in the former category. Such performances do not involve "melodic" instruments save for the occasional use of a shawm (*sornāli*). *Kooththus*, by contrast, vary widely by region, though generally they center on a drum called *maththalam*. In the east, *kooththus* do not typically use melodic instruments, while in the north they often use harmonium and sometimes the *maththalam* is supplanted by *tabla* (Malaiyaha Tamil *kooththus* in the hill country, by contrast, use the *parai* frame drum). In Brahmanical temples and many auspicious contexts, *nadaswaram* and *thavil* are used. Tamils have made profound contributions to Carnatic classical music and Bharata Natyam (South Indian classical dance), but I am concerned here with the musics of ritual, folk, and drama, which Sri Lankan Tamils tend to consider their indigenous tradition.

First on the list are rituals Shanmugalingam (using an old anthropological term) says belong to the "little tradition," that is, non-Brahmanical forms of worship. Examples include the Naraciṅka Vairavar sacrificial dance; Vathanamar dance; Kāttavarāyaṉ dance, and rituals appeasing other locally significant gods: Māriyammaṉ, Kāliyammaṉ, Gangathevi Kaṅkātēvi, Neelasothayan, Praththi, Caṅkili Kāḷi, and Muttukkiḷavi (2012; Ranasinha n.d.). Second are rituals that drive away spirits inflicting disease, held mainly at Kali temples. Third are "domestic rituals" in which a priest heals devotees through possession at one's home—rituals akin to Sinhala *yak tovils*, since they involve "dramatic dialogues, singing and dancing, mime and music," with the ritual occurring "in the presence of the neighbours and relatives of the household" (2012). Fourth are rituals associated with regionally significant temples (*tēcattukōvil*) at Kokkadichcholai, Mandur, and Tirukovil (McGilvray 2008: 71; Whitaker 1999). One example is the re-enactment of the marriage of Murugan and Valli at the Mandur Kovil (a Sinhala version of this is held at the Kataragama pilgrimage site; Obeyesekere 1981). Also in this category are a hunting festival that involves a symbolic shooting of an arrow into cooked rice; a reenactment of maidens becoming enchanted by Murugan such that they fall unconscious; and a ritual where women of the Mukkuvar caste "beat" members of the Vēḷāḷar caste softly with plantain leaves,

---

[20] Shanmugalingam (2012) is the only source that has this information neatly summarized in English, so I rely heavily on him here. I have incorporated information from elsewhere (Maunaguru 1992, 1993, 1998; Balasugumar 2009) and from interviews conducted in Batticaloa, Kalmunai, Akkaraipattu, Mullaitivu, Jaffna, and Colombo.

as the latter carries an idol of Murugan (Shanmugalingam 2012). One might also include in this category regionally famous Hindu festivals, like the Draupadi fire-walking festival (*tīmiti*) at Pandiruppu (McGilvray 1998: 66). Music at such festivals may include *uṭukkai, parai*, and/or the *nadaswaram/thavil* combo—the choice is determined by numerous factors, such as the nature of the event, which deity is being worshipped, local temple politics, and the availability of musicians. In Kalmunai, for instance, I met some *thavil* drummers who had been invited to come from their home in the hill country to play at a Hindu festival.

The hunting festival mentioned above seems to draw on or mimic rituals of the Väddas, the indigenous community. In Batticaloa there is one relatively well-known ritual associated with the region's Väddas, the Kumara Tēvar ritual (Shanmugalingam 2012). While these Väddas speak Tamil, the ritual is in Vädda *basai* (Vädda language). Curiously, the priest who performs it is the Kappuhan, while a priest who goes into trance is a Kattadi—names reminiscent of the Sinhala ritual specialist of the deity cults (*kapurala*) and demon cults (*kattadiya*). The ritual last seven days and involves collecting honey (and—it should be stressed—its status after the war is unknown).[21]

Fifth, the Kompu Viḷaiyāṭṭu brings rain and calms Kannagi, the goddess who burned down the South Indian city of Madurai in the *Cilappatikāram* epic (the same goddess as Pattini, who is worshipped by Sinhalas). It involves a game of tug of war between two groups from the village. Kompu Murippu is a festival lasting several days in which Vacantan Kooththu (see below) is performed with other songs and games (Ranasinha n.d.). Sixth on Shanmugalingam's list is a near-extinct phenomenon, Mahudi Kooththu (in Batticaloa) or Mahedi Kooththu (in the north). It is a friendly competition or "staged conflict" between ethnic and/or religious groups. It seems to have been a way to relieve social tensions. Shanmugalingam writes that it involved "Betting; accomplishing one's success in the bet with the help of magic and trick; hunters charming the snakes playing their musical instrument called 'Mahudi'; fantasy brusque and obscenity are all found in this performance" (Shanmugalingam 2012).[22] In the north, it enacted a "conflict" between Brahmins and Muslims, or between Brahmins and Catholics; in Batticaloa, the narrative might include "migrant Malayalees" or a European man and wife (Shanmugalingam 2012). A humorous event, it included song, dance, and drama. Since Muslims were driven out of the north by the LTTE in 1990 (only a few have returned after the war), they are no longer around to perform this ritual.

By far, the most important category of music, dance, and drama in Batticaloa (number seven on Shanmugalingam's list) is *kooththu*. The genre is derived from the South Indian *terukkuttu* (street theater), which has roots in the Sangam era

---

[21] According to Ranasinha (n.d.), the ritual is performed by Tamils, with the ritual language being called *verduvar basai* ("hunter's language").

[22] The *magudi* is a small double-reed instrument (Paige 2010).

Figure 3.3 A Tamil drummer holding a *maththalam* drum, Batticaloa.

but appears to have crystalized into its current form by the seventeenth century (Hiltebeitel 1988: 147–149; Bass 2012: 154). Many *kooththus* are named after the lead figure in the drama (e.g., "Kaman Kooththu" is the story of Kaman). One favorite is Vacantaṉ Kooththu ("The Drama of Vacantaṉ"), a stick dance performed in May during harvest season at temple festivals that helps young children gain skills they need for performing in other *kooththus*. Vacantaṉ Kooththu is also found in Jaffna and Trincomalee, where it uses some of the same music but is held on the proscenium stage rather than in the theater in the round (*vatakkalari*), which is used in Batticaloa.[23] *Kooththus* are performed in *vadamodi* or *tenmodi*, two stylistic categories of great importance that I describe in the next section.

---

[23] Sri Lanka's *Sunday Leader* (December 1, 2014) published a story describing the origins of the drama. According to them, it originated in nineteenth-century Jaffna with Sattambiyar Viswanathar, a farmer and teacher who, having no children, taught the songs to Vallipuram Guruswami, who passed them down through his family: "The songs would speak of the cycles of sowing seed and reaping the harvest of crop, the circling of birds in the skies, in a devotional manner, seeking the protection of Veerapaththirar, an avatar of Shiva." The genre, they say, uses *mridangam*, harmonium, and *talampota* (finger cymbals), with dancers playing percussion by clicking sticks. The current elder of the tradition, Sivapragasam (b. 1941), was displaced from his native Kadduvan (in Jaffna) due to the war but has since settled in nearby Kokkuvil.

Finally, an eighth category is "Aryanized" or Brahmanical forms of worship, which may involve trance but center on the reenactment of scenes from the Mahabharata and Ramayana epics. Examples include Cūraṉ Pōr, Pūttappōr, Kacamukācuraṉ Pōr, and Kamcaṉ Pōr. The performance of Cūraṉ Pōr I saw in Jaffna involved the movement of large statues of characters from the Hindu epics on chariots, accompanied by the *nadaswaram* and *thavil*. Footage of a *cūraṉ thalai kadal* emanating from the famous Nallur Kandaswamy Kovil in Jaffna in 2015 showed enormous kettle-shaped drums (*murasu*) played with a large *parai* (*periya parai*) as a statue of the *asura* Śūrapadmā was wheeled through town.

For the sake of space and lack of knowledge, I will not include Trincomalee on this list, since the region has received little anthropological attention save for a few pioneering studies (e.g., Gaasbeek 2010). Given the region's position between Jaffna and Batticaloa, Trincomalee reportedly contains cultural aspects from both regions. Shanmugalingam (n.d.) notes the region is known for "Karaiyal," a ritual offering associated with Māriyammaṉ organized by families who have her as their lineal goddess, with other regional cults being Kāttavarāyaṉ, Vīravākku Tēvar, Vaṉṉittēvar, Nāyaṉmār and Bhairava. He also mentions a masked "dragon dance" (Vētāḷa Āṭṭam) that used to be associated with Thennamaravadi (a village totally destroyed by the war), which involved the *parai* and was held at the Kantha Sasti (Murugan) festival (Shanmugalingam 2012).[24] It is impossible for me to say anything more about the music and dance of the region at this point.

While the east coast is more or less evenly split between Tamils and Muslims, the southeastern Ampara and northeastern Trincomalee districts have seen an acute influx of Sinhala settlers since the 1950s due to state-financed resettlement projects; today they are divided almost evenly between Tamils, Muslims, and Sinhalas.[25] As Korf (2009: 105) notes, "Tamil nationalists considered this to be an attempt to make Tamils a minority in their own homeland," while some Sinhala geographers have sought to justify the settlements by stating they were built on unoccupied lands or in places that in ancient times housed Sinhala settlements. After several massacres of Sinhalas in the north in 1984, the government armed Sinhala farmers in the north and east, including those in the Allai Extension Scheme. Following the brutal massacre of almost 150 Sinhala civilians (including monks and nuns) at Anuradhapura in 1985, "an orgy of violence was orchestrated

---

[24] In 2004, Tamilnet.com reported that Thennamaravadi was "in a ruined state without a single dwelling." Six hundred residents from the town who were displaced by the war settled near Mulliayawallai village in Mullaitivu District, forming a new village called Ponnagar. The article states they were set to vote for the first time since becoming IDPs (internally displaced persons). https://www.tamilnet.com/art.html?catid=13&artid=11610

[25] These controversial resettlement schemes include the Gal Oya dam project in Amparai and the Allai Extension Scheme in Seruvila, Muthur, and Eachchilampattai divisions in Trincomalee, as well as Kantalai and Morawewa in the east, and parts of the northern Dry Zone. The Department of Census and Statistics (2007) reported that the Sinhala population in Ampara and Batticaloa jumped from 61,996 in 1963 to 229,000 in 2007.

in Kottiyar Pattu [bordering the south of Trincomalee harbor] that culminated in the destruction of every single village within walking distance from a Sinhala village by a mob comprised of soldiers from outside and local villagers" (Gaasbeek 2010: 18).[26] It will take many researchers to determine the musical dynamics enacted by these waves of movement and displacement—yet another project for a budding ethnomusicologist, who should study the long history and current dynamics of ethnic relations through music in Trincomalee.

The North

Once again, we can split the genres into more purely "ritual" domains and "drama" (*kooththu*), noting overlap between them (once again I stick here just to Hindus; I say a bit about Christians, particularly Catholics, and Muslims in the next chapter). Trance rituals appeasing local deities include Kāliyamman, Vairavar, Vīrabhadra, and Annamar (a caste deity for the Nalavars and Pallars). As in Batticaloa, there is a hunting festival ("Vettai Thiruvizha"), where devotees dress up as animals and dance to *nadaswaram* and *thavil*.[27] Way up in Karainagar, a tiny island connected to the Jaffna Peninsula by a small paved road, was a plough harnessing festival in which a priest and dancers reenacted the history of the community, a "migratory myth" that "reflects the fertility cult and the 'Pallu Nadagam' of Tamil Nadu and Sri Lanka". Finally, one prominent ritual in Mullaitivu is the "Seven Maidens" festival ("Saptha Kanniyar Vilzha"): seven young girls are dressed in costumes and taken to the temple, where songs and dances are performed and a priest hands them seeds; they then head to the paddy fields with farmers for ploughing (Shanmugalingam 2012).[28]

Finally, Shanmugalingam (2012) provides a list of dramas (*kooththus*) from the north:

1) "Vada modi koothu"
2) "Then modi koothu"
3) "Thenn paṅku" or "Thenn mettu"
4) "Vada paṅku" or "Vada mettu"
5) "Vasakappa" or "Vasappu"
6) "Kāttavarāyan koothu"

---

[26] Gaasbeek (2010) writes that since the early 1980s, about 5% of Kottiyar Pattu's pre-war population has been killed, over half of the houses have been destroyed at least once, and almost everybody has had to flee his or her village two or three times.

[27] I have seen footage of devotees in Jaffna riding on fake horses in a manner reminiscent of the Javanese *Kuda Lumping* or Malay *Kuda Kepang*, a form of trance that is deemed un-Islamic by religious authorities in Malaysia and Singapore.

[28] Shanmugalingam (2012) notes the affinity between this and the Sath Pattini cult in Sinhala culture, as both are traced to the cult of Kannagi.

7) "Kovalan koothu" (Mullaitivu).
8) "Nondi nadagam"
9) "Pallu nadagam"
10) "Vilasam"

Balasugumar (2009) says the Jaffna *vadamodi* style is more closely associated with the Vaddukoddai and Uduppiddy areas, while *tenmodi* is more associated with the coastal areas. The problem with this is that Vaddukoddai is quite near the coast. Perhaps Balasugumar means *vadamodi* is associated more with the north and *tenmodi* with the coastal areas to the south (*vada* = "north" and *ten* = "south"), however, I have yet to be able to map *vadamodi* and *tenmodi* in an easy north-south bifurcation.[29] According to one observer, *vadamodi* in Jaffna is associated with Hindu epics and Puranas, stressing heroism and bravery, more dancing, less singing, with the influence of "North Indian melodies," while *tenmodi* is associated with Christian stories, stresses the theme of love, and involves more singing, less dancing.[30] *Tenmodi koothths* seem to be associated primarily with the coastal fisherman caste, the Karaiyars, many of whom are Catholic. Kovalan Kooththu is reportedly more associated with Jaffna and the Vanni, while Kāttavarāyan (also known as *sinthu nadai koothu*) is reportedly associated with Jaffna. Both are considered Kataivali Koothus, associated with pilgrimages when people walk long distances and sing on their way (ibid.). Vāsāppu ("Vasahappa") is composed in prose ("vasaha") and poetry/song ("pa") and performed for up to four nights; the tradition has a special association with Mannar. Here we see *"vada"* and *"ten"* doing more work, as there the songs associated with Vāsāppu are *tenpānku* and *vatapāngu*. According to Balasugumar (ibid.), the latter in Mannar is called Yazhpana pānku ("Jaffna mode"), which would suggest that it spread there from Jaffna. Balasugumar also believes these to be based less on dancing and more on song and plot. It may take literally dozens of researchers to determine the history, regional reputations, recent histories, and status of these genres after the war; the above is intended merely as the first sketch in the ethnomusicological literature of the geography of Sri Lankan Tamil traditional musics.

The Hill Country

As up country (Malaiyaha) Tamils were brought by the British to work as laborers on tea plantations in the late nineteenth and early twentieth centuries,

---

[29] In his book on *terukkuttu*, Frasca (1990: 50) notes that "within Tontaimantalam [in Tamil Nadu, India] . . . regional styles fall into two groups called *vatapānku* (northern style) and *tenpānku* (southern style), which refers to the areas north and south of the Pālāru River that divides Tontaimantalam approximately in half." It may be that the divisions between *"vada"* and *"ten"* denote a previous north/south division for *kooththus* in Tamil Nadu.

[30] http://www.eelavar.com/arts/

their music and dance is more similar to genres in South India. To stick with Shanmugalingam (2012) a bit longer, he states there are three main styles of music drama associated with Malaiyaha Tamils: "Arjunan Tapacu" ("The Penance of Arjuna," originally from the Thanjavur area of Tamil Nadu), "Ponna Sangar" (originally from Kongu, Tamil Nadu), and "Kaman Koothu" (from Tiruchirappalli, Thanjavur, North Arcot, and South Arcot, in Tamil Nadu).[31] According to Bass (2013: 154), *kooththus* foster unity between workers on an estate, forging a sense of unity against those from other estates. He mentions Kaman Kooththu is the most important for up country Tamils but is now a dying tradition and rarely performed. The main instruments are *thappu* (the frame drum known as *parai* in South India), *uṭukkai*, and *talampota* (finger cymbals). Bass (2012: 154) notes that Paraiyars now often refuse to take part in Kaman Kooththu, leaving a key moment of the drama, when a Paraiyar announces the death of the hero Kaman, without drummers. Since no one comes forward to take their low-status place in the drama, productions are canceled. As with the Kohomba Kankariya for the Sinhalaese, Bass notes that Kaman Kooththu is in a process of revitalization as a staged display of Up Country Tamil ethnicity, but unlike the Sinhala ritual, it is Tamils themselves rather than the state that is sponsoring the transformation.[32]

The Politics of Regional Identities

It appears that in some contexts in the north, some *kooththus* have been transformed into an "art song" tradition that uses harmonium, with performers standing still instead of dancing (I witnessed a staged performance like this in Colombo). I think the addition of the harmonium and tabla may have come through (or been influenced by) *isai nadagam*, a late nineteenth-/early twentieth-century South Indian style of drama (developing out of the Parsi theater) that flourished before the advent of film (Seizer 2005). This would reinforce the description (above) of Jaffna's *vadamodi kooththus* having "North Indian melodies." In any case, the important point here is that the harmonium is used frequently in northern *kooththus* but not so much in Batticaloa, where the genre revolves

---

[31] Shanmugalingam (2012) notes that in the up country, there are numerous rituals performed by laborers on estates, such as for Ratha Muni (wheel god), performed by factory workers to protect themselves, Plant Nursery God ("Thavaranai Muni"), Crop God ("Kauvathu Muni"), Cable God ("Kambi Muni," for purposes of safeguarding the tea leaves as they made their way up cable lines in the old days), Tender Shoot God ("Kolunthu Sami," a ritual performed by female tea pluckers).

[32] Bass (2012: 154) tells a fascinating story that begs for further research. In the 1960s and 1970s, a prominent cultural activist and educator, S. Thiruchenduran, tried to modernize Kaman Kooththu by shortening the drama and putting it on the concert stage. Thiruchenduran repatriated to India, but his modernization project was picked up by a Tamil Christian, Frances, who has drawn upon Thiruchenduran's scripts since 1989 to reformulate the genre, though sticking with the traditional instrumentation of *mridangam*, harmonium, and *talampota*.

around dancing, singing, and drumming on the *maththalam* with no "melodic" instruments. Thus there is a considerable difference in sound between eastern and northern *kooththus*.[33]

In his ethnography of Batticaloan *kooththu* actors during the war, Thompson (2005) asserts the Batticaloan *kooththu* is considered "more authentic" because it adheres to the traditional style (with the *maththalam* and without the harmonium). He describes a performance of a Batticaloan *kooththu* troupe in Jaffna during a festival organized by the LTTE in 2003 (a performance made possible by the ceasefire in operation at the time, it was a significant cultural event); Thompson remarks the Batticaloan troupe "received some criticism of their performance at this occasion":

> A newspaper review reported their *kooththu* as "crude" . . . During the conflict *kooththu* performances from Batticaloa had barely existed for local audiences—and therefore this voyage north was a major venture for the group—but the *kooththu* that they performed existed in the imaginations of many sections of the Tamil community rather than as a witnessed event. . . . [One Batticaloa performer] noted during our discussions that there is a romantic vision of *what kooththu from the Batticaloa region is*. . . . The people I met in Jaffna, who urged me to see the *real kooththu* by visiting Batticaloa, were now perhaps those people critical of the example at the festival—war-structured nostalgia looking disdainfully on the war-torn practice (his italics; Thompson 2005: 67).

In my view, Thompson's story captures how the addition of harmonium, *mridangam* (and sometimes *tabla*), and the proscenium stage in Jaffna, combined with a drumming style that I suspect is influenced by *isai nadagam*, has influenced the *kooththu* in Jaffna more so than in Batticaloa, leading to the perception that the Jaffna style is "newer," "more refined," and "more developed" than in Batticaloa, which retains the older style.

What follows is a more detailed description of the technical aspects of the Batticaloa *kooththu* that emphasizes the differences between *vadamodi* and *tenmodi*. According to Kartigesu Sivathamby, the *kooththu* in Batticaloa "was preserved among all castes, from the agrarian caste to the service castes, from the fisher caste to the artisan castes."[34] The scriptwriter is the *ettu annaviyar* and the

---

[33] Consultants in Mullaitivu reported that in some contexts they use the harmonium and *mridangam*, in other contexts the *maththalam*. It will take more researchers to determine how this instrumentation varies regionally, but it seems to me that a huge determining factor is whether the *kooththu* is held outdoors (the *maththalam* is loud and perhaps more associated with outdoor performances).

[34] Kartigesu Sivathamby, "Annaviar Chelliah: Little-Known Man behind Well-Known Tamil Theatre," *Northeastern Herald*, August 8, 2003. By contrast, Jayaraman reports that in the up country, the Kaman Kooththu was a "structural display of caste hierarchy and the relative social position of individuals and groups on an estate" (cited in Bass 2012: 158). I do not think Sivathamby's statement

leader of the performance is the *annaviyar*, who in traditional settings sits with his *maththalam* drum in the *vaṭṭakkaḷari* (theatre-in-the-round), from which he drums and guides the action. The *annaviyar* trains the dancers; in performance, he is the sun, the *vaṭṭakkaḷari* is the solar system, and the performers are planets that move around the *annaviyar* (Sinniah Maunaguru, personal communication; see Maunaguru 1998).[35] Other musicians in the Batticaloan *kooththu* include a *sallari* (finger cymbal) player and chorus (*capaiyōr*) who are also actors.[36] *Kooththus* generally begin with a *kochaham*, a three-line, recited or half-sung introduction, which in Batticaloa's *tenmodi* style is followed by *theru*, the singing of nonsense syllables (Thompson 2005: 82). After this comes the *thalisai*, an introductory section that helps set the scene of the play. Following the *thalisai* is the *viruttam*, a "prose song" in which characters are introduced.[37] Following the *viruttam* are songs that allow for a character to sing and dance, and then the character dances as the chorus repeats the melody.

Theoretically, an *annaviyar* is able to pick which style (*vadamodi* or *tenmodi*) to perform, but certain villages are more associated with one or the other. This falls on an east-west bifurcation: villages closer to the seaside (the "sun-rising side") are said to prefer *vadamodi*, while villages on the other end of Batticaloa lagoon (the "sun-setting side") prefer *tenmodi* (Maunaguru, personal communication). James Thompson (2005: 82) remarks that,

> while the distinction between [*vadamodi* and *tenmodi*] styles was widely appreciated [in the village of Kannangkuda], one of the consequences of the war was that the clarity of the division in performance was starting to be lost. In this village [the performers] would keep both

---

should be taken here to mean that the *kooththu* in Batticaloa has always been egalitarian. For example, members of the washerman caste were employed to hold the screen covering characters before they entered the stage (*vaṭṭakkaḷari*) in the older version of the style known as *vadamodi kooththu* (according to a consultant; today no such screen is used).

[35] *Annaviyar* derives from *annanthu nokkal*, meaning "looking upward": this demonstrates the respect shown to the *annaviyar*, who is typically a village elder (*-ar* is an honorific suffix; Sivathamby 2003).

[36] Another core component of *kooththu* is the *eaddu parpor*, who stands in the *vaṭṭakkaḷari* and holds a text of the *kooththu* being performed. The script is written on palmyra leaves collated in a rectangular book (*eaddu*) or written onto a copy of the original (the person is sometimes called the *copy parpor*). The function of the *eaddu parpor* is to read the lines of the play. Thompson (2005: 83) mentions his informants could not agree whether the origin of the *eaddu parpor* lies in the previous illiteracy of the villagers, a reason that would make them irrelevant today, given Sri Lanka's high literacy rate. Perhaps the continued use of the *eaddu parpor* is that he provides an aura of officialdom and spectacle to the event: his presence lends gravity and "truthfulness" to the event being performed—he is a physical avatar of the power of the text. Thompson remarks that the *parpor* is "a dramaturg live on stage, who teaches the knowledge of the epic."

[37] Thompson remarks that "the *thalisai* is in verse and more 'melodic' than *viruththam*. In Tamil, the latter is said to be sung in a 'dragging' manner, the former in a 'shrinking' manner" (2005: 82).

Figure 3.4 Kooththu musicians pose with a *kooththu* text in Akkaraipattu.

very separate, but the lack of experience among some newer *annaviyars* meant that a mixing of the *vada-* and the *ten-* was being seen more often.

The differences between *vadamodi* and *tenmodi* are structural and stylistic. In *vadamodi* style, the *annaviyar* traditionally "stands at the centre and enables the unrestrained flow of the drama through his efficient drumming. In the *tenmodi* tradition he is also an interlocutor, talking to the characters especially the less important ones. Thus he drums and acts."[38] In *vadamodi*, characters introduce themselves; in *tenmodi* they are hidden behind a curtain and introduced by the chorus. *Tenmodi* is considered "male" because it is quicker and its characters "braver"; *vadamodi* is "female" because of its slower tempo (Thompson 2005: 89). While today there are no significant differences between the costumes in each tradition, in the past a *karappu* costume (made of cane) was used in *tenmodi*, while in *vadamodi*, people used to dance with beads. These differences were apparently altered with the advent of film, which must have had a huge impact on *kooththus*.

After the success of Sarachchandra's modernization of the Sinhala *nadagam*, a Tamil professor at the University of Peradeniya in Kandy, Suppiramaniam Vithiananthan (1924–1989), asked why there had not been a comparable revival of *kooththu*. As chairman of the Tamil Drama Panel of the Arts Council of

---

[38] Kartigesu Sivathamby, "Annaviar Chelliah: Little-Known Man behind Well-Known Tamil Theatre," *Northeastern Herald*, August 8, 2003.

Ceylon, he organized an inter-school competition in 1959 to discover local talent for a *kooththu* modernization project (Sivathamby 2003, 2005). This led to his discovery of students Maunaguru, Perinpanayagam, and Kanagaratnam, and he organized his first student *kooththu* production in 1961–1962 with the *annaviyar* Kathiramalai Chelliah (1925–2003) from Batticaloa.

The *kooththu* they chose was *Karnan Pōr* (*The Battle of Karna*) from the *Mahabharata*. Chelliah's task was to "train the girls and boys to dance the *kooththu*, increase the performance capacity of those who already had some experience in the dance form and play the *maddalam* to bring out the dramatic potential of the *arttams* (dances)." The production used male and female actors, while in the past only men were involved. The women had already trained as Bharata Natyam dancers, so they had to learn the *kooththu* style. Vithiananthan discarded the *vaṭṭakkaḷari* to put the production on the stage, moving the *annaviyar* to "behind the scenes." He also "fused" Brecht and Stanislavsky "and along with this was the more crucial part of making the dance steps an integral part of the dramatic exposition."[39] *Karnan Pōr* was followed by three more plays by Vithiananthan and Chelliah: *Nondi Nadagam* (1963), *Ravanesan* (1965), and *Valivathai* (1967).

The actor who played the lead in *Ravanesan*, Sinniah Maunaguru, became a professor at the Eastern University in Batticaloa and a leading *kooththu* choreographer, playwright, actor, and scholar. Born in the Seelamunai area of Batticaloa, his father was a temple priest versed in traditional medicine and astrology. Maunaguru says he grew up around "drum beats and cymbals. Music is deeply ingrained in me."[40] After his apprenticeship to Vithiananthan, he moved to Colombo where he found "the national identity was being thought of deeply."[41] He describes this period (the 1970s) as a "golden period of theatre productions in Colombo with Tamil and Sinhala plays being staged on the same platforms and drawing audiences of all three communities (Sinhala, Tamil and Muslim)." The period was brought to an end by the start of the war in 1983, whereupon "All Tamil cultural activities in Colombo, including drama disappeared. Most of us relocated to Jaffna and so the cultural events that had been gaining ground in Colombo, took root in Jaffna. For a period we flourished again until the LTTE grew heavy handed and shut us up."[42]

Moving to the University of Jaffna, where Vithiananthan was vice chancellor, Maunaguru was inspired to "teach the people who had largely forgotten it that we had our own indigenous forms of dance and Bharatha Natyam (imported from India) was not the only form of Tamil dance."[43] This move was opposed by some invested in that South Indian tradition, who

---

[39] Ibid.
[40] http://www.thehindu.com/features/metroplus/society/interview-with-sri-lankan-tamil-theatre-personality-s-maunaguru/article7662357.ece
[41] https://eyeofthecylone.wordpress.com/2012/05/08/professor-maunaguru-icon-of-indigenous-tamil-culture/
[42] Ibid.
[43] Ibid.

conveniently forgot that Bharatha Natyam was a courtesan dance of India which had been stylized and made socially acceptable only in the 1930s through the efforts of Rukmini Devi Arundale [the Brahmin woman who transformed South Indian temple dance into Bharata Natyam; Allen 1997]. I have nothing against that dance form but I opposed the myth making and the attempted burial of our own roots as not being good enough. Despite all the opposition, I coached the children [in *kooththu*] and even brought them to a production in Colombo where audiences were appreciative and asked what this "new" form of dance was.[44]

One can see from this statement that there was a lack of awareness of *kooththu* in Sri Lanka outside the Tamil-majority regions and that the genre was not as highly regarded as Bharata Natyam.[45] Over his long career, Maunaguru produced numerous plays on social issues, such as *Sangaram* ("Destruction," first staged in 1969) on the oppression of the lower castes and *Sakthi Pirakkuthu* (first staged in 1986) on the oppression of women.[46] He has continued to stage *Ravanesan*, including a performance at the 2011 Jaffna music festival; the drama is now considered "a modern classic amongst the Tamils."[47]

In sum, Vithiananthan's modernization project positioned *kooththu* as a Sri Lankan Tamil musical theater form, emblematic of the proud history of the Sri Lankan Tamil people but akin to Sarachchandra's Sinhala *nadagam* revival in the Sri Lankan national context (which, as mentioned in Chapter 1, it is historically related to). During the war, however, *kooththu* gained an international reputation as a vehicle for the LTTE. For example, when I expressed my interest in doing research on *kooththu* to my Indian Tamil *veena* teacher in New York City in the mid-2000s, she asked if I was sure the performers were not members of the LTTE. Regardless of practitioners' feelings about the LTTE, the *kooththu* was able to survive better in regions under LTTE control, since the rebel group supported the genre. By contrast, in Tamil-majority areas under government control, the tradition fell on hard times. Since *kooththu* rehearsals are held in someone's yard in the evening and at night at temple festivals, performances were often curtailed during the war. Performers in Seelamunai (two kilometers north of Batticaloa town) told

---

[44] Ibid.

[45] While I cannot fully gauge the *kooththu's* reputation today, there is certainly a broader appreciation of it; for example, in the late 1990s, the Eastern University in Batticaloa added the study of "Eelam's music tradition" (Balasugumar 2009) to its syllabus.

[46] Inspired by his wife, Chitra, Maunaguru's feminist play depicts "the Goddess Kali with her several hands, having ultimate power over the people. She divided herself into individual ordinary women who then became oppressed. After many trials and tribulations when the women figured out they had to organize themselves as one again, they became all-powerful and defeated their oppressors."

[47] https://eyeofthecylone.wordpress.com/2012/05/08/professor-maunaguru-icon-of-indigenous-tamil-culture/

me no performances were held there between 1990 and 2003, though I have no way of confirming this. In Chapter 5, I describe in more detail the silencing and persistence of Tamil music and dance during the war.

In 2010, shortly after the war concluded, Maunaguru staged *Ravanesan* in Colombo in the *vadamodi koothu* style, with synopses for the audience in Sinhala, Tamil, and English. The content of the play, culled from medieval poet Kamban's version of the *Ramayana*, "shows specifically the encounter between Ravana and Rama each justifying their Dharma in their own terms."[48] In a turnaround from the *Ramayana*, Ravana (the "evil king of Lanka" in the epic) is the protagonist of the story. While in Vithiananthan's version he was depicted as a proud Tamil king, in Maunaguru's staging he is a tragic figure.[49] His wife Mandothari begs him to release the kidnapped princess Sita in order to avoid war with Rama, but he is filled with hubris and ignores her plea, and is eventually killed in a useless war. The play highlights how "in the normally masculine theater of war, women are left out of debates and decision making"; just as Ravana ignored Mandothari, so "Sita, the abducted woman, is used by Rama as his excuse for war." The play ends with Mandothari mourning over Ravana's body; she is portrayed as "the only heroic figure in the play" and "is left at the end . . . to imagine a possible future."[50] Keep this use of Ravana in mind, for as I show in Chapter 6, Ravana is now treated by some Sinhalas as the progenitor of Sinhala music history.

---

[48] http://thirdeyesouthasia.blogspot.co.uk/2010_03_01_archive.html
[49] http://www.island.lk/2010/02/28/features6.html
[50] Ibid.

4

The Cartography of Culture Zones

Social Relations and the Conversion of Sonic Money

The last two chapters positioned Sinhala and Tamil musics in a binary. In this chapter, I break the binary down by briefly describing traditional musics from a few other Sri Lankan communities; I then question the validity, usefulness, and politics of cutting Sri Lanka up into communally defined culture zones by considering histories of communal interaction through traditional musics. My aim is to pivot toward a less ethnically divisive framework, one that acknowledges communal similarities, interactions, and histories of musical giving across the island.

The Muslims

Most of Sri Lanka's Muslims are of "maritime Indo-Arab origin" (McGilvray 2004: 274), Sunnis who adhere to the Shafi legal school. Their number includes a small number of Malays. As mentioned in the last chapter, the east coast is a checkerboard of Muslim and Tamil villages, some divided into Muslim and Tamil neighborhoods; Muslims form a slight majority in the southeastern Ampara District. In the build up to war, Muslim youths participated in some Tamil insurgent activities while some Muslim politicians joined Tamil political parties but "this relationship, always difficult . . . deteriorated—with assistance from the state—into a complete polarization between the communities" (Haniffa 2007: 1). For their refusal to join the LTTE, Muslims were "targeted, displaced, and dispossessed" by the rebel group, with 75,000 expelled from the Northern Province in October 1990 (Haniffa 2007: 52). The 2004 tsunami devastated Ampara (which received more casualties than any other region), killing 18,000 Muslims (Haniffa 2007: 53). Today, Muslims remain ubiquitous throughout the island, prominent in places like Colombo, the all-Muslim town of Kattankudy (just south of Batticaloa), Puttalam (on the west coast), and historic Muslim neighborhoods like the one inside the walled city of Galle (in the south). In Oluvil in the southeast, an all-Muslim school (South Eastern University) was founded in 1995, whose first students were transfers from the Eastern University in Batticaloa—thus reflecting the increased ethnic bifurcation of Sri Lanka's educational system during the war.

Here I draw on McGilvray (2004), one of the only scholars to have discussed Sri Lankan Muslim devotional musics. He notes the "surprising vitality and growth of popular Sufi devotionalism in Sri Lanka," despite opposition from conservative Muslim factions (274). Sufi mystics, the Bawas, perform on tambourines (*dahira, dāf, rabāna*) and chant at death anniversaries (*kandoori*) of Sufi saints at shrines (*dargah*) and hermitages, places "of saintly visitation and mystical meditation" (275). A well-known hermitage is Daftar Jailani, located on a "generalized Muslim pilgrimage route" (273) from the southern ports of Galle and Weligama to Adam's Peak, a pilgrimage site in the central highlands (called Adam's Peak by Muslims and Christians, and Sri Pada by Buddhists). Founder of the Qadiriya order, Sheikh Muhiyadeen Abdul Qadir Jailani (known in Tamil as Muhiyadeen Andavar, d. 1166 CE in Baghdad), is believed to have meditated at Jailani for twelve years after making the pilgrimage to Adam's Peak; McGilvray (McGilvray 2004: 276) says the site was rediscovered in 1875 by an Indian Muslim from the Lakshadweep islands in India, and the annual *kandoori* began in 1890.[1] A core component is the flag-raising ceremony, after which *mauloods* are recited. At night is a performance of *rifai ratib*, devotional music performed by about a dozen to twenty Bawas with tambourines. The Bawas belong to the Rifai order; *ratib* is a kind of *zikr* ("remembrance"). While the Bawas perform, a few take turns performing self-mortification, such as drilling a spike into their head or cutting their tongue with a knife.

I have seen the same practices at Kataragama, the southeastern pilgrimage site that attracts Buddhists, Hindus, and Muslims; similar accounts were reported in Kataragama, Colombo, and Kalkudah in the 1930s (McGilvray 2004: 281). At the Beach Mosque in Kalmunai, on the east coast, I witnessed the flag-raising ceremony, which was preceded by Bawas carrying the flag in procession, accompanied by tambourines and chanting as a man danced with a sword. The Beach Mosque is associated with the Saint of Nagoor (sixteenth-century saint Hazrat Seyid Abdul Qadir Shahul Hamid), whose main shrine is at Nagoor in Tamil Nadu, with other shrines in Penang (Malaysia) and Singapore—carving out an eastern Indian Ocean Sufi geography. McGilvray (2004) lists Jailani, Kataragama, the Beach Mosque, and the *dargah* of Faqir Muhiyadeen at Porvai near Akuressa (in the south) as the island's famous Sufi pilgrimage shrines. In 2016, I was given

---

[1] Interestingly, the beginning of the festival includes an all-female recitation of the Talai Fatiha ("an intercessory prayer to the wives of the earlier Prophets and to the Prophet Mohammed's daughter Fatima"), composed by Sayyid Muhammad (d. 1316), a South Indian known popularly as Mappillai Lebbe Alim (McGilvray 2004: 278). Opening the event this way, McGilvray says, "seems to set a tone of gender equality and co-participation that is felt throughout the festival, despite spatial separation of the sexes within the Jailani mosque itself" (McGilvray 2004: 278).

a CD of a Sufi (Naqshbandi) devotional group from Malaysia that was coming to Colombo to perform, so there are some connections between Sri Lankan and Malaysian Sufis. McGilvray (2014) notes connections to the Lakshadweep islands off the southwestern coast of India, as a prominent *shaykh* from eastern Sri Lanka, Makkattar Vappa, was recently named leader of a Sufi order from Androth Island in Lakshadweep (he maintains genealogical ties to a locally entombed saint of Yemeni Hadhrami ancestry; McGilvray 2014).

These Sufi musical connections demand more musicological attention, as do the local politics of Sufi musics in Sri Lanka. The Bawa face pressure from Islamic reformist groups who are anti-Sufi and anti-music (McGilvray 2008; Spencer et al. 2015). In 2006, a mob in the conservative town of Kattankudy destroyed the homes of over a hundred followers of M. S. M. Abdullah, a charismatic spiritual leader who had gained over 15,000 followers through his books and songs. Abdullah was issued a fatwa by Wahhabis for promulgating "Hindu" beliefs through his teachings. His followers were subjected "to grenade attacks and . . . were victims of regular thefts by those opposed to their presence in the traditional village."[2] Their meditation hall, built in 1996, was burned down a year later, and several businesses of Abdullah's followers were destroyed. In an interview I conducted with Abdullah's son, I was told his 181 songs were recorded with Sinhala, Tamil, and Muslim musicians in Colombo, sung in Tamil and using combinations of *sitar, tabla, mridangam*, violin, harmonium, and keyboards. Thus his music mixed musical instruments and sensibilities associated with Tamils, North Indians, Sinhalas, and South Indian/Sri Lankan Muslims. The Wahhabis' eradication of such practices is akin to Sinhala and Tamil nationalist attempts at ethnically purifying musical genres.[3]

The Christians

While "Muslim" is an ethnic and religious category in Sri Lanka, "Christian" is a religious designation that includes Sinhalas, Tamils, and Burghers (Eurasians) of various denominations. The Christian musical geography is equally if not more complex than the Muslim one because of the diversity of the community: one must untangle relations between Sinhala and Tamil Christian musicians; between Sinhala Buddhist and Sinhala Christian musicians; between Tamil Hindu and Tamil Christian musicians; between Sri Lankan Christian musicians and

---

[2] Dilrukshi Handunnetti and Arthur Wamanan, "In the Name of Religion," *Sunday Times*, April 29, 2007.

[3] There are surely many other Sri Lankan Muslim musical genres, most unknown even to Sri Lankans. One is the *Kali Kambattam* ("beat and play"), a stick dance associated with the east; a group from Akkaraipattu performed this at the 2011 Jaffna music festival. I consider Muslim contributions to Sinhala popular musics in the "Checkpoint" following Chapter 5.

European musical influences and connections; and regional differences, such as between west coast Christians and those in Jaffna or the east. There are also differences between how different denominations use music. I described the importance of the *kooththu/nadagam* genre for Tamil and Sinhala Christians in the introduction; what follows here is a broader overview.

Catholic music in Sri Lanka is synonymous with Jacome Gonsalves (1676–1742), a Goan missionary and writer fluent in Konkani, Latin, Spanish, Portuguese, Sinhala, and Tamil, and more recently with Friar Marceline Jayakody (1902–1998), a songwriter and poet who was parish priest of Duwa (a section of the Sinhala Christian-dominated town of Negombo). In the early eighteenth century, Gonsalves introduced the Pasan genre (plaintive chants), grouping them into a book (Pasan Potha), which is still sung during Lent; he also composed Tamil *opparis* (women's lamentations sung at funerals), and several early Sinhala *nadagams* were on themes from his writings. When Friar Jayakody began his service at the church in Duwa (from 1939), the annual Passion Play performed there used life-sized puppets, a tradition dating from Gonsalves's time. Jayakody replaced the puppets with actors (except, initially, for Jesus and Mary) basing his new play on Dorothy Sayers's *The Man Born to Be King* (Sinhala: *Dukprathi Prasangaya*), a popular radio show in the 1940s first broadcast on the BBC. Over the years, the Duwa Passion Play grew to include some 250 actors and is now considered one of the finest in Asia.

As with many musicians of his generation, Jayakody studied at Rabindranath Tagore's school for the arts at Shanthiniketan, Bengal. Trained in violin, he composed (according to one estimate) eight hundred songs, though many of these are surely lyrics rather than melodies.[4] He played a role in getting Ananda Samarakoon's song "Namo Namo Matha" chosen as the national anthem (see Chapter 5), since he trained a choir to sing it during the first Independence Day celebrations in 1949. One example of his songs is "Sigiri Landakage," from the 1956 film *Rekawa*, a lullaby sung in the film by a mother to her baby; Jayakody wrote lyrics, and the song was sung by Sinhala Christian singer Latha Walpola (1934–), with music composed by Sunil Shantha (1915–1981).[5] Walpola has set numerous Jayakody hymns to music.

Musicologist Devar Surya Sena (1899–1981; born Herbert Charles Jacob Pieris) is known for his collections and performances of Sinhala folk songs (Chapter 6) and as the composer of a "Ceylon Liturgy" (1932), a Catholic mass still in use today (Surya Sena 2008). Surya Sena drew on Sinhala folk music for inspiration: "The majestic theme of the Gajaga Vannama seemed to fit the Sanctus; a suggestion of the Boatman's Song–Sivpada tune seemed just right for the Agnus

---

[4] http://www.sundaytimes.lk/030126/tv/3.html

[5] The influential Catholic composer Sunil Shantha (née Don Joseph Don) made such a broad contribution to Sinhala-language popular music more generally that I consider him in my discussion of the twentieth-century *sarala gi* genre in Chapter 6.

Dei. Bit by bit themes for each part of the service up to the Gloria were given to me. I was merely a channel. Some unseen power seemed to be directing."[6] The music was first performed in Baddegama (in the south) in 1932 with talampota (finger cymbals) and North Indian instruments (as was the custom at the time) tambura, dilruba, and tabla. In 2015, during the second Sunday of Lent, Surya Sena's liturgy was performed in a trilingual ceremony at St. Andrew's Scots Kirk, a Presbyterian church in Colombo: the Kyrie, Nicene Creed, Sanctus, and Agnus Dei were sung in Sinhala, while his 1950 setting of W. S. Senior's famous poem, "Hymn for Ceylon," was sung in Sinhala, Tamil, and English, accompanied by tabla, talampota, and organ.[7]

The study of Tamil Christian music is under-researched and virtually impossible to say anything about here. I will say merely that I learned that Tamil Catholic priests (as reported by a priest I interviewed in Trincomalee) often compose songs in the South Indian Tamil Christian style, borrowing melodies from videos found on YouTube. These typically involve Western instruments not widely found in Hindu musical contexts, such as guitar, keyboards, electric bass, and drum set. One of my Tamil interlocutors in Jaffna told me his father, a well-known Hindu and composer of Hindu devotional music, wrote some of the songs now heard routinely at the Our Lady of Madhu shrine, the important Catholic pilgrimage site that attracts Protestants, Buddhists, and Hindus.[8]

Kaffirs and Burghers

Africans were brought to the island by Arab merchants to work as laborers in the ninth century (Jayasuriya and Angenot 2008). Today's Afro-Sri Lankans, the Kaffirs, are believed to be descendants of slaves and soldiers brought by the Portuguese from about 1630 (according to popular belief, from Mozambique).[9]

---

[6] Sivpada is a popular meter for Sinhala poetry; the Gajaga Vannama ("Elephant Vannama") is an important part of the Kandy Perahera (a procession with many elephants). "The Boatman's Song," sung in Sivpada, belongs to a tradition of "work songs." I consider Sinhala meter and work songs farther below in this chapter. http://www.sundaytimes.lk/150419/plus/celebrating-surya-senas-musical-endeavour-with-the-sinhala-liturgy-145115.html

[7] http://archives.sundayobserver.lk/2001/pix/PrintPage.asp?REF=/2015/03/29/mon30.asp

[8] Before the war, attendance at the shrine's August festival had reached a million. The church has a statue of Our Lady of Good Health (Our Lady of Velankanni), an apparition of the Virgin Mary that appeared in Velankanni, Tamil Nadu. Its location is due in part to the persecution of Catholics in Jaffna under the Dutch, and was expanded by the Jesuit Saint Joseph Vaz. By the late 1990s, the site was a de-militarized zone and some 15,000 refugees were taking shelter there; however, the site suffered from shelling, and 44 Tamil civilians were killed there in fall 1999. In 2001, the statue of Mary was taken in procession to Sri Lanka's parishes to pray for an end to war.

[9] "Kaffir" has a derogatory meaning throughout the world, but this is the term Sri Lanka's African community uses to refer to itself, and it does not have negative connotations in Sri Lanka.

The Kaffirs are originators of the dances Kaffiringha, Chikothi, and Manja; Sri Lanka's most popular twentieth-century music, Baila, is descended from a mixture of these and related Portuguese genres.[10] An ensemble emerged that includes various combinations of guitar, mandolin (*banderinha*), frame drum (*rabāna*), triangle, and violin (*viaule*, a thirteen-stringed instrument). It's worth noting the ubiquity of such music across the Indian Ocean: one finds versions of it in the former Portuguese colonies of Goa (India) and Melaka (Malaysia); there are similar rhythms and dances performed in the Séga genre of Mauritius (which emerged from marooned African slaves) and the Maloya genre of Réunion. Baila was popularized by Wally Bastiansz (1914–1985), a policeman who developed a subgenre ("Chorus Baila") that spread like wildfire, with M. S. Fernando and Maxwell Mendis among the famous performers of subsequent decades. The genre spawned a "debate" version (somewhat like a rap battle), a "calypso" version (with performers wearing straw hats; De Mel 2006), and has since incorporated influences from global pop forms (like disco), though in the past few decades it lost popularity to Sinhala Pop (contemporary Sinhala-language pop music) and "Western music" (rock and hip hop; Sheeran 2002).

Today there is a small, highly publicized Kaffir community in Sirambiyadi, near Puttalam, and reportedly others in Trincomalee, Batticaloa, and Negombo (Jayasuriya and Angenot 2008). The Sirambiyadi group has received acclaim for revitalizing *manja*. The songs contain a few lines in Portuguese creole, accompanied by *dholki* (a drum) and *rabāna* (tambourine), with coconut shells, spoons, and bottles. Songs start slow and end with fast percussion and dancing. As with most Sri Lankan folk musics, there is no "melodic" instrument. The Sirambiyadi group has recorded a CD and performed well-publicized concerts, such as the one in 2008 at the popular Barefoot Café in Colombo. In 2010, they were the subject of a documentary film; in 2013 they were featured in the United States on National Public Radio on the show *Afropop Worldwide*. A tour group now arranges visits to Sirambiyadi so that tourists can meet the Kaffirs and see them perform in their village setting.

---

[10] Sources are not in agreement on the origins of these genres. The Sri Lankan newspaper *The Nation* writes that, "With Creole, there sprung a unique form of music and dance called 'Kaffirinha' based on African 'manja' and Portuguese 'fado' music, a joint creation by Portuguese and the Kaffirs." Manja is taken as the "African" side of the collaboration, which bequeathed "Kaffrinha." Manja is "a creole of the Portuguese word manha, which comes from marchinhas or 'little marches'" (*Sunday Times*, November 9, 2008). Another source says "Kaffrinha" "describes the music and dance popular among the eighteenth and nineteenth century Burghers [Eurasians] that has since influenced popular Sri Lankan music" ("Getting to know the Kaffirs through music and dance," Maura O'Connor, *Sunday Times*, November 9, 2008). According to this reading, the Burghers' dance was "Kaffrinha" because the term acknowledges the origins of the dance (perhaps manja?) with the Kaffirs. "Chikothi" was a slower and statelier version. The Baila was pioneered by Burghers out of the Kaffrinha (or on another reading, the Kaffrinha is one version of the Burghers' Baila) and eventually transformed into a popular music genre played by virtually all Sri Lankan communities.

As Kannan Arunasalam says in his film about the Kaffirs, "The recent discovery of their music has made all things Kaffir hugely popular in Colombo, chic even." But he acknowledges that while the exposure has helped publicize their culture, it has been a double-edged sword: "At times, they've been treated like exotic animals in a human zoo by the media." Another commentator was told the Kaffirs were "fed up being treated like a circus freak show!"[11] Arunasalam remarks, "There's a romance about a people on the cusp of disappearing. You see it in Hollywood films featuring Native Americans. Here in Sri Lanka, you see Kaffirs portrayed at times as a simple, smiling people, as though their centuries-old culture can be reduced to a collection of songs."

One writer mentions that upon arriving in Sirambiyadi, she noticed that "they do not look radically different from Sri Lankans"; thus her first question was, "What is the major difference between them and the Singhalese majority?" She was speaking with Ignatius, his mother, and two other Kaffir women. One of them answered, "Our music and dance, which has been passed down from generations is what makes us different. . . . We use the rabāna and a drum we call the dholki." The *rabāna* frame drum is ubiquitous throughout the Indian Ocean Region, though in Sri Lanka it is associated with Muslim and Sinhala culture; the dholki is used casually in Sri Lanka for entertainment but it is more associated with India and not with the musics of any other Sri Lankan ethnic group. I find it interesting that it is these instruments the Kaffirs (or at least the person cited above) take to mark their music as unique, for what is being harped upon is not the music's "African-ness" but the Kaffirs' uniqueness among Sri Lankans.

I fear the link between music and identity is allowing a discourse on ethnicity to usurp a history of musical giving between Portuguese, Africans, Sinhalas, Tamils, and Burghers embodied by the Kaffirs' music and its historic influence on the Burghers and Sri Lankan Baila. This indeed is a double-edged sword: the Kaffirs feel they must perform their music and dance authentically to retain their cultural identity; but the broader discourse in which their search for recognition exists simultaneously recognizes their music's syncretism while using it as a vehicle to distinguish their ethnic difference from Others. This is what happens in the music and identity episteme.

In 2015 I interviewed Burghers at an association gathering in Batticaloa. Warm and charming individuals, we had a long talk about Burgher music. They sang me a couple of *their* Portuguese creole songs. We talked about the Burghers' influence on Baila. I noticed their style of singing had similarities to the Kaffirs' songs. Eventually I asked the Burghers what they thought about the relationship between their and the Kaffirs' music: both sing in a Portuguese creole, both are a mix of Portuguese- and African-derived styles. The room grew silent. After an awkward pause, one of the Burghers gently corrected me, saying their music did

---

[11]. Sadly, this blog is no longer active: http://isrilankan.com/sri-lankan-africans-from-puttalam-visiting-my-long-lost-relatives/

not have a connection to the Kaffirs: the Burghers' music, he said, was Portuguese. Looking back now, I realize the Burghers have become a part of the ethnicized culture zone discourse: their music, demonstrating a mix of Portuguese, African, Dutch, English, and (depending on the community of Burghers) Sinhala and Tamil culture—is now read as ethnically Burgher, traced just to the Portuguese heritage. At the time, I was concerned mainly with moving the discussion on from what I felt was a substantial roadblock I had created. So I asked them to continue singing. One of the Burghers then stood up and began a song, which I immediately recognized. It was the old American civil war tune "Battle Hymn of the Republic," which became a Baila tune with Portuguese Creole lyrics in the late nineteenth century (Ariyaratne 1985), the melody taught to Burghers by American missionaries.

The Cartography of Culture Zones

Zoomed out, one might distinguish only Sinhala and Tamil culture zones; zoomed in a bit, one distinguishes between, for instance, "Tamil" Jaffna and Batticaloa, and "Sinhala" Kandy, Sabaragamuwa, and low country; farther in, one distinguishes distinct ethnic and/or religious towns, like all-Muslim Kattankudy and Christian-dominated Negombo; farther in, one finds isolated ethnic groups like the Vāddas in Dambana (in Badulla district, south of Kandy); still farther in, one finds distinct ethnic neighborhoods like the Malay area of Kirinda (southeast) and the Kaffirs in Sirambiyadi. Do we want to assign music history to an entire ethnic or religious group, such that we assume "Vādda music" is shared equally by all Vāddas, or do we prefer a music history that emphasizes regional differences?

While the former seems historically unsupported, the latter is challenged by a subgenre of Sri Lankan studies that emphasizes how "hybrid" identities have diminished over the past few decades as group boundaries hardened. For example, the Vādda population outside Anuradhapura has reportedly become more Sinhalized, while the Vāddas living outside Trincomalee have become more Tamilized (Obeyesekere in Silva 2002; Brow 1996). Negombo's Tamil Christian population, known for its bilingualism and dialect of Tamil, has reportedly become more Sinhalized, while today's ethnic Tamils on the west coast are now associated mainly with the village of Udappu and Maradankulama (the latter a place that, according to Bastin (2002: 152), contains villagers who mainly speak Sinhala but are Saivite Hindus). Rajasingham-Senanayake (in Silva 2002) argues some villages in the northern Vanni (south of Jaffna) had a mixed Sinhala-Tamil culture before the war. The village of Panama was known for its intermarried Sinhala/Tamil population (Yalman 1967). What was music like in Panama before the war? What is it like now?[12] Are these different Vādda groups now going for Sinhala

---

[12] According to Gaasbeek (2013: 170), "To all intents and purposes, Panama is now a Sinhala-Buddhist village with some Tamil families living on the margins."

or Tamil music, respectively, or do they perform variations of the same "Vädda music"? Do we consider the Sinhala Saivite Hindus in Maradankulama to perform "Sinhala" music, or are they Sinhalas who patronize Tamil musicians when they go to a Hindu temple? Do they perform "Sinhala popular music" but "Tamil religious music"? Many researchers will be needed to answer such questions, but a good place to start is by acknowledging that music in the recent Sri Lankan past did not relate to ethnicity but function—these sorts of questions, filtered through the discourses on identity that drive the island's ethnic politics, are what is eliminating such "hybrid" musical cultures.

Thus I suggest that while the cartography of ethnicized culture zones is the stuff that makes up Sri Lankan cultural history, it is a significant contributor to the island's communal fracturing. An outgrowth of liberal aesthetics, the cartography makes Sri Lankan cultures appear as though they emerged in distinct regions without engaging one another; it ignores diversity within regions; it makes today's ethnic fracturing seem as though it has always been there; and it hardens ethnic boundaries by forcing people to choose sides. The framework makes the large minority presence throughout the island seem inconsequential and separate from the traditional musics of Sinhalas and Tamils (who, in turn, are deemed to have separate music histories that "belong" to different parts of the island and little connection to one another). In order to understand the discursive power of the cartography of culture zones, consider this map from a classic text by anthropologist M. D. Raghavan (1967; Figure 4.1)—don't worry if you can't read the text, for it is the placement of images I want to draw your attention to.

Note that the entire north and east—the Tamil and Muslim heartlands—are empty. The implication is that there are no people there, no dances there, or no dances that are Sri Lankan. The display of a lack of Tamil dances implies Tamil dances in Sri Lanka are Indian. Any historical connections between Tamil dances in the north and east and Sinhala dances in the lower part of the map are not represented, nor for that matter are interactions represented between Sinhala dances and non-Sinhala dances in regions where the Sinhala dances are placed. Each Sinhala dance appears to have arisen *sui generis*. Because music and dance now signify histories of community, this visual representation is a political claim that Tamils are not Sri Lankan, even if that was not intended by Raghavan (who was an Indian Tamil scholar). This visual depiction of an essential connection between ethnicity, dance, and territory is the logical endpoint of liberal aesthetics; as Tariq Jazeel (2013: 16) puts it, "It is these spatial rationalities—these geographical instantiations of Sri Lankan modernity—that do the work of hegemony, helping to secure the primacy of ethnicized Sinhala identities as well as the otherness of Tamils, Muslims, and [Eurasian] Burghers in the Sri Lankan context."

Such visual depictions of the Sri Lankan arts have not since disappeared. Even when Tamil arts are placed on the map, they are routinely kept in a space of foreignness. Consider a 2004 issue of *The World of Music* journal dedicated to the laudable mission of discussing Sri Lankan female musicians (Claus-Bachmann

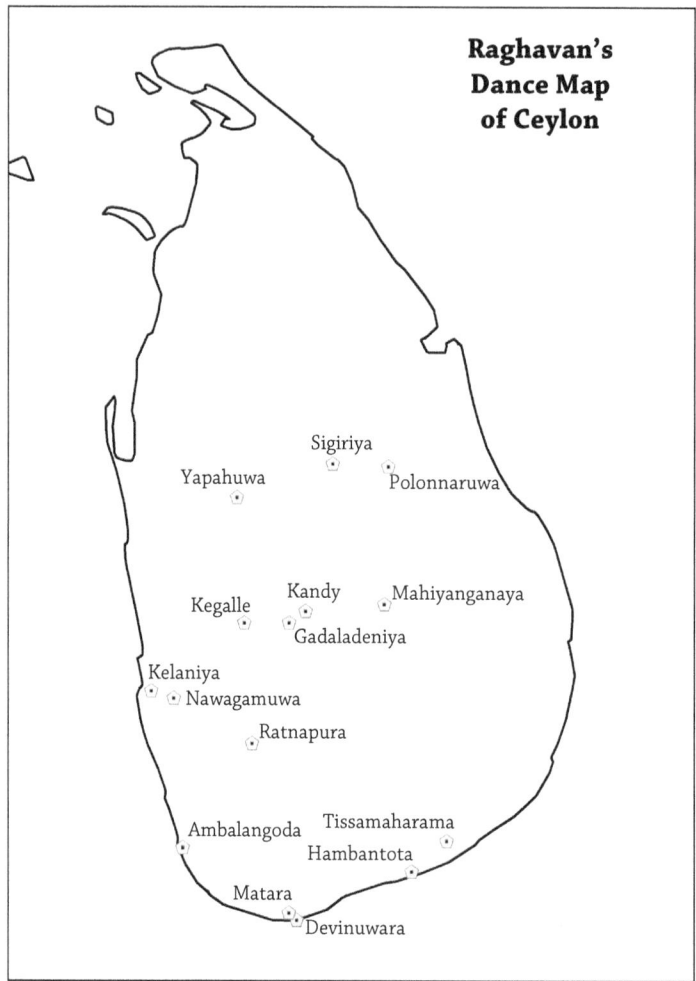

Figure 4.1 A recreation of M. D. Raghavan's "Dance Map of Ceylon" found in his *Sinhala Nätum* (1967: xiv). Map by Girmay Misgna. Used with permission.

2004). The issue's introduction contains a chart with photos of musicians from different ethnic groups, with the following captions: "Reconstructed, canonized traditional music representing the dominance of the state" (over an image of Kandyan drummers), "Low-country music as example for regional culture" (over an image of low-country dancers), "Veddha music culture as example for minority culture" (over a photo of Vädda people), "Sinhala reggae and hip-hop as examples for subculture" (over an image of a reggae band), and "Tamil music as example for *migrant* culture" (over an image of Tamil musicians at a Hindu temple; my italics). The description of Tamil musicians as "migrant culture" implies a recent and potentially temporary presence that is contradicted by the fact that Tamils have been on the island—by conservative estimates—for at least a thousand years.

When considered with maps that straightforwardly present the placement of ethnic groups throughout the island, the above geographic depictions of traditional culture seem as though they reflect the way Sri Lanka *is*. Consider, though, how easy it is to rip apart the following map of Sri Lanka's culture zones (Figure 4.2): here ethnicity and religion are conflated ("Muslim," an ethnic and religious category in Sri Lanka, appears equivalent to "Christian," a multiethnic religious category); Kandyan ethnicity is projected *way* farther north than the hill country (bizarrely, the Vavuniya region is shaded half Kandyan and half *low country* Sinhalese even though it is a traditional Tamil-majority area); the area surrounding Badulla (in the middle) collectively is shaded all colors, as though the aspiring cartographer couldn't figure it out. Here the ethnic fetish (Willford 2006) obscures the ubiquity of ethnic interaction and hybridity in Sri Lanka.

The geographic placement of communities on a map is the assumed *starting point* for discussions of Sri Lanka's artistic traditions; it is not a discourse whose legitimacy is typically questioned. The framework is what Thongchai Winichakul (1997) calls a "geo-body," a "territorial-national identity dependent on the technology of mapping for its conception and distribution" (Klima 2002: 22). Let's turn now toward de-legitimizing and getting rid of it.

Connections between Musical Givers

Tanaka (1997: 160) describes Sinhala drummers playing at a Hindu temple festival (a Draupadī Goddess Festival at Cattiyur, near Chilaw).[13] He describes a (Hindu) Bhadrakali festival in the same area where "Three Sinhala drummers from Munnesvaram and a musician group of the [Tamil] Karaiyar called *pacanayār* (literally those who sing *bhajana* or devotional songs) play the drums and cymbals (*tāram*)" (105). I have seen video footage of Sinhala *hēvisi* drummers playing several steps ahead of but in time *with* Tamil *nadaswaram* and *thavil* players inside the Muneeswaram temple in Chilaw (with the deity's circumambulation of the temple), a mixed Hindu/Buddhist temple complex

---

[13] "There are ... three groups of musicians involved in this festival. One consists of [Tamil] Karaiyars, who sing accompanied by drums and cymbals during the *karakom* pot procession and worship. The second group is a trio from a professional [Tamil] caste (Mēḷakkāraṉ) from Munnesvaram. They play drum, harmonioum, and an oboe-like instrument (*nadaswaram*). Two or three Sinhalese drummers from the outside also usually perform. Both of the latter groups play music at the processions of festival images, but the Sinhalese are not allowed to enter the temple" (Tanaka 1997: 160).

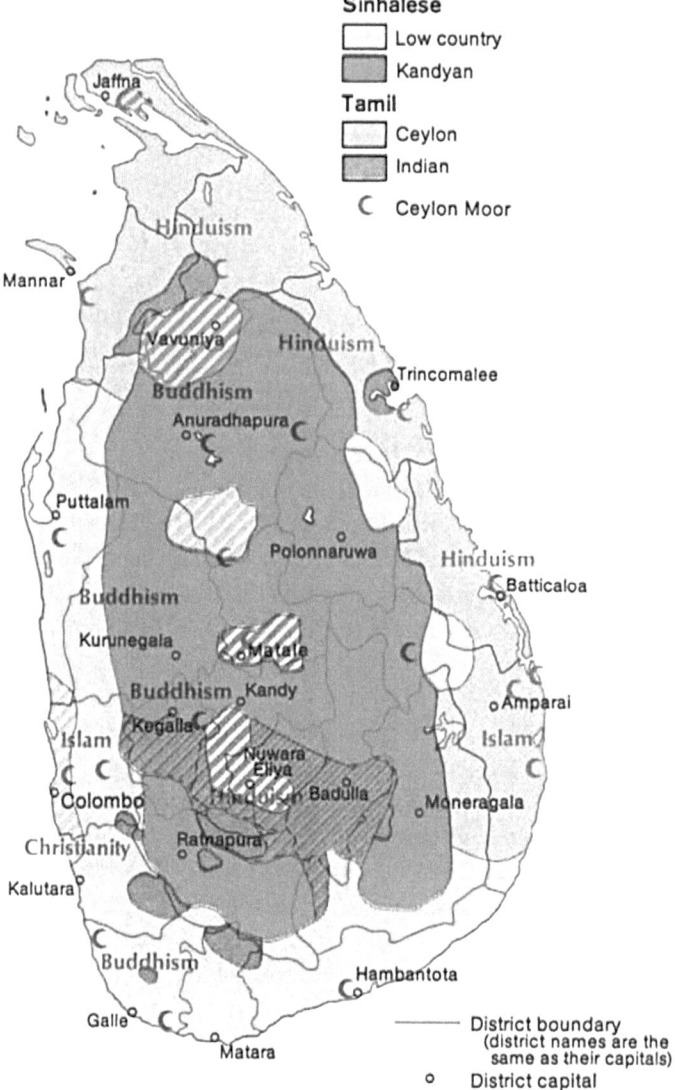

Figure 4.2 An "overly ethnicized" map of the island. Courtesy: University of Texas Libraries. U.S. Central Intelligence Agency, 1976.

that also attracts some Catholic and Muslim worshippers.[14] I have already noted some shared musical experiences for Sinhala and Tamil Catholics at

---

[14] In the video, Sinhala drummers march ahead of Tamil *nadaswaram* and *thavil* players, but the Sinhala *thammättama* drummer plays along with the *nadaswaram*. There is a clear spatial separation between the groups, and the relations are not necessarily positive. See "Sri Munneswaram

Madhu (with some Protestants, Hindus, and Buddhists), and I met one Tamil in Jaffna (a Hindu) who composes Christian music. McGilvray (2008: 252) writes that Tamil drummers used to play at Muslim weddings, circumcision ceremonies, and mosque festivals in Akkaraipattu, in the east. He says Paraiyars would "sometimes also be asked to stage a public-drumming and dance exhibition at the mosque, for which they received additional remuneration" (252).[15] According to Dewaraja (1994: 113),

> In 1930, in Rambukkana many Muslim boys had received their education in Buddhist monasteries. Many of them studied Sinhala and indigenous medicine. Facilities were provided for the Muslim boys to say their prayers and attend Koranic classes, while living in the temple. . . . Muslims made voluntary contributions toward the [Buddhist] vihara and they participated in the [Buddhist pageant] Esala Perahera. The [Buddhist] drummers voluntarily stopped the music when they passed Masjid [the mosque].

At Kataragama, a pilgrimage site holy to Buddhists, Hindus, and Muslims, a complex arrangement of communally defined sounds occur in differently demarcated spaces, such as Sufi drumming on the grounds of a mosque, and Beravā drumming at *devales*. This can be seen as mutual accommodation and competition for multiethnic/multireligious audiences (those watching the Sufis perform at Kataragama are not just Muslims but a hodgepodge of festival goers, including foreign tourists).

Communal difference is acknowledged in such cases, and one group's musical gift does not belong to the Other. But what these examples demonstrate is that musical gifts can be offered alongside those of Others, be witnessed by Others, and/or halted out of respect for Others. Each tradition has grown up under the visual and aural gaze of Others, while at important shrines (e.g., Madhu and Kataragama), people come from far away to contribute to musical traditions that ostensibly "belong" to a different culture (and culture zone) than the one they belong to.[16]

Devasthanam, 18th festival of the annual festival, 2013," https://www.youtube.com/watch?v=xJ7df9um7iI.

[15] According to McGilvray (2008: 252), such performances were actively discouraged by Muslim authorities since the mid-1950s, though some of these customs, such as Paraiyar drumming at Muslim circumcision ceremonies, were still occurring during his fieldwork in the 1970s.

[16] I recognize that the witnessing of another group's musical gifts can turn ugly. As Obeyesekere (1981) and Goonasekera (2007) attest, Kataragama was largely usurped by Sinhalas in the latter half of the twentieth century. The Tamil practice of carrying *kavadi* (a structure symbolizing one's burden to be vanquished through penance to the god Tamils call Murugan and Sinhalas call Kataragama) has long involved the performance of *nadaswaram* and *thavil* for Tamil devotees. Tamil interlocutors complained that Sinhala devotees, in adopting the practice of *kavadi*-bearing, use a

Reframing Culture Zone Discourse

More controversially, there are similarities between Tamil *kooththu* and Sinhala Beravā drumming, and between Tamil Paraiyar and Beravā *hēvisi* drummers, that beg for a rethinking of culture zone discourse. For example, sections of Sri Lankan Tamil *kooththus* and Beravā rituals begin with introductory, exclamatory singing; *kooththus* use nonsense syllables (*theru*), which Beravā call *tanama*. Ankle bells used in *kooththu* are called *selange*, which the Beravā call *selambe*. Sinniah Maunaguru (personal communication) notes that *kooththu* dancers dance pictures with sacred significance (*yantra*?) on the grounds of the *vaṭṭakkaḷari*; Halverson (1971) claims Beravā dancers sometimes dance *mandalas* (Buddhist pictures with ritual significance) on the ground. Stories about gods are common to each tradition: Pattini is honored in the Beravā rituals Gam Maduva and Devol Maduva, while as the Hindu goddess Kannagi, she is featured in the Kannagi Kooththu, associated with Mullaitivu.[17]

In each genre, a line of drumming (in Sinhala, a *pada*, in Tamil, a *tālam*) uses the same words as those for dance steps. A rhythmic composition, dance, and sequence in a drama are often given the same name. Beravā drums and the Sri Lankan Tamil *maththalam* are not typically performed without dance or drama. In the *kooththu*, there is a *tālam* played when the king enters the stage, which sounds like the gait of the king; in the *kōlam* masked dance drama associated with the south, rhythms are associated with the primordial first king, Mahasammata. Batticaloan *kooththu* master Sinniah Maunaguru (personal communication) says there are thirty-two compositions (*tālams*) in the older Batticaloan *kooththu* tradition; there is an older Sinhala meaning of *tālam* as thirty-two compositions taught to dancers after learning their initial five poses or *sutra-mātras*—though this congruency may have more to do with the auspiciousness of thirty-two than a historical connection. Wirz (1954: 19) describes low-country Sinhala *tālams* as "rhythmic movements of the arms, legs, feet, and hands to the accompaniment of a drum"; the word *tālam* is not common in Beravā rituals, but it is used to describe a section of dance steps and rhythms in the Bera Pōya Hēvisi (Sykes 2018b).

---

pappara ensemble as their backing music, an ensemble that uses a Western-style bass drum and trumpets, associated with drunken celebrations at cricket matches. Sinhala drummers now even play *thavil* in some ensembles. Such *pappara* ensembles may play Baila tunes, a genre associated with drinking and partying, which Hindus find inappropriate for the religious context. This is a classic example of cultural appropriation.

[17] In photography exhibitions in Colombo, Jaffna, Batticaloa, Delhi, and New York (as well as on a trilingual website), anthropologist Malathi de Alwis and photographer Sharni Jayawardena have promoted the shared history of Kannagi/Pattini. While putting together their exhibit, they found many Sri Lankans did not know these are Tamil and Sinhala versions of the same deity, "perhaps an indication of the extent to which the two main ethnic communities on our small island have become alienated." Interview, *Sunday Times*, February 16, 2014.

This is not how the word *tālam* is used in India. There, *tāla* (North India) and *tālam* (South India) refer to beat cycles: rhythmic cycles with stressed and unstressed beats that drum words are slotted into. In Sri Lankan Beravā and (at least in the Batticaloan) *kooththu* tradition I studied, *tālam* describes small-scale *combinations* of drumming and dance in a particular dramatic sequence. Indian *tāls* are akin to Western time signatures; Sinhala and Batticaloan notions of *tālam* are akin to an entire rhythmic sequence matched to dance steps in a section of drama without reference to a "meter" (beat cycle or time signature). This is not to say the Sinhala and Tamil traditions are the *same* but that one can make a case for a Sri Lankan approach to rhythm that is different from South India, which Sri Lankan Tamils and Sinhalas to some extent share.

In my meetings with *annaviyar* in Batticaloa, drummers taught rhythms (*tālams*) as sentences (whole compositions) without acknowledging beat cycles. As in Beravā drumming, the rhythm came from the drum words, conceptualized at the level of syllables and words, without placing these "in a *tāl*" (as one does in India). This makes them sound sloppy to Indian and Western ears. And it requires vocalists to take liberties with *their* rhythms to fit the drumming. For example, a Batticaloan Tamil commentator says, "There are no measures to control the sound of music in *kooththu*. The vocal management is in the breath of the performers."[18] Suraweera (2009: 96, 172) notes Sinhala ritualists sometimes stretch their singing so it ends with the *pada*.

There are also similarities in how the Batticaloan Tamil *maththalam* drum, the Kandyan *gäta beraya*, and the low-country *yak beraya* are played that distinguish these from South Indian drumming styles. Compared to South Indian and Jaffna drumming styles, Sinhala and Batticaloan *maththalam* drumming keeps the arms *way* outstretched, hitting the drum *very* forcefully, without emphasis on the fingertips. I have seen Batticaloan Tamil drummers hit the drum with something resembling what Suraweera (2009) calls the "flick thumb" technique (used in low country and Kandyan drumming) where one swivels the hand to hit first with the thumb and first finger, then with the middle finger through the pinky. Similar swivels in South India place the hand *much* closer to the drum, with emphasis on the clean articulation of notes through controlling the fingers. By contrast, in Sinhala and the Batticaloan Tamil traditions, the whole hand turns, another factor that makes Jaffna observers think the Batticaloan style is "crude."

When playing *mridangam*—the drum associated with Carnatic classical music—one achieves a change in pitch by gently pushing the bottom of the hand into the drum (which changes the pitch) while playing with the fingertips on the same hand; by contrast, in the Batticaloan *maththalam* and Sinhala drumming traditions, one smacks one's hand against the drum and forcefully pushes into the drum head with a finger or fingers (rather than the bottom of the hand). The drum roll is also played similarly, with the "flick thumb" technique on one hand and fast

[18] http://thirdeye2005.blogspot.com/2012_03_01_archive.html

strikes with the whole palm on the other, in a "triplet" formation. Again, something similar happens in South India but at a *much* more restrained level, based more on the fingers than the palm, with the hand held closer to the drum. South Indian drumming traditions use a black dot (paste) in the middle of the drum, which warms up the tone; no dot is typically used for Sinhala *beras* or Batticaloan Tamil *maththalam*. More research will need to be done to determine the history of paste on drums in South India and Sri Lanka; while it is useful for performances with microphones, most Batticaloan Tamil staged performances of *kooththus* do not, in my experience, use the paste. This gives Batticaloan *kooththu* drumming a loud, high-pitched tone, surprisingly similar to the Kandyan *gäta beraya*.

In sum, to compare the Batticaloan *maththalam* with the South Indian *mridangam* because both are played by ethnic Tamils is misleading. If you find some footage with a clear view of a Batticaloan drummer playing *maththalam* standing up in the *vaṭṭakaḷari*, and compare that to Kandyan and low-country Sinhala drummers, you will notice *so many* similarities in how the drum is played that comparing it with footage of Keralan *maddalam* drummers and South Indian Tamil *mridangam* or *maththalam* drummers you will immediately notice the similarity between the Sri Lankan styles and differences from the Indian drumming styles. The question is what to *do* with these similarities, not to deny them. Doubters can go to YouTube and search (in this order) *gäta beraya*, Batticaloa *kooththu*, Kerala *maddalam*, and Tamil Nadu *terukkuttu*, and hear the similarities between the Sri Lankan drums and differences from the Indian drums for oneself. You can then look up *yak beraya* and hear the great difference in sound between that (the low-country Sinhala drum) and *all* of the above-mentioned drums: for while the *yak beraya* operates through a music theory similar to the Kandyan *gäta beraya*, it is shaped differently and has a booming, low tone that is radically different from the up country *gäta beraya* and Tamil *maththalam* (I'll consider possible reasons below). Bear in mind that because of modern changes to the northern Sri Lankan *kooththu* tradition (in which the harmonium, *mridangam*, and occasionally *tabla* are used) and the recent (nineteenth/early twentieth centuries) influx of Tamils from South India to work on tea estates (who play the *thappu* frame drum in their *kooththus*), the similarities between Sinhala and Sri Lankan Tamil drumming styles I'm talking about here are only immediately discernable when listening to the eastern Batticaloan style—though I would not be surprised if similar styles can be found in rural areas elsewhere, such as Mannar and Mullaitivu.

What Does It Mean?

Frasca (1990: 89) notes in his study of the South Indian *terukkuttu* (ancestor of the Sri Lankan *kooththu*) that despite the use of the word "*raga*," "fully two-thirds of [its *rāgs*] have equivalents in the *pan* system" (the ancient Tamil musical system that was once paired with the *parai* and *yazh*). Thus, he says, "the music of this ritual theater is probably primarily derived from the ancient musical system of the Tamils rather than the Carnatic system that evolved only much later." He continues that, "Many scholars who propose an independent pre-Carnatic Tamil *icai* [music] system maintain that the identification of the musical modes of forms such as the *terukkuttu* using the raga terminology and titles of the Carnatic system was imposed at some point upon the earlier *pan* system by musicians and musicologists who were influenced by Sanskritic rather than Tamil traditions."

I suggest a discourse on "Carnatic music" has been mobilized over the past century in Sri Lanka, giving the impression of homogeneity among Sri Lankan Tamil musics that was not historically there. In the South Indian Carnatic tradition, *rāgam-taṇam-pāllavi* refers to melodic improvisation, improvisation on syllables, and a refrain or one-line composition set to a beat cycle or cycles. Curiously, in one interview with a Batticaloan *kooththu* performer, I found he used these words to refer to the following: *rāgam*, the initial exclamatory singing of the story, which furthers the plot of the drama (what I described in Chapter 3 as the *kochaham* and/or *thalisai*); *taṇam*, a more musically structured section in which a character dances to the specific *tala* meant for him (the *viruttam*); and *pāllavi*, a more freely structured space for dance, where the main character stops singing and a chorus takes up his melody. These terms may have come from South India and been mapped onto a *kooththu* structure that predates them. I suggest Batticaloa retains this older system to a greater extent than the north, because the latter is closer to Tamil Nadu. The esteemed Batticaloan *kooththu* master Sinniah Maunaguru (1992, 1993, 1998) has made similar arguments (and received criticism from some Tamils for doing so). Here is Maunaguru's reply to his critics:

> People ask me, "Why do you portray the Tamils of different regions as having different traditions? Why especially do you portray the North and the East as having distinctly different cultures?' . . . It's because the Tamils of the North and the East do have distinctly different cultures. I don't see anything wrong with it. A culture that has diversity and variety within it is a rich culture. Cultures with uniformity across them are poor cultures. The Tamil culture is a rich culture and I try my best to showcase it in all its diversity.[19]

Even if we think the Batticaloan Tamil *maththalam* and Sinhala drumming did not influence each other, it is possible both developed through earlier influences from Kerala. Since Sri Lankan Tamils may be keen to trace their heritage to Tamil Nadu rather than Kerala (where Malayalis, and not Tamils, are the dominant ethnic group), and Sinhalas may be keen to trace their heritage as far back on the island

---

[19] "Professor Maunaguru: Icon of Indigenous Tamil Culture," https://eyeofthecylone.wordpress.com/2012/05/08/professor-maunaguru-icon-of-indigenous-tamil-culture/). Maunaguru has also been vocal about similarities between Batticaloan traditional arts and those of the Sinhalese.

as possible, an awareness of Keralan connections has been lacking in popular discussions of Sri Lankan culture (but not in academic scholarship; Obeyesekere 1984; McGilvray 2008). The *maddalam* is used in Kerala's Kathakali dance-drama, where it is held in a similar fashion as the Sri Lankan Tamil *maththalam*. Reed (2010) makes the case that the up country Beravā ritual the Kohomba Kankariya (and hence Kandyan Dance) is influenced by the Kathakali. Obeyesekere (1984) has posited that Pattini worship came to the island from Kerala. According to one source, the *terukkuttu* of South India does not typically use *maththalam* but an upright *mridangam* with the left side facing down ("shorter and squatter than its classical counterpart, thus providing a higher pitch") and a horizontal *dholak* that is "modified by the addition of a small bamboo stick for striking the right head" (Wolf 2000: 913).

We have three options: the *maththalam* was played in the Indian *terukkūttu* the way it is now used in Batticaloa, after which it spread to Sri Lanka but faded away in Tamil Nadu and Jaffna; the drum was imported at an earlier date from Kerala; or both are true. While the *maththalam* is well-attested in South Indian Tamil literature, it seems in our present era the drum has been largely replaced in Tamil Nadu by the *mridangam* because the latter is quieter and more suitable for indoor, staged performances. Interlocutors in Jaffna viewed the *maththalam* as the "ancestor" (they used the English word) of the *mridangam*.[20] It is also possible that the *maththalam* developed in Batticaloa somewhat cut off from northern Sri Lanka and South India for a couple hundred years when northern Sri Lanka was ruled by the Dutch and Batticaloa contained vassal states of the Sinhala-led Kandyan Kingdom, and that styles of drumming in Kandy and Batticaloa developed similarities during this time. I also suspect modern, South Indian conceptions of rhythm were influenced by Western approaches in the colonial period to a greater extent than in rural Batticaloa.

Finally, let me address the possibility of physical encounters between Sinhala and Tamil musicians in the medieval period. After Sinhala society broke into competing southwestern kingdoms, *devale* worship flourished (the supplication of Hindu deities at shrines, or *devales*, attached to Buddhist temples), the kind of worship at the center of Beravā *deva tovils*. I suspect that during this period of contact between Sinhala and Tamil cultures (thirteenth through sixteenth centuries), which I have argued is when Beravā regional traditions (Korales) were sedimented, Beravā rituals developed through some influence from Malayali (Keralan) and Tamil (Sri Lankan and South Indian) drumming and dance. The *kooththu* in South India is thought to have achieved its current form more or less by the seventeenth century. Beravā ritual drumming is not Tamil *maththalam* drumming, but I suggest they developed from a

---

[20] The ubiquity of the *mridangam* in modern Tamil Nadu may have led *terukkūttu* drummers at some point to forego the *maththalam* and take a *mridangam* and turn it upright, to approximate the sound they used to get from the *maththalam*. This is a hunch, but even if correct, it does not preclude the possibility of earlier influences from the Keralan *maddalam*.

similar constellation of influences and perhaps encounters with one another in the late medieval and early colonial periods.

This view may seem banal to outsiders, so I need to emphasize how controversial it is in Sri Lanka. Popular discourses on Sinhala and Tamil cultures define each group as having thoroughly distinct histories of music and dance. The Sinhala version traces Sinhala music to the indigenous Väddas, the prehistoric god-king Ravana, and thus the pre-Buddhist period (see Chapter 6). The Tamil version traces the history of music and dance to the ancient Indian treatise the *Natya Shastra* and to South India (see below, this chapter). Both perspectives elide the possibility that they share mutual influences from (late medieval/colonial-era) Kerala; that there are *internal* divisions in their respective cultures (between upcountry and low-country Sinhalas, and between Jaffna and Batticaloa Tamils); and that certain techniques demonstrate histories of encounter or mutual influence.

Consider the entry for "drums" in the *Encyclopedia of Sri Lanka* (Gunawardena 2005: 120). It mentions "Sinhala" drums *gäta beraya, yak beraya, davula, thummediya* (a clay pot drum, clearly derived from the *ghattam* drum prevalent in Tamil Nadu) and the Arab- and Malay-derived *rabāna*. The implication is that these are the only Sri Lankan drums that are "native" to the island. This is a sleight of hand because, as I have shown above, each of these drums developed through interactions with non-Sinhalese communities on and off the island, while some (the *davula, thummediya*, and *rabāna*) are probably direct imports. While I *do* assert they are "native," this does not mean that comparable drums played by Sri Lankan minorities, like the *maththalam*, should not be considered "native."

There has now been a whole generation (at least) that has grown up in a world where Sinhalas and Tamils are treated in the educational system as though their music and dance is not historically connected. Even when "Tamil dance" (*kooththu* or Bharata Natyam) is on a school syllabus, its historical separation from "Sinhala dance" (e.g., Kandyan Dance) is assumed. Consider Subashini Pathmanathan's (2014) article comparing Bharatha Natyam and Kandyan Dance.[21] She notes that Bharata Natyam grew out of the temple dances (*sadir*) in South India, and Kandyan Dance grew in part out of the temple dances (*digge nätum*) of Sri Lanka; but she ignores the possibility that the *digge nätum* was historically related to *sadir*. Instead, the author places each, via the ancient text the *Cilappatikāram*, back in the mist of time, asserting they grew up independently from one another:

> Silappathikaram, the Tamil classic, describes Santhi Koothu which consists of four main Koothu forms, namely, Chokam, Mei Koothu, Abhinaya, and Nadakam. Chokam is the pure Nirtha dance [presumably Nirtha is *nritta*, the "pure dance" category listed in the *Natya Shastra*]. The Mei Koothu consists of three main categories: Desi, Vaduku, and

---

[21] Subashini Pathmanathan, "Similarities between Kandyan Dance and Bharata Natyam," *Sunday Observer*, October 12, 2014.

Sinhalam. Desi was a dance form of the Tamil country. Vaduku was a dance form belonging to Telugu Desam, and the word Sinhalam, was apparently a reference to a dance form belonging to Sinhala country. Unfortunately apart from the word Sinhala, there is nothing about the dance form in Silappathikaram. Even the great Tamil poet Subramaniya Bharathi spoke of building a bridge to Sinhala Deepa. Traditional Kandyan dance is a pure Nirtha dance firmly based on Thala, Laya, and on Thandava Karana stance and based on rhythm. Like Bharatha Natyam, the Kandyan dance was also danced in temples, and temple festivals. But both dance forms enjoyed the royal patronage.

I propose the author has it backward: Tamil women's temple dances (i.e., *sadir*) and various kinds of Tamil drama came to Sri Lanka, were adopted by (or influenced) Sinhalas, who transformed them into distinctly Buddhist genres (e.g., *digge nätum*) and/or adopted elements to influence genres that had been around in some different form (e.g., the Beravā's Kohomba Kankariya ritual that bequeathed Kandyan Dance). By emphasizing Kandyan Dance's royal patronage, the author forgets the importance of the low-caste Beravā in producing the genre; and "Kandyan Dance" was only patronized by kings at a late date (the late eighteenth century), at a time when the Kings of Kandy were of Tamil Nayakkar descent. In the above quote, the *Natya Shastra* is used to ethnically purify Kandyan Dance, to place it back in a time before it existed, while making it sound like its "royal patronage" existed centuries before Kandyan Dance (as we know it) existed.

There are serious implications for this myth of thoroughly separate histories for Bharata Natyam and Kandyan Dance. Satkunaratnam (2009: 59) notes that Bharata Natyam was classified initially by the famous Kalakshetra institute in South India as transcending "a localized South Indian and Tamil identity in favor of a national and pan-Indic one." At the All-Ceylon Dance Festival in 1950, the dance was described as "Indian," "Oriental," and "Indigenous" (59). The dance's popularity grew considerably in Colombo after the founding of the Saiva Mangaiyar Kalaham established a School of Music and Dance in 1945, and the Ceylon Tamil Women's Union established the Kalalaya School of Music and Dance in 1948 (73). It has since achieved a surprising popularity among Sinhala women. However, when beginning her research on the history and performance of Bharata Natyam in Colombo, Satkunaratnam was given the phone number of the Chitrasena Dance Company, the famous institute whose importance in the transformation of Kandyan Dance into a staged tradition is well documented (Nurnberger 1998a). The woman who answered the phone asked why the researcher was in Sri Lanka, and when she found out Satkunaratnam wanted to study Bharata Natyam, the woman "interjected abruptly," stating, "Bharata Natyam is an Indian dance form. Indians do Bharata Natyam. We have nothing to do with Bharata Natyam. Instead, our focus is on our dance, Sri Lanka's dance called Kandyan Dance. I am curious as to why you are working on Bharata Natyam. Wouldn't you go to India to study that? Where are you from?" There has been a kind of nuclear escalation of authenticity and boundedness that is a form of historical amnesia, a dangerous forgetting of a shared cultural history, a forgetting that is willfully legitimized through the insertion of Kandyan Dance into the ancient *Natya Shastra*, to act as though it arose *sui generis* on the island, devoid of outside influences.

Needless to say, the issue is tricky: for as I have already suggested, Carnatic classical music and dance are indeed from South India and *are* developments that came into Sri Lanka. But this does not mean that the Sri Lankan Tamil *kooththu*, or the forerunner of Bharata Natyam (*sadir*), or other dances from Kerala or Tamil Nadu or elsewhere did not influence Kandyan Dance (and vice versa!). The Chitrasena teacher's belief in the naturalness of borders–the idea that the boundaries of the island have always been a rigid political and cultural boundary (Sivasundaram 2013)—demonstrates a lack of recognition that cultural influences have *always* crossed into Sri Lanka and helped develop Kandyan Dance in the first place, such as through the adoption of the *talampota* (finger cymbals, which are not used in low-country tradition) and the adoption of terms (e.g., the Tamil *varnam* became the Sinhala *vannam*, the term *adavu* is used in both traditions). Such histories of connection are written out by observers like Pathmanathan through a sleight of hand: "Kandyan Dance appears to have grown out of Natya Sastra, as there are discernible similarities between the classical dance forms of India."[22]

The Southeast Asian Connection

The *yak beraya*'s skins are made from the inside of a cow's stomach, while one skin on the *gäta beraya* is made of monkey skin: there is a joke that the low-country drum sounds like the rumbling of a cow, while the *gäta beraya* sounds like a pesky monkey. Frankly, the *yak beraya* is the lowest-sounding drum I have heard in South and Southeast Asia. As a straight drum (*mihingu beraya*), it neither looks nor sounds anything like the *maththalam* or *gäta beraya*, even if all have somewhat similar approaches to drumming as unmetered speech.

Kulatillake suggests there was a seeping of Javanese cultural elements in the courts of the Kotte Kings during the reign of Parakramabahu VI (1412–1467). This king, he says,

> enjoyed healthy alliances with Malaysian royalty. The institution of the Bandāra gods and the ritual of Kohomba Kankariya from which the Kandyan style of dancing is supposed to have originated provide

---

[22] Subashini Pathmanathan, "Similarities between Kandyan Dance and Bharata Natyam," *Sunday Observer*, October 12, 2014.

reasonable indications of the influence of these Malaysian cultural elements, particularly in the field of dancing. . . . Masked dancing associated with the cult of deceased spirits and such instruments like the *devol* or the *ruhunu bera* and the tambourine *rabāna* are supposed to be Malaysian imports (Kulatillake 1976: 5).

By stating the *yak beraya* is of "Malaysian" origin, Kulatillake (1974: 58, 128) must be referring to the *gendang* (used in the palace *nobat* ensemble), which is a variation of the *kendang* in Java and Bali; similarly straight-shaped drums are pictured on the ruins of Borobudur in Java. These drums resemble the *yak beraya* because they are long, relatively thin, with a straight shape. But one could just as easily claim the gendang/kendang are of South Asian origin, and the *gendang* uses taut buffalo or cow hide and does not sound like the *yak beraya*. Given the simplicity of the shape, practically anyone could invent a straight, long drum, but for that very reason, it is surprising such drums are rare in South India and Sri Lanka, the only examples being the *yak beraya* and *chenda* (the latter is from Kerala but played vertically, with sticks, and is higher-pitched).

It is notable that the *yak beraya* is absent from medieval treatises and sculptures of musicians. Bandara (2004) claims the earliest reference to a *yak beraya* is the eighteenth-century painting in the Silabimbaramaya temple in Duranduwa (near Hikkaduwa, southwest coast). The drum also appears in Kandyan era paintings in the Mulkiragala Raja Mahavihara in the south, near Tangalle (Ramanayake 1986: 14). While a "straight drum" (*mihingu beraya*) is depicted on a pillar at the Brazen Palace, Anuradhapura, that drum is smaller than today's *yak beraya*; Ramanayake (6) mistakes it for a *maddalaya* (the Sinhala term for *maththalam*), believing that name a synonym for *mihingu bera*, which is wrong, since *maddalaya* is not a straight drum—it bulges in the middle and has tapered ends. Another possibility is that the drum depicted in Anuradhapura is a *patawa*, an ancient drum (no longer used) that is almost exactly straight across (there is a slight bulge), though shorter in length than the *yak beraya*, which was supposedly used for the female temple dances (*digge nätum*).[23]

The Vädda Connection

At this point I've argued that the *gäta beraya* and *yak beraya* have separate origins (or at least connections) off-island, one in South India, the other possibly in Southeast Asia (though we should not rule out the possibility it is indigenous to the low country). I now want to add one other issue to the mix, the question of what drums are used by the indigenous Väddas. I think the Väddas are important

---

[23] Kandyan drum master Panibharata says the *patawa* looked similar to the *gäta beraya* but had larger drum heads and was made of calf skin (Ramanayake 1986: 6).

Figure 4.3 East Coast Väddas, Vakarai, early twentieth century, holding a drum shaped like a *maththalam*, from C. G. and Brenda Z. Seligmann (1911: Plate LXVIII). Photo courtesy of Cambridge University Press.

because they further challenge the ethnicized culture zone discourse by providing a link between Sinhala and Tamil drums. Little research has been conducted on Vädda musics save a chapter in C. G. and Brenda Z. Seligmann's classic 1911 study. The authors include a photo of east coast Väddas (in Vakarai) holding a drum shaped, unsurprisingly, like the *maththalam* used by nearby Tamils.

Many east coast Väddas were displaced by the Gal Oya Dam project in the 1950s, and later by war and the tsunami. Some were forced into IDP camps. In research conducted in 2010, Premakumara De Silva (2011: 128) located dispersed Vädda settlements that extend "from the eastern and north eastern slopes of the hill country to the Eastern and North Central parts of the country," including Dambana, Rathugala, Pollebedda, Dalukana, Henanigala, Vakarai, Muttur, Anuradhapura and Panama.[24] Against the common trope of the Väddas as immobile jungle-dwellers, he notes that due to displacement, 45% of "Dambana" Väddas came to Dambana in the last generation, and only 12% of Väddas in Vakarai said they were living in their original village (De Silva 2011: 135–136).

No one, to my knowledge, has conducted research on Vädda music since the Seligmanns' study; we do not know how all this displacement changed Vädda drumming. Nevertheless, over the course of my research I developed a hypothesis: Vädda drums change (or used to change) in shape from a "Tamilized" *maththalam* construction in the east to a "Sinhala-ized" construction in

---

[24] He estimates the total Vädda population to be not more than 10,000 (De Silva 2011: 134).

geographically central villages (closer to Sinhala society), like Dambana. This would mean, for instance, that Vāddas in the east would use goat and cow skin (as is used for the *maththalam*), while those in Dambana would use monkey skin (as is used for the *gäta beraya*). Perhaps the more in between Sinhala- and Tamil-dominated villages one went, the more Vādda drums were a hybrid combination of Sinhala- and Tamil-looking drums. But, if the Tamil-ized Vāddas use *maththalam* or a drum like it, what do Sinhala-ized Vāddas use? Does their drum look like a *gäta beraya* (with a bulge in the middle, similar to the *maththalam*, but longer and skinnier) or like a *davula* (short and fat with no bulge, played with a stick rather than both hands)? The Vāddas who used to live in Sabaragamuwa province used to play *davula* (Ramanayake 1986: 10), but the *davula* is associated with Sabaragamuwa Beravā rituals; in the hill country region, though, the *davula* is associated just with Buddhist temple and funeral ceremonies—so would Dambana's Vāddas use such a "Buddhist" drum in their rituals of ancestor worship ("Naa Yakku"), or do they have their own, unique drum? And if so, have the Vāddas now professing Buddhism switched to the *davula*?[25]

Thanks to the wonder that is YouTube, I was able to test my hypothesis. One should not hasten to make judgments from YouTube (!), but in a Sri Lanka that is still hard to travel to in many places, it is useful if used carefully. And what I found is that the Vāddas in Dambana use a short, fat drum that looks like a *davula*—though their drums look a bit longer in shape than the Sinhala *davula*.[26] The videos show Vāddas playing the drum with two hands (as one does with the *gäta beraya*) and not with a stick, as Sinhalas do with the *davula*. As if to confirm my hypothesis, one observer mentions that Vāddas from Dambana use monkey skin to make their drums.[27] In combing through videos and photographs of today's east coast Vāddas, I did not find an image of a *maththalam*, as captured in the Seligmanns' photograph, but I did find a member of a Vādda community from Kaluvanken, Batticaloa, using a *straight-shaped* drum that does *not* look like a *maththalam*, gäta beraya, or *davula*. Rather, it is much longer—closer in size to a *yak beraya*—though the head of it is wider than those on the *yak beraya*, more resembling a *davula*. Nor does the drum use an outer ring on top of the main drum skin, as the *yak beraya* does. The drum is striking—I haven't seen anything in Sri Lanka like it.

For some readers this game of comparison may seem silly—and indeed it is. For one might assume one could decide to make a drum of any size if one wishes. And Sri Lankan drums tend to be built proportionally for the drummer who will play it, by measuring from the elbow to the fingertip, so the issue of length may

---

[25] De Silva (2011: 166–167) writes that, "currently . . . 74% of the Veddas call themselves Buddhists whereas 18% call themselves Hindus. Only 2.75% of the Veddas currently worship and believe in their traditional deities and ancestors and have not acquired Buddhism, Hinduism, Christianity, or Catholicism. Nearly 2.0% worship and believe in the traditional deities while following Buddhist, Hindu, Christian, and Catholic faiths. However, only 2.5% have adopted Christianity and Catholicism."

[26] For example, search for "Kiri Koraha Dance from Vedda People in Dambana."

[27] John Gimlette, *The Telegraph*, August 25, 2013.

Figure 4.4. A Vädda drummer from Batticaloa plays a drum with a shape unlike others in the Sri Lankan context—longer than a *davula*, fatter than a *yak beraya*. Photo courtesy of Jeyasankar Sivagnanam.

be a red herring. For instance, the drum in the back of the above photo looks more like a conventional *davula*—perhaps the drum featured in the photo is just a *davula* that is longer than normal. And yet, those knowledgeable about Sri Lankan drums will know that the choice of how to make a drum is not usually arbitrary. One would never make a *gäta beraya* for a low-country drummer or a *yak beraya* for a *kooththu* drummer (the longer size also looks similar to the drum being built by Väddas in a photo taken by the musicologist C. de S. Kulatillake that I have reproduced in Chapter 6). One might also remember my anecdote about how the Kaffirs have claimed the *dholak* as their own; I suggest the Dambana Väddas have claimed the *davula* as their own (though perhaps a longer-shaped *davula*), and that the "Batticaloa" Vädda drum above may be a remnant of a time when Vädda villages gradually shaded from Tamil into Sinhala culture and vice versa, with the drum somewhat in between a *davula* and *yak beraya*.

Further Connecting Sinhala and Tamil Drumming

There are acute similarities between the (Tamil) Paraiyars and (Sinhala) Beravā *hēvisi* ensemble. As mentioned in the last chapter, the Sri Lankan Tamil *parai* does not look like the South Indian *parai*; rather, it looks almost identical to the Sinhala *davula* (see Figures 4.5 and 4.6).

The playing styles between the Sinhala *davula* and Sri Lankan Tamil *parai* do differ: the *davula* is played with one hand and one stick; the Sri Lankan Tamil *parai*

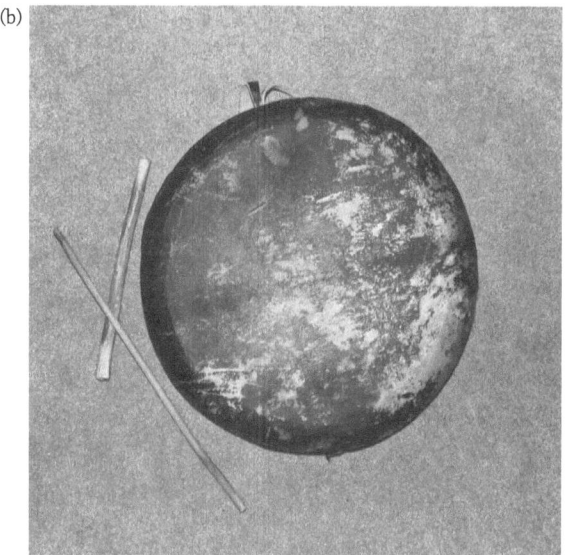

Figure 4.5 The Sri Lankan Tamil *parai* (a) and the South Indian Tamil *parai* (b): the drum in the (b) is single-sided, and thin. Figure 4.5a by the author, Figure 4.5b courtesy of Prabhunkl, CC BY-SA 4.0.

is sometimes played with two sticks. The Sri Lankan *parai* comes in different sizes; it seems the larger version (*periya parai*) is found in Jaffna and Mullaitivu. And the *davula* and *parai* are clearly similar to barrel-shaped drums in India (such as the drum from Karnataka called *dollu*). Nevertheless, their similarity is striking. Both are played at funerals, and both used to play the role of the "messenger drum"; the use of the *davula* for this was called *anda bera*.

McGilvray's book (2008: 248) features a photograph of a drummer playing a *tappāṭṭam* (Figure 4.7). In an earlier publication (Sykes 2013), I naively thought this was derived from the Sinhala *thammättama*, used in the *hēvisi* ensemble. I have

Figure 4.6 The Sinhala *thammättama* (left) and *davula* (right).
Photo courtesy of Roger Vetter.

since found out this drum bears some resemblance to a number of differently sized kettle-shaped drums in ancient Tamil society, including the large *murasu*, the *kinai*, and an older drum (or drums) also called *parai*. The Tamil version of this uses one drum while the Sinhala version (the *thammättama*) uses two.

Premalatha Panchadcharam states that during the Sangam period (circa 300 BC to 200 BCE), the large *murasu* kettledrum was used to rally soldiers and announce defeats.[28] He provides drawings of the *murasu* and *parai* as both being kettle-shaped drums, the latter similar to today's *tappāṭṭam*; it seems that the frame drum was adopted as the *parai* in Tamil Nadu at a later date, though more research will be needed to determine how that history unfolded. McGilvray (personal communication) posits that discrimination against Paraiyars was so great that they may have stopped using the *parai* (frame drum) and switched to the *davula*, which they borrowed from the Sinhalas. Kulatillake (1974) suggests the *davula* is of "ancient Persian" origin, and that it descended from comparable drums (*duhul, dolk, dolak,* or *dolki*) in India. Who got it from whom is impossible to tell, but I think the drums point to a similarity, if not a historic interaction, between Sinhala and Tamil musical cultures that needs to be recognized in musicological discussions of the island. As one Tamil interlocuter put it, "either we got it from them or they

---

[28] Premalatha Panchadcharam, "Parai—The percussion instrument nurtured by Ancient Tamil Nation," *Tamil Diplomat*, January 10, 2016.

Figure 4.7 A Tamil drummer playing the *tappāṭṭam*, which looks like one half of what makes up the Sinhala *thammāttama* drum. Photo courtesy of Dennis McGilvray (see McGilvray 2008: 248).

got it from us." Perhaps the *tappāṭṭam* is a newer version of the ancient *parai* that used to be played with the *yazh* (harp), and that it was adopted by Sinhalese before both were displaced by round, barrel-shaped drums (variations on the *dhol*) from India—that's my contribution to the guessing game.

In both Sinhala *hēvisi* and Batticaloan Hindu temple ensembles, the barrel- and kettle-shaped drums are accompanied by small double-reed instruments (not to be confused with the longer and more famous *nadaswaram*). The Sinhala version is called *horanāva*; the Tamil version is the *sornāli* (clearly, one of these words is derived from the other).

A fascinating component of Batticaloa Paraiyar tradition that McGilvray (2008: 263) mentions is that they were required to do dance routines with their music, "similar in some ways to choreography observed in the [Sinhala] Kandy Perahera" (the Äsala Perahera). I believe what McGilvray saw was the Parai Mela

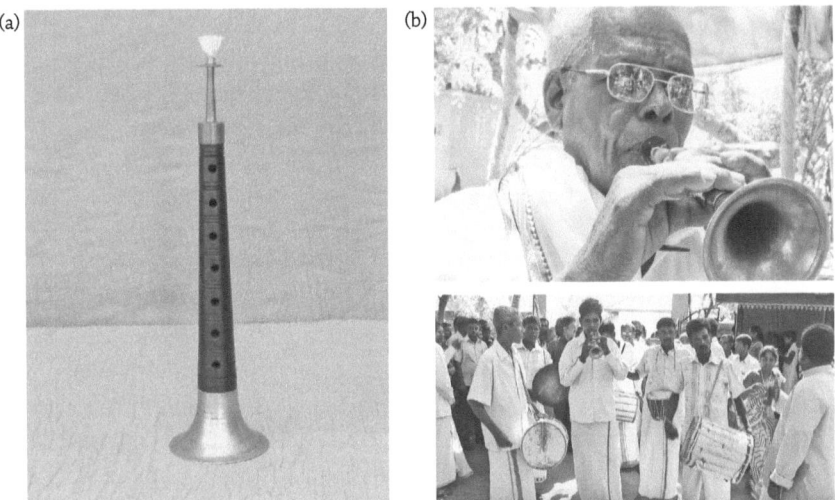

Figure 4.8 Sinhala *horanäva* (a) and Sri Lankan Tamil *sornāli* (b [top], played by master Parasuraman). Tamil sornāli, parai, and *tappāṭṭam* players (b [bottom]).
Photo on 4.8a courtesy of Roger Vetter; photo on 4.8b courtesy of Jeyasankar Sivagnanam.

Kooththu. It would be easy to assume the Kandyan version was derived from the Tamil version, but considering the esteem the Kandyan Äsala Perahera procession is held in, and the historical relations between Batticaloa and Kandy, I suggest the similarities in performance may come from the other direction.

Finally, there is the issue of the *yazh* (the harp that gives Jaffna its Tamil name) and the *veena* associated with ancient Sinhala culture described by Kulatillake (1991: 67–69). Mention of the *yazh* goes back in Tamil culture to the *Thirukkural*, written by Thiruvalluvar (who lived sometime between the third and first centuries BCE). The Sangam literature spoke of five kinds of lands associated with five kinds of *yazhs* and *parais*.[29] A later work, the *Cilappatikāram*, identifies four kinds of *yazh*: *periyazh* (twenty-one strings), *makarayazh* (nineteen strings), *cakotayazh* (fourteen strings), and *cenkottiyazh* (seven strings). Also known are two shapes for the *yazh*, one resembling a peacock and one like a bow (Sambamoorthy 2010, Plate I). According to Kulatillake, there are fourteen kinds of "Sinhala *veenas*" (stringed instruments) mentioned in the ancient Pali and Sinhala sources, and further mention in the literature of the Kotte period (fifteenth through sixteenth centuries). The *Samantapāsādika Vinaya* commentary of Buddhaghōsha states that the *veena* is "a despicable instrument that promotes lust and passion" (Kulatillake 1991: 67–69), and in this capacity it was used by Māra as a weapon to distract the Buddha from meditating. Surely this is one reason the instrument

[29] Ibid.

died out among the Sinhalese, though it is also says that when Māra dropped the instrument and fled, it was picked up by the god Sakka, who gave it to the god Pancasika (Kulatillake 1991: 67–69). It does not take a rocket scientist (nor, for that matter, a scholar of Pali) to see that the *veena* described in such sources has some historical relation to the *yazh*. The drawing Kulatillake (1991: 67) supplies of Pancasika's *veena* has ten strings, but it looks rather like the seven-stringed Tamil *cenkottiyazh*.

Harps were also once found farther north in India and in mainland Southeast Asia; today, the harp called *saung* is still played in Myanmar, while in Cambodia, a revival of pre-Angkorian harps (*pin*) is currently underway, as several musicians and scholars are seeking to recreate harps based on old sculptures.

What to make of these similarities, and of the politics of the relations between the harps and ethnic identities in the Tamil world and mainland Southeast Asia? Well, Buddhism flourished in South India from the third century BCE until it began to decline around the seventh century CE. The Buddhist presence in South India is attested in many sources, notably the *Puranānūru, Cilappatikāram,* and *Manimekalai* (the earlier circa 100 BCE to 200 CE, the latter two of less certain dating and likely a few hundred years later). Chinese pilgrim Hiuen Tsang wrote about the giant stupa he saw at Kāñchipuram in South India in 640. Peter Schalk surveyed material remainders of Buddhists in South India (e.g., coins, inscriptions, texts, and so on) and concluded that, "none is before the fourth and none after the fourteenth century" (Schalk in Deeg et al., 2011).[30] It seems the decline started happening in the south as early as 600 CE on account of a lack of kingly patronage (Schalk 2013: 30), but Buddhist/Saivite syncretism in Tamil Nadu continued for many centuries. During the height of the seafaring Tamil Chola Dynasty, from the tenth through twelfth centuries, raids were conducted on sites in Southeast Asia, including the Burmese kingdom of Pegu, the Maldives and Malabar Coast, northern Sri Lanka, parts of Srivijaya in Malaysia and Indonesia, and southern Thailand. This—and of course, centuries of trade—may be the origin of those harps in mainland Southeast Asia. My point here, though, is that I am suggesting against *both* Sinhala and Tamil normative perspectives that the *yazh* may not have been related just to a purely "Hindu" Tamil culture, nor that the Sinhala *veena* was related just to a purely "Sinhala Buddhist" culture. Rather, the medieval period throughout South and Southeast Asia was characterized by numerous periods and places that showed mixed Buddhist-Saiva (Hindu) practices. The harp probably circulated between communities and regions, adopting a Hindu veneer in the Sangam literature and a Buddhist one in the Pali literature, while in some contexts, a mixed

---

[30] The last Tamil Buddhist document appears to be a thirteenth-century inscription displaying a syncretic form of Buddhism and Saivism (Schalk 2002, section 5.7). The Sīmālankāra written by Vācissara in the first half of the thirteenth century describes methods used by the Coliyans (residents of the Tamil Chola empire in South India) to determine monastic boundaries.

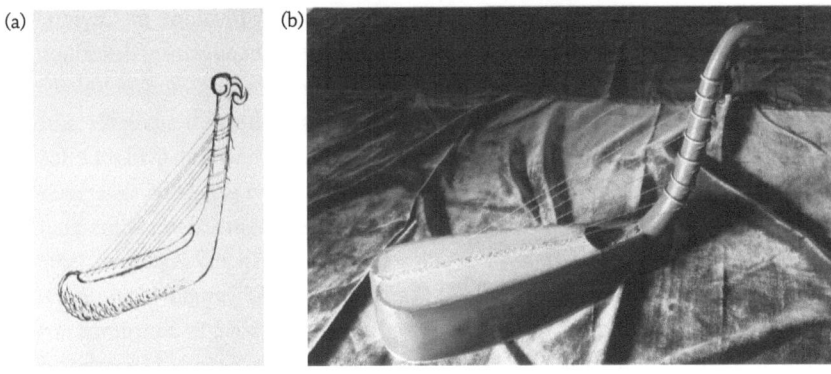

Figure 4.9 (a), drawing of Pancasika's Buddhist *veena* (based on a drawing in Kulatillake [1991: 67]), (b), a seven-stringed Tamil *cenkottiyazh*. Drawing by Lee Veeraraghavan. Photo on 4.9b courtesy of Ludwig Pesch.

Buddhist-Saivite culture may have conceived of the instrument in a different way. Of course, this does not preclude the possibility that Sinhala and Tamil societies had their own versions of the harp—and this, precisely, is my point.

Thus my concern here is not to determine who got what from whom, nor to say who more rightly owns an instrument. Rather, my point is that these histories of relations challenge the validity of the ethnicized cartography of culture zones as the only way to discuss the traditional arts in Sri Lanka. We can come up with different culture zones *in addition* to the normative ethnicized one. Instead of having to group the "Sinhala" up-country and low-country drumming together, on the one hand, and "Tamil" Jaffna and Batticaloan drumming, on the other, we can add at least three more cartographies: (1) one that marks three culture zones: Tamil Nadu and Jaffna; Batticaloa and Kandy; and the low country and Southeast Asia; (2) one that groups Kerala, Tamil Nadu, and the whole island together; (3) one that groups the whole island as musically different from South India. These proposed culture zones are not intended to discount the standard version, but to suggest that maps that do not emphasize ethnic division are *also* correct.

Medieval Sinhala Musics and the Question of "Relations"

Mid-twentieth-century studies of medieval Sinhala culture note that treatises from the medieval Polonnaruwa period and a few centuries after (up through the *sandesa* poems of the Kotte period) describe the Sinhalese playing musical instruments and adopting musical practices that were some combination of Hindu/Indian/Tamil origin. While I have made the case for histories of interaction and mutual influence, we must be careful in conceptualizing those interactions. In his classic *Society in Medieval Ceylon*, Ariyapala (1956: 262) states forthrightly that, "the available material . . . helps us to establish that it was the Indian tradition of classical music that was prevalent in Ceylon." He claims the thirteenth-century Sinhala treatise the *Thupavamsa* describes the Sinhalese playing "Tamil" musical instruments (*mridangam, maddalam, thappu,* and *nagaswara*). However, I have been unable to find these in available editions of the text.[31] This is significant because the earliest material evidence for the *nagaswaram* (as *nagasura* or *nagaswara*) currently known is a 1496 inscription in Tirumala, Andhra Pradesh (Terada 2008: 109).[32] Ariyapala also claims that the thirteenth-century *Saddharma-ratnāvaliya* uses the term *mihingu bera* (straight drum) as a synonym for *maddala bera* (Tamil drum) (Ariyapala 1956: 261), but no evidence is provided for this—this is significant because in contemporary Sri Lanka, *maddala bera* is not a straight drum and *mihingu beraya* is another name for the *yak beraya*. However, the thirteenth-century *Pujavaliya* does mention the *udekki* (*udukkai*) drum that is widespread in Tamil culture, and the fifteenth-century *Saddharmālaṃkāraya* mentions the *ottu*, a Tamil conical reed instrument similar to the *nadaswaram*, which plays drones.

According to Ilangasinha (1992: 149), the *Oruvala Sannasa* depicts Tamil Brahmins having a strong influence on the Kotte court, leading to Tamil becoming an important language in the *pirivenas*, monastic colleges for Buddhist monks. Studies at the *pirivenas* included "prosody (*chandas*), ornaments of speech (*alankāra*); logic (*tarka*), astrology (*nakṣatra*), and medicine (*vaidyaśāstra*)" (Ilangasinha 1992: 149). At the Vijayabāhu Pirivena, "they were allowed to learn not only Buddhism but also other religions (*samayāntara*)" (150). *Sandesa* poems of the fourteenth and fifteenth centuries describe female Sinhala dancers dancing to images of "Hindu" gods at Devundara, in the south near Matara (Sarachchandra 1952: 14–16).

We operate through a severe anachronism if we define the above practices as "Indian classical music" (all three terms are modern inventions). From a conservative Sinhala perspective, the above influences are deemed "intrusions" into a Sinhala Buddhist culture that predates them. And let's acknowledge they have a point. For uniquely Sinhala musical instruments and ideas are *also* present in medieval sources, demonstrating a distinctly Sinhalese musical system. The fifteenth-century *Saddharmālaṃkāraya* mentions drums that, to my knowledge, are found nowhere in Tamil culture (or for that matter in Kerala or Southeast Asia). Here is a partial list (culled also from Ariyapala 1956: 57, 99, 106, 130, 412, 462): *mihingu bera, gäta bera, panā bera, paṭaha, loho bera, talappara, vīrandam, tammäṭṭa, nisāna, rodu bera, ekäs bera* (one-sided drum), *dūdu bera, däduru bera, ḍavura, koṭumbara,* and *deṇḍima*. The meanings of some are probably lost to history: *ālavaṇṇi* (Sdhlk 129, 412); *tanti* (Sdhlk 412; according to Ariyapala, this is a lute), *ekacchidra,*

---

[31] His source is Hettiarachchi's 1947 edition (pg. 41), which is out of print; I have been unable to locate it.

[32] According to Raghavan (1949: 159), the *nagaswaram* is mentioned in *literature* from earlier in the fifteenth century, but that still post-dates the *Thupavamsa* (Terada 2008: 109).

mani parva, kaulasvara, kamsutalam, daladara, dalaham, loham, and *vijayodhvani* (Sdhlk 462, 305, 129). The thirteenth-century *Pujavaliya* lists drums including the *davura bera* and *ḍahara bera* (606) and mentions the conch (*sak*; 170, 283), *sinnam* (according to Ariyapala a kind of trumpet; 606), *timbili, vangī* (veena), *panā bera; kulal* (501; the *kuzhal* is a reed instrument from Kerala), *kālam* (501), and *horanāva*. Ramanayake (1986: 2) lists drums found in the "Sinhala and Pali literature" but does not list his sources; he includes *gata bera, pana bera, ekas bera, mihingu bera, maha bera, roda bera, karandi bera, ghosa bera, talappara, virandam, tammättam, timbuluvi, davul, morahu, mallari, sirivili tappu, tatsara, dakki, udakki, mandala, damaru, sindi, madvani, prutu bimba, dundubhi, anda bera,* and *gatapahatu*. Some of these are easily identifiable (e.g., *davul*); others have a known meaning in other contexts (*mallari* is an important part of the *nadaswaram* repertoire); others (e.g., the *prutu bimba*) are less identifiable (*ghosaka beraya* and *mihingu beraya* are synonyms for *yak beraya*, but I do not know if that is the drum referred to here).

The thirteenth-century Sinhala chronicle the *Thupavamsa* (the story of the relic shrine built in Anuradhapura by King Dutugämunu, circa second century BCE) provides a list of instruments that resounded when the Buddha achieved Enlightenment: "The gods who remained in the sky beat divine drums. But it was not just these alone" (Berkwitz 2007: 113). The text lists veenas—*vangi vina, nakula veena, bhrnga veena*—followed by drums: *gäta bera, panā bera, ekas bera, mihingu bera, maha bera, loho bera, tappu, tappara, virandam, tantiri, thammättama, nīsāna, ranaranga ghosā, däkki* (large hourglass drum), *udäkki* (small hour-glass drum), *maddala, davura,* and *saksinnam* (Berkwitz 2007: 113). Later in Anuradhapura, a drummer is sent around the city to announce the laying of the ceremonial brick of the Great Relic Shrine (201). As Dutugämunu is being adorned for the ceremony with numerous jewels, necklaces, anklets, and crowns, "and thus being decorated like Sakra, king of the gods" (ibid.), he sets off in procession to the sound of the drums listed above, accompanied by numerous "trumpets" (*randārā, rididārā, dalaham, lōham, gavaraham, vijayodhvni, ottu, tantiri, and patasiri*) and veenas (to which the text adds two others: *ksudra veena* and *ālavatti*).

Sinhala categorization works via use and are not fixed to the object; terms like *maha bera* ("great drum") and *gäta bera* ("auspicious drum") could have been applied to different drums at different times. Scholars are not in agreement about what drums these names refer to, and some might have referred to multiple drums: for example, Kulatillake thinks *pana bera* is another name for *udäkki*; Panibharata believes it referred to any drumming before the king or elite (Ramanayake 1986: 4). The presence of these drums in the thirteenth-century *Thupavamsa* is a writer's imagination of what music was like in India at the time of the Buddha's Enlightenment and Sri Lanka in the second century BC: they cannot be taken as proof that these instruments (such as the *thappu*) were played by Sinhalas at this time. The presence of *thappu* simply means Sinhalas were aware of the drum and the writer imagined it in the distant past in India. Perhaps most important to note is that Dutugämunu's procession was reliving the Enlightenment: he is dressed up as the king of the gods and the list of instruments is virtually the same as those described as being around at the Enlightenment. Today's low country drummers, when they play in the Bera Pōya Hēvisi, are reliving this moment, too, and they believe their drum—the straight drum, *mihingu bera* (which is on the list above)—was present when the ceremonial brick was laid for the Great Relic Shrine.

Sinhala medieval literary texts discuss rules governing meters for poems, such as *Siyabas lakara* (written in the tenth century), *Elu sandes lakuna* (1270–1293 CE), *Muwadevdawata, Sasadavata* and *Kavsilumina* (Ariyapala 1956: 258; Alawathukotuwa 2015: 13; Cumaratunga 2000). Kulatillake (149–185) and Weerakkody (2011: 1001) emphasize the importance of the Samudragosha meter to Sinhala sung poetry, which has "18 matras and the pause (yathi)—falling on the tenth and the subsequent eighth matra" (Alawathukotuwa 2015: 15). Sinhala chanting is theorized in the *Samantapasadika*, a fifth-century Pali commentary by Buddhaghoṣa that describes three forms of chanting, the Suttas, Jatakas, and Gathas (*pirit*, or Buddhist chant, belongs to the Suttas; Jatakas are tales of the former lives of the Buddha; and Gathas are versified renditions of the Pali Canon; Weerakkody 2011: 1000).

No consideration of Sinhala poetry is sufficient without considering eḷu (hela or helu), a Prakrit (Middle Indo-Aryan) language that allowed Sinhala authors to participate in and refuse being enveloped by the "Sanskrit cosmopolis" that swept across South and Southeast Asia at the turn of the second millennia (Pollock 2006; Hallisey 2003). Eḷu emphasized the nasalized ä sound that is so important to the Sinhala language, while rejecting Sanskrit loanwords and aspirated consonants "to create an autonomous literary space that gestured toward but remained separate from the cultural-political world articulated in Sanskrit" (Berkwitz 2016: 328). This culminated in a number of treatises on "grammar, prosody, poetics, and lexicography that enabled it to craft aesthetically refined works of literature that would accord with accepted literary standards" (328). Eḷu made a comeback in the mid-twentieth century, as writers and musicians attempted to revive it and channel it into the creation of a pure Sinhala language and music that would be free from Indian influence (Field 2013).

This tendency to emphasize chant, meter, and sung poetry was stressed by twentieth-century Sinhala scholars who sought to find a pure and uncorrupted Sinhala music in folk songs such as "lullabies, reaping songs, fisherman's songs, boatman's songs . . . [and] swing songs" (Aravinda 2000: 130; Abeysinghe 1991). As I describe more fully in Chapter 6, prominent twentieth-century musician and scholar Devar Surya Sena (1899–1981) collected these songs and publicized them in Europe and Ceylon as the nation's most esteemed traditional music. Before Surya Sena and educational initiatives by twentieth-century musicologists, most notably W. B. Makulloluwa (2000), this music was known as "poetry" (*kavi*) rather than "song" (*gi*); Surya Sena changed the name of some genres like *jana kavi* and *gemi kavi* to *jana gi* and *gemi gi* (Aravinda 2000). These poetic genres have a very small pitch range: perhaps up to five pitches. Surya Sena classified them as "song" to show the Sinhalese have their own folk music, but doing so left them vulnerable to being judged as having "primitive" melodies. The Sinhalese traditionally used the word "song" (*gitaya*) for genres with a larger pitch range, such as *nadagam* and *praśasti* (panegyric songs); thus they recognized a division between sung poetry and song.[33] A key component of the identity episteme in Sri Lanka, I suggest, has been the transformation of sung poetry into "music," and the transformation ignores the fact sophisticated Sinhala meters arose because Buddhists discouraged "songs" on account of their sensuality.

The oldest meter in Sinhala poetry is Gī, which is sung in a "recitative" style (Kulatillake 1991: 53). Examples have been found on inscriptions from the third century BC. *Padas* in Gī are unequal in length, and in Kulatillake's view they may have been an outgrowth of Pali Gāthās. When sung, Gī demonstrates a small range of pitches. One example Kulatillake provides (1991: 53) is of the opening of a *kōlam* (masked theater) drama in which the Gī has four *padas* of 9, 11, 9, and 14 *mātras* (beats). Gī meters are in low-country rituals as salutations to the Triple Gem (Buddha, Dhamma, Sangha) and as introductory preludes describing birth stories of gods (*upath kavi*), though the singing of Sanskrit verses (*shloka*) are also used as "eulogies to divinities" (Kulatillake 1976: 4).

The most common folk song meter is *sīvpada* ("four lines"), which as its name implies, contains a four-lined verse structure. The lines usually ended in "consonantal assonance" (*eli-väta*; rhyming with the same consonant/vowel combination; Kulatillake 1976: 4). This simple structure should not be taken to mean singing in this meter is easy. Kulatillake (1976: 54) notes some contain as many as thirty *mātras* in a line and rhythms *within* such lines of three, four, or seven beats. So a four *mātra* verse consisting of "va-ra-la-sa" will be recited with "va" and "ra" on beats one and two, followed by a pause, with "la" on beat four (followed by a pause) and "sa" on beat six. Though I did not get this advanced in my training on *yak beraya*, Kulatillake asserts this has resulted in Sinhala drum music "expressing . . . the quadruple rhythm in a complex pulse of $\frac{3}{4}$." An example of this is the famous Gājagā (elephant) Vannama heard in the Kandyan Perahera (Kulatillake 1976: 9). It seems to me much of the genius of the Kandyan Vannams (integral to Kandyan Dance) is that they use some of these folk song meters but with *gäta beraya* drumming fit *into* them, with the addition of *talampota* (finger cymbals) to keep time; such a system did not develop in the low country.[34]

---

[33] The history and content of *praśasti* "songs" begs further research. Ariyaratne (1989: 179–181) suggests they closely resembled the Tamil *cintu* (Sinhala *sindu*), a "five-line composition with a shortened first line (*pallavi*) and a long second line (*anupallavi*)," and they appear to have flourished during the days of the Nayakkar dynasty in Kandy, particularly at the court of King Narendrasinghe (1707–1739; [Sheeran 1998: 966]).

[34] Kulatillake (1991: 55) describes the *sindu* as "another style of metrics" different from Gī and Sīvpada, though I think this is more properly thought of as a song genre. The form was used to narrate the former lives of the Buddha or recount stories about villages (56). Kulatillake (55) states that it contains three Sīvpada or twelve lines and did not require *eli-väta* at the end of each line; one of the most widely used meters in the *sindu* contained lines split between twenty *mātras* and ten *mātras*, with a vibrato elongation (*yati*) on the twentieth *mātra*.

To Kulatillake, the Samudraghōsha meter and a genre of folk song called Seepada grew out of the Sīvpada meter.[35] Seepada became important for the Sinhala "messenger" (*sandesa*) poems of the fifteenth and sixteenth centuries, and consists of unaccompanied quatrains. Roberts (2004) provides a list of other folk song genres: *patal kavi, gäl kavi, paru kavi, nelum kavi, nalavi gi, pel kavi, kurahan kavi, prasasti, têravili, tavalam kavi, stotra viraha*, and *varnana* ("the songs of miners, carters and boatmen, transplanting songs, lullabies, songs sung at night while guarding chena crops, *kurakkan*-harvesting songs, eulogies, riddles in verse, songs of the pack cattle people, poems of erotic desire and devotional religious verse").[36] While such genres exhibited a small pitch range, they required memorization and dexterity, encouraging "tease and play on words".[37]

Finally, a third meter of importance—one that I suggest may have influenced Beravā drumming—is the *chanda* system. Sanskrit Vedic literature shows examples of *akshara-chandas*, "syllabic meters" where the number of the syllables makes up the meter. While *gana-chandas* were present in early Sanskrit verses, they developed later, "the result of an attempt by the Pali theologians to deviate from the Sanskrit metres" (Kulatillake 1976: 3). The *gana-chandas* involve arranging clusters (*gana*) of three syllables into groups of short/light (*laghu*) and long/heavy (*guru*) properties.

Each long syllable is given two *mātras*; each short syllable is given one. Different arrangements or clusters of syllables are considered good or bad luck. The inauspicious clusters are in "odd" combinations of beats: for example, "Anti-bacchic" is four *mātras* with pulses on beats 1, 2, and a heavy accent on 3. The system also allowed for the building of clusters upon clusters of nested *gana-chandas* that, as a whole, would be auspicious or inauspicious. For example, Kulatillake (1976: 4) describes Mällnee, an auspicious *gana* meter with five clusters, as having its first two syllables as Tribrach (☉), the middle as Molassus (☉), and the final two as Bacchic (☉).

If readers are wondering if this belief in good and bad *ganas* still matters in Sri Lanka, consider that the lyrics to the national anthem were changed shortly after it was adopted in the 1950s on account of its inauspicious ordering of syllables, which some believed were the root of the island's political problems (see Chapter 6). I suspect some *bera padas* (lines of drum poetry) involve similarly auspicious or inauspicious combinations of *mātras* (perhaps the former are played for

---

[35] "Samudra Ghōsha" is listed in the *Thupavamsa* in a list of drums (Berkwitz 2007: 204). It is also described as a "conch" and "musical instrument" associated with the South Indian Pallava Dynasty (Heras 1933: 53–54), which sounds more right to me, since "samudra" is a Sanskrit term for "seven seas" (hence its association with the conch). The Sinhala poetic meter of the same name is named as such because it is supposed to sound like waves.

[36] Michael Roberts, "The Instance of Pre-Modern Sinhala Society," *Colombo Telegraph*, November 25, 2014.

[37] Ibid.

deities, the latter for *yakku*). I was not told of any such combinations, however, and I suspect this is where the drumming becomes directly efficacious. I also suspect certain kinds of repetition (say, repeating a *pada* 108 or 32 times) may be used in addition to this efficacious ordering of *mātras* to enhance the efficacy of auspiciously ordered *padas*. This shows why an incorrect performance of the *yak beraya* can bring about bad luck.[38]

In sum, all this should be enough to demonstrate one can identify a Sinhala approach to meter and vocality that marks a division between efficacious speech (i.e., *pirit*) and sung poetry acceptable in Buddhist ritual contexts, and songs for entertainment. There appears to have been a consistency in this approach over the centuries, with circulation between Sinhala performers granting unity to such concepts: for example, poets from Alutnuvara (in Kegalle district) had a great reputation as poets and were recognized in the Kandy *kavikāra badda* (the department for poetry in the Kandyan Kingdom; Roberts 2004). Certain aspects of this poetic knowledge were used by Sinhala musicians in the twentieth century, most famously W. D. Amaradeva (the doyen of Sinhala "classical" music) as a means to mold a modern Sinhala music, out of the belief that Sinhala music in the mid-twentieth century had become too influenced by North Indian music (see Chapter 6).

Sinhalas also had unique genres at the courts of medieval kings. For example, Parakkamabahu IV of Dambadeniya (fourteenth century) had a daily routine that included four music and dance sessions at the palace; he maintained two ensembles, one for festivals celebrating the Buddha's tooth relic (*daladagei vijjatun*) and the other for court services (*rajagei vijjatun*). Later, the royal dance unit in Kandy, *nätum illangama*, was "constituted only of women according to the Malabar fashion" (Kulatillake 1991: 35), but King Narendrasinghe (1707–1729) installed the *kavikara maduwa*, the royal institute of poets, with singers known as *kavindra*, or *kavikāra*, and poets came from places like Matara and Uva, who received land and titles in return for their poetry.[39] An official, the Muhandirm Nilame, was placed in charge of each unit in the Kavikara Maduwa. The genres that emerged there include uniquely Sinhala genres like Hatan Gee (war ballads), Viraha (erotic songs, sung mainly in Sivpada; Kulatillake 1991: 52), *viridu* (eulogies), and *sanvada* (comical poems).[40] The Vannams, it seems, grew out of the viraha; Kulatillake (1991: 52) describes them as "a phono-metric composition."[41]

---

[38] A Telugu treatise, the *Nruthya Mālākhyāva*, and a nineteenth-century Sinhala treatise, *Vādankusaya*, describe how Kandyan drumming is based on Sanskrit rules for organizing syllables (Sedaraman 1966: 120).

[39] Michael Roberts, "The Instance of Pre-Modern Sinhala Society," *Colombo Telegraph*, November 25, 2014.

[40] Ibid.

[41] During the late Kandyan period (eighteenth century), there was a flowering of poetry in the deep south in Matara whose sonic/musical aspects have yet to be studied.

However, despite the uniquely Sinhala quality of these genres, many of them need to be understood as emanating from the selective adaptation of the "Sanskrit Cosmopolis" (and its understandings of the royal court) in the Polonnaruva and Post-Polonnaruva periods. They also say nothing about how the Beravā thought of themselves or what they did. It may be that because of the Buddhist prohibition against music, caste bias against the Beravā, colonial era claims by British observers that Beravā drumming was Hindu in origin, the lack of consideration of the Beravā in older sources, and the Sinhalas' investments in song and poetic meters, twentieth-century Sinhala scholars focused on poetry and meter, generally ignoring the Beravā (see Chapter 6). Beravā drumming was subordinated to dance in the national imagination. But this had the effect of making Sinhala sung poetry stand in for a full-fledged "song" tradition, which it was invented *not* to do.

My *yak beraya gurunnānse* told me a story about an incident that really irked him: he was confronted by an Indian singer (he was performing in India) who said the Sinhalese do not have "rāga" (the melodic system common in Indian musics). He had a ready reply: in the ritual texts he inherited from his father, the word *swara* (notes) is used to describe a scale (quite like the Indian solfege system of sa-re-ga-ma-pa-dha-ni, but this was labeled ma-du-de-mu-di-te-rati). He sang the scale and applied the Sinhala style of singing with a lot of vibrato at the end of a line of sung poetry, called *yati*, characteristic of much Sinhala sung poetry. Thus he feels he won the battle by demonstrating the Sinhalas have *rāga*. But what this game of "Indian-ification" does, I suggest, is wage a battle with Indian music on the latter's turf, which is a losing game. This is not because Sinhala music is worse, but because the Sinhalas have their own musical values that differ from Indian ones—and that Sinhala and Sri Lankan Tamil traditional musics to a certain extent share. This is an emphasis on sung poetry, drumming, and drama, with a small pitch range but fantastic acting, storytelling, dancing, verbal innuendo, and drumming as repetitive poetic sentences.

I suggest the smaller pitch range and emphasis on lyrical content and complex poetic meters was a *choice* medieval Sinhalas made—a conscious limitation to avoid "music" to produce sounds appropriate for Buddhists—and that this gave the Sinhalese room to grow in. My argument is that on several occasions from the medieval Polonnaruwa period through the late medieval period, the stipulation that Buddhist monks and kings must not propitiate music and dance essentially halted the development of a court musical tradition and eliminated Sinhala investment in "melodic" instruments, putting the weight on the backs of the Beravā to develop Sinhalese "music," who responded with their drumming-as-speech so that it would be acceptable as an offering to the Buddha and gods. In the process, I suggest, *yak beraya* drumming developed into a "melodic" drumming tradition, occupying wide tonal spaces (through fluctuations in the drum head) that might otherwise have been filled by "melodic" instruments, with an arrangement of auspicious/strategically inauspicious syllables through a *mātra* system intended to make them sound "non-musical."

Music History as a Duck/Rabbit

Where does this leave us in our discussion? Sinhala music is like the famous picture of a "duck/rabbit" described by Wittgenstein (a picture that can be seen in two different ways depending on how one looks at it). Music history appears to give us a *choice* between (1) seeing the Sinhalas as a hybrid musical culture, forever taking outside elements and transforming them, *or* (2) one can view the Sinhalas as having a unique tradition separate from "Hindu" accretions, which periodically "invaded" Sinhala culture, only to be thrust out by orthodox monks at various moments of "Buddhist revival." These *seem* like contrasting claims, and they are usually treated as such. To make any comment that Tamil Hindus influenced Sinhala music is discounted by nationalists, who point to the ancientness of Sinhala culture; to make a claim about ethnic purity is discounted by those favoring the discourse on hybridity. But I suggest we don't have to choose between these perspectives, because both are right: the Sinhalese have always had a unique system—developed through Buddhist strictures and an interest in sung poetry and drum-speech—but they have also always taken in outside influences and developed their traditions through such encounters. Buddhism is originally from India, after all, and the Kandyan *gäta beraya* is not South Indian, even though it probably developed through encounters with Tamil drums. The idea that one *has to pick a side in this debate* is based either (1) on a false premise that there has always been a sharp binary between Sinhalas and Tamils, Aryans and Dravidians, Buddhism and Hinduism, and Sinhala and Carnatic musics, or (2) on the false premise that such categories are meaningless because everything is ultimately hybrid. Choice 1 ignores that Buddhism was once widespread among Tamils, and that medieval Sinhalas (according to the treatises above) may have once played instruments now marked "Tamil." And yet, Choice 2 ignores that the *gäta beraya* seems always to have been classified as Sinhalese, and that the Sinhala *maddalaya* was referred to even in the early medieval period as *Demala bera* (Tamil drum). I think it is essential for post-war Sri Lanka to draw a truce between this debate: lines between communities were drawn, but outside practices were consistently incorporated.

The crux of my argument, though, is that by emphasizing a *medieval* (i.e., Polonnaruwa and Kotte) phase of Indian/Hindu/Tamil encounters through music, the instruments we recognize today as distinctly "Sinhalese" (the *gäta beraya, yak beraya, davula, thammättama,* and *horanäva*) and distinctly Tamil (the *maththalam*, the *mridangam*) are kept out of the discourse on musical encounter between Sinhalas and Tamils. I think the reason there is a gut reaction against (or an absence in public culture of) the argument that the Paraiyars and Beravā *hēvisi* drummers, and *kooththu* and Beravā ritualists, are historically related and developed similarities in playing style, instrumentation, sound, and function, is that these are the instruments that Tamil and Sinhala nationalists have latched onto, respectively, as authentic to each group. One invested in the link between music and identity might be inclined to use this history of relations to make an argument about identity, saying that it shows each community is basically the same. But this is where the progressive argument for peace loses out by being just as invested in the link between music and identity as the ethnonationalists. Rather, I suggest we can mobilize a discourse on musical giving and describe music as a *technique* through which communities with different identities have often interacted with, given, and/or taken music from each other.

Musical Giving in Ethnonationalism

Consider the extreme ethnic purification that shaped uses of Beravā drums during the presidency of Mahinda Rajapaksa. Observing the Independence Day celebrations in February 2010 (a heavily politicized, nationalistic event, for it was the first Independence Day since the end of the war), Eva Ambos (2012) noticed a shift in the state's "heritage politics": she asserts that the state's position on traditional culture went "from a multicultural to a transcultural paradigm." Here's what she means by this. She notes that both paradigms "embrace purity as a value," but they have the following difference:

> Transculturality here should be thought of in a double sense: Firstly, as transcending culture, whereby an official image of a religious and ethnic neutral nation state is developed; and secondly, as an appropriation of the other. While the multicultural paradigm consists of ideologies which exclude everything that is interpreted as "other" as invading and corrupting Sinhalese-Buddhist culture to keep it pure, the transcultural one is to absorb the "other," to incorporate it into a hegemonic Buddhist-Sinhalese framework and to redefine it in relying on purity as a value (Ambos 2012).

Included in her idea of the absorption of Otherness are low-country Beravā, who in the Independence Day celebrations were incorporated into a homogenizing up-country Sinhala Buddhism that posits ethnic unity in the public sphere. The celebrations revolved around a display of Kandyan culture performed not just in Kandy (celebrations were held in Colombo and elsewhere), to people not from Kandy (that is, to all Sri Lankans and the international community), by people not from Kandy (that is, by Sinhalese from various regions wearing Kandyan dress). A key part of the celebrations was the performance of the up country Kohomba

Kankariya ritual for then-president Rajapaksa, who hails from the low country. The ritual was not so much the absorption of an up country ritual by a low country president as the other way around.[42] The photo Ambos provides for her article shows hundreds of *davula* and *thammättama* drummers (who surely in virtue of their sheer number, are mostly non-Beravā), lined up in Kandyan dress with flags. Why not pick Sabaragamuwa dress for the *davula* and *thammättama* drummers? While the *davula* is part of the Kandyan *hēvisi* ensemble, the *davula* is associated with Sabaragamuwa, the area that is considered to have the oldest Beravā traditions. If the state is trying to portray ancientness and authenticity, why pick Kandyan traditions if Sabaragamuwa ones are assumed to be older? Through the projection of a local Kandyan ritual as transcendent, the syncretic heritage and regional differences between Beravā traditions are elided: "The . . . emergence of an idealized image of 'Buddhism proper,' informed by middle class values, requires the purging [of] 'non-Buddhist' elements, which eventually leads also to a rejection of rural practices, often characterized by syncretism" (Ambos 2012). I suggest this is an extreme example of what is basically happening at every turn to Beravā drumming now, as it has been appropriated by the state in a way that openly subsumes low country ritualists to the hegemony of Kandyan traditions, and that conceptually separates Beravā ritual musics and dance from all of its historical connections with non-Sinhala Sri Lankans, the Indian subcontinent, and Southeast Asia.

Conclusion: The Musicological Potlatch

In Western and Sri Lankan musicological discourses alike, the music of a community that is foreign to one's own is generally not considered a part of one's own music history unless it has influenced one's own compositions and/or performance techniques. Listening to Others is not a part of one's own music history unless those Others are deemed to have changed a self or community that is conceived as having originated before its encounters with Others. Our normative musicological languages thus embed a linguistic distortion that, even when we act supposedly as outside observers (presumed to be excluded from music history *qua* music history), becomes the *form* of music history itself. Sonic relations disappear—or are conceptually transformed—when music appears as the emerged qualities of an inwardly stable person, ethnic group, religion, or nation.[43]

---

[42] This rhetorical use of Kandyan drummers and dancers to legitimize sovereignty is not new. For example, Kemper (1991) notes how President Premadasa had himself inaugurated as president inside the Temple of the Tooth in Kandy, projecting himself as in the line of the precolonial Kandyan kings.

[43] As Bourdieu puts it in his *Outline of a Theory of Practice*, "The 'knowing subject' . . . inflicts on practice a much more fundamental and pernicious alteration which, being a constituent condition of the cognitive operation, is bound to pass unnoticed."

To use terminology promoted by Levi Bryant (2011), the normative musicological mark of distinction indicates self-sound as constituent parts of a collective ("community") rather than as distinct units (self and sound) that can be situated *apart* from one another in different collectives, or situated with other communities in a single collective. Not only does this discount positive examples of inter-ethnic communal relations from a community's music history, it also means that alienating uses of music, such as Rajapaksa's use of the Kohomba Kankariya, are not deemed a part of Tamil music history in Sri Lanka, despite the fact such actions are watched by Others, who adjust their cultural practices according to the discursive and physical spaces lent to them by the state.

The musicological potlatch—the conceptual destruction of musical gifts that arises through the competitive drive to promote music as metonymic for communal identity—is founded on an amnesia of the (visual and aural) gaze, which "is fundamental to human consciousness" (Hansen 2012: 3). As Lacan famously put it, "the subject depends upon the signifier and . . . the signifier is first of all in the field of the Other" (1977: 186). Over the course of the next two chapters, I suggest the anxiety that developed in mid-twentieth century Sri Lanka out of the belief the Sinhalas have no classical music arose not just through comparisons with European classical music but also with already-classicized Indian genres. The genre now known as Sinhala "classical" music (called *sarala gi*; see Chapter 6) has long used North Indian instrumentation like *sitar* and *tabla*, with its purity founded on its drawing on indigenous Sinhala elements, like Buddhist lyrical themes and poetic meters.[44] As I show in Chapter 6, this equalizing gesture led to the purging of Sinhala engagements with North and South Indian musics in the 1950s to create a "pure" Sinhala music and thus "postcolonial demarcations of ethnic boundaries, and with them hierarchical assertions of an ethnosymbolic hierarchy . . . can produce uncanny doubles" (Willford 2006: 2).[45] In conclusion, "we might ask whether the disavowal or surmounting of the Other"—this drive to invent and hold onto a culture supposedly devoid of outside influences—"can produce uncanny doublings which, in turn, fuel overidentification with the ego ideal, or in Heidegger's words, 'ensnare' the subject" (Willford 2006: 2).

The musicological potlatch is an overidentification with the ego ideal that ensnares the subject through its compelling narrative about community, which

---

[44] As Bennett (2001: 96) puts it, paraphrasing Latour, "To be modern . . . is not only to create purity and to create hybrids but also to celebrate the first activity and officially deny the second. The power of modernity as a political and conceptual regime relies on the relegation of hybridization to the status of an open secret."

[45] "True belief, involving the constant reiteration of identity, is one possible symptom of an ascribed identity's fragile hold. At the same time, the function of a master ideology, such as a national ideology, is, ironically, to partially master the alienation and uncertainty that is produced by the Other, which might, in turn, be produced by the master ideology itself" (Willford 2006: 5).

discounts how the community emerged in the first place through relations and competitive engagements with Others that view, listen, and give music to them. Once we realize music ontologically *is* an act of giving, the potlatch readily appears as a violence enacted through the community's desire for recognition, though I do not want to define the recovery of musical giving as a foolhardy attempt to go back to the Real (in Lacan's terminology). Musical giving never generated a pan-ethnic utopia, nor a world beyond identity and difference.[46] But there was a time when sound mattered more because of what it *does* for people through its being offered than for what it says about one's community, and I contend this should matter for the study of music—and for politics and histories of community—in Sri Lanka.

---

[46] We might pause, though, and acknowledge the awe Sunil Goonasekera (2007: 8) expresses when considering the Sinhala- and Tamil-language songs (performed not just by Buddhists and Hindus but also Christians and Muslims) played over loudspeakers at the multi-religious Kataragama shrine. He remarks, "These are . . . loud, vociferous, yet tuneful discourses by the middle and working class people on working with cultural others by contributing appropriate elements from one's own culture for mutual enrichment. They occur in the popular domain and are meaningful to the vast majority of people in this country irrespective of the ethnic and cultural differences among them. Judging by the sheer complexity of the ethnic and cultural interactions involved in the making of these songs, and their tremendous popularity, one gets the feeling that they were made in an ethnic heaven to be played in utopia."

PART III

THE DISCURSIVE ERASURE OF MUSICAL GIVING

5

Beyond the Musicology of Disaster

War, Tsunami, Post-War

> There is something about both death and giving that draws each other to haunt the other, something that silences us with the seeming impossibility of speaking about these matters.
> —Alan Klima (2002: 246)

In fall 2004, I took a four-month, pre-dissertation trip to Sri Lanka. I spent most of my time fumbling about looking for a research project. Tourist guidebooks say the low-country arts are associated with the southern coastal town of Ambalangoda, so I visited the town. I have a memory of swimming off Ambalangoda's shore, looking back at palm trees swaying in the wind. Little did I know that the places I was visiting, including the place where I was swimming, would be destroyed just days after I left, when a tsunami hit on December 26, 2004. As a newcomer to Sri Lanka, most acquaintances I made during that trip were made just in passing; social media was not fully developed. I met many locals and foreigners at seaside hotels, and I'll never know who lived or died. I also carry around much guilt for not having returned for the immediate cleanup. At the time I blamed this on my newfound commitments as a graduate student, but deep down I know I was too scared to witness death and destruction up close, especially in a place I had committed to studying professionally but had barely gotten to know personally.

Recalling the tsunami for Sri Lankans is, say, what recalling September 11 is for Americans: a national tragedy one is sick of hearing about, that now happened long ago, in which one may or may not have been affected, in which everyone knows someone who died, or knows someone who knows someone who died. Everyone remembers where they were, how they would have died themselves if they had boarded that bus or train, and everyone remains traumatized by imagery from that day. Thus it is with some embarrassment that I recall the tsunami here—I feel that I have to, because it was in the aftermath of the tragedy that I learned Sri Lankans use musical gifts as technologies of care.

When I returned a year after the tsunami, I couldn't find that spot where I swam off the coast in Ambalangoda: the shape of the coast had changed and people were living in tents by the shore with U.N. logos on them. Interlocutors reported a jump in the amount of *yak tovils* performed. Besides this indigenous way of using music to cope with disaster, non-governmental organizations had arrived in droves, local and foreign, some with musical troupes in tow. I saw a cultural show at the Galle Face Hotel in Colombo, where staged excerpts of *yak tovils* were performed to raise money to help those affected by the tsunami: I'm not sure the irony of using a de-ritualized, staged version of a healing ritual to raise money for the purpose of healing was grasped by anyone there. Back in Ambalangoda, I learned that the person who stayed in my room before I moved in was a clown who had come to the island to entertain children with songs on guitar. When I returned for a thirteen-month stay in 2007–2008, compilations of songs about the tsunami were still circulating, with proceeds going to local charities. I played drums on one of these, called "Another Monsoon Sunday" (the title refers to the tsunami), written by the local band 10 Second Rule. Composer Eshantha Peiris, a friend and former conductor of Sri Lanka's national symphony orchestra, created an art music version of post-tsunami reflection and healing with his *26/12/2004*, a symphonic work in which a pastoral musical opening takes a violent turn when the tsunami strikes (Figure 5.1). This culture of memorializing disaster, I suggest, is a middle class equivalent of *yak tovil* rituals.

By this time, tsunami warning systems had been set up on the coasts, towers that emit deafening sounds to warn people of impending waves—another use of sound as a technology of care. I saw footage someone filmed of a frightening moment when a tower malfunctioned, causing people to run inland in terror as a worker, realizing the alarm should not have gone off, climbed up and screamed to people below that they didn't have to run. I had entered a post-disaster soundscape.

In early 2006, a woman seated next to me at dinner spoke of how, shortly after the tsunami, a young girl she knew began to speak in a garbled, affected voice. After the problem refused to go away and her behavior became more erratic, the child's parents held a *yak tovil* for her, hoping the ritual would cure her. In the middle of the event, the ritualist asked the child *"Who are you?"* and the girl, gasping for air and barely able to breath, replied that she was the child's aunt, who had died in the tsunami. She was choking on water and that was why she couldn't speak properly: making a motion with her hand above her mouth, she said, "I can't talk because the water's up to here."

I'm not sure how a fieldworker should cope with such events. My initial reaction was to avoid producing a study of disaster that, like a compilation CD or mixtape, would function as a curatorial project in which disasters are collated, or worse, enshrined. Like the stereotype of Africa as a "dark continent" haunted by failure (Ferguson 2006, Mbembe 2000), Sri Lanka as a site of disaster has long haunted the country's identity in the international community, with a profound effect on "development" and "modernity" on the island, as well as the

Figure 5.1 Eshantha Peiris' *26/12/04* captures the terror of the 2004 tsunami: after depicting a pleasant morning on the coast, section "L" marks the moment when the waves hit the shore. Score courtesy of Eshantha Peiris.

confidence and stability of its peoples.[1] The more time I spent on the island, the more "disaster" seemed an insulting way to situate the musicians I worked with. While such tragedies were undoubtedly terrifying for musicians, they were never understood as an integral part of someone's musical identity, nor do Sri Lanka's diverse musical traditions, some of which date back hundreds of years, seem reducible to a narrative on the country's postcolonial problems. In interviews, interlocutors positioned music as the *antithesis* to disaster: music

---

[1] This reputation has been swiftly changing since the war, as in the past several years Sri Lanka has garnered widespread publicity on travel blogs and websites, proclaiming it ready for travelers and open for business.

appeared as the "before" and "after" of disaster; as resilience in the wake of disaster; as the transcendence of politics; and as joy, humanity, and entertainment. Frankly, many of those I interviewed in the former war zones were thrilled I was not another NGO worker there to ask them about disaster. While ethnographers are supposed to situate their object of study within the social context in which they find it, my interlocutors generally defined music as alien to that context.

Yet whenever I tried to place music in a safe space free from disaster, "disaster" surfaced as the elephant in the room. Here I wish to partake, briefly, in that mixtape of disaster I had hoped to avoid. My aim is twofold: first, turning from the tsunami to the war, I will confront how the disaster affected musicians, without suggesting that their music is reducible to it; second, I argue that the issue of how to situate Sri Lankan musics in relation to the island's recent history of disasters is best approached through a recognition that Sri Lankan traditional musics in their original contexts are responses to and ways to protect people from disaster.

After a nonchalant interview with a *kooththu* performer in Akkaraipattu, someone mentioned casually in English (a language the interviewee didn't know) that the man standing in front of me had seen his son shot by the LTTE. One interview I conducted in Mullaitivu was held as a framed photograph of the man's daughter—who was abducted by the LTTE and never returned—hung above us on the wall. In 2008, music students I met in Batticaloa said they often couldn't get to the Eastern University for classes because of checkpoints or roadblocks. A theme that routinely came up in conversations with Tamil musicians in Jaffna is that their instruments were often flagged at checkpoints because soldiers feared they were hiding bomb-making materials. One Jaffna Tamil musician told me his instrument probably saved his life during the time of the Indian Peacekeeping Force (IPKF) in the late 1980s. He was driving home on his scooter from a gig with his drum; when approaching an intersection, he noticed civilians lying on the scorching pavement in the afternoon sun. An IPKF soldier pointed his gun at him and told him to lie down as well. The soldier was telling people in the intersection, one by one, to "come with me." It seemed he was deciding whether they would be killed or not. One girl my interlocutor knew, who was out buying medicine for her father, was raped; he heard this happening while lying on the pavement. When it was finally his turn, the soldiers were perplexed about his *mridangam* (drum)—it was in a carrying case and they worried it was hiding bomb-making materials. They decided to let him survive if he could take the drum out and play it, proving he is a drummer. Perversely, here the musical gift becomes protective through its ability to display the identity of the performer as a drummer. Similarly, one time a Tamil musician in Jaffna was leaving a wedding gig when fighting between the LTTE and government forces left two people dead, whose bodies he saw lying in the street; the military detained him because they were suspicious of the carrying case that held his drum; after tearing the instrument apart and checking for bomb-making materials, they let him go.² Another musician said the tuner for his *mridangam* was mistaken for a weapon at a checkpoint; the soldiers were also suspicious when they saw powder on his hands (used for drumming) and worried it was residue from making a bomb. One Jaffna Tamil musician reported Sinhala soldiers paid visits to his house to borrow his *mridangam* to play at their camp; sometimes, they would ask if he could drum for them while they were blowing off steam at night. To my surprise, he said he was not scared of these Sinhala soldiers, as they treated him respectfully on such occasions. I heard about one drummer who got his hand cut off for playing for the LTTE, though I have no idea who it was who did the cutting.

During the IPKF period, the son of the eminent *nadaswaram* player N. K. Pathmanathan was in Sri Lanka on holiday from India (where he was studying music) and was killed by the Indian army when, not being used to having military around, he poked his head up to see what was going on and got shot, an incident recalled by several musicians in Jaffna.³ One time the IPKF raided a music school in Jaffna looking for weapons and saw only musical instruments; in deference to the instruments, the soldiers took off their shoes and stepped around them (a common practice throughout South and Southeast Asia), all the while using their weapons aggressively as they poked around the room. The respect shown to the instruments but not the local people was not lost on my interlocutors.

One musician in Jaffna (I'll call him Rajan) told me how during the IPKF time, at one point a battle raged between the Indian army and LTTE at the junction across from his house. Fighting went on for hours, and a shell landed on his house, destroying half of it. The armies eventually moved on, but the battle continued between two soldiers firing at each other at close range. After an uneasy silence broke out, Rajan looked out his window and saw the bodies of both soldiers, dead, lying next to each other, their blood running into the same gutter. He recounted this story to me nonchalantly, in the midst of a conversation about his father's band who played popular music in Jaffna in the 1960s/1970s.

Rajan's story is one of persisting through decades of violence to forge a career recording music, even when he was physically immobile and could rarely perform live. After the Sri Lankan military took control of Jaffna in 1995, he fled to the jungle around Mullaitivu, working as a driver and recording patriotic songs for the LTTE. He returned to Jaffna after the 2002 ceasefire, but with the government in control of the city, he was unable to leave home without crossing checkpoints in every direction, risking detainment and torture. So he stayed home as much as possible—and was thus trapped in his home for almost ten years (the war ended

---

[2] I encountered my own (albeit less life-threatening) version of this in 2008 when I drove with a bandmate to a gig in Colombo with a Western-style drum kit and a soldier pulled us over, worried my drum stands might be a weapon.

[3] Kartigesu Sivathamby, "A Music Maestro and Leader of a Community—Nagalingam K. Pathmanathan." *Northeastern Herald*, July 25–31, 2003."

in 2009, but it took a few more years for the checkpoints to truly ease and freer movement to be allowed). Sometime during this period, Rajan got an Internet connection. He began recording songs at his home studio and sending them over the Internet to his brother (who had escaped and moved to Tamil Nadu), who got them released in South Indian films. Rajan was unable to play many live concerts during these years, but he developed a career making CDs of devotional music for Hindu temples.

When the LTTE was in control of Jaffna from 1990 to 1994, one musician told me, they could perform whenever they wanted but had no electricity. Once the government took control of the area, electricity gradually returned, but they could only perform during daylight hours because of curfews. At that time, she said, to go from her house in Jaffna to Vadamarachchi (28 kilometers) would require going through twenty to thirty checkpoints and take many hours. By her reckoning, by that point 90% of Jaffna's musicians had left. Someone else said, "Most of the people died or went abroad." Musicians remember periods when they had to change professions: one I met developed a second career as a wedding photographer. Temple festivals were often held in the mornings or not at all; people could generally play music (*thavil* and *nadaswaram*) inside temples but would not broadcast it on loudspeakers outside. One musician said his family moved from Jaffna to India from 1987 to 1991, returned in 1992, left for Colombo in 1995, returned to Jaffna in 2002, left during the conclusion of the war between 2006 and 2009, and then returned to Jaffna. A *parai* drummer in Mullaitivu told me that when he was forced to flee to an IDP (internally displaced person) camp he hid his *parai* inside his chimney, tying it with string. He said they had nothing in the camps: they were behind a fence, no temples, no festivals, no music, they could only wait—and when he finally returned home, his chimney was empty, his drum stolen.

An entire book needs to be written about the experiences of Tamil musicians during the war—this is not that book. Yet while I am resistant to the "disaster porn" I have provided above, ignoring it would be just as perverse. Eventually I had to accept, against the wishes of some interlocutors, that the idea of music as a safe space from disaster is problematic. As the above shows, war changed the configuration of musicians and genres in the north and east, while in the south, the tsunami washed away the spot where I watched my first Devol Maduwa. More to my point, once one ropes music off as safe from disaster, its value appears too easily to reside only in its long-term value to the community that performs it— musical giving becomes obscured by the terms of the music and identity episteme. And this makes it hard to recognize *similarities in purpose* between Sri Lankan forms of musical giving.

For example, let's return to the story about the *yak tovil* for the little girl. Such rituals are moments when the trauma of historical events are confronted and shaped. To understand the value of this ritual simply as the expression of the identity of the "performer" and "audience" when situating it in a historical narrative discounts the ritual's transformative capabilities, which provide its reason for being. Through that framework, rituals become less about psychological maneuvering and more about authenticity and ancientness. They become less about the way ritual helps and more about the communal identities of the people who turn to it. As we saw above, the identity produced by ritual in this case was not an ethnic or religious identity but a familial one: the deceased aunt of a shattered little girl. It would be more appropriate to situate low-country drumming in a history of *help* and of *kin*.

Let's compare this case with a Tamil anecdote recounted by the anthropologist Patricia Lawrence (1997). She undertook her dissertation research in Batticaloa at the height of the war there in the mid-1990s.[4] Lawrence says one time she was at a Hindu festival when Sri Lankan army forces raided it to round up men assumed to be LTTE militants. A ritual officiant, possessed by the Goddess Kali, frantically chased the soldiers around the temple grounds, his tongue sticking out *as Kali*. I can think of no other incident that more profoundly ropes together the divine, personal, political, profane, and *musical* under one roof (for becoming Kali in such a context surely is not possible without drumming). What could be a more liberating expletive than to have Kali inside you, sticking your tongue out at the soldiers who devastated your community, killed your brothers and sisters, ruined your life? The exasperation, fury, and divine laughter embedded in this incident was a force to be reckoned with: the soldiers couldn't take it, as they were chased out of the temple. The fact that music is so prevalent in temple festivals (it probably occurred before, and perhaps during and after, this incident), the fact that dancers possessed by Kali and other gods moved during the war to music in arenas that were at once safe and unsafe spaces, should draw our attention to ethno/musicology's failure to draw a truce between the eventful history of music and the musicful history of the event: is Kali's engagement with soldiers in this incident a part of music history? Or does music history become something else in such moments?

Now, consider the similarities between how *musical meaning* emerged in both these cases—for the first event belongs to a Sinhala Buddhist context, the latter to a Tamil Hindu one. Musical meaning in both was relational: it emerged through connections between the living and dead, gods, supernatural power, ritualists, trauma, violence, fear of the divine, fear of death, and so on. Undoubtedly, there are significant soteriological differences between the offerings made in a *yak tovil* and those by Tamils for Kali: this must be emphasized. But both are variations of a similar ethos, of sonic transactions with the divine in order to protect humans in this world. Such connections and the similarities between them are made peripheral to cultural history when we transition from a retelling of these events to histories of "the" culture of Sinhalas and Tamils. Through a cultural history

---

[4] Personal communication, 2008. The following story is a canonic one in Sri Lankan studies.

of community, such connections and the similarities between them become interpreted as "surplus" meaning, what Bataille (1988: 26) calls "the movement that exceeds." A standard ethnicized music history dispels or contains this surplus in the drive to attach music to a community. Rather than view sound/music as a gift and way of caring for others, the normative music history interprets it as an arrow pointing back to those who "perform music," saying, "this is you." It is in such moments of translation that ethno/musicology creates its own potlatch, destroying musical gifts through the act of representing them—a foundational, destructive irony of music history.

The Musical Gift Writ Large

The point I want to stress, though, is that the erasure of musical giving is a social context that determines significant aspects of the world in which people live. Consider how the late Kartigesu Sivathamby, one of Sri Lanka's most revered Tamil intellectuals, spelled out for me (in an interview) the significance of the erasure of a Tamil Hindu musical offering to Sri Lanka's Sinhala president and prime minister in the climate of war:

> After '83, so many things have happened here, Sir.[5] The whole pattern has changed. After '83, with '83, there is a fear that you cannot have, except in very closed-door circumstances, open Tamil music performances. *Do you know what would happen?* Do you know that, in Colombo, during the time July–August, during the time the festival is held at Kataragama, there is a Vel festival.[6] And they (used to) bring in great Indians to play here.[7] And that has completely stopped since '83. They (would) start playing at the temple in Pettah, then the procession comes and stops in front of the president's house, then the president comes out, they play there, then they come to Temple Trees [the prime minister's residence], the prime minister used to be there, they play there, and then they come to the temple. People are afraid now. Do you know how the average Sinhalese man looks at Carnatic music? He calls it the *dosa kadai* ["dosa shop," i.e., a Tamil restaurant], because that is where the Carnatic [South Indian Tamil] songs are played. You see, there has been, from the time of the 1930s–1940s, there has been

---

[5] July 1983 was the official start of Sri Lanka's civil war.

[6] The festival he refers to is the Hindu festival held in July–August in Colombo that honors the deity Murugan. Devotees march from a Tamil *kovil* (Hindu temple) in Pettah (the market district) to Wellawatta in the southwest of the city.

[7] He means Indian musicians from Tamil Nadu, although Sri Lankan Tamil musicians would have also performed.

this sort of sense of internal rivalry, which made the Sinhalese go for Hindustani music and not Carnatic music [my italics].

How should we understand this frightening yet informative description of the rupture in musical relations between Sinhalese and Tamil communities that occurred "from the time of the 1930s–1940s," culminating in the rupture of 1983? I explore this history in the next chapter; here I want to emphasize that Sivathamby is pointing out how, with the official start of war in 1983, a history of respect shown between Sinhalas and Tamils through a musical offering, where Tamil musicians honored the Sinhala president and prime minister in the context of a Hindu festival, was erased by mutual enmity and fear. After this, he says, Tamil music was driven indoors and resignified as a potentially dangerous activity. A musical gift cannot be made to a this-worldly sovereign if the sovereign fails to protect the community. Here the failure of the musical gift is indicative of the failure of the social contract.

An important outcome of the erasure of such musical gifts, Sivathamby makes clear, is that for a long time, *silencing* became the context in which Tamil musicians were forced to act in Sri Lanka. Consider the scratching of records (in both meanings of the term) described by a Tamil consultant knowledgeable about the history of the Sri Lanka Broadcasting Corporation (SLBC). He said there was once an excellent Tamil *sarala gi* singer (this is typically considered a "Sinhala" genre) named S. K. Pararajasingham, and

> SLBC did all those recordings [of his]. At the time I was supposed to be an advisor [to the radio station], but later, politics changed, and we fell out. And then [the new director] took over. And the worst part was, the staff had such an animosity towards us [Tamils]. What they had done is, they had virtually scratched off all those recordings [of Pararajasingham's] which we had made. This happened around 1979, 1981.

Some interlocutors told me that *all* the recordings made by Tamil musicians at SLBC were scratched with safety pins in the early 1980s, though I have been unable to verify this. This was around the time of the burning of the Jaffna Public Library (in 1981), an act of cultural genocide in which thousands of irreplaceable Tamil documents were destroyed.

The scratching of records with safety pins is a metonym for a process of silencing that is a social context created *by* others through which one's creativity is forced to act. Tamil musicians in Sri Lanka were not silenced per se but their musical contributions were redirected through *silencing*: the hiding of Tamil sounds behind closed doors; the resignification of Tamil sounds as a threat to Sinhala lives; the redefinition of Tamil sounds as "Indian" rather than "Sri Lankan"; the transformation of Tamil sounds (through phrases like *dosa kadai*) into a symbol of a debased form of humanity. *"Do you know what would happen?"* Sivathamby asked about the possibility of "open Tamil music performances": this statement highlights the possibility of a musicology of fear, one foundation of which would be the study of the erasure of musical giving.

The Resilience of Musical Giving

While many Sri Lankans continue to suffer from structural violence and poverty, it should be emphasized that the tragedies and some of the anxieties mentioned above now belong firmly to the past. Today, Jaffna, Trincomalee, and Batticaloa are vibrant cities with new restaurants, thriving temple festivals, and traffic-clogged streets. Visitors to Sri Lanka will hear Carnatic music blasting at Tamil establishments across the country, inside and outside Hindu temples (through loudspeakers), in Hindu processions, and at concert halls. According to 2015 statistics from the Ministry of Settlement, 5,600 Tamils have returned to the island since 2011—not a huge number, but promising nonetheless.[8] When I visited the Muslim town of Kattankudy in 2015, it had been significantly refurbished, with shiny new buildings and roadside decorations, due to an influx of money from foreign Muslims (and Sri Lankan Muslims working abroad). A museum on the history of Muslims in Sri Lanka had opened to much fanfare. The new mood is demonstrated from another angle by the emergence of Arjun Coomaraswamy, a Sri Lanka-born, London-based R&B performer, whose remix of the song "Why This Kolaveri Di?" went viral in India. He won Best Urban Act at the 2012 UK Asian Music Awards. From Colombo and born to a Sinhala mother and Tamil father, Arjun has sung a Punjabi-flavored fusion song and a Sinhala remix of the classic song "Oye Ojaya" for the Sri Lankan music market.[9]

Indian musicians have started returning to the north. In October 2011, Chennai-based Carnatic vocalist T. M. Krishna became the first Indian musician to tour the north in nearly three decades.[10] Organized by the Indian High Commission and Indian Cultural Centre in Colombo, Krishna performed in Jaffna's Veerasingham Hall, followed by concerts in Kilinochchi and Vavuniya. Krishna said that after his Kilinochchi concert an "elderly gentleman with tears in his eyes came up to me and said that this was the happiest moment in the last thirty years of his life."[11] After the Jaffna concert, Krishna met several hundred

---

[8] Gazala Anver and Maryam Azwer, "Returning Home after the War: Not Refugees Anymore," Roar.lk, December 1, 2015.

[9] "Arjun Commaraswamy: Sri Lankan Born R&B Artist in UK," uslanka.net, October 8, 2013.

[10] The last Indian musician to tour northern Sri Lanka before the war was reportedly the playback singer M. L. Vasanthakumari in 1983, who had to quit midway through because of the start of war. Arunabha Deb, "A Varnam in Jaffna," *Indian Express.com*, October 16, 2011.

[11] T. M. Krishna, "Beyond the Scars: 'I Have Never Met Another Community That Treats Artists the Way These People Do,'" *Transcurrents.com*, October 23, 2011.

students from the Ramanathan Academy of Fine Arts (RAFA), the major institution for music and dance in Jaffna.¹² Krishna returned to Jaffna in August, 2012, when he organized a small festival that included performances and lecture-demonstrations by vocalist P. Unnikrishnan and Bharatanatyam dancer Alarmel Valli.¹³ Krishna said he hopes Jaffna can regain the status it once held as a cultural hub and suggested that in fifteen years the situation might again be like it was in the 1930s, when musicians from India routinely traveled back and forth between India and Jaffna: "I hope we [Indians] get world-class musicians from Jaffna."¹⁴

The memory of Jaffna's Carnatic music legacy has reemerged in India of late. In 2016, a documentary about a highly regarded though largely forgotten *thavil* player from Jaffna who made it big in South India in the 1960s, Yazhpanam Thedchanamoorthy Pillai, won the award for Best Arts/Cultural Film at the 63rd National Film Awards in India. The film contains interviews with Carnatic musicians proclaiming him a genius, such as R. K. Srikantan, musicologist B. M. Sundaram, and drummer Palghat Mani Iyer (who proclaimed Thedchanamoorthy "the eighth wonder"). Actor Sivaji Ganesan was a fan, and Thedchanamoorthy played with several well-known *nadaswaram* players of his day, including Karukurichi Arunachalam. After living in Thanjavur for a few years, Thedchanamoorthy was haunted by depression and moved back to Jaffna, where he died at the young age of forty-two: "He came, he conquered and he perished," is how his cousin put it.¹⁵ Director Amshan Kumar remarked that, "At times, Indian Tamils project a sense of superiority over Sri Lankan Tamil artists. But Thedchanamoorthy rubbished it by being the best thavil player of the time."¹⁶

From the late nineteenth century through 1914, Indian musicians regularly visited Jaffna by taking the "Boat Mail" service, which brought a passenger by train from Madras (now Chennai) to the South Indian port city of Tuticorin (a journey of around twenty-two hours), followed by a steamer to Colombo. After the bridge to Pamban island was built (the island owned by India that houses the Rameswaram pilgrimage site), the railway route was changed to end at Dhanushkodi (the southeastern tip of Pamban), where a ferry brought passengers the 31 kilometers (19 miles) to Talaimannar, a small settlement on Mannar Island. In 1964, the service

---

¹² RAFA was established by the son-in-law of Sir Ponnambalam Ramanathan, S. Nadesapillai, to promote Carnatic and Sri Lankan Tamil music and dance. It was taken over by the University of Sri Lanka after the establishment of a Jaffna Campus, producing its first graduates in 1998 (Notes on RAFA provided by a consultant, Jaffna, 2015).

¹³ This event was sponsored by RAFA and the Svanubhava Festival Committee in Chennai through the Indian High Commission, the Sri Lankan government, and governor of the Northern Province. "Alarmel Valli, T. M. Krishna and P. Unnikrishnan to perform in Jaffna, Sri Lanka." *Kutcheribuzz.com*, August 14, 2012.

¹⁴ T. M. Radhakrishnan, "Indian Carnatic Vocalist T. M. Krishna Enthralls Jaffna, Kilinochchi, and Vavuniya." Transcurrents.com, October 7, 2011.

¹⁵ Meera Srinivasan, "A Jaffna Thavil Maestro's Thanjavur Connection," *The Hindu*, June 13, 2016.

¹⁶ Vishal Menon, "The Thavil That United Tamils," *The Hindu*, April 3, 2016.

was discontinued after about a hundred people were killed when the train they were on at Pamban was washed out to sea during a cyclone, the tracks destroyed. By that point, though, musicians were routinely flying from Chennai to Palaly airport in Jaffna (and vice versa). During those years, a musician in Jaffna told me, his father so routinely performed in South India that one month he made the trip from Palaly to Chennai ten times. He said the flights stopped in 1979 (the Sri Lanka air force moved onto the site around 1976). In 1982, the site became an "Air Field Unit," and then a high security zone, and from 1990 to 1995 it was the only government-controlled area in Jaffna, a critical stronghold for the government who used it to send materials to GoSL soldiers. But things have now changed. In 2013, I took the newly relaunched flight between Colombo and Palaly, and in summer 2015, it was announced that Sri Lanka plans to hold discussions with the Indian government to reopen the ferry service. At the time of writing, though, Indian musicians can only get to Jaffna by flying to Colombo and taking a long train or bus ride north, flying past Jaffna to drive up to it. I think Indian musicians would be among the first to celebrate the return of the Boat Mail—as long as they could get to their gigs on time.

From the 1980s through 2009, when Jaffna became one of the most isolated places on earth, its people became one of the most international. Families dispersed to Australia, Canada, London, and many other places besides. They became leaders in the worlds of Bharata Natyam and Carnatic music in the diaspora. Musicians who stayed during the war years told me they are pleased to see so many people with new ideas and lifestyles move back to or visit Jaffna. In 2015, I met two *thavil*-playing brothers in Jaffna who studied music in Chennai in their youth, and after living in Jaffna, they moved back to Chennai during the war and stayed there; they were in town to perform at a temple festival, and regaled me with stories of concerts played in Singapore, Sydney, the United States, and elsewhere. A famous *nadaswaram* player in Jaffna in the 1970s and 1980s, Kuttaalingam Maanikkam, had two daughters who grew up to form a *nadaswaram* and *thavil* duo, including Rajeswary Suntharalingam on *nadaswaram* and Pushparani Thiruchelvam on *thavil* (according to the *Indian Express*, one of just two female *thavil* players in Jaffna and probably all of Sri Lanka).[17] The duo has played in India, Malaysia, and Singapore.[18]

Meanwhile, the *parai* is having a renaissance. The drum has been prevalent at the multi-ethnic and international Galle and Jaffna music festivals (the first one in Jaffna was in 2011), arranged by the Sri Lanka-Norway Music Cooperation (SLNMC) and the NGO Sevalanka. Emerging in the post-war period, the SLNMC now organizes a "village level performance program" aimed at preserving and reviving folk traditions. They have arranged events to raise awareness

---

[17] P. K. Balachandran, "Lanka's Woman Thavil Players Fading Away," *The Hindu*, May 21, 2013.
[18] Dushiyanthini Kanagasabapathipillai, "Two Jaffna Sisters Playing the 'Nathaswaram' and 'Thavil' in Male Dominated Music Sphere," *Ceylon Today*, Friday, April 5, 2013.

and de-stigmatize the *parai,* and have raised money for musical instruments, performances, and travel expenses for *parai* drummers.[19] Gillian Howell describes one gathering held by SLNMC at the Swami Vipulananda Institute of Aesthetic Studies at the Eastern University in Batticaloa, where elder drummers came and taught rhythms to Tamil students. As Howell puts it, such events help "preserve and celebrate the knowledge of the elder musicians by training the next generation of performers, and of sidestepping the hostility toward the *parai* drum within the musicians' own communities."[20] The silencing of Tamil music thus seems to be a thing of the past—though it is debatable whether it has been eliminated altogether.

Economies of Reconciliation

How does one suture relations previously formed through musical giving? The activists' work above is geared toward addressing the status of the *parai* among Tamils, and re-connecting Sri Lankan and Indian Tamil musical worlds. This is necessary work, but would Tamil musicians feel content to once again honor a Sinhala president with a musical offering? I'm not sure they would, nor am I sure that they should. Is the emergence of inter-communal musical relations (e.g., Sinhala-Tamil musical relations) necessary for reconciliation and healing in postwar Sri Lanka? I don't think so: I suggest constant dialogue with Others is less important for peace than simply a lack of violence and hostility. Yet as I show throughout this book, Sri Lanka's music history is filled with communal interactions to such an extent that the existence of a completely musically divided island, with little or no inter-communal musical interactions is actually a new state of affairs. I suggest we remember Pierre Clastres' (2010: 256) statement that "it is not that war is the effect of segmentation, it is segmentation that is the effect of war." While a lack of violence toward Others is necessary for peace and security, I suggest a key part of reconciliation should be the promotion not just of inter-ethnic artistic collaborations but of cultural histories of ethnic interaction—which after all is the aim of this book.

I conclude this chapter by considering some examples of individuals and organizations doing important work on music as reconciliation in post-war Sri Lanka. My aim is to ask questions relevant for their projects and this book: What constitutes a successful use of music for reconciliation? What *are* peace, healing, reconciliation, and music, anyway? (I suggest NGOs have spent more time querying the former three terms than the latter.) Is there a role for articulating narratives of musical similarity and historical relatedness between Sri Lankan

---

[19] Gillian Howell, "Access All Areas: Researcher," http://musicwork.wordpress.com, June 6, 2016.
[20] Howell, "Access All Areas."

communal musical cultures in staged performances? I argue that when activists hold onto the identity paradigm, they are more likely to reinforce divisions produced by ethnonationalists; the promotion of histories of musical giving—in which a group is acknowledged to have a separate identity but as being historically connected to Others—is a more productive way to use music as reconciliation.

The Failure of the Musical Gift

In 2015, I came across a fascinating experiment being undertaken by a Sri Lankan NGO. Based on the "El Sistema" model pioneered in Venezuela, where European classical music is brought to poor communities to productively occupy their time and steer them away from drugs and gangs, this NGO (who will remain nameless) was described in a news article I read as bringing Sinhala and Tamil youths together through European classical music. Intrigued, I contacted the organization. I was unable to get an interview with the head of the NGO, but I spent a day with their teachers and taught Western-style drum set to Tamil schoolchildren in a rural town in the Vanni district.

It did not take long to realize something is drastically wrong with how this this NGO operates. The organization is based in a Sinhala town in the hill country; it provides music lessons for Sinhala schoolchildren there. Lessons are held for Tamil schoolchildren in the rural Tamil village in the Vanni. The two groups of students don't learn together. The same teachers teach music in both places, alternating their weeks of teaching in each place. The teachers are Sinhala, and they live in the Sinhala town, and on the weeks they teach in the Tamil village they stay at a house rented by the NGO. They seemed to have minimal contact with the Tamil kids and their families. While the news article I read made it sound like the Sinhala and Tamil children are taking lessons and performing together, this could not be farther from the truth. After being around for several years, the NGO had organized just one performance where the Sinhala and Tamil children performed together, and for this the Tamil kids were bussed to the Sinhala town.

The situation appeared even more problematic when I spent time with the teachers. While undoubtedly kind individuals, they made noticeably little effort to interact with the Tamil schoolchildren. The one I worked most closely with did not use their names or converse with them through any basic Tamil vocabulary, even a basic greeting like "*Vanakkam*" ("Hello"). There was a severe language barrier, which European classical music, as supposedly enlightening high art, was mobilized to overcome.

When I asked the teachers about this, one was clear about the universal power of European classical music. It is something that has been shown to help children: "There have been studies," he said. When I asked the Sinhala teacher why he was teaching music to the Tamil kids, he said (and here I place my emphasis), "*They* were affected by the war. We are bringing music to help *them*." It did not dawn on this person that he, too—that all Sri Lankans—were affected by the war. Nor did it dawn on him that he could have learned something musical *from* the Tamil children. Nor, it seemed, did he think Sinhala and Tamil music could have been equally shared—given—between the teachers and students in class. Unsurprisingly, it was clear to me the Tamil kids saw these teachers as another example of a masculine Sinhala presence (the teachers were all male) that might as well have been the state. The teachers were Power, and they were giving the kids European classical music to help them because *they* were the ones who had suffered in the war. How nice.

This NGO's work is the clearest example I found of the failure of musical giving. Here, the "new orthodoxy" of "the nongovernmental organization (NGO) as the primary agent in its vision of development" (Stirrat and Henkel 1997: 67) and its concomitant discourse on generosity merges with the subordination of the will of one intelligence to another, what Rancière calls "stultification" (1991: 13).[21] We can see from this example that it is wrong to romanticize music by treating it as a leveling phenomenon, as for instance Fukushima (2011: 11) does when she says that, "Classical music has no borders, for which reason musicians from different backgrounds can play together. . . . By sharing music stands and playing together, they come to respect each other for their respective music skills." By contrast, the example I provide here shows that music can construct and reinforce borders even when it is mobilized to erase them. Activists working with music need to think critically about how they are defining music, and how best it might work to positively connect people.

While I don't want to appear as though I was a hero who came in and changed the situation at the school in a day, the whole system was so distressing that I tried, if not too subtly, and at least somewhat politely, to change the situation. I asked the kids to play Tamil rhythms on the Western drum set; I played some of my rhythms for them; I played some *baila* rhythms on the drum kit, a genre nowadays associated with Sinhala culture. I learned their names. I talked to them a bit in Tamil. It made a huge difference. The Sinhala musician was visibly surprised and said something about how he couldn't believe these were the same kids he had gotten used to teaching. To be clear, I don't blame him or the other Sinhala teachers for how their teaching gig was set up—they are musicians, and they need jobs. I believe they sincerely cared about helping the children, and I don't fashion myself a musical Santa, bestowing musical gifts. But the whole event made me see how music, *as a gift*, can be offered in ways that are alienating. Here the musical gift, offered as a way to reforge the social contract, contributed to its lack of fruition.

---

[21] "What starts off as a pure gift, an act of seemingly disinterested giving, morally and ethically divorced from the mundane world, becomes in the end an object or a service intimately entwined in the mundane and interested world" (Stirrat and Henkel 1997: 69).

Post-War Musical Giving

Luckily, several organizations in Sri Lanka have better utilized music to promote peace, healing, and reconciliation, even if they have not described their activities through a language of sonic generosity. The aforementioned Galle and Jaffna Music Festivals emerged in 2009 and 2011 (respectively), the aim being to strengthen "reconciliation between Sri Lankan communities across ethnic and religious boundaries through music, especially traditional folk music, which very beautifully depicts Sri Lanka's multi-ethnic and multi-cultural identity."[22] First held in Galle in 2009, alternating each year between Sinhala-dominated Galle and Tamil-dominated Jaffna, the concerts are produced by the Sevalanka Foundation with help from Concerts Norway and Aru Sri Art Theatre. The Jaffna festivals have brought Sinhala and non-Sri Lankan musicians to the region for the first time in decades. One highlight of the Galle Festival in 2016 was the performance of Thappu, an all-female Kilinochchi-based group of Tamil drummers who play the *thappu* frame drum. At one point during the festival, they collaborated with Thurya, an all-female Sinhala drum troupe who play Sinhala drums (the *gäta beraya, yak beraya, davula*, and *thammättama*).[23]

The mother of all reconciliation concerts was held on March 6, 2012, when Kalasuri Arunthathy Sri Ranganathan arranged for one hundred musicians from all districts of Sri Lanka to perform together. Hailing from Jaffna, she has long worked at the Sri Lanka Broadcasting Corporation and founded the Aru Sri Art Theatre group in 2004. The group promotes reconciliation through "harmony concerts" and dance dramas. The 2012 concert was hosted by the Kadirgamar Institute, which has organized an annual National Conference on Reconciliation since 2011. The event featured a multi-ethnic "Oriental Music Orchestra," with musicians from India, Norway, Bangladesh, and Palestine, who performed with Sinhala, Tamil, Muslim, and Burgher musicians from all of Sri Lanka's provinces. The troupe was invited to perform in April 2012 in Bintan, Indonesia, and in Singapore at the Sri Senpaga Vinayagar temple, where Tamil and Sinhala dancers performed Bharata Natyam. I do not know what music was played in the Southeast Asian concerts, but the repertoire for the Sri Lanka event included a South Indian Carnatic composition from one of the foundational "trinity" of Carnatic composers, Mutthuswamy Dikshitar, as well as a North Indian Hindustani composition and a Sinhala composition. The instruments played included "Tamil" instruments such as the *veena, mridangam*, and violin (which has

---

[22] "A Musical Way of Life," *Sunday Observer*, January 31, 2016.

[23] One organization that deserves mention but whom I only conducted a few interviews with is the famous Center for Performing Arts, founded in Jaffna in 1965, which now has twenty-five branches across the island. The CPA uses the arts for conflict resolution and to promote coexistence. I have not ignored them purposely, but rather their work seems to use theater more so than music. It deserves a full study of its own.

long been indigenized by Tamils), the *sitar* (a North Indian instrument often associated with Sinhala culture), *tabla* (North Indian drums associated with both Sinhala and Tamil communities in Sri Lanka), and the usual Sinhala drums (*gäta beraya, yak beraya, davula* and *thammättama*).[24]

Musicmatters is a school and DIY performance space in Colombo, founded in 2010, to introduce (according to their website) "an alternative model for Western music education in Sri Lanka."[25] They also host a monthly "Big Ears Music Series" and an annual music festival that brings in international performers. Founded by the aforementioned composer and pianist Eshantha Peiris (who is also my research assistant) and jazz (and *yak beraya*) drummer and scholar Sumudi Suraweera, the institute includes a few foreign teachers, such as New Zealand bassist Isaac Smith.[26] With a grant from Deutsche Gesellschaft für Internationale Zusammenarbeit GmbH (GIZ), Suraweera and Peiris (who are Sinhalese) launched the Musicmatters Trans-coastal Collective, a collaboration with Tamil music students from the Swami Vipulananda Institute at Eastern University in Batticaloa. The idea for the project, Peiris says, was to "encourage critical thought processes in Sri Lankans through promoting experimental music." They drove the eight or nine hours to Batticaloa to meet with the principal of the Vipulananda Institute, who approved the project. Subsequent rehearsals were held in Batticaloa, with the Colombo musicians driving instruments there for rehearsal. The group played at the Musicmatters festival in 2015, generating much press, and a concert in Batticaloa was held in early 2016. While the Tamil members of the ensemble have shifted a bit, those who performed at the Colombo concert were Lavanya Mahadeva, Kisnaveni Palasingam, Selvaraj Rajiv, Baskaramurthi Satheeswaran and Meiyanathan Ketheeswaran.[27]

The Musicmatters collective are trained as rock and jazz musicians, and in their concerts, they are known for long-form improvisations. Peiris describes how they first imagined the Trans-coastal collaboration:

> Our intent for the project was to use songs from Batticaloa as a starting point for longer improvisations. So during the first few meetings we asked the Batticaloa musicians to sing me songs from Batticaloa, which we then transcribed. They found it rather strange that we were interested in Batticaloa songs, since they seemed to attach more value to South Indian and Jaffna music. The songs they sang for us

---

[24] A similar event was the Interfaith Music Festival held in February 2012, organized by Mother Sri Lanka Trust and the Art of Living Foundation: the event brought together children from across Sri Lanka to perform Buddhist, Hindu, Christian, and Islamic music and chanting on a single stage.

[25] http://www.musicmatterssrilanka.com/

[26] Suraweera also wrote a PhD thesis on Raigam Korale drumming (2009).

[27] "Exciting, Confusing: We Are Talking Music!" *Sunday Times Magazine*, August 30, 2015.

were ... mostly *kooththu* songs as documented by Maunaguru, which they had been taught as part of their degree program."[28]

As with any collaboration between musicians conversant in different musical styles, the musicians had to figure out how to play together. The Colombo musicians first intended to develop "shared improvisational techniques," but this proved difficult because of the inability to have regular rehearsals and due to the language barrier between Sinhala and Tamil. Peiris says the Colombo musicians first borrowed a *maththalam* from *kooththu* master Sinniah Maunaguru, but the Tamil students were more comfortable with what he called "Indian instruments," the *tabla* and harmonium.[29] Eventually, a format developed in which the Batticaloa musicians' songs formed the foundation for the music while the Musicmatters folks would fill out the sound and improvise off the material. The result, according to Peiris, is perhaps more a "juxtaposition rather than a collaboration," but he notes the ensemble has important symbolic value and I would add it has received rave reviews.[30]

Tanya Ekanayaka is a globally recognized performer, composer, and linguist who grew up in Kandy and conducted research in linguistics and musicology for a PhD from the University of Edinburgh. A renowned pianist (she records on the Naxos label) and part-time faculty member at Edinburgh University, Ekanayaka is a fellow of the Trinity College of Music–London.[31] Ekanayaka's recitals include her own compositions, some of which draw on Sri Lankan "folk melodies" that are "reinterpreted, transformed and integrated within musical frameworks inspired by the Western classical works of the same program."[32] In 2012, she accepted an offer from SCJ87, an Australian nonprofit formed by graduates of the 1987 batch of students at St. John's College, Jaffna, to hold a workshop in Jaffna to encourage students to heal by expressing themselves through music. The workshop was held at Chundikuli Girls' College. One observer of the event reported that Ekanayaka

---

[28] Maunaguru is the professor at Eastern University whose influence on *kooththu* I considered in Chapter 3. It's interesting to consider the preference shown here among the Batticaloan musicians for what Peiris describes as "South Indian and Jaffna music" rather than the local *kooththu*.

[29] It's interesting to me, given my discussion in Chapter 4 of the *maththalam*'s origins in South India and its reputation as the ancestor of the *mridangam*, that Peiris describes the *maththalam* here as "Sri Lankan" and the *tabla* and *harmonium* as "Indian." It is also significant that in India, these latter two instruments are more commonly defined as North Indian rather than South Indian. And, in the mid-twentieth century when Sinhalese musicians cultivated close connections with North India (see the next chapter), these latter instruments were defined as North Indian but arguably more associated with the Sinhalas than Tamils.

[30] I regret I was unable to include the Tamil musicians' perspectives here, as I found out about this collaboration late in my research.

[31] DBS Jeyaraj, "Post-War Jaffna Children feel the Healing Touch of Music," *Daily Mirror*, September 9, 2012.

[32] DBS Jeyaraj, "Post-War Jaffna Children feel the Healing Touch of Music," *Daily Mirror*, September 9, 2012.

made sure to put the students at ease, some of whom seemed initially tongue-tied. Ekanayaka encouraged "any mode of musical expression . . . even thumping on chairs and drumming on tables was encouraged. Also musical traditions ranging from Carnatic music to Christian hymns were recognized and deemed acceptable."[33] The students were broken up into groups, which they named themselves (names they came up with included "Gangsters" and "Rock Stars"). A workshop attendee describes what happened next:

> Each group was asked to select five words indicative of their past or shared experiences. Then they had to make a sentence incorporating all five words. Thereafter they had to express the essence of the meaning conveyed in the sentences through some form of music. The students had to convey the meaning of words through their own music composition. Musical creativity as a substitute for language was urged.
>
> The results were amazing. Tanya was very much impressed by the versatile creativity of the young students. Music was successfully utilized as an alternative language to facilitate mutual healing. They shared their narratives among each other through the language of music. Tanya thought the collaboratively composed musical compositions were beautiful and creative; the students in her opinion were extremely gifted and spirited.[34]

Ekanayaka's project demonstrates the sheer fun of music for students recovering in a former war zone—this much is obvious, but should not be discounted. For my purposes, though, it will be useful to dig beneath the surface to consider the discourse surrounding the event. Ekanayaka said afterward that while "effective communication forms the basis of human existence," its breakdown "between individuals, communities and nations . . . underlies the pain and tragedy that prevails between many of them all over the world."[35] Language is the "principal medium through which humans deceive one another"; while music, she claims,

> does not possess many of the marvelous attributes that human language does (such as enabling us to conceptualize in ways that no other species can), it possesses a certain feature which makes it particularly powerful in the context of trying to rebuild relationships between people. This feature can be described as the absence of deceit. In other words, it is impossible to deceive another through the medium

---

[33] DBS Jeyaraj, "Post-War Jaffna Children feel the Healing Touch of Music," *Daily Mirror*, September 9, 2012.

[34] DBS Jeyaraj, "Post-War Jaffna Children feel the Healing Touch of Music," *Daily Mirror*, September 9, 2012.

[35] D. B. S. Jeyaraj, "Healing Touch of Music."

of music: I'm simply unable to lie through the language of music. Therefore, when individuals communicate with one another through music (by performing to and listening to others perform), the particular act of communication will by nature be devoid of deceit and it is this reality which I feel renders musical communication so conducive to affecting healing both within and between us.[36]

What she says next makes an appeal to the supposedly abstract nature of music, a claim that (like the above) will raise eyebrows amongst ethnomusicologists, for whom music is typically considered impossible to understand outside its social context:

When I refer to musical language as being incapable of being used to deceive, I'm basically referring to musical language in the abstract. After all, music *has* been used to indoctrinate and condition—nations and individuals have used it in this way for centuries. Take anthems for example and how they are used to foster patriotic feelings. I'd say that the reason for this has to do with the association of certain kinds of musical forms with certain kinds of sentiments and so it is that over generations . . . individuals will experience certain feelings or have certain sensations when listening to such forms of music. However, my argument about music as being incapable of deceit relates to music *in* the abstract, the phenomenon of musical language per se in its unadulterated form and which by nature *is* abstract. So in other words, one cannot conceptualize through music in the way that we do so through language. And it is in the zone of conceptualization that deceit manifests.[37]

The Director of the Program in Peacebuilding and the Arts at Brandeis, Cynthia Cohan, makes a similar statement when she says that, "Nondiscursive modes of expression may be the only route available to people as they seek to construct meaning from and gain power in relation to the violations they have experienced" (2003: 268).

Such statements, though, seem odd in the wake of the workshop's use of language: the students were told to come up with their own words and then express them through music. I suggest what is missing here is a language of the gift. What made the workshop powerful was that Ekanayaka traveled all the way to Jaffna to *give* her music to the students and encourage the students to *give* their music

---

[36] DBS Jeyaraj, "Post-War Jaffna Children feel the Healing Touch of Music," *Daily Mirror*, September 9, 2012.

[37] DBS Jeyaraj, "Post-War Jaffna Children feel the Healing Touch of Music," *Daily Mirror*, September 9, 2012.

to her. It was not music's removal from the social that enabled this "absence of deceit" but the opposite. The event was powerful because this mutual interaction enabled through musical giving was forged through the students having a large amount of agency, such as their genre choice and naming of their groups. Ekanayaka's analysis is a good example of how Western liberal assumptions about music obscure our ability to recognize the power of sonic generosity.

If I appear critical, though, I actually mean to laud Ekanayaka's efforts. I suggest the idea that deceit manifests itself in conceptualization is relevant in some ways for a better recognition of musical giving. For it is precisely this gap between the conceptualization of what music "is," who it belongs to, and so on (its semiotic element), and the malleability and perhaps evasiveness of sound as it gets resignified by social actors who put forth new conceptualizations, that lends people the *choice* to use music to recognize difference and/or to mobilize histories of similarity and positive relations between communities through music. In other words, I suggest that the ethnicized cartography of culture zones is a deceit, willful or not. Ekanayaka's workshop demonstrates how the mobilization of a *discourse* on musical giving might facilitate broader awareness of how the *act* of giving music can lead to changes in the perception of histories of social relations, the "distribution of the sensible" (Rancière 2009). This is quite different from the investment in music as healing in virtue of it being a "nondiscursive mode of expression."

Does It Work?

> Art invites reciprocity. It involves people in reciprocal relationships of sensitivity toward others. A work of art is inherently other-regarding in a way that is rarely the case in political discourse or debate.
> —Cynthia Cohen (2003: 269)

As the above examples demonstrate, it is the sheer ubiquity of the use of music to promote healing and reconciliation in Sri Lanka that is most striking. Such efforts do not have the same goals or the same methods, and thus they do not achieve the same results. It will be helpful to mark a difference between healing and reconciliation by noting that Ekanayaka's intervention is aimed at using music to overcome trauma (I'll call this "music as healing"), while concerts like Arunthathy's aim to patch up ethnic relations (let's call this "music and reconciliation," which of course is also a form of healing). Both are important, but here I focus here on the latter.

It does not take much effort to see that the more successful uses of music as reconciliation described above have at their base a commitment to sonic generosity founded on respect for Others and equality between peoples—e.g., the Sinhala musicians from Musicmatters encouraging the exchange of songs with Tamil musicians in Batticaloa, rather than the Sinhala music teachers patronizingly giving European classical music to their rural Tamil students. As much as I would like to agree with Cohen's suggestion (above), art is only "other-regarding" if we strive to make it so. Cohen (2003: 267) writes, "children's sense of ethnic or national identity is created in part through the 'externalization' of pleasurable and wholly good impulses onto symbols of the in-group. In a parallel process, unpleasurable phenomena or impulses labeled as "bad" are attached to symbols associated with the enemy." As Volkan puts it, "since our enemies . . . serve as a reservoir of our unwanted selves, they are unconsciously seen to some extent as being like us, although on a conscious level they should not seem to be the same as us since they contain our unwanted aspects—those characteristics we vigorously reject" (in Cohen 2003). One threshold for projects using music as reconciliation is to consider whether they rehumanize the Other by generating the feeling that the Other has positive attributes we associate with ourselves.

Where this gets tricky, though, is that the ubiquity of the music and identity episteme means that uses of music aimed at rehumanization tend to occur through the belief that music simply *is* about the expression of one's personal emotions and/or music's ability to project one's communal identity, including one's historic connection to land. This way of thinking is only capable of humanizing those within one group and dehumanizing those outside, since it always emphasizes communal differences. While inter-ethnic collaborations through music are positive in that they show to the world that two supposedly opposing groups can respect each other enough to play music together, such collaborations may simultaneously project seemingly essential, insurmountable differences between them, even as they harness music to transcend those differences. The link between music and identity is a part of the problem, not the solution.

Consider the important Galle/Jaffna music festivals. In such concerts, different regions of the country are deemed to have their own separate musical traditions; representatives of those traditions perform in succession onstage. The festival is held one year in the "Sinhala" area of Galle and the other year in the "Tamil" area of Jaffna, and the festival aims to unite the island by bringing groups from different regions into contact with one another. While these festivals are steps forward—they are arguably the most significant musical development in Sri Lanka's postwar period—I do worry the emphasis on regional difference reinforces the notion that Sri Lanka has always been musically divided along ethnic and regional lines. Furthermore, the collaboration between Thappu and Thurya, while fruitful, visually and aurally displays differences in musical instrumentation between Tamils and Sinhalas. Arunthathy's large-scale concert involved the rendering of pieces associated with Sinhala and Tamil culture back to back. Of course, Sinhalas and Tamils *do* have separate musical traditions and instruments. The benefit of such collaborations is that they publically promote the idea that Sinhalas and Tamils can play music together; they also visually and aurally present differently defined Sri Lankans playing together united, and in Arunthathy's concert, musicians respectfully sonically embodied the musics of the Other. I don't want to discount any of this. But I do wonder if there is *also* room to demonstrate that Sinhalas and Tamils have a somewhat shared music history, and whether this could be mobilized to show that the island is not naturally or essentially divided, regionally, ethnically, or musically.

On closer analysis, we can see the above uses of music do recognize, even if implicitly, that musical giving is a way to protect oneself and Others. As with Ekanayaka's workshop, though, such investments in musical giving tend to be discursively subordinated to a discourse on identity, which remains hegemonic. "Identity" is what structures how musical giving is situated in concerts and festivals: groups are defined *first* by difference and then put on stage and told to interact. By contrast, I contend that reconciliation will require *downplaying* music's historically constructed, relatively recent ability to promote ethnic and regional pride.

Sometime around 2006, I asked a female Tamil musician to reflect on a "concert for peace" she played with a Sinhala musician. I asked her if such concerts "worked" and she laughed and said, "Do we have peace?" The implication was clear: such concerts may help people feel better and act as an escape valve, but they are useless without the political process. From such a perspective, it matters little whether musicians give musical gifts to Others if sovereign powers do not humanize Others. According to this view, the arts are feel-good mechanisms that are politically useless. Sri Lankans performed peace concerts before and after the war, and the end of the war seemingly had nothing to do with them.

Such criticisms are fair, but I think they once again utilize a Western-derived notion of music as expression and identity that is founded on the erasure of musical giving.[38] I think the broader issue is that musical giving's protective powers are more noticeable and effective when they are arranged on a large scale: the equivalent of a mass uprising for peace, reconciliation, and communal healing that does not subordinate one community's beliefs or traditions to another, while recognizing commonalities and shared heritage. For many years, the political situation was such that Sri Lankan peace activists could only act incrementally because doing so more brazenly or at the level of a mass movement would be viewed as an affront to warring factions and could result in retributive violence. Furthermore, when we look more deeply at concerts for peace, it becomes obvious

---

[38] Even without the intent to rehumanize the Other, the mere recognition that one incorporates the sounds of the Other in one's music does complicate cultural narratives on racial purity, something W. E. B. Du Bois recognized long ago in his *Souls of Black Folk* (1903). Du Bois asks, "Our song, our toil, our cheer, and warning have been giving to this nation in blood-brotherhood. Are not these gifts worth giving?" Reflecting on this passage, Ron Radano (2003: 282) writes that, for Du Bois, "In the context of American race relations, the gift of black song . . . seriously undermined the binary logic of race. By taking a gift without thought of reciprocating, whites claimed blackness for themselves, committing a selfish act. But this gesture also reveals an inadvertent generosity: it complicates racial purity together with the absolute power of whiteness."

such events are often organized by reputable, middle-class individuals and held in the country's most esteemed concert halls, sometimes with foreign dignitaries and government officials in attendance; they are preaching to the converted or people who go along with the motions while ignoring the message. There is an invisible line—the line of protest—where the use of music for peace has been tolerated, so long as it doesn't step over that line and argue for widespread change. The idea that music is epiphenomenal to politics is thus useful for the promotion of ethnic violence.

Ras Ceylon

In 2012, hip hop artist Ras Ceylon stepped over that invisible line. Hailing from Oakland, California, of Sinhala parentage, Ras is a Rastafarian who plays hip hop influenced reggae music. Long active on the U.S. West Coast music scene, he relocated temporarily to Sri Lanka in 2012, after releasing his album *Gideon. Force V2: Repatriation Time*. The album generated two hit singles in Sri Lanka, "Repatriation Time" and "Heal Lanka," the former spending eleven weeks on TNL Radio's Criminal Records Most Wanted Countdown (four weeks in the number one position) and five weeks on the YES Home Grown Top 15. He performed in Jaffna, Negombo, Kandy, and Colombo, and was interviewed widely in the press, including feature-length stories in the *Sunday Times* and *Ceylon Today*.

"Repatriation Time" makes bold statements in ways that are uncommon for Sri Lankan music. The lyrics proclaim that "all beings are born free / with equal rights and dignity" and mention the Universal Declaration of Human Rights, saying "there is a place for the Other of mankind." He proclaims that there should be "no forms of slavery" and that "the truth became a casualty / 'cause the victors write history / but it really ain't no mystery why the masses are in misery / trapped in captivity lab rats we been literally taken out of our homes and natural zones but it's set to be—repatriation time." The lyrics describe Ras' "repatriation" to Sri Lanka, the land of his ancestors, but his claim that the "victors write history" while "masses are in misery" was surely provocative coming just a few years after the Sri Lankan government (according to UN estimates) killed 40,000 Tamil civilians while exterminating the LTTE to finish the war. The video for "Repatriation Time" shows a dreadlocked Ras wandering near Kandy Lake, rapping as Kandyan dancers and *gäta beraya* drummers (and one *yak beraya* drummer) play behind him.

Ras began work on a video for the album's second single, "Heal Lanka," which he intended to roll out with a press campaign, including behind the scenes interviews and a trailer. The song begins with a sitar sample from an evergreen light music (*sarala gi*) song over a hip hop beat, followed by straightforward lyrics: "We've been fighting too long / my island needs to heal / there's so much innocent lives lost / too many children have been killed / We got good at burning bridges but now who is down to build? / Peace can only come through unity / for all Sri Lankans that's the deal." The production company sent out a casting call to Sri Lankans between the ages of eight to twenty-six who are "a figure of representation for your ethnic background (Sinhala, Burgher, Tamil or Muslim)." The website Decibel.lk praised the song as a "post-war anthem" that "is not the regular deal you'd hear. Not to be confused with some sugary appeal for peace, the song's strong, political questioning lyrical content makes it an anthem for an age of Sri Lanka that wants to move forward and make 'that change.'"

In March, 2013, radio stations began pulling "Heal Lanka." Ras received notice the song had been banned because of its lyrics. One radio station told him that "due to the current political climate in Sri Lanka" they would be taking the track off the radio "until the situation gets better." According to multiple reports, his film crew was physically roughed up by men later found to be associated with the Ministry of Defense and Urban Development.[39] After postponing the video's release, post-production work was eventually halted because of continued intimidation. Ras continued to speak out in videos posted online, including one in June 2014 after violent attacks by the extremist Buddhist group Bodu Bala Sena on Christians and Muslims. He says in that video, "Let's heal Lanka. . . . it's up to Sinhalese people, like myself, and you, and whoever, to stand up and say, 'No more war in Sri Lanka; we don't want another July 1983,' because what's happening now is way too similar, we've seen it before, and we know what happens."[40] As of late 2015, Ras posted on Facebook that a "Heal Lanka" documentary film is in the pipeline but the video has yet to be released.

It is clear what made Ras's message more politically dangerous to the Rajapaksa regime (then in power) than Arunthathy's concert for peace. Ras is Sinhalese, and he cannot be dismissed as a Tamil agitator; he is from the West, but he is not white, nor does he visually embody elite, upper-class values but Rastafarianism.[41] Ras's lyrics are anti-colonial, anti-imperialist, and anti-violence. Thus he cannot be accused of making a call for a return to Western imperialism, an accusation typically leveled at Western critics of the Sri Lankan government. He does not espouse the Tamil cause in particular, but healing for all Sri Lankans. He recognizes the deaths of innocent children regardless of ethnicity, calls for building bridges between ethnic groups, and identifies groups that drive violence regardless of their background, including the BBS, something local Sinhalese may have felt uncomfortable doing publicly. In other words, Ras's positionality is such that none of the criticisms typically used to discredit people making his kinds of claims can be used against him. And because of the wide appeal of reggae and hip hop among

---

[39] Nate Rabe, "'I Feel There Is a Void for Reality in Music': Ras Ceylon, Sri Lankan American Hip-Hop Activist," Scroll.in, January 24, 2016.

[40] "'Heal Lanka' Trailer (Still Decolonizing)." YouTube video, June 27, 2014.

[41] In a recent interview, Ras mentions that he recently converted to Islam; he is married to the Muslim hip-hop artist Alia Sharrief (Nate Rabe, "'I Feel There Is a Void for Reality in Music': Ras Ceylon, Sri Lankan American Hip-Hop Activist," Scroll.in, January 24, 2016).

the Sri Lankan masses, he had the ability to take his message to the masses and was starting to do so through tours. The response to this by the Rajapaksa government was something like "Cannot compute," "System overload," and "Shut it down"—and that is precisely what they did.

The State Giveth

I'll conclude this chapter with one more anecdote of musical giving as an act of peace and reconciliation on a large scale. Sri Lanka's national anthem was composed by Sinhala musician Ananda Samarakoon (1911–1962) in October 1940.[42] The chief inspector of schools for the Southern Province at the time, T. D. Jayasuriya, asked Samarakoon (then a teacher at Mahinda College, Galle) to compose a patriotic song. Samarakoon came up with "Namo Namo Matha," dubbing it a "Jatika Geeya" (national song). The tune was performed in *sarala gi* style (see next chapter) on Radio Ceylon in 1942 with a printed version appearing in 1943, followed by a recording on the H.M.V. record label. The Lanka Gandharva Sabha organized a contest to choose a national anthem in 1948, and the initial winner (a song by P. B. Illangasinghe with music by Lionel Edirisinghe) was discredited because its composers were on the selection committee. Samarakoon's song was the next choice, and it was adopted as the official anthem in 1951. According to one source, Samarakoon's song was among those performed in both the Sinhala and Tamil languages at the first Independence Day ceremony in 1949, though the official Tamil language version ("Namo Namo Thaye") was reportedly commissioned from the poet M. Nallathambi in 1950.[43] The Tamil version of the anthem was first broadcast on Radio Ceylon on February 4, 1955, sung by two women, Sangari and Meena.[44]

According to journalist D. B. S. Jeyaraj, whose work I draw on here, the Tamil version of the anthem was sung widely throughout Colombo and Sinhala-majority areas of the country in Tamil and Muslim schools in the 1950s and 1960s, even after the enactment of the Sinhala Only language law (which made Sinhala the official language of government) in 1956.[45] The performance of the Tamil version

---

[42] The information in this paragraph draws on: Sumana Saparamadu, "The Origin of Our National Anthem," *Sunday Observer*, January 30, 2011.

[43] Anjule Maheeka Weeraratne, "National Anthem Was Sung in Tamil in 1949 Too: Vajira." *Daily Mirror*, September 2, 2016.

[44] DBS Jeyaraj, "National Anthem: From 'Namo Namo' to 'Sri Lanka Matha,'" DBSJeyaraj.com, December 31, 2010.

[45] As is well-known, the title of Samarakoon's song and some of its lyrics were changed to "Sri Lanka Matha" following the wishes of a committee in 1961. In the years following the election of S. W. R. D Bandaranaike in 1956, the country had experienced numerous problems, from ethnic violence, strikes, protests, and natural disasters; a faction of Buddhist monks and others complained that the "gana" (the cluster of syllables) that started Samarakoon's song was inauspicious: it began with "na-mo-na," a short-long-short combination that was deemed unlucky, and it was assumed this had

of the anthem declined significantly with the onset of Tamil militancy, and by the 1970s, Jeyaraj says, sometimes only the music of the anthem was played at state functions in Tamil-majority regions.[46] The Federal Party and Tamil United Liberation Front (TULF) developed their own anthems, songs that praise "mother Tamil" (Thamizh Thaai Vaazhthu).[47] After the LTTE gained territorial control in parts of the north and east, the Tamil version of the anthem "was virtually discontinued."[48] The 1978 Constitution defined Tamil as a national language and included a clause that recognized the Tamil version of the anthem; but "what prevails now," Jeyaraj wrote in 2010, "is a "mixed" state of affairs where Sinhala and Tamil are being used to sing the national anthem in Jaffna on different occasions."[49] With the conclusion of war in 2009, the permissibility of the Tamil version of the anthem emerged as a factor for determining what tone the Rajapaksa regime would take toward Tamil-speaking minorities in the post-war period and the possibility for reconciliation between Tamils and the Sri Lankan state.

In a meeting on December 8, 2010, Rajapaksa's cabinet met to discuss a proposed official ban on the Tamil language version of the national anthem. The proposed ban met with fierce opposition, and Rajapaksa tabled the proposal. However, reports surfaced that he quietly signaled to government officials and military personnel to enforce the Sinhala version of the anthem in the Tamil-majority regions. An unofficial ban of the Tamil version was put in place. News surfaced that Tamil students at the University of Jaffna, with little or no knowledge of Sinhala, had struggled to sing the Sinhala version of the anthem at a National Safety Day celebration (commemorating the sixth anniversary of the tsunami) where Prime Minister D. M. Jayaratne was chief guest.[50] Sinhala politician

---

doomed the country. Samarakoon, who long-suffered from depression after the death of his young son, had fallen into financial hardship (he did not own the copyright to the anthem). He complained about the changes and wrote in a letter that death would be preferable. He was found dead on April 5, 1962, having overdosed on sleeping pills.

[46] Jeyaraj, "National Anthem."

[47] Jeyaraj says there were three "versions of a 'Tamil Eelam national anthem' . . . sung during the past decades when Tamil ultra-nationalism and separatism rode high." These include "Vaalha Eezhath Thamizhaham, Vaalha Endrum Vaalhave" ("Long Live Eelam Tamil Homeland, Long Live Forever") by Paramahamsathasan; "Engal Eezhath Thamizh Thirunaadu, Kalai Vaazhum Ponnaadu" ("Our Great Eelam Tamil Land, the Golden Land Where Arts Flourish") by "Thirukkovil" Ariyanayagam, and "Vazhiyave, Vazhiyave, Vazhiyave, Engal Thanga Maamanith Thamizh Eezham" ("Long Live, Long Live, Long Live, Our Golden Gem Tamil Eelam") by Kasi Anandan. Jeyaraj, "National Anthem."

[48] According to Jeyaraj, the LTTE did not have their own official anthem but they did have a mandatory song played for the hoisting of the tiger flag, written by the LTTE's "poet laureate" Puthuvai. Rathinathurai, called "Eruthu Paar, Kodi Eruthu Paar" ("See It Being Hoisted, See the Flag is Being Hoisted"). DBS Jeyaraj, "National Anthem: From 'Namo Namo' to 'Sri Lanka Matha,'" DBSJeyaraj.com, December 31, 2010.

[49] Jeyaraj, "National Anthem."

[50] "Sri Lanka National Anthem Row Reignites," BBC.com, December 28, 2010. "Jaffna Students Forced to Sing National Anthem in Sinhala," *Daily Mirror*, December 28, 2010.

Wimal Weerasekara dismissively called the Tamil version of the anthem "a joke" and suggested, provocatively, that Tamil students prefer the Sinhala version.[51] Coming so soon after the end of war in 2009, the government's actions struck some as a colonizing gesture, and as a significant blow to reconciliation.[52]

One can imagine the joy some Sri Lankans felt when, on February 4, 2016, the government of Maithripala Sirisena (whose government had been in power for just a year) made a remarkable act of sonic generosity: they announced that during the Sixty-Eighth Independence Day celebrations (to be held in March at Galle Face, Colombo), the national anthem would be sung in Sinhala and Tamil. Jeyaraj (who is of Sri Lankan descent but a longtime resident of Canada) summed up his emotions after watching the event online:

> During the past decades I have seen many official commemorations of Independence Day occur. However for the first time in my life I witnessed a scene via the Internet which I thought would never ever happen during my lifetime. I saw and heard a youthful choir of boys and girls exuberantly rendering the Sri Lankan National anthem in my mother tongue—Tamil. It took 2 minutes and 32 seconds. The singers were students of Bambalapitiya Ramanathan Hindu Ladies College and Colombo Vivekananda College. They sang harmoniously. After several decades the national anthem was being sung with official approval at the state sanctioned commemoration of Independence.
>
> I was in a state of emotional ecstasy. I did something which I have not done before when Sri Lanka's national anthem was being played. I cried! I am not ashamed to say that!! I kept clicking replay to see the clip over and over again. My eyes turned moist and tears kept trickling down my cheeks. I even sobbed a few times involuntarily. It was with the greatest difficulty that I controlled myself. When the "Rupavahini" camera panned on the distinguished gathering, I saw those very important children of the Sri Lankan mother—most of them Sinhalese—standing respectfully erect as the words rang out clearly in Tamil. It was truly a defining moment![53]

---

[51] "Sri Lanka National Anthem," BBC.com,

[52] Uninformed politicians, notably Weerawansa, insisted Sri Lanka is the only nation with a national anthem allowed in two languages. This generated a backlash from observers who provided examples of national anthems sung in multiple languages or in the language of a minority group, with examples of the former including South Africa (in five languages), New Zealand (which has Maori and English versions), and Canada (French and English versions), and the latter including Singapore (which is in Malay, the language of the minority) and India (a Tagore song in Bengali). "National Anthem and National Identity," Notebook of a Nobody by Shanie, *The Island*, December 17, 2010.

[53] Unsurprisingly, there was a conservative backlash. Sri Lanka Freedom Party parliamentarian Sarath Weerasekara proclaimed, "We are totally against this measure. . . . It is illegal and the betrayal of

> Tagore → Samarakoon → Ceylonese Government → Tamil Population → [Rejected by Tamils (1970s–2000s)/Withdrawn by Government (2010)] Sri Lankan Government → Tamil Population

Figure 5.2 Sri Lanka's national anthem as a musical gift.

While it is perhaps unsurprising that the "Sinhala anthem only" faction was generally unaware that many countries have national anthems sung in multiple or minority languages, I find it surprising that they seemed also unaware that Sri Lanka's national anthem itself had not arisen *sui generis* from the mind of Samarakoon but was a musical gift from India. According to Bengali journalist Haroon Habib, Indian poet and Nobel Laureate Rabindranath Tagore (1861–1941) wrote the song "Nama Nama Sri Lanka Mata" in Bengali as a gift for Samarakoon in 1938 when the latter was residing at Tagore's school for the arts in Santiniketan, Bengal.[54] On this reading, Sri Lanka's national anthem was a musical gift from Tagore to Samarakoon to the Sinhala-led government to the Tamil population, and after being ignored for a few decades—after it was hoarded by the Rajapaksa regime—it was re-gifted back to the Tamil community (Figure 5.2).

I suggest the easiest way to promote reconciliation through music is "from the top down," when the state recognizes that musical giving protects people. Sirisena's act was a turnaround of how musical giving is traditionally used in Sri Lanka: in the past, music had been a gift *to* the sovereign (and to gods to protect people and the king) rather than from the sovereign to protect the people.

Conclusion: Beyond the Divided Island

> The language of reconciliation is often explicitly backward-looking: working through the past, coming to terms with the past, confronting or reckoning with the past, settling accounts.
> —Erin Daly and Jeremy Sarkin (2007: 22)

In his book *The Moral Imagination: The Art and Soul of Building Peace*, John Lederach (2005) argues that four capacities are necessary for building a moral imagination that transcends violence. These include "the capacity to imagine ourselves in a web of relationships that includes our enemies; the ability to sustain a paradoxical curiosity that embraces complexity without reliance on dualistic polarity; the fundamental belief in and pursuit of the creative act; and the acceptance of the

---

our race." Galagoda Aththe Gnanasara, leader of the Buddhist monk party the Bodu Bala Sena, stated that any version of the anthem besides the Sinhala one would be unconstitutional.

[54] Other observers have claimed Tagore simply helped Samarakoon write the song.

inherent risk of stepping into the mystery of the unknown that lies beyond the far too familiar landscape of violence" (Lederach 2005: 5). He goes on to say that achieving these capacities requires understanding "the geographies and realities of what destructive relationships produce, what legacies they leave, and what breaking their violent patterns will require" and that we should "explore the creative process itself, not as a tangential inquiry, but as the wellspring that feeds the building of peace." As he memorably puts it: "Our thesis requires us to explore the survival of the artist's genius and gift in the lands of violence" (Lederach 2005: 5).

Lederach's intervention is important for my purposes: he succinctly makes the case that the creativity inherent in artistic giving is essential for contesting the idea that Sri Lanka is a divided island, and that defeating the latter *geography* is integral for moving beyond communal violence in Sri Lanka. Of course, this is easier said than done. Verdeja (2009: 3) notes that reconciliation is

> a complex, multileveled process that is best understood as *disjunctured* and *uneven*, with multiple moral claims often in competition with one another. Rather than posit a model, on one hand, equating reconciliation with social harmony between former enemies or, on the other, as a condition of minimal peace with no exploration of past injustices, I [suggest] a conception that emphasizes the importance of shared notions of moral respect and tolerance among erstwhile adversaries as a realistic and morally defensible idea of what we should expect in transitional societies [his italics].

The argument I have pursued here is that tolerance and reconciliation in Sri Lanka can be built by (1) recognizing the protective power of musical giving to gods, people, and from one community to another; (2) mainstreaming the idea that Sri Lanka's cultural history is founded, in part, on the giving of "culture" from persons and communities to one another; (3) promoting the idea that the island is not divided between a Sinhala south and a Tamil north, nor between ethnically defined towns and villages, but is built on various communal movements and entanglements that have always involved respectful engagements between peoples who are welcoming of difference; and (4) acknowledging that the acceptance of these points must not be used as an excuse to subordinate one region's or group's practices or presence to those of another. Adopting the musical gift as a framework for reconciliation, I suggest, is a decolonizing gesture that displaces the identity paradigm by returning to Sri Lankan aesthetics. What is needed is to look inward to forms of Sri Lankan generosity and use the *positive* impulses that lie therein to redefine Sri Lanka's musical geography.

Checkpoint

The Malays Who Sing in Six Languages

It was fall, 2006; I was in the Kandyan hills, staring down at greenery everywhere; a few roads were visible in the distance. The scene was beautiful and the weather gorgeous. Visible in the distance was the lake that forms the center of Kandy town, next to which lies the Temple of the Tooth, Sri Lanka's most famous Buddhist temple. Near the temple are *devales* (shrines) honoring the Four Warrant Gods (*hatara varam deviyo*) and an old palace (now a museum) that once served as the court of the Kandyan Kingdom (1521–1815).

As I looked across Kandy Lake that day, I found myself not in the home of a Kandyan drummer or in a Buddhist temple but at my friend Tony Hassan's house, staring at the scenery from his music studio—a tiny room with a drumset, electric guitars, microphones, amplifiers, and no windows (let alone sound-proofing!). Looking at his drumset perched literally on the edge of a cliff, I realized why the Buddha insisted music should be avoided by those making an attempt at nirvana: I easily imagined loud rock drums cascading throughout this Buddhist heartland, jarring some poor *bhikkhu* (Buddhist monk) from his meditative state.[1] A member of Sri Lanka's small Malay community, Tony is a devout Muslim and retired construction worker who spent years living in Abu Dhabi. He is also a lifelong musician whose passion is drumming and singing in pop bands. Tony used to perform professionally in the 1970s when his group, Kandyan Rubies, played at hotels, weddings, and other functions in Kandy. Tony invited me to his house that day because he wanted to show me his studio and introduce me to his friends from the Hill Country Malay Association. The Malays, Tony said, are famous in Sri Lanka for their musical abilities.

As we sat in Tony's kitchen and drank tea, I asked about Kandyan Rubies: what kind of music did they play? I figured Tony's band must have consisted only of Malay musicians and that they played for that community (or the broader Muslim

---

[1] Two major Buddhist fraternities in Sri Lanka, the Malwatte and Asgiriya *nikayas*, have their headquarters close to Tony's house.

community) only. I was wrong. Tony's band consisted of Sinhalas, Tamils, and Malays, and they sang in Sinhala, Tamil, Hindi, English, Malay, and Arabic. Malay songs were reserved for Malay weddings, Arabic songs were more for Muslim audiences (and played prominently when they performed in the Middle East), while evergreen classics ("light music," or *sarala gi*) were typically sung in Sinhala, though some of these were Sinhala versions of Hindi and Tamil film songs.[2] The band sang less frequently in Tamil, but they did include some famous Tamil songs. They chose which songs to sing based on who was in the audience and what they thought the audience wanted to hear.

I was stunned. This was only my second trip to Sri Lanka and I had read widely about the island's "ethnic conflict," learning that its roots were sewn before and during Kandyan Rubies' heyday in the 1970s. Tony's band seemed to occupy an ambiguous space between the three ethnic groups—Sinhala, Tamil, and Muslim—that formed the discursive ground upon which my knowledge of the island's cultures was then shaped. My first thought was that his band was a "hybrid" anomaly facilitated by his status as a Malay living in Sinhala-dominated Kandy. Because Sri Lankan Muslims typically speak Tamil and Sinhala is the main language in Kandy, I reasoned, Tony was in a unique position to move between different Sri Lankan musical genres.

Just then, Tony's friend Marhoum Saudara Cassiere arrived. He struck me as a gentle person, immensely proud of his Malay heritage.[3] One of the first things Cassiere told me was that he is the only person who remembers the old Sri Lankan Malay *pantuns* (traditionally sung at weddings), a genre descended from a Malaysian genre of the same name.[4] He wore a Muslim cap (*kufie*) on his head,

---

[2] I don't remember if Tony said his repertoire included "Surangani," but that song is a classic example of why language does not always mark which community a song belongs to: the song originated as a Baila tune, produced and written by Sri Lankan Tamil pop musician A. E. Manoharan, who made a bilingual Sinhala/Tamil version; the song was later remade in a Konkani language version in Goa, and in Tamil Nadu by composer Ilayaraja for the film *Avar Enakke* (which was an immense hit in Tamil Nadu).

[3] Sri Lanka's Malay community are descendants of laborers brought from Java during the period of Dutch rule in the coastal provinces (1605–1795), and descendants of a regiment brought by the British from Malaya that was settled in what is today known as "Slave Island" in Colombo. There is also a village in the southeast, Kirinda, with a distinctive Malay neighborhood (Slomanson 2013). In Kandy, Malays are largely intermarried with Sinhalese.

[4] It is often said Sri Lanka's entire Muslim population speaks Tamil as their native language, but I found this to be false. While most Muslims do speak Tamil as their native tongue, there are those in the hill country, south, and west of the island for whom their native tongue is Sinhala, English, or (more rarely) Sri Lankan Malay. For example, two Muslim friends of mine come from a middle-class family in Colombo; their families speak English at home, they speak Sinhala in public and did so at school, and neither knows Tamil (though they have relatives elsewhere who do). It is high time for academics writing on Sri Lanka to stop simply saying that all Sri Lankan Muslims speak Tamil as their native tongue.

Figure C2.1 Marhoum Saudara Cassiere.

and his facial features struck me as characteristically "Malay." Tony said Cassiere is much in demand for reciting the Qur'an at Malay funerals.[5]

I could not help but think, "Now *here* is an authentic Sri Lankan Malay musician!" I expected Cassiere to launch into *pantuns*, or perhaps another genre of Muslim folk song. He seemed the antithesis to Tony's cosmopolitanism—a village folk musician. Cassiere took out his *rabāna*, a tambourine metonymic for Muslims in Sri Lanka. But over the next two hours, Cassiere (a man of 70-plus years) gave me a private concert of Sinhala, Tamil, Malay, Arabic, Hindi, and English pop songs. He had *boundless* energy and a musicality that was immediately recognizable; he sang from the same pool of songs as Kandyan Rubies, but added *pantuns* and a difference in instrumentation (the *rabāna*).

As I have continued to research Sri Lankan music over the years, I have concluded that Tony and Cassiere are not anomalies. Rather, they put a Malay spin on a wide range of songs and genres—a way of interacting with music—that can be labeled "Sri Lankan music." While a Sinhala musician would probably not play Malay *pantuns*, he or she might well have played some of the songs Cassiere sang for me, such as the American pop song "Hotel California." I think it is best to avoid thinking of Cassiere's performance as "cover songs" or live "karaoke." His

---

[5] Sadly, Cassiere passed a way a few years after this meeting.

was a performance that drew on a common repertoire formed through histories of Indian Ocean musical encounters—musical giving—between variously defined Sri Lankans, Indians, English-speaking Westerners, Arabs, East Africans, and Malays. This repertoire is shaped by one's ethnicity, since songs *are* often associated with one group rather than another; but some songs migrate between groups and multiple versions exist in different languages. Sri Lankan musicians draw on this repertoire strategically, depending on the makeup of the audience. While the question of which ethnic group originated which song is relevant, just as important for Sri Lankan music history is who owns what musical gifts and which they deem appropriate to give to whom on what occasion. A typical concert of Sri Lankan pop musics, I suggest, is a choice of musical gifts given cleverly and respectfully to the audience. I'll never forget the gleam in Cassiere's eye when gave me "Hotel California" as a token of respect for my background as a North American (I didn't tell him I'm not from California). A few years after I met Cassiere and Tony, I met a Tamil musician in Jaffna who told me his father used to tour around the island in the 1960s and 1970s: he would play Tamil and Sinhala songs to Sinhala audiences in the south, and would learn which songs were locally popular before performing in that place. The same musician later joined the LTTE and fled to India.

A Brief History of Musical Giving in Sri Lankan Popular Musics

Sinhala has long been the language of the marketplace; just because someone sang in Sinhala didn't mean that the song was "Sinhala." Language was a medium, not a marker of identity (Mitchell 2009). Some of the most famous "Sinhala" singers of the twentieth century were not Sinhala. Mohideen Baig (1919–1991) was a Tamil Muslim from Salem, Tamil Nadu, who migrated to Sri Lanka in 1932. He became famous for singing Buddhist devotional songs in Sinhala, and as a playback singer in Sinhala films (he is supposedly the only Sri Lankan to duet with famed Indian playback singer Lata Mangeshkar). Baig also sang in Tamil, Urdu, and Hindi.[6] He is perhaps most famous for "Buddhang Saranang Gatchami" ("To the Buddha I Go for Refuge"), now a standard played in Sri Lanka during Vesak, the holiday commemorating the birth, Enlightenment, and death of the Buddha. Baig reportedly once told his son, "I am from the country the Buddha was born in. . . . So I like singing Buddhist songs. Whatever religion we belong to, we are born from a mother. All religions show us how to live better. From the Buddhist songs I sang, I learnt a great deal. Until I die, I will sing for Sinhala Buddhists. The love I gained from this country's people is the biggest triumph of my life."[7]

---

[6] Jayanthi Liyanage, "Recalling the Muse," *Daily News*, November 4, 2009.
[7] Jayanthi Liyanage, "Recalling the Muse," *Daily News*, November 4, 2009.

Another notable Muslim musician of the era was Mohammed Ghouse, who helped introduce Baig to Radio Ceylon when he arrived in Sri Lanka. Ghouse was already a known film composer when he gave a break to the young Sinhala musician W. D. Amaradeva (now regaled as Sri Lanka's most famous classical musician) by hiring him to play violin in his orchestra. Rukmani Devi (1923–1978), a Tamil Christian singer, was born in Nuwara Eliya (in the hill country) and grew up in the Tamil-dominated neighborhood of Colombo called Wellawatte. She moved to the Sinhala Christian-dominated town of Negombo after marrying comedian and actor Eddie Jayamanne. Hailed as the "Nightingale of Sri Lanka," with an acting resume of over one hundred films, she was arguably the most famous female Sri Lankan singer of the gramophone era. She was so beloved that after she died in an auto accident in 1978, thousands of Sri Lankans of all stripes turned out for her funeral. These are not minor figures in Sri Lankan music; they are some of its biggest stars.

The Ceylonese film industry was a significant site for musical encounters between Sri Lankans and Indians from the 1940s through the 1960s. As one writer put it, "for three decades . . . Tamil Nadu's film industry was part and parcel of the Sinhala cinema," with "artistes and technicians" from the Tamil-majority Indian cities of Madras, Coimbatore, Madurai, and Salem being "the pioneers of the Sinhala film industry."[8] The music for the first Sinhala feature film, *Kadawunu Poronduwa* (1947), and the later *Banda Nagarayata Pemineema* (1952), was composed by Malayali (Keralan) musician Narayan Iyer (Samaranayake 2013: 18). The first film made by a Sinhala director (Shanthi Kumar Seneviratne), the 1947 *Asokamala*, had music composed by Ghouse and sung by Amaradeva, Baig, and Tamil singer Bhagyarathi (Samaranayake 2013: 18–19). A number of South Indian singers were featured in Sinhala films in the 1950s and 1960s, such as A. M. Raja, Ganadasala, T. M. Soundararajan, Sirigali Govindarajan, J. P. Chandrababu, B. P. Sirinivas, K. Rani, Yamuna Rani, P. Susila, P. Leela, Jikki, and A.P. Komala (Samaranayake 2013: 21). Premaratne Samaranayake, whose book I draw on here, also mentions that the shop Cargills sold a recording with songs from the Tamil film "Chinthamani," sung with Sinhala lyrics (Samaranayake 2013: 22). Sunil Ariyaratne (1986: 110) describes the classic Sinhala songs "Bhava heena gune dutu da" and "Athi supembara sara komala giri devi" as covers of the Tamil songs "Aandavane muruga" and "Theruvilvarandi," respectively. Most of the songs from the early Sinhala films, though, were covers of Hindi film songs. The song "Sandyawe Sriya," a classic from the 1947 *Kadawunu Poronduwa* sung by Rukmani Devi and Hugo Fernando, for instance, was a cover of the Bollywood song "Pardeshi Balma Badal Aaya," performed by Zohra Ambala in the film *Rattan* in 1944. A blogger has painstakingly chronicled Sinhala covers of Hindi film songs, listing 225 covers appearing in Sinhala films from 1947–1960.[9] More recent Sri Lankan

---

[8] DBS Jeyaraj, "Indigenous Tamil cinema in Sri Lanka before 'Black July,'" *Daily FT*, September 26, 2015.

[9] http://musicfilmlk.blogspot.com/2009/08/origins-of-sinhala-film-cover-songs.html

singers A. Vardaraja, S. Anthony, R. Shivanandan, A. M. U. Raj, Suriyakumar Muttulage, Kalawathi, Sujatha Attanayake, and Chadrika Siriwardana have sung songs with Sinhala or Tamil lyrics (sometimes with the same tunes, such as the song "Suriyakumar Muttulage"). I am not suggesting such songs were gifts to Sinhala musicians, but rather than taking such songs and making them one's own positions them as gifts to give an audience who will recognize them.

While I earlier described the Baila's mixed African, Portuguese, and Sinhala heritage, there is also a Tamil version of Baila made famous by Nithi Kanagaratnam and A. E. Manoharan in the mid-1960s and 1970s. Nithi Kanagaratnam began playing in English bands in Colombo, performing Tom Jones and Engelbert Humperdinck songs, but found success with his Tamil language baila song "Chinna Maamiye," which he first played at a cricket match in Jaffna.[10] In a 2010 interview, Kanagaratnam says he composed six solo albums while studying at Allahabad Univerisity in India in the late 1960s and early 1970s, including the Baila classic "Kallukada Pakkam Pogatha," a song against alcoholism that was adopted by M. G. Ramachandren, chief minister of Tamil Nadu at the time, for a campaign against alcohol abuse.[11] Now a professor of pharmaceutics at Victoria University in Australia, Nithi still composes songs in English and Tamil, and translates songs from Sinhala into Tamil.

A. E. Manoharan (or Ceylon Manoharan) has acted in over 250 films, including alongside film star Sivaji Ganesan. Manoharan achieved fame in Sri Lanka and India in the 1970s for his pop songs sung in Tamil, Sinhala, and English, particularly the aforementioned "Surangani," which was released on the Colombo-based Sooriya label in the early 1970s. Manoharan toured the island in the mid-1970s and later performed internationally in the UK, Singapore, Canada, and elsewhere.[12]

The legacy of Sri Lankan musical multilingualism and multiethnic performance lives on in hip hop. Krishnan Maheson, who rapped in English in the 1990s, appeared on Sinhala rapper Iraj's 2004 self-titled album, rapping in Tamil on the songs "Ran Ran Ran" and "Ninda Noyana Hendewe."[13] Krishnan's brother, Gajan, performs as a duo with a Tamil rapper, Dinesh Kanagaratnam, whose 2006 album features rappers performing in Sinhala and English. The well-known Sinhala pop duo Bathiya and Santush released a bilingual song ("Yalpaname," referring to Jaffna) with Tamil lyrics sung by an Indian singer, Hariharan.[14] I met one Tamil musician who says he performs "Sinhala" drums (i.e., *gäta beraya, yak beraya*, and so on) with other Sinhala members of his group

---

[10] Prince Frederick, "To the Baila Beat," *The Hindu*, November 11, 2016.

[11] Prince Frederick, "To the Baila Beat," *The Hindu*, November 11, 2016.

[12] "Sri Lankan Music Maestro A. E. Manoharan," *Tamilweek.com*, April 7, 2006.

[13] Marianne David, "Krishan Asian Avenue," *Sunday Leader*, September 18, 2005.

[14] Ironically, the music video for the song was produced by a company called "Aryan films." Thanks to Eshantha Peiris for alerting me to this and helping with this section.

as an introduction to their set of pop songs they perform in Sinhala, Tamil, English, Hindi, and Arabic for Sri Lankans living in Dubai. Later on in my fieldwork, when I recorded with the rock band 10 Second Rule, it dawned on me that the band was composed of two Sinhala musicians (brothers), two Muslim musicians (cousins), an American (myself), and our recording was produced by two Tamil musicians. This did happen in Colombo, however, and would not have been possible in some other parts of the country.

Of course, it would be wrong to give the impression that all Sri Lankan music involves interactions between individuals or songs borrowed from different ethnic groups. The above runs the risk of "throwing the baby out with the bathwater." Once one starts noticing the ubiquity of Sinhala borrowings of non-Sinhala musics, the need arises among some to counter with examples of Sinhala creativity and originality to *prove* the Sinhalese do more than just copy the songs of Others.

I want to stress, then, that I am *not* providing the above as a debunking of Sinhala musicality, nor as an argument that Sinhalas have not created original music. Rather, I am responding to the extreme ethnic purification Sinhala-language pop music that has occurred in recent decades, in a manner similar to the purification of Beravā music and dance. In a 2015 article for the *Daily Mirror*, Gamini Akmeemana describes being in the Colombo 08 neighborhood on Vesak, watching *dansals* (alms-giving stalls) hand out food and drinks.[15] She listened to the music; present were classic songs on Buddhist themes by W. D. Amaradeva, Victor Ratnayake, and Narada Disasekara. She realized that Baig's "Buddhang Saranang Gatchami" was missing. After doing some digging, she noticed the song

> was axed from Vesak programs almost everywhere during the racist Rajapaksa regime. There was no public outcry or protest. No explanation was given. The reason was that the singer was a Muslim. But this was never stated officially, will never be admitted. Nor was there an official ban. The axing of Baig's Buddhist devotional song remains one of those all-too-frequent Sri Lankan gray areas and a shameful episode in the history of the country's cultural diversity.

Akmeemana notes the song has seemingly returned to rotation during the time of the Sirisena government, but that the feeling that ethnic purification equals patriotism has not. On a visit to a supermarket, she met a woman who asked if she was pleased with the music that was playing. Apparently the woman had asked the management on several visits to stop playing Western music. The woman told Akmeemana, "I thought, 'how absurd!' This country belongs to us Sinhalese! We

---

[15] Gamini Akmeemana, "Things Unspoken in the Serendib Island," *Daily Mirror*, May 25, 2015.

are spending Sinhalese money here! We have a right to listen to Sinhala music!" While I empathize with the woman's dislike of some Western pop music, the assuredness not only that the country belongs just to Sinhalese but that there is such a thing as a pure "Sinhala music" that involves only Sinhala performers with no minorities involved (on no foreign-made instruments, in a recording studio without foreign technology, and so on) is a blatant erasure of thousands of years of Sinhala music history, in which Sinhala music has always been unique but always incorporated the musical innovations of Others.

This kind of purity ad absurdum reached its apotheosis in early 2016 when a controversy erupted around the song "Danno Budunge." Written by playwright John De Silva (1857–1922) for his play *Sirisangabo* (1903), the song was composed in the *nurthi* style that thrived in Colombo in the late nineteenth century (see Chapter 6), derived from the Bombay Parsi theater. De Silva's lyrics depict three princes observing the ancient Sinhala capital of Anuradhapura. The music was composed with Visvanath Lawjee, a musician from Bombay. De Silva grew up with a formal Christian education, and even though the lyrics are Sanskritized, "Danno Budunge" "sounds more like a Christian hymn than a Buddhist devotional verse."[16] The song was "a true hybrid product."[17] Devar Surya Sena included the song in his collection of De Silva's music that he printed as sheet music in Indian musical notation.[18] Singer Hubert Rajapaksha then popularized it in the 1920s in a slightly operatic-sounding rendition on a recording for Ceylon Cargills Ltd. The song acquired more patriotic overtones in the early independence days, when it was performed as an unofficial national anthem before Samarakoon's "Namo Namo Matha" was picked. It has been recorded many times since by some of Sri Lanka's most famous singers, including W. D. Amaradeva and Rukmani Devi.

At the 2016 Independence Day Celebrations on Galle Face Green, Colombo, Sri Lankan British Soprano Kishani Jayasinghe sang a version of "Danno Badunge" in European operative style, with Sri Lankan musicians accompanying her in a "light music" (*sarala gi*) style.[19] Wearing a sari but standing still and emoting in the style of opera singers (with heavy vibrato), she was accompanied by an orchestra that included Sinhala drums (which were there just for show, as they were inaudible). The performance created one of the largest firestorms of debate I have ever witnessed, anywhere. Jayasinghe was "hooted by the crowd and pilloried by television and

---

[16] Sasanka Perera, "Shrillness of Nonsensical Cultural Politics and the Social History of a Song," *Groundviews*, February 8, 2016.

[17] Eshantha Joseph Peiris, "The Politics of Musical Taste, the Inadequacy of Good Intentions, and Not Saying 'No!' to Racism," *Groundviews*, February 16, 2016.

[18] Eshantha Joseph Peiris, "The Politics of Musical Taste, the Inadequacy of Good Intentions, and Not Saying 'No!' to Racism," *Groundviews*, February 16, 2016.

[19] Originally a lawyer, Jayasinghe gave it up to pursue a career in opera; according to the *Daily Mirror*, she was the first Sri Lankan singer to perform at the main stage of the Royal Opera House. Kamanthi Wickramasinghe, "Dilemma over 'Danno Budunge,'" *Daily Mirror*, February 23, 2016.

electronic websites."²⁰ In a style reminiscent of bloviating U.S. talk show hosts Bill O'Reilly and Rush Limbaugh, she was lambasted on Sri Lankan television. In an article Jayasinghe wrote addressing the controversy for the *Sunday Times* (March 6, 2016), she claims to have received over *half a million* emails in response to her performance, emails that "opened my eyes to what really bubbles underneath the surface of what otherwise might seem a benign and tolerant society."²¹ The problem was that she was singing a "Buddhist," "anti-colonial" song in a European style. This should ring familiar with U.S. readers because it was basically the debate on cultural appropriation that has been prevalent in recent years on U.S. college campuses. As typically happens, people say what they're thinking in the YouTube comments: one commentator, Chamindu Yashod, demonstrates the vitriol:

> What the f**k is this s**t? You b**ch just ruined our national feeling. Sri Lanka is just f***ed up to the end right now. The woman singing in this video should have thought twice before doing something like this. This is a Buddhist song which u just westernised. F**k the current [Sirisena] government. We Ain't afraid to speak the truth. F**k maithree. F**k mangala. F**k ranil.²²

Some commentators chastised her for borrowing a melody from Richard Wagner, though one positive aspect of the controversy is that esteemed Sri Lankan musicologists, like Sunil Ariyaratne, were quoted in Sri Lankan newspapers providing background details for the song noting that the Wagner attribution is incorrect. Clearly, Jayasinghe's rendition compromised what some view as the purity of Buddhism and the nation. One critic, responding to an article defending Jayasinghe, responded,

> I would like to ask the author to imagine "Amazing Grace" being rapped, in a U.S. church on the fourth of July, even in the birthplace of rap many would shudder even at the thought of that, section of the Sri Lankans would have felt the same way listening to "Danno Budunge" in an operatic rendition, especially at the Independence celebration, there is something called common sense, this rendition displayed how out of touch the organizers were with the rest of Sri Lanka.²³

In her response to the controversy, Jayasinghe lists her "favorite responses" from critics, one saying she should be reborn a mute in her next life, one that she should

---

²⁰ Gamini Akmeemana, "Insulting a Lady Who Dared to Differ," *Daily Mirror*, February 17, 2016.
²¹ Kishani Jayasinghe Wijayasekara, "My Experience of Independence," *Sunday Times*, March 6, 2016.
²² The names at the end are prominent left-leaning political figures, including President Maithripala Sirisena and long-running icon of liberal politics in Sri Lanka, Prime Minister Ranil Wickremesinghe.
²³ Perera, "Shrillness of Nonsensical Cultural Politics."

die in a traffic accident, another that "not only should I suffer for this act during the course of my lifetime, but also . . . my innocent children should suffer . . . and bear the pain of it too."[24] She says those three messages came from women.

In an article on the Jayasinghe controversy, Eshantha Peiris discusses the seeming impossibility of creating dialogue with "the ethnic and national purity crowd" and suggests what is needed is less futile attempts at persuading than a broader attention to root causes:

> I suggest that we can learn a few things from the healing strategies of traditional rituals. When Sri Lanka's inter-communal "getting-along" factor is in a state of imbalance due to a history of power inequalities, and when negative forces threaten to further disrupt the social ecosystem, is it not worth trying to "appease" the negative forces by asking about what's really bothering them? Before we criminalize racism, and create more hidden resentment in the process, could we not inquire into the root causes that allow top-down racist propaganda to be so easily reproduced on bumper stickers? If we truly care about processes of social reconciliation, then I think we should at least consider the possibility of employing empathetic dialogue with all involved. "But those idiots won't listen to us!" That may turn out to be true anyway, but there's certainly no doubt about it if we continue to call them idiots, in English.

Indeed, my efforts here are aimed at intellectuals who read English, rather than the Sri Lankan masses; but Peiris is right that, as with traditional rituals, reconciliation through the arts can only be facilitated by asking people what's wrong in languages they understand. What needs to be instituted from the "top down" and "on bumper stickers," I suggest, are actions that better facilitate a broader recognition of people who embody histories and respect shown to Others through music, and the publicization of such figures to generate an ethnically united Sri Lankan cultural history. When Cassiere gave me "Hotel California," he was acting like Baig did in his rendering of Buddhist messages in Sinhala. Baig did not pretend to be Buddhist—he was a proud Muslim—but he displayed no antipathy towards Buddhists. Nor was Baig a traitor to Sri Lanka by singing Buddhist songs in the way he knew how (he was from India). Regardless of whether Baig's decision to perform Buddhist songs was made for commercial reasons or out of sheer generosity, or a combination of both, Baig performed Buddhist songs to give Sri Lanka's Sinhala Buddhist population something they could cherish. Many Sinhalese felt love for Baig in return, whose musical gifts they still appreciate as gestures of respect. Likewise, Cassiere's performance of "Hotel California" for me was a musical *inhabiting* of the Other, a harmonious "occupation" that simultaneously recognizes difference but also the right to occupy the same musical spaces

---

[24] Wijayasekara, "My Experience of Independence."

as Others. What Sri Lankan musical giving demonstrates is a recognition and enjoyment of the Other's sounds and that the musical Other occupies a part of oneself. And this is precisely what Jayasinghe was doing when she gave Sri Lankans her song—their song—in a style associated with the West (that had influenced the original version of the song to begin with). One might wonder why her critics did not turn the lens around and laud her for "muddying" the domain of "pure" Western music with a Sri Lankan patriotic song? From one angle, that is about as "anti-colonial" a gesture as it gets.

Looking back on Cassiere's performance, his songs went a long way towards showing me techniques common to traditional musics in Sri Lanka, regardless of ethnicity, religion, and region. Rather than view him as a minor figure (a "minority") in a Kandyan region defined solely by Buddhism, let us define him as emblematic of Sri Lankan music as a whole. (1) He interpreted a common repertoire spread across multiple languages according to his own performance style, which was framed according to his religious and ethnic affiliation. (2) He demonstrated his individuality by creatively matching lyrics, melody, and instrumentation. This is a characteristic with deep roots in Sinhala folk song (Aravinda 2000), where it has always been possible to move lyrics around to different melodies. (3) Cassiere sang with no "melodic" instrument, his performance consisting of percussion and vocals. This is characteristic of Sri Lankan traditional musics throughout the island (e.g., those performed by Buddhists, Hindus, Sufis, and Väddas). (4) In practically every song, Cassiere's rhythm was a $\frac{3}{4}$ meter with an accent on the beats 1 and the "and" of 2. Played quickly, this is the rhythm associated with Baila; I met older Sri Lankans who called the slower version of it *khemta*, a six-beat meter in Hindustani light-classical music.[25] It is not just a triple feel, though, but a duple over triple rhythm, or "hemiola," which is characteristic of African musics and may indeed have been popularized across Sri Lanka through the spread of Baila Kaffrinha. The rhythm is also found throughout South India, but I suggest there is a particular Sri Lankan way of playing it, and its ubiquity in Sri Lankan musics is one of the island's defining musical features. One hears it in genres as diverse as Baila (the beat is fast; the "duple" meter is clappable, while the bass line plays in the "triple" meter), Sarala Gi (light classical music generally sung in Sinhala, generally slower; in the song "Basa Seethala Gagule" by Ananda Samrakoon, for example, the triple meter the foundation, the duple rides on top), certain moments in Beravā rituals (such as the basic *gaman matra*, or walking beats, played in the *yahan daekma* sequence of a Devol Maduwa; here the triple feel is emphasized by drummers, the duple by dancers walking in a circle), Sufi drumming (such as the song "Ulagam Iraval" performed by Bawa Nasurudeen, where his *rabāna* frame drum emphasizes both duple and triple),[26] Tamil Christian

---

[25] Jayantha Aravinda (personal communication).

[26] This can be found on Ceylon Muslim Digital TV: "Ulagam Iraval | Bawa Nasurudeen | Fakkeer Baith | Ceylon Muslim Digital TV," YouTube, August 4, 2016.

Figure C2.2 The standard "Sri Lankan" rhythm, known as a hemiola.

Figure C2.3 The standard rhythm found in the song "Ran Asipata," by the "militant monk" Ella Gunawansa Thero (Seneviratne 2000: 242).

Figure C2.4 The standard rhythm found in "Pachchai Vajale Panam Kadal Valiye," a song praising the LTTE (YouTube, December 13, 2010).

hymns,[27] jazz and rock groups adding "Sri Lankan flavor" to their music,[28] and both the martyrs' songs of LTTE Tamil militants and Sinhala nationalist songs written by militant monks (see Figures C2.2–C2.4). These genres have radically different styles and ways of playing music, but the hemiola remains nonetheless. It's like how Cuban musicians take a genre (e.g., rhumba) and boil it down to a rhythm that can be played *inside* other genres.

Sure, there is a longstanding genre of Sinhala militant music called *gaman hēvisi*, which involves rhythms (played on the *thammāttama*) that are obviously absent in LTTE songs. The Ella Gunawansa Thero song above ingeniously incorporates the *thammāttama* in a duple feel over the triple feel of the song. Most of the other songs on that album do not use a hemiola; many use traditional

[27] A Tamil Christian example is the music performed by Rev. G. Ambrose in Trincomalee (the duple is clapped by the audience over the triple meter rhythm): "REV. DR. G.AMBROSE TAMIL WORSHIP SONG (SRI LANKA)," YouTube, May 16, 2014. Strangely enough, the hemiola is virtually absent in Sinhala Christian music, which is generally in a straight $\frac{4}{4}$ or a $\frac{3}{4}$ waltz feel.

[28] Try the Sri Lankan jazz/rock fusion band Thriloka's cover of the Sinhala folk classic "Kuveni Asne" (part of the up country Kohomba Kankariya ritual), featuring Pabalu Wijegoonawardane on the *yak beraya* (scroll to the end): "K uweni Asne Rehearsals with Thriloka," YouTube, July 19, 2015.

gaman hevisi rhythms. The music has a distinctly Sinhala feel to it, even as it uses sitar and Western-sounding flute. Similarly, the theme for the Sinhala nationalist Buddhist monk party, the Bodu Bala Sena (by Sunil Edirisinghe), begins with a seven-beat pattern (presumably a *gaman hevisi* pattern, though I am not sure) and transitions into a $\frac{4}{4}$.[29] This could hardly be more different from the numerous LTTE songs that contain instruments and lyrical imagery associated only with Tamil music and culture.[30] Differences matter, *but so do similarities and shared aesthetic sensibilities*. Sinhala Buddhist processions (*peraheras*) are surely the Sinhala version of the Tamil tradition of circumambulating with an idol at temple festivals, which is the Tamil version of the Sufi Muslim procession to a mosque for a flag-raising ceremony, which is the Sufi version of Christian processions down city streets on saints' days, which is the Christian version of the Väddas' pilgrimage to Kataragama, which is the Vädda version of a *perahera*. Each of the above characteristics (#1–#4) can be found to varying degrees across Sri Lankan musics. They allow us to see there is an island-wide Sri Lankan musical aesthetic that is *different* from Indian music, and that Sri Lankan communities interpret in their own ways.

The most important lesson I learned from Tony and Cassiere is that one can be *both* a proud member of a specific community and a proud Sri Lankan: the two are not incommensurable. The musicality of Tony and Cassiere, and their ways of being with, on, and of the island are examples for Sri Lankans and the world. It is their everydayness I wish to highlight: their respect for Others and embodiment of an integrated Sri Lanka should not be deemed abnormal, outdated, a recent accretion, or peripheral to the nation (Tony and Cassiere, I suggest, play *Kandyan* music, and to think otherwise is to misunderstand Kandy's historic diversity in an attempt to define it as an exclusive, homogenous place). An obituary written about Cassiere says about his practice of gathering families together in Malay homes on Sundays and Thursday evenings to recite "Yaseen and Haddad Ratheeb and other [passages] from the Qur'an" that, "To 'survive' with this practice in the face of divergent views held by the numerous brands of Islamic 'fundamentalism'/ fanaticism that have sprouted up recently, is a tribute to his religious fervor."[31] The question is not whether such individuals are important enough or relevant to Sri Lankan music history, but what damage is done when we forget them.

---

[29] "Bodu Bala Sena Theme Song by Sunil Edirisinghe," YouTube, December 14, 2012.

[30] There is a specifically Tamil way of playing the hemiola, common in Tamil film songs: it's incredibly fast, the beat emphasizing the duple, but the bass playing more of a shuffle feel as opposed to the triple, as in the baila. For example, listen to the LTTE song, "Kaalai Vidiyum": "Kaalai Vidiyum—LTTE Song—Tamil," YouTube, May 20, 2013.

[31] Maas Jaam Cassiere, "He Always Had the Time for Any Traditional Function," *Sunday Times*, March 2, 2008.

Checkpoint

Sound as Commodity (Identity) versus
Sound as Gift (Identity + Relations)

<u>Music history conceived via musical commodities</u> = sounds expressed by a person or group → congeal into a form → are experienced/bought/taken by others → inner emotions and history of person or group deemed expressed → music history articulated → differences between groups perceived.

<u>Music history conceived via musical giving</u> = music created by others → given to others → reinterpreted by others → given to other others or back to the original givers → recognition that the culture of others is a part of one's own culture history of sonic generosity articulated → similarities and relations between groups perceived.

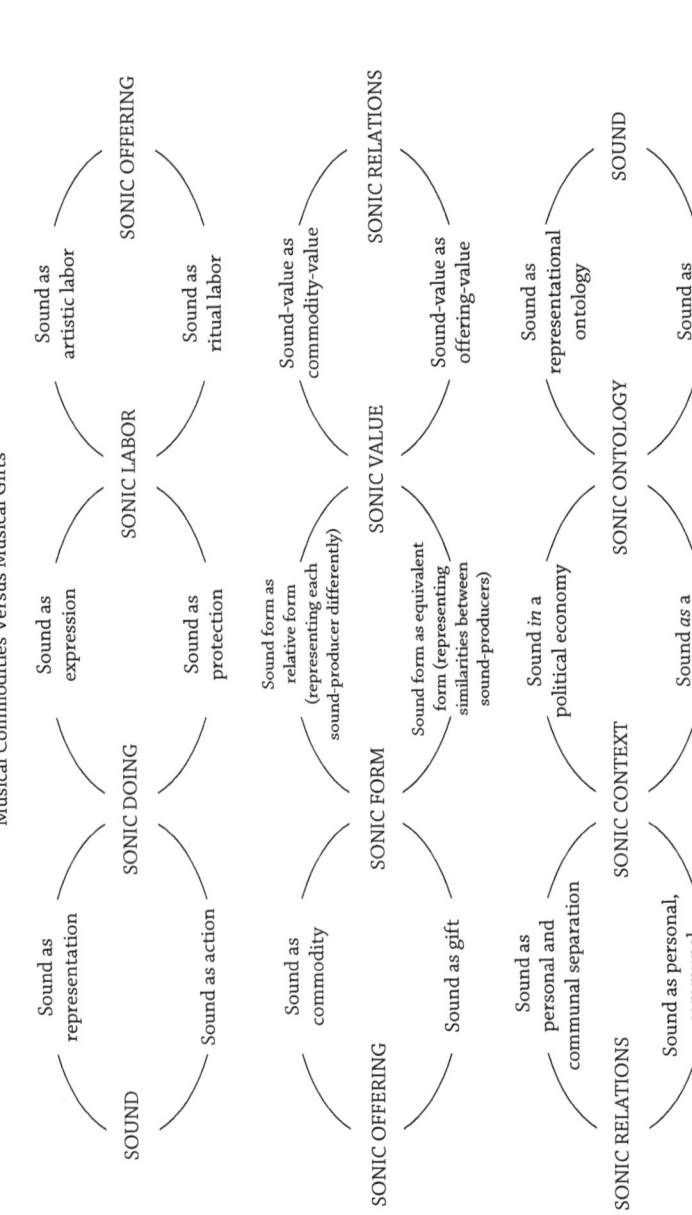

Musical Commodities Versus Musical Gifts[1]

[1] The binaries here are based on David Harvey's (2010) visual analysis of Marx's Das Kapital.

6

The Island Space

Music, Buddhism, and the Sinhalas

> Islandness, in this sense of identity confronting difference, informs primordial issues of philosophy: how, conceptually, we connect and disconnect parts and wholes, for example, and how we connect and disconnect one thing and another.
> —Marc Shell (2014: 3).

In this chapter, I show how the link between music and identity was instituted in Sri Lanka. I do so via two arguments. First, the British bounding of the island as a political space separate from India—what Sivasundaram (2013) calls the "islanding" of Sri Lanka—facilitated in the late nineteenth and early twentieth centuries a narrative of diffusion in which Sinhala and Tamil musics were deemed to have *come from* India. This had the effect of making it seem as though each community has distinct musical genres that originated outside the island. Second, I show that over the past few decades, Sinhala nationalists jettisoned the *movement to* discourse by locating Sinhala musics on the island in the prehistoric time of the mythical god-king Ravana. This "archive fever" (Derrida 1996), I contend, is the result of the music and identity episteme applied to an "islanded" island: it positions the musics of the Sinhalese and indigenous Vāddas as "Sri Lankan" and the musics of other communities as ultimately foreign.

The Islanded Island

In her work on the Andaman islands (just east of Sri Lanka), Aparna Vaidik (2010: 10) notes the British colonists operated with a specific notion of island history: islands are receptacles for migrating cultures in which culture is moved and then confined, as if in a prison. One sees this view in television shows like *Lost* or *Gilligan's Island*: travelers wash up an island that history seems to have passed by; the interior is unknown and perhaps populated by prior generations of maroons; if locals are discovered, they exhibit traits that seem to have come from an earlier era elsewhere, which appear to have persisted unchanged or developed as if in a Petri dish.[1]

Marc Shell (2014: 16–18) notes the tenacity of the islands as "isolates" view in Western culture. Eighteenth-century astronomical writings, such as Thomas Wright's *An Original Theory of New Hypothesis of the Universe* (1750) and William Herschel's *Construction of the Heavens* (1785), likened galaxies and planets to islands. In his *Critique of Pure Reason*, Kant drew on the island metaphor to describe the boundaries of objective knowledge: "This domain [of possible truth] is an island enclosed by nature itself within unalterable limits" (cited in Shell 2014: 16).[2] The British musical establishment has its own version of this discourse in the long-running BBC radio program *Desert Island Discs* (which premiered in 1942), where famous people were asked what gramophone records they would take with them if they were stranded on a desert island, "assuming of course, that you had a gramophone and an inexhaustible supply of needles."[3]

The peripheral musicological status of Sri Lanka was surely facilitated in part by this notion of islands as "isolates." The island's coasts were captured by British East India Company officers from the Dutch in 1796; because they did so under orders from Henry Dundas (Secretary of War), the East India Company and British Crown laid equal claim to it. But the island was deemed valuable for strategic rather than commercial reasons, so the initial experiment in joint "Crown Company" rule, whereby Sri Lanka was ruled from Madras presidency in South India, gave way in 1802 to rule as a separate Crown Colony, "Ceylon" (an English corruption of the Portuguese corruption (Ceilão) of "Sinhala"). The island was then controlled from the Colonial Office in London and thus "it shared its nineteenth century rulers with Fiji and New Zealand, rather than Madras and Bombay" (Spencer 2014: 2). The British developed a distinctly modern infrastructure that included extensive surveillance of the seas, as well as the bringing of populations

---

[1] According to this view, the further one goes inland, the more cultural "survivals," holdouts from culture contact, and potential danger one finds. Conrad's *Heart of Darkness* is not about an island but similarly, Lauren Benton (2010: 40) notes, "a certain timelessness attaches to the novel's associations of upriver isolation, loss of bearings, violence, and cultural dislocation. Simply raising the topic of rivers and their place in colonizing calls up surreal images of a slow ascent into a zone where all norms become distorted." The importance of the inland Kandyan Kingdom as a hub of Buddhist authenticity for postcolonial Sri Lankans, for instance, is surely a result of this islanding discourse but inverted, with the inland regions defined as a place of historic safety from colonial incursions.

[2] Shell (2014: 18) notes the OED defines "island" as originating from Old Norse and Old English: the historically prior Norse definition meant "water-land," which "stresses that the noun *is* (the first part of the word) properly means 'water' and indicates the mixture of water and land at the limiting, or defining, of 'coast'"; by contrast, the Old English definition meant "something like 'insulet,'" involving "the separation, or 'cutting' off, of land from water at the coast" (18). The latter definition is ironic, since the British colonists themselves came from an island.

[3] "The History of Desert Island Discs," BBC.com.

from disparate parts of the island into contact with one another through railroads and a road system. According to Sivasundaram (2013),

> Ever since the British bounded Sri Lanka in this way, it has not been able to take on a non-islanded political geography. The making of the island as a separate unit of governance in turn dictated a colonial policing of the movement of peoples, so that belonging on the island equated with a different identity than did coming from the mainland or elsewhere in Asia.

Thus, as Vaidik (2010: 10) puts it, *contra* the colonial view on island history that it was "human intervention [that] played a significant role in minimizing the effects of isolation, which geography at times imposed on island spaces," colonial imaginations and bureaucracies had "the reverse impact of reinforcing the spatial metaphor whereby the geographical isolation of islands, instead of being broken, was reinforced, reconfigured and even enhanced." Through the islanding process, Sri Lanka's coasts came to be seen as gateways that let cultural influences *in*, after which they appeared to have developed in distinct ethnic and religious communities, separated from outside contact, deemed to belong to certain regions of the island. Tamils were no longer seen as naturally and continually engaging with South India by crossing the Palk Strait, but as minorities in Sri Lanka.[4] As Spencer puts it, "Attempts to dredge a deeper channel between the island and the mainland provide a nicely concrete metaphor for the ideological separation [between India and Ceylon] in early colonial rule" (Spencer 2014: 2).

Being From versus Movement To

Literature by Caribbean writers overflows with challenges to the British colonial idea of islands as receptacles: a famous example is Kamau Brathwaite's notion of "tidalectics" (a rejoinder to dialectics), which stipulates that "in the culture of the circle 'success' moves outward from the center to the circumference and back again" (1983: 42; DeLoughrey 2011). The idea that the success of Sri Lanka lies in its synthesis of cultures that came from elsewhere—its creolization—and its giving this synthesis back to global culture *could* have defined the island in the modern age.[5] Consider how British Captain Robert Percival described the

---

[4] Tagliacozzo (2009: 102) argues the same process happened in the South China Seas and Indonesia, where it was only "as Dutch control over the Indonesian archipelago started to take a more bounded shape," that "some . . . indigenous notions of travel and far-flung community became more difficult to maintain."

[5] The concept of "creolization" in the Caribbean, Eisenlohr (2007: 23) writes, "has been understood as both a refuge from the essentialism of a purist search for origins and a central trope in several

cosmopolitan nature of Colombo (today's capital, founded by the Portuguese) in 1803:

> There is no part of the world where so many languages are spoken or which contains such a mixture of nations, manners and religions. Besides European and Cingalese, the proper native of the island, you meet scattered all over the town almost every race of Asiatic: Moors of every class, Malabars, Travancorins, Malays, Hindoos, Gentoos, Chinese, Persians, Arabians, Turks, Maldivians, Javians and Natives of all the Asiatic isles, Parsees or worshipers of fire. . . . There are also a number of Africans, Cafrees, Buganese, a mixed race of Africans and Asiatic; besides the half-castes, people of color and other races which proceed from a mixture of the original ones. Each of these different classes of people has its own manners, customs and language. (Choi 2012: 3)

Unlike Cuba, Sri Lanka had no twentieth-century intellectual like Fernando Ortiz to achieve widespread acceptance via the idea that cultural mixing through music is central to the island nation's identity. Nor did the Sri Lankan state take a syncretic genre, like Baila, and publicize it as national folklore in virtue of its syncretism, as Castro's government did with the ritual musics of the Afro-Cuban Lucumi religion.[6]

Since European settlements in the Caribbean devastated native populations, today's Caribbean communities are of much more recent vintage than those in Sri Lanka, some of whom trace their heritage back over two millennia. Nevertheless, the roots of all Sri Lankan populations (except the small indigenous Vädda population) lie in a *movement to* the island, and this generates a problem for those who would prefer a *being from* discourse: how can one acknowledge one's practices as *being from* the island when one has to admit one's community arose through a *movement to* it? If one admits one's community originated elsewhere, one's practices might seem to contain foreign elements and not be "of the soil"; if one admits elements of one's practices grew up on the island *after* other communities migrated to it, one risks making one's practices seem comparatively new and as having grown up through contact with other communities or after *their* practices were formed. This generates anxiety for the *being from* crowd, who feel they must

---

Caribbean nationalisms striving for local authenticity" (e.g., Mintz and Price 1992 [1976]; Trouillot 1998; Rommen 2015).

[6] Eisenlohr (2007: 14) notes the same resistance to creolization is happening in Mauritius, an Indian Ocean nation with no precolonial history, in which several groups maintain diasporic connections to India: "cultural forms recognized as creolized are confronted as a threat rather than embraced as expressions of cosmopolitan identity reinforced by increased cultural flows across national borders."

Figure 6.1 A photo of Väddas taken circa mid-1970s by musicologist C. de S. Kulatillake; they appear to be building a drum. Courtesy of the Kulatillake family.

place their communal identities and practices on the island back in a time before anyone else was around. In order to understand how this has played out in discussions of Sinhala traditional music, it will help to take a brief detour and discuss the presumed historical relations between Sinhala musics, the Väddas, Prince Vijaya (the mythical progenitor of the Sinhalas), and the mythical god-king Ravana.

Indigenizing Sinhala Music History: The Väddas and Ravana

The Väddas (also called the Wanniya-laeto) were stereotyped by an earlier generation of anthropologists as "primitive" because of their jungle habitat and profession as hunters; as Obeyesekere (2002b: 1) puts it, "The Väddas were once a classic group of aboriginal peoples who lived in the margins of Sinhala Buddhist civilization."[7] Obeyesekere and others have challenged the notion

---

[7] He cites Tylor's depiction of them in an 1881 publication: "In the forest of Ceylon are found the Väddas or 'hunters,' shy wild men who build bough huts, and live on game and wild honey" (Obeyesekere 2002b: 164).

that the Väddas are or have always been "primitive" (Obeyesekere 2002b; Brow 1996). He argues that in the northeastern jungle of the Bintanne Plains, where Väddas were living in poverty when studied by the Seligmanns for their 1911 monograph, there was a flourishing town, Bintanne-Alutnuvara, as late as the seventeenth century. According to Dutch and Portuguese chroniclers, the city protected families of Sinhala kings when they needed safety from invaders. The Väddas were known for their loyalty to the Sinhala crown. Kandyan King Rajasinha II was born in Vädda territory. Seventeenth-century Portuguese writer Fernão de Queiroz discusses the respect shown to Väddas by the Kandyan king:

> Once a year the Väddas send two deputies with honey and little presents to the king. When they arrive at the gate of the palace, they send word to his majesty that his cousins wish to see him. They are immediately introduced. They then kneel, get up, and inquire of the king, rather familiarly, about his health. The king receives them well, takes their presents, gives them others, and orders that certain marks of respect be shown them on their retiring from the palace (cited in Obeyesekere n.d.).

While the Väddas now live in isolated villages in the north-central and northeast of the island, it is known they once lived in other regions. In an earlier publication, Obeyesekere (1984) suggests that today's Sinhala-majority Sabaragamuwa province may have been named after a Vädda population that once lived there, since Sabaragamuwa means "land of the hunters." No one is sure what happened to those Väddas, but Obeyesekere (2002b) suggests some became Sinhalas (and the opposite transformation probably occurred, too).

The status of Väddas as respected kinsmen who are different from the Sinhalas is an important component of the founding myth of Sinhala civilization. The Sinhala origin myth, famously recounted in the *Mahavamsa* (compiled by Buddhist monks in the fifth century CE and after), states that in the sixth century BCE, North Indian Prince Vijaya was banished from his kingdom because of "numberless acts of fraud and violence" (Bullis 2000: 31). Landing in Sri Lanka with seven hundred followers, he is greeted by Upulvanna (Vishnu), who sprinkles water on him and ties a protective thread (*nool*) around his arm. Because of the thread, when Vijaya's followers are held captive by a demoness (*yakkhini*, sometimes described as a member of the Yakkas, one of the four indigenous populations at the time), he is protected; Vijaya forces the *yakkhini* (named Kuveni) into submission, and takes her as his queen. The moment their relationship is consummated is when she grants him sovereignty over the island. The story of their union is the earliest mention I have found of Sri Lankan musics, since it may have been written as early as the fifth century CE, and it describes an event said to have happened around a thousand years before that:

This (destined) ruler of the land, while reposing there with the *yakkhini*, hearing the sounds of song and music, inquired of the *yakkhini* regarding the same [about "the future advantages that were to result" because of their union]. Thereupon, she being desirous of conferring the whole sovereignty on her lord, replied, "I will render this Lanka habitable for men."

In the days following the celebrations, Vijaya routs the local population with Kuveni's help, making the island safe for newcomers. The couple has two children (a boy and a girl) and they appear set to live happily ever after. But seeking to better his political fortunes, Vijaya abandons Kuveni for a princess from the Tamil city of Madurai. Distraught and banished to the jungle with her children, an enraged Kuveni puts a curse on Vijaya and his kingly successors.

Obeyesekere (2002b: 17) takes this story to demonstrate that, "in the Buddhist scheme of things there are no 'indigenous peoples,' no 'aborigines,' no 'wild men' and 'tribes' of the Western imagination": this is because the Väddas are descended from the children of Vijaya and Kuveni, while the Sinhalas are descended from Vijaya's and his men's unions with Tamil women from Madurai. Rather than understand the Väddas as having existed *before* the arrival of the Sinhalas, in classic Sinhala tradition the Väddas are kinsmen of the Sinhalas, though they were banished to the jungle, deemed to live on the outskirts of Sinhala society.[8] In local legend, the up country Kohomba Kankariya (which forms the foundation for Kandyan Dance) originated to heal Vijaya's successor, King Panduvas, when he suffered from Kuveni's curse.[9]

The first drummer in Sri Lanka, my *gurunnānse* told me, was Pulastya, son of Brahma and grandfather of Ravana. Pulastya was the father of Vaisravana, one of the Gods of the Four Quarters (the cardinal directions) and father of the Rakshas, one of the four indigenous groups (the others were the Yakkas, Nagas, and Devas). According to my *gurunnānse*, over time, some Rakshas "became Väddas." As mentioned in the introduction, the Bera Pōya Hēvisi ritual was given by Pulastya to the Väddas, who gave it to the Beravā. As one drummer in Pelmadulla (Sabaragamuwa province) put it to me in English, "Sinhala drumming *is* Vädda drumming." It is after all these events occurred that the Buddhist missionary

---

[8] Obeyesekere (2002b: 5) notes that when Väddas perform rituals at Buddhist shrines, such as at Kataragama or Mahayangana, the rituals function as "a mechanism for incorporating Väddas into the religious and social structure of adjacent agricultural communities, while at the same time recognizing their separateness."

[9] There are many Sinhala ritual traditions that reference Kuveni's curse. Kapferer (1997: 63) mentions that the *punava* pot ("leopard" pot, leopard being a form of Kuveni) is used at shrines to Devol Deviyo by those wishing to put a curse on others, while in the south of the island, articles said to have protected King Panduvas are put in front of the patient in the major healing rituals.

Mahinda, son of the Indian Buddhist King Asoka, brought Buddhism to Sri Lanka (third century BCE).[10]

Now, consider the following statement (made in 2006) by retired Lieutenant Colonel A. S. Amarasekera: after mentioning that "the Buddha has pointed out that the root of all evil is ignorance and false view," he says

> The identity of the indigenous population is used to identify a country. Thus England is the land of the English people, Germany, the land of the German people, France, the land of the French people, Japan, the land of the Japanese people, China, the land of the Chinese people, Malaysia, the land of the Malay people etc. . . . The skeletal remains of a human found in the Balangoda caves [in Sri Lanka] were carbon dated and found to be over 28,000 years old. There is legendary belief of an advanced civilization in this country over 5,000 years ago in the Ravana era. This belief extends further to a Maha Bali civilization 10,000 years ago, a Tharaka civilization 15,000 years ago and a Manu civilization 30,000 years ago.[11] However, written history in the Mahavamsa takes us back 2,500 years to the advent of Vijaya. At that point of time the country was known as Sivhela as there were four clans living here. They were the Devas, the Yakkas, the Rakshas and the Nagas. Vijaya and his Sinha clan that migrated to this country integrated with the above mentioned four indigenous Hela clans and were together identified henceforth as Sinhala and their country was known as Sinhale.

In Amarasekera's narrative—which I take as representative of what today is a fairly standard Sinhala ethnonationalist view—the *movement to* is submerged into a *being from* such that it matters little if Tamil settlements on the island go back a thousand years or more since Sinhala society goes back 30,000! This is a perspective that objectifies the island, sees it from outside, views it as naturally enclosed—islanded—and as capable of forever being transgressed except by Sinhalas, whose *being from* is rooted back in time through their equation with *all four* of the island's primeval indigenous peoples. It matters little that the actual existence of people who identify as Sinhala developed tens of thousands of years after those remains found their resting place in the Balangoda caves; nor does it matter that countless migrants to the island over the centuries (surely some of

---

[10] According to legend, Vijaya arrived on Sri Lanka at the moment the Buddha achieved Enlightenment; during the Buddha's lifetime, he gave the god Vishnu a warrant (*varam*) to protect the whole island. According to the *Mahavamsa*, the Buddha made three trips to the island, deeming it a place where his religion would flourish and be protected.

[11] Lt. Colonel A. S. Amarasekera, "Original land of Sinhale," *Sunday Times*. These are civilizations that, according to "Sinhala folklore" (Amarasekera's words), existed in Sri Lanka before the coming of Vijaya.

Amarasekera's ancestors) intermarried over the years with Sinhalas and might *also* have a claim to that ancestry. In Amarasekera's narrative, the *Mahavamsa's* origin story about the Sinhalas—the classic text that has long been the founding document of Sinhala identity—has been jettisoned.

In Gombrich and Obeyesekere's (1988: 449) seminal book on modern transformations of Sinhala Buddhism, they describe meeting a Sinhala musician who makes the case that the island's music history goes back to the time of Ravana:

> An advocate of the study of Indian music is reported to rest his case on the claim that Sri Lanka excelled in that field in the time of Ravana. Ravana was the demon king of the island in the Sanskrit epic, the Ramayana, but hitherto Sinhala history has ignored him; nevertheless, his rule is now being assigned to the primordial time before the Buddha. Thus the past is not merely being credited with ever more inventions, but also extended back beyond what has always been regarded as the point of origin of the Sinhala people. Modern conditions appear to have stimulated the popular mythopoetic imagination.

It is key to register the surprise of the authors in this passage, for it hints that in the 1980s, the musical connection between the Sinhalas and Ravana was a new thing. It is also necessary to note they use the term "Indian music," a vestige of a late-colonial perspective that Sri Lankan musics are "Indian."

Nowadays Ravana is ubiquitously described as the progenitor of *Sri Lankan* musics. He is used to promote an ancient Sinhala presence that distances Sinhala musical identity from India. For example, in recent years there has been a newfound interest in the Ravanahatha, described on its Wikipedia page as an "ancient bowed violin" that "originated among the Hela civilization of Sri Lanka during the time of the demon king Ravana." The entry goes on to say that according to the *Ramayana*, the Hindu god Hanuman picked up the Ravanahatha and brought it to India, where it developed into North Indian bowed instruments, after which it made its way via trade routes to Arabia, the Mediterranean, and Europe, where it developed into the violin and viola. Thus in a twist of the colonial narrative of musical migration from India to Sri Lanka, Ravana allows Sri Lanka to appear as a progenitor of Indian and European musics!

My friend Pabalu Wijegoonawardene, a *yak beraya* drummer, founded the music drama troupe the Ravana Brothers, which explores the status of Ravana as progenitor of Sri Lankan music history. He produced a drama about Ravana and scored its music; the group's website provides much information on Ravana, his importance to Sinhala culture, and the places he supposedly lived in Sri Lanka. It is key to note, though, that Pabalu is no Sinhala chauvinist: Ravana was a Hindu devotee of Shiva; Pabalu views Ravana as a *pan*-Sri Lankan musical progenitor (much the way Maunaguru positioned him in his *Ravanesan*, discussed in

Chapter 3). Here, the colonial narrative on Beravā rituals being pre-Buddhist in origin allows for a grounding of Sri Lankan music that cuts across ethnicity and religion.

Pabalu's inclusiveness, however, lies in stark contrast to ethnonationalist appropriations of Ravana, who is now treated as a historical rather than mythological figure. This and the contemporary resurgence of the Ravanahatha are examples of what Derrida calls "archive fever": an "authoritarianly transparent and authoritatively concealed" discourse that is the "consignation in an external place [in this case, the island imagined as external] which assures the possibility of memorization, of repetition, of reproduction, or of reimpression," which Derrida associates with the Freudian death drive. As Derrida says, "There would indeed be no archive desire without the radical finitude, without the possibility of a forgetfulness which does not limit itself to repression."

Elsewhere (Sykes 2011), I argue this archive fever is a postcolonial response to colonial era writers who positioned Sinhala musics as though they came from "India" only to have degenerated in the hands of the Sinhalas. In the next section, I show that efforts (in the early to mid-twentieth century) to view North India as the ancestral home for Sinhala musics enhanced the idea of Sinhala musical lack, driving a musical wedge between Sinhalas and Tamils, and contributing toward the above-mentioned archive fever.

The Fetishization of North Indian Music

A prominent idea amongst Sinhala Buddhists in the late colonial period was that Sinhala ethnicity has Aryan roots. Sir William Jones (1746–1794) posited Central Asia as the cradle for North Indian and European cultures, noting affinities between Latin and Sanskrit; through the work of philologist Max Muller, by 1861, this connection was being discussed in racial terms (Sheeran 1997: 152).[12] Proof of a Sinhala connection with Aryan heritage was found in the Sinhala language, which was categorized as part of the Indo-Aryan language family (like Hindi). Since Tamil was classified as a Dravidian language, the Aryan connection became a way to differentiate Sinhalas and Tamils (Daniel 1996). For the Buddhist revivalist Anagarika Dharmapala (1864–1933), the Aryan connection established a link with a noble past: "In the most glorious days of our beloved Lanka our ancestors were in touch with our Indian cousins, but now we are estranged on account of our anglicized habits, so utterly unsuited to the Aryan spirit" (Guruge 1965: 518; cited in Sheeran 1997: 156). The Vijaya tale also placed Sinhala heritage in North

---

[12] Sheeran (1997: 152) notes that the "flattering conclusion" garnered by the comparison between North India and Europe is "suggested probably most plainly in the deployment of the term *arya*, the Sanskrit term for noble, as in 'the ancient Aryan civilization.'"

India. For these reasons, some Sinhalas in the early-to-mid twentieth century viewed North India as the ancestral home for Sinhala music.

This preference for North Indian music, though, was a historical development and not something that had always characterized Sinhala music. It emerged in the late nineteenth century, when a visiting Parsi theater troupe from Bombay performed a wildly popular version of the Urdu play *Inder Sabha* in 1877 at the Floral Hall in Colombo. C. Don Bastian (1852–1921), who would later edit the first Sinhala language daily newspaper (the *dinapatapravrtti*, starting in 1896; Peebles 2006: 64), decided to stage his own version of the genre, which he called *nruthya* (or *nurthi*), after the Sanskrit term for "expressive dance" (*nritya*).[13] Bastian went on to produce musicals like *Romeo and Juliet* and *Franklow and Ingirlee*, which were seen by Ceylonese of all stripes, as well as the British governor. The genre was continued by Sinhala playwright John de Silva (1857–1922), who "brought to the stage a more modernistic blend that was rapidly domesticated to cater to local tastes" (Wickremasinghe 2014: 87) through his collaborations with Visvanath Lawjee, a composer from Bombay (Field 2014: 1046). De Silva is remembered as an early Sinhala nationalist for his plays on historical themes, such as *Sirisangabo Charitaya* (1903) about the king of the ancient Sinhala kingdom of Anuradhapura (ruled 252–254 CE), *Sri Vikrama Rajasinghe* (1906) about the king of Kandy (ruled 1798–1815), and *Devanampiya Tissa* (1914) about the Anuradhapura king who introduced Buddhism to the island (ruled 307–267 BCE). He also produced Shakespearean dramas.[14] *Nurthi* deserves a place in a broader Indian Ocean history of the Parsi theater, which also went to Malaya and spawned the multiethnic musical theater genre called *bangsawan* (Tan 1993), and to Indonesia, where it developed into the *komedie stamboel* (Cohen 2006). Musically speaking, *nurthi's* biggest accomplishment was laying groundwork for the spread of North Indian (Hindustani) music in Ceylon, which would dominate the recording industry and radio until the 1950s. In line with the budding Arya philosophy of the time, De Silva "advocated a song form that valorized Buddhism and North Indian music as authentically Sinhalese" (Field 2013: 14), though the genre was made and consumed by Sinhalas, Tamils, Muslims, Burghers, and the British.[15]

---

[13] Field (2014: 1046), paraphrasing Ariyaratne (1983: 56–58), notes that "nine songs found in six different *nurthi* musicals in the 1880s were imitations of the melody from the most popular Indar Sabha song, 'Rajahumayi Kavmaka.' One such musical featured five different song-lyrics set to this tune."

[14] Ruwini Jayawardana, "Nurthi the Living Art," *Daily News*, April 29, 2009.

[15] *Nurthi* songs were among the first to be recorded with the new gramophone technology, which was introduced to the island in 1900, with Sinhala records available from 1903 (Wickremasinghe 2014: 81). The Gramophone Company made just 44 recordings in Ceylon between 1900 and 1910, a tiny amount compared to the 4,000 in India, 93 in Java, 97 in Thailand, and 121 in Malaya (85). Here we encounter a theme that runs throughout this book: it is not *that* the Theravada Buddhist laity looks down upon music, but that people *assume* they will, that stops musical innovation: "It was perhaps felt by exhibitors [of the gramophone] who toured Asia with their talking machines that in the predominantly Theravada Buddhist society where congregational practices or participation in community life

From the 1930s through the 1950s, a number of important Sinhala musicians went to Rabindranath Tagore's school for the arts in Santiniketan, Bengal, and returned with training in Hindustani classical music. Sheeran (1997: 152) remarks that "granting such recognition to Hindustani music would ally the Aryan Sinhalese with what was regarded as a superior musical and racial ancestry while simultaneously suggesting considerable ancestral and geographical distance between Sinhalese and Tamil cultural traditions." It was Anagarika Dharmapala himself who first suggested the idea that Sinhala musicians should accept the leadership of Tagore. Dharmapala's ties with the Tagore family had arisen through his friendship with Raja Jotindro Mohan Tagore, the older brother of musicologist Sourindro Mohun Tagore (Sheeran 1997: 191–194).[16] In 1955, the "Report on the Commission on Broadcasting and Information" (RCBI) stated that "we agree with the view expressed by the Sinhalese Advisory Committee, and several others who gave evidence before the Commission, that North Indian classical music should be the basis for any Sinhalese national music" (cited in Sheeran 1997: 194). The sitar had become all the rage in Sri Lanka, though it was used differently than in North India: it was used to play short melodic phrases in between lines of singing, and for the opening melodies of a song, rather than in long improvised performances.

However, the discourse on folk music that emerged through the Shantiniketan experience encouraged Sinhala musicologists to look to rural areas of the island to "find" Sinhala folk music. It was assumed Buddhism had stunted the growth of Sinhala music, but that authentic Sinhala music was located in the songs of farmers and fishermen. For example, after nine months at Shantiniketan, Devar Surya Sena and his wife Nelun Devi returned to Ceylon to collect such music, becoming the world's first experts in Sinhala folk song (Sheeran 1997:172). At the early date of 1928, the duo performed Sinhala folk songs with sarangi accompaniment for the Duchess of York (later Queen Elizabeth), while in 1935 they made the first broadcast of Sinhala folk tunes on Radio Ceylon (Sheeran 1997: 172). After only a year in Ceylon, the couple set off for England, where they debuted at Grotrian Hall (in 1932) with mixed results (Surya Sena 1978: 88–89).[17] These attempts to "find" Sinhala folk music were arrested by a lack of confidence: in his autobiography, Surya Sena admits that when he returned home after performing

---

were not the norm, that the lure of recorded songs would not be powerful enough to attract crowds" (82–83). In fact, the gramophone *was* used by lay Buddhist preachers and *bhikkus* (monks): for example, Anagarika Dharmapala used the gramophone "with a magic lantern to reach out to Sinhalese people in rural areas" (89) and about a decade later, the monk H. J. Saranankara, "incumbent monk at the Isurumuniya Temple in Anuradhapura," used the gramophone while preaching.

[16] Dharmapala's opening of a Department of Pali Studies at Calcutta University also strengthened ties between Sinhala Buddhists and Calcutta (ibid.; Kemper 2015).

[17] According to Surya Sena, Indic musicologist Fox-Strangeways praised the duo's singing because their vocal intonation lacked the nasalization of Indian singers and sounded "Anglophone" (Surya Sena 1978: 89).

for the Duchess, he "plunged with zest into the task of resurrecting Sinhala music. I was convinced it had existed" (64).

The Advisory Committee's discussions on Sinhala music reported in the 1955 RCBI show a fear that Sinhala music was too watered down by outside influences: *nurthi* was defined as "a distinct Sinhalese tradition" but the committee was concerned too many others saw it as a "mixture of Western, Indian, and hybrid Bengali music with a veneer of Sinhala folk music" (Sheeran 1997: 194). The Committee warned such a perception leads many to view the Sinhalas as having no music (194). However, instead of accepting cultural mixing as a part or definitive of Sinhala music, the committee warned against "the deterioration of the musical taste of the listeners" and discouraged "blind imitation and indiscriminate borrowing" (195). Sinhala music had to be guarded from dilution, but exactly what Sinhala music is (or was) needed to be determined. The fear of degeneration was based on the view that popular music is corrosive: "In another five years," the RCBI warned, "the Sinhalese farmers will be singing film songs at the customary ploughing and reaping of their fields if the present policy of indiscriminate dissemination of film music is allowed to continue" (186). Such a view of popular music was shared by guardians of Indian culture at the time, notably B. V. Keskar, then–Minister of Information and Broadcasting at All India Radio (AIR), who in 1953 banned Bollywood songs from Indian airwaves; this made Radio Ceylon immensely popular in the Subcontinent, for it played a lot of Bollywood music at the time.

In sum, we can take the RCBI's 1955 report, coming just before a wave of Sinhala Buddhist nationalism would transform the country, as a turning point for Sinhala music: no longer was it assumed Sinhala music came from India; it was assumed that *either* the Sinhalas once had a native musical tradition that had declined through outside influences, *or* the Sinhalas never developed their music because Buddhism didn't let them.[18]

The Apotheosis of the Islanding of Sri Lanka: The Development of a "Pure" Sinhala Music Tradition

Despite the evident successes of Hindustani-influenced musicians, the effort to develop a less "North Indian–sounding" Sinhala music emerged during the same period (Ahubudu 1960). W. D. Amaradeva (1927–2016) is perhaps the most influential performer in this genre (*sarala gi*, "light music"), a vocalist and violinist who over a long career has merged Sinhala folk music idioms, Buddhist

---

[18] Where was Beravā drumming in such discussions? I suggest Anglicized Sinhala scholars looked past it, either out of a caste bias or belief that a country's music needed to be founded on melodies rather than percussion. Also, because of Beravā secrecy, the elites were also not familiar with the intricacies of Beravā drumming—they were more likely to learn piano or harmonium.

lyrical imagery, and Hindustani instrumentation, including sitar and harmonium.[19] With a foundation in Hindustani light music and training at Santiketan, in the 1950s, Amaradeva studied with Kandyan dancers and drummers (such as the famous Pani Bharata) to develop a style of song (*janagayana*) that included Kandyan traditional melodies with longer verses built in to flesh them out as popular songs.[20] The influential Sinhala Christian musician Sunil Santha (1915–1981) studied at Shantiniketan and went on to study Hindustani classical music at the Bhatkande College of Music in Lucknow in the early 1940s, but after returning he began composing, as Michael Roberts puts it, "for the Sinhalese ear."[21] Santha secured a position as a recording artist at Radio Ceylon and recorded over a hundred songs for them between 1946 and 1960.[22] Perhaps his most famous music incorporated poetry from the influential Hela Havula movement, founded by Munidasa Cumaratunga (1887–1944). A language "purist," Cumaratunga's movement aimed to eliminate Sanskrit influences from the Sinhala language by returning it to an earlier form called Hela.[23] Garrett Field (2014: 1044; 2017) perceptively notes that while John De Silva's *nurthi* movement "created an inner domain of song with Buddhism and North Indian classical music at the core and the West threatening from outside . . . Cumaratunga created an inner domain of song with a pure Sinhala language at the heart and North India threatening from outside." Radio Ceylon was instrumental in developing these nationalist strands of Sinhala music.

In sum, the islanding process generated a narrative of diffusion, which produced the need to search for authenticity. This generated anxiety about whether the Sinhalas "have" music, on account of the idea that Buddhism had stunted the growth of Sinhala music, the prevalence of Hindustani music at the time, and the "hybrid" nature of some genres (e.g., Baila). This wound up generating

---

[19] *Sarala gi* continued on even as the North Indian influence on Sinhala musicians waned, through artists like Victor Ratnayake (b. 1942) and Sunil Edirisinghe (b. 1949). The genre is now often referred to as Sinhala "classical" music.

[20] Pani Bharata (1920–2005) was an influential figure in his own right, son of a dancer in the Algama village from Kegalle and a fantastic drummer and dancer who would become Head of Aesthetic Studies in Colombo. In the 1930s, accompanying the fine artist J. D. A. Perera and performing with Perera's wife, the dancer Chandralekha, he played in India for the Maharaja of Travancore, and earned a scholarship to study at Santiniketan in the 1940s.

[21] Tony Donaldson, "Sunil Santha: A Search for Sinhala Music," Tuppahi.wordpress.com, March 12, 2015.

[22] Donaldson notes (ibid.) notes that Santha formed his own unique ensemble that included Hawaiian guitar, bamboo flutes, and occasionally rabāna.

[23] Donaldson (ibid.) explains "hela": "The Sinhala word 'hela' is rooted in the word 'Heladiva,' which literally translates as 'Isle of the Sinhalese.' When 'hela' is paired with another word, it refers to something particular about the Sinhalese 'nation.' The term 'Hela Havula' became widely used in the 1960s to refer to a 'gang,' 'group' or 'batch' of like-minded persons striving to promote a refined and disciplined style of the Sinhala language (*svabasha*), while 'Hela Gee' refers to a distinct type of Sinhala song."

worries of derivativeness, and the need to find or create musical traditions that could be rooted in the soil. But even though this was a proud project—it is not my aim to debunk it here—it emerged from a state of anxiety, because Sri Lanka is a space that has always been characterized by extensive migration and cultural diversity. And the recognition of this only reinforced the need to combat the narrative of musical diffusion.

By the late twentieth century, when all hell had broken loose and the country was engulfed in civil war and myriad communal conflicts large and small, the definition of Beravā music and dance had radically changed. The worry that Beravā rituals are "Indian" or "Hindu" had long subsided—and to be clear, that is a *good* thing. Beravā drumming is not Indian or Hindu. But that doesn't mean Beravā drumming (or any other Sinhala musical genres) did not arise through acts of musical giving from and to non-Sinhala communities. One can say any kind of Sinhala music is Sinhala and Sri Lankan without meaning that it arose *sui generis* on the island, back in the mist of time, in the Balangoda caves.

Conclusion: An Islanded Britain and Islanded Others

In April 2012, in Tamil-majority Batticaloa, four statues were destroyed, presumably by the Sinhala-dominated police or military. These included statues of: Swami Vipulananda, the Tamil musicologist and poet from Batticaloa; Pulavarmani Periyathampi Pillai, a Tamil poet; Robert Baden-Powell, the founder of the Scout Movement; and Mahatma Gandhi.[24] Such attacks, whether intended for this purpose or not, destroy physical reminders of Sri Lankan historical connections with India and Europe, as well as Sri Lankan Tamil contributions to the Sri Lankan arts. Such extreme vilification of Sri Lankan connections off the island long ago reached shocking proportions. While Sinhala society has long been influenced by Indian and European cultures, such acts show an attempt to purge such connections from the Sinhala psyche. The islanding process has reached its apotheosis.

Sri Lanka is not alone in this endeavor. Just ask this Brit, lamenting in the pages of the *New York Times* in 2016 after Britain voted to leave the European Union: "Do we open ourselves up to new things, even if they might be unfamiliar, risky, unexpected, sometimes even undesirable? Or do we close ourselves down: a small island, trapped in its own smallness?"[25] He concludes:

> All I can do is look out at the nature from the window of my room in Alresford. I'm from here, so I can't be sure whether or not this is just another type of nihilism, but I think: Well, if all this nature is bigger

---

[24] "Gandhi, Vipulananda, Poet Periyathampi, Baden-Powell Desecrated in Batticaloa," Tamilnet.com, April 6, 2012.

[25] Tom Whyman, "Hell Is Other Britons," *New York Times*, June 25, 2016.

than us, then I want it be get even bigger. I want it to become so big that it will consume all of our smallnesses, invalidate them, smother them out. Not just Alresford. I want a demented, throbbing, fecund nature to overrun this whole country, to overturn the wretched consequences of the laws that we have, in our stupidity, set for ourselves.

This is a call for de-islanding. And it is vitally important to realize that to make such a call—in Britain or Sri Lanka—is not the same as a call for a return to imperialism. Rather, it is a call for the encouragement of positive human connections that can be made and remembered without the intervening of manmade borders and the ideologies it sets in place, the type that imperialism *and* ethnonationalism imposes.

Jonathan Spencer (2014: 4), borrowing from Subrahmanyam's notion of "connected histories," calls similarly for a "connected anthropologies." Spencer (2014: 4) puts it thusly: "Islands like the island of Sri Lanka are perhaps best thought of not as closed entities but more as sieves or colanders, through which persons, ideas and theories pass, leaving odd bits and pieces behind on their passage." Such a discourse, when developed in full, will situate Sri Lanka's communities as being *from* the island and as connected with musicians and music histories all around the Indian Ocean and, surely, Britain and elsewhere. Such a discourse will show how Sinhala musicians borrowed from India and Sri Lankan Others while being, forming, and remaining themselves. As Spencer puts it, "if we attend to the movements of migrants across the Bay of Bengal, we find ourselves thinking in terms of a rather different region, a region which includes Singapore and Penang, as well as Colombo and Kolkata, and therefore a region which undermines the coherence of received ideas about Southeast as well as South Asia." The accusation that such a call is for a return to imperialism, which Spencer says he received from a Sri Lankan audience member when he presented his paper, is to reimpose a smallness on islands that was created *through* imperialism. It is also to ignore that throughout the long history of Sinhala engagement with non-Sinhala cultures, Sinhala musicians have kept their identities while absorbing, resignifying, and re-gifting beliefs, practices, and sounds offered to them by Others.

PART IV

REDISCOVERING MUSICAL GIVING

Checkpoint

Re-Connecting Sinhala and Tamil Musical Cultures

> To discover the various uses of things is the work of history.
> —Karl Marx, *Das Capital* (1981: 1)

The A9 Road

Sri Lanka's A9 road runs north-south for 321 kilometers, connecting Kandy with Jaffna. Scenic and often barren, it passes through the historically important towns of Matale, Dambulla, Anuradhapura, Vavuniya, and the former capital of the LTTE, Kilinochchi. Due to the war, the road was officially closed in 1984. Once a means to connect the predominantly Sinhala hill country with the predominantly Tamil and Muslim north, the war turned the A9 into an icon of disaster, a symbol of a divided nation. Its closure meant contact with friends and family in the north was difficult if not impossible; for those still in the north, the region came to resemble a "camp," with travel into and out of the region severely limited.

With the government's retaking of Jaffna in 1995, Kilinochchi became the LTTE headquarters and effectively an independent country, with a time zone that ran a half hour behind the rest of the island. In the wake of the 2002 ceasefire, the LTTE, deeply in need of funds, realized it could collect taxes on traffic along the A9. The road was reopened in 2002 under heavy restrictions for the first time in nearly twenty years. It was closed again in 2006 as heavy fighting erupted again, and then reopened to civilians after the end of the war in December 2009.

While international journalists have tended to write about the A9 as a road that connects "Sinhala" and "Tamil" Sri Lanka, thereby reinscribing differences between these populations even while using the road as a metaphor for connection, playwright and activist Dharmasiri Bandaranayake saw the opening of the road as an opportunity. Starting after the 2002 ceasefire, he began working with *kooththu* master Sinniah Maunaguru to take Sinhala musical theater (*nadagam*) artists to the north and Tamil musical theater (*kooththu*) artists to the Sinhala-dominated

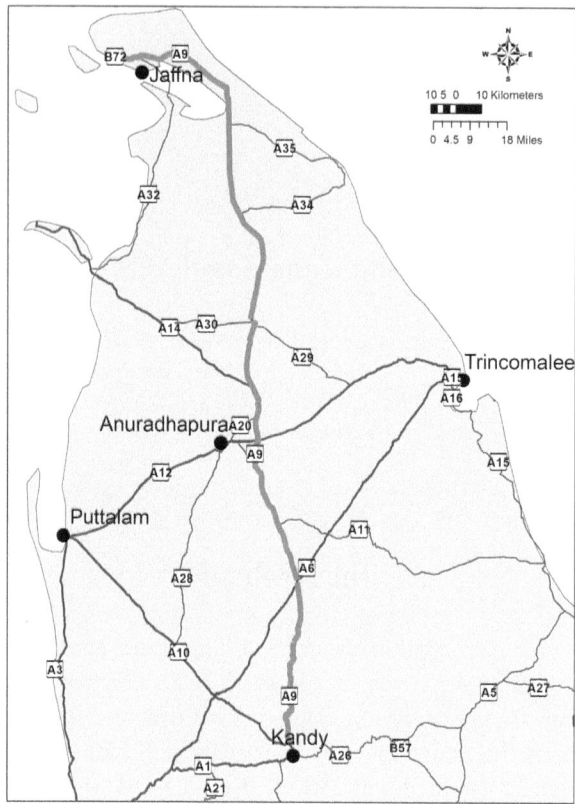

Figure C3.1 The A9 Road. Map by Girmaye Misgna. Used with permission.

south, to host workshops and performances demonstrating to residents in both places that Sinhalas and Tamils have a shared cultural heritage.[1]

Bandaranayake's applied musicology project occurred immediately following one of his most politically controversial projects, and is intimately related to it. It is worth going into that project first, for it will show both his public notoriety and the extreme danger he faced in undertaking the A9 project. On December

---

[1] Bandaranayake is a major figure of Sri Lankan film and theater. His films *Suddilage Kathava* (1986) and *Bavaduka* (1997) won Best Director at Sri Lankan film award ceremonies; his plays have garnered awards for Best Play, Best Director, and Best Actor and Actress at state drama festivals starting in the 1970s. In 1998, during a period of extreme terror in the south, Bandaranayake was forced to flee to India after receiving death threats for his adaptation of Sartre's *Men Without Shadows*, which was viewed as critical of the JVP (Janatha Vimukthi Peramuna, the social revolutionary group, now a political party, that was responsible for two uprisings in twentieth-century Sri Lanka; see Chapter 1). Among his documentaries chronicling the war, most notable are 1987's *Echoes of War* (which was banned), 1990's *Across the Fence* ("conceived as a social appeal for Sinhala and Tamil education as a long term contribution to helping extinguish war flames of the ethnic crisis"), and 1995's *The Refugees*

10, 1999, Bandaranayake premiered a Sinhala-language adaptation of Euripides' anti-war play *The Trojan Women* (*Trojan Kanthavo*) to a packed house in Colombo. The play featured seventy actors and musicians, with funding from the Royal Netherlands Embassy in Sri Lanka and HIVOS (a Dutch NGO). Bandaranayake's reasons for reviving *The Trojan Women* were unequivocal:

> I chose this play as my contribution to the efforts to end the civil war raging in our land and to bring lasting peace to our society. Even twenty-five centuries after its creation, *The Trojan Women* remains the most powerful and foremost anti-war play produced in world theater. It has been the most powerful weapon in the hands of artists using the arena of theater in the struggle against war and barbarism. Staging this play and taking its unique dramatic message to all corners of the land, I believe, is the most powerful service and contribution that I can make as an artist to the efforts to end war.[2]

A week after the premiere of *Trojan Kanthavo*, the home of the play's lead actress was destroyed. A report written by Bandaranayake with an anonymous journalist describes what happened:

> The first attack had taken place around midnight of December 25, 1999; a vehicle, identified as a double cab, had entered the farm from the main road and has stopped. A group of men came out of the vehicle, firing at random from machine guns at the house, throwing two hand grenades. . . . The hand grenades had been thrown into the open verandah on the right side of the house . . . extensively damaging the walls.

The actress was not home but her house's caretakers barely escaped with their lives. On January 2, 2000, the attackers returned and destroyed the house, along with the actress's film archive. Then on January 26, the play's musical director and his musician wife were attacked. An anonymous letter written to the *Sunday Times* describes what happened:

> Thugs forcibly entered the home of xxxxx and xxxxx, two pop music singers. The couple had pistols held to their heads, their hair was cut off

---

(about refugee camps). For this work he received numerous awards, including a selection by Sri Lanka's Film Critics Society as one of the ten best directors of Sri Lankan Cinema, the Bunka Prize for special achievement in theater and cinema from the Japan–Sri Lanka Friendship Cultural Fund (1996), and an honorary citizenship from the city of New Orleans (1990).

[2] Panini Wijesiriwardana, "Sri Lankan Artist Speaks About Death Threats by Sinhala Extremists." World Wide Socialist Web, December 2003.

Figure C3.2 Dharmasiri Bandaranayake. Photo by Vikalpa Sri Lanka [CC BY 2.0].

and they were doused with petrol. The attackers forced loaded pistols into the singers' mouths and threatened to kill them unless they promised not to appear on "anti-government" political platforms. xxxxx and xxxxx had sung at a UNP rally during last year's presidential elections and xxxxx provided the musical score for *Trojan Kanthavo*. The attack took place in front of their two young children and xxxxx's mother.[3]

The victims of both attacks had supported the opposition party, the UNP, in recent elections.[4] Due to the threat of more violence, the musicians and lead actress were forced to leave the country, and all scheduled performances of *Trojan Kanthavo* were canceled. Bandaranayake launched a campaign on behalf of the victims, to find the perpetrators and bring them to justice.

Ever-defiant and riding a wave of media attention because of the attacks, Bandaranayake made plans to bring his actress and musicians back to Sri Lanka, and to go ahead with *Trojan Kanthavo*. In response to these and other attacks against artists at that time, and in response to growing cases of state censorship against artists,[5] Bandaranayake founded the Trikone Center for the Arts, a

---

[3] I have written "xxxxx" to obscure the names of the victims mentioned.

[4] Sources suggest the Presidential Security Division, which had been accused of similar incidents at the time, were responsible for the attacks (though the government denied involvement).

[5] For example, Lasantha Alagiyawanne, a People's Alliance provincial council member from Veyangoda, organized attacks against artists campaigning for the UNP on December 16 of that year,

nonprofit whose mission is to promote peaceful coexistence through the arts and protect the rights and free speech of artists.

One of the first of Trikone's objectives was to tour *Trojan Kanthavo* to different parts of the island. Unsurprisingly, those involved received death threats for these efforts, two of which Bandaranayake translated for me and gave me permission to reprint. The first is aimed at a member of his troupe:

Letter #1:

Madam (xxxxx),

What is this absurdity that you are trying to commit? Are you trying to put the lives of the innocent band of actors in the drama troupe in danger by taking Dharmasiri's (anti-war play) *Trojan Women* to the North and the Hill country?

Can the war be stopped by showing this? Isn't it better to do good to the country by conducting your own workshop? Ask Dharmasiri, his son and the daughter-in-law to be careful when they travel about.

It was reported in the media that you are going to Vavuniya. Stop taking part in this adventure.

We are connected to the LTTE.

Jaya and Vaman.

In a formal statement, Bandaranayake wrote: "I am reluctant to believe that it was the LTTE which has sent these letters. . . . It is highly uncharacteristic of the LTTE to issue decrees on behalf of the hill country over which they have no control." The second was aimed directly at him:

Letter #2:

Dharmasiri Bandaranayake,

We express our deep sorrow at your attempt to take your play to the North and Hill country. Even if you expose it through the media, it would not be easy for you and your drama troupe to escape from us. From today onward, we will be watching (xxxxx), (xxxxx), your son, and your daughter-in-law.

---

in which several were hospitalized (*Sunday Times*, June 28, 2000). A prominent example of state censorship at the time was the banning of Prasanna Vithanage's 1997 film *Purahanda Kaluwara* (*Darkness on a Full Moon Day*), which depicted the brutality of the war.

It will be beneficial if you could immediately abandon the plans to go North. You will face a great catastrophe if you don't.

Subramaniam and Group

The lead actress, the one whose home was destroyed, wrote an open letter to the media describing her commitment to the project and determination to proceed:

> I consider it a great fortune that I could participate in the play, *Trojan Kanthavo*. Is that the last role that I'm going to act? Every second of those five months I saw my own country burning. I saw it in my sleep, too. Have I been able at last to tell my country the destruction wrought by the current war? . . . When the Tamil sisters who came to see the play embraced me and congratulated me, what warmth they displayed. Did they see me as a Sinhala woman? They treated me on that day as a human being, as one of them. There were many occasions when it occurred to me, how far we artists have gone beyond such narrow things as national, religious and caste divisions. . . . All my possessions have been burnt by vandals. What great wonder of fate is this? It is as if god has made me through this ordeal an even more tempered artist. Just as Hecabe rises from the ashes and dust so will I. I shall expose to the entire world the true character of this politics of the power lust (*Sunday Times*, June 28, 2000).

Trojan Kanthavo won Best Play, Best Direction, Best Supporting Actress and Actor at the State Drama Festival in 2000. In 2001–2003, the Trikone Arts Center toured the play through the south, north, hill country, and Dry Zone (Galle, Tangalle, Kandy, Anuradhapura, Badulla, Ampara, Batticaloa, Trincomalee, Chilaw, and Jaffna). On March 4, 2002, Bandaranayake and one of the victims of the attacks met with then-president, Chandrika Kumaratunga to (in Bandaranayake's words) "urge her to not let the artists of Sri Lanka fall into this tragic state and take appropriate action." Two years after the incidents took place, investigations into the crimes were initiated. So far as I know, to this day no one has been arrested.

Just following the reopening of the A9, Bandaranayake took part in the LTTE's five-day festival of music, dance, and drama held in Trincomalee in 2003. TamilNet. com claimed the festival was held "to create awareness among Tamils and to promote peace when the next round of talks takes place between the Government of Sri Lanka (GoSL) and the Liberation Tigers of Tamil Eelam (LTTE) in Japan."[6] The chief speaker was Puthuvai Ratnathurai, Head of the Arts and Cultural Unit of the LTTE. Bandaranayake performed his Sinhala-language version of *The Trojan*

---

[6] "Music, Dance, Drama Festival to Be Held in Trincomalee," Tamilnet.com, February 10, 2003.

Women, with handouts in Tamil. He told me his inclusion in the event showed the LTTE at the time was interested in using the peace process to create links with "nonracist artistic tendencies in the south." Whatever one might make of this, it highlights the alternative reality and post-war future briefly glimpsed during the ceasefire, which was soon thwarted.

It was about this time that Maunaguru and Bandaranayake staged a joint *kooththu-nadagam* workshop in Colombo, in the hopes that it would stimulate discussion on the historical similarities between Sinhala and Tamil cultures. The workshop was met with protests by conservative Sinhala factions and postponed initially due to the threat of violence. Eventually the workshop was held, with police guarding the premises. A hundred or so Sinhala and Tamil musicians, dancers, and interested amateurs occupied a single room, guided through lectures (in Sinhala, Tamil, and English) on the shared history of the *kooththu* and *nadagam*. The audience was taught dance steps and drum patterns from each tradition. The event culminated in a moving performance: the Sinhala actor who played the lead in Sarachchandra's original version of *Sinhabahu*, who flew in from London for the event, performed an excerpt from that play; this was followed by Maunaguru, who performed an excerpt from Vithiananthan's *Ravanesan*.

What were Maunaguru and Bandaranayake doing with their Sinhala-Tamil workshop? Why was it so powerful? Why did something seemingly so banal as a musical theater workshop make people so mad? On the one hand, we might be tempted to say the workshop acted out the totally constructed nature of identity discourses. Through the demonstration of a shared Sinhala-Tamil cultural history, the arts were used to make a mockery of ethnonationalist views of essential differences between the communities. On this reading, the workshop's participants were dancing on the ashes of ideologies that had long controlled their lives and killed their brothers and sisters. Yet it is more accurate, I think, to say that in the workshop, Maunaguru and Bandaranayake used the arts as *proof* that Sinhalas and Tamils are not that different from one another. The power of the project lay in its debunking of the identity episteme on its own terms.

One another analysis is possible, however. It seems to me the power of the workshop lay in its use of *both* the gift and identity paradigms simultaneously: the workshop used the link between music and identity to promote a particular view on the relationship between Sinhalas and Tamils, and this view was *offered* to everyone in the workshop *and* to the factions protesting outside. It was an investment in sound (and dance, and theater) as a form of protection and healing. It has been a goal of this book to show the commonality of musical giving across Sri Lanka; to promote the idea of a shared music history between all Sri Lankans; to question for the world's music history what is lost when we forget about musical giving; and to question the implications of re-attending to it. I am not quite sure what would happen if it were to be recognized, routinely.

Conclusion

The Regulation of Happiness in Post-War Sri Lanka

> Happiness is a human right. It's neither a luxury nor a triviality. It's given to you at birth, but you must recognize its existence. It's as important as the breath of air in your lungs. If people aren't happy, the world is not right.
> —Pharrell Williams, *New York Times* (2014)

In the American pop star Pharrell Williams' now-iconic video for his song "Happy," people are shown singing, dancing, and clapping to the song in cities throughout the world, all within the same twenty-four hour time period. An implicit rejection of the turbulent news headlines of our era (with their incessant displays of violence and grief), the video makes a claim to the ubiquitous presence of happiness in the world, as well as for the ability of music and dance to serve as a means to achieve it. Writing in an op-ed for the *New York Times* in December 2014, Williams says he is grateful for the warm reception his video received, which at that point had reached just over one billion views. The reason for the video's success, he says, is that "happiness is the truth, and it's contagious"; the world is now so connected through social media and sites like YouTube, that once the happiness bug caught on, people were inspired to show their happiness to others. Williams gives his thanks in particular to some young Iranian men and women who were arrested after they posted their video, "Happy in Tehran," and forced to make public apologies: "It's those people, inspired and brave, making their own videos and sharing them on YouTube, who showed me how happiness can connect us all."

Williams' essay is well-written but filled with platitudes about music that make ethnomusicologists cringe. He claims "music is universal" and because of this, it proves "how similar we are as human beings by taking us all to a common place, a shared feeling, an emotion or an understanding of something that is often inexplicable. It can make us all smile—and few things on this earth are as beautiful." Elsewhere in the essay he says music transcends "language, religion, and even geography." Of course, ethnomusicologists typically strive to avoid such syrupy statements, and as area studies specialists, we go out of our way to tell readers and students that music is not universal, because it requires knowledge of distinct cultural values and concepts that function in specific social contexts.

It might come as a surprise, then, that I want to conclude this book by emphasizing that my efforts throughout have been to make the case that Williams is right—though I will support him with a few caveats. First, I have argued that the ethnomusicological tendency to fight against trite universalisms about music and stress the particular are noble endeavors that nevertheless wind up reinforcing perceptions of essential, natural, and historical differences between ethnic and religious groups, the types that drive communal conflicts. By conceptually bounding communities and working to understand what defines them, we sometimes bound them in artificial and historically inaccurate ways. Yes, there is a growing literature in ethnomusicology that agrees with me on this, even if tacitly: for example, several studies have emerged of musician-activists forging meaningful relations between Israelis and Palestinians (e.g., Belkind 2014; Brinner 2009). But what would the history of European music look like, say, if we routinely emphasized that many European classical instruments have a historical connection to the Middle East? What I have attempted to do in this book is question how we can treat social relations through music as foundational for the particular musical communities we study, and for the music histories of nations. This does not have to be perceived as trite or syrupy, but rather as a core component of cultural recognition, human rights, and peace.

I am particularly open to Williams' statement that music transcends "language, religion, and even geography," but I hope it is clear that I think music is less a "transcendence" of cultures and their differences than a means to forge interactions between communities despite their differences. Music connects not because it is universal and somehow "above" culture but because the particulars of a music connects with the particulars of Others' lives to produce new forms of music and subsequent shared music histories. The normative approach in ethnomusicology, I contend, has been to either discuss groups in isolation in the context of a nation-state, or to discuss connections between a group in a nation-state and the West—and in doing so, we have been generally less attentive to how music articulates meaningful relationships between different groups within a nation-state. Instead of simply critiquing the public's claims to musical transcendence, perhaps it would be more useful to more fully consider how the ability for music to produce happiness can be channeled to bridge differences within fraught social contexts.

In 2014, the well-known Sri Lankan website *Groundviews* published a cynical take on the "Happy" phenomenon.[1] The writer of the article, Sanjana Hattotuwa, noted that a website catering to Australians of Sri Lankan descent, Aus News

---

[1] Sanjana Hattotuwa, "Happy Sri Lanka," *Groundviews*, June 10, 2014.

Lanka, provided links to numerous homemade Sri Lankan versions of the "Happy" video, and took them to be evidence that Sri Lankans are now "enjoying peace, stability, and economic progress. We can see that from the faces of locals and the tourists. Visit Sri Lanka!" Indeed, the Sri Lankans in the "Happy" videos are photogenic, well-dressed, smiling, and dancing around some of the more expensive areas of Colombo. Hattotuwa makes an important point:

> The videos are—by design or unwittingly—deeply political because they project a specific, carefully tailored image of post-war Sri Lanka. There are no "Happy" geo-remixes from the North and East, where families, even today, cannot mourn their dead. There are no "Happy" people from the drought-affected districts, a catastrophe of passing interest at best for the majority outside the affected areas. Free Trade Zone workers and Sri Lanka's tea-pluckers aren't in any of the "Happy" videos, perhaps because they are too busy working long shifts for meager pay. Tellingly, the places these "Happy" videos are shot at are geographically a stone's throw away from, but don't focus on or feature locations like Slave Island or Java Lane in Colombo—areas where tens of thousands have been forcibly evicted from their homes. Doubt many of them are happy today. . . . Clearly, happiness in post-war Sri Lanka is unequally shared, and no greater insight can be found than looking at the silences, gaps, and absences in these "Happy" videos.

He goes on to provide compelling details of what happened behind the scenes in some of the videos. In early 2013, a remake of an earlier viral video, "Harlem Shake," was organized at Galle Face Green ("an open, public space, in broad daylight") and some policemen asked the producers to stop filming. In another case, a single person dancing to "Happy" while another person filmed were told they had to stop filming because they were in a high security zone.[2] One person being filmed singing "Happy" on a train was met with terrified looks from some older passengers, who seemed to have no idea why people were singing and dancing in public on a train.

This national security mindset, which has overtaken much of the United States and Europe in recent years, produces a security apparatus that fears any movements in public it can't recognize. As the "Happy" phenomenon shows, happiness thrives on the possibility of its public fruition in sometimes random, unpredictable ways; it is indeed a contagion, one worth spreading. But in order to make the world safe for happiness, the security apparatus snuffs it out. As Hattutowa says, "It is one thing for civil society to campaign against web

---

[2] Hattotuwa notes that since the Emergency Regulations ended in 2011, high security zones "aren't legal."

censorship and the intrusion of a security mindset into civil affairs. It is another for young producers, actors, and citizens, in the pursuit of happiness, to encounter first hand a war mentality that endures, and indeed, grows far beyond barracks." The war mentality, built on a fear of instability, is prone to overreact. It can easily escalate a situation and let it get out of control; it is also prone to be more present or absent in public life depending on the political winds, and thus its existence is premised on the possibility of its future absence. It builds stability through instability, safety through fear, and calmness through anxiety: a fearful presence that warns what will happen in its absence.

I have aimed to show in this book that liberal aesthetics is *ipso facto* not correct: many cultural practices that *do* belong to distinct communities are formed in public space through engagements with Others. The security mindset, though, tells you to stay at home unless (say) you have been booked for a concert, in which case you come out of hiding to perform onstage. This winds up generating what the system takes for granted—the development of closed, physically separate, communally defined cultural practices. And once such divisions are routinized, as they were during Sri Lanka's war years, they are projected back in time to define a place as ethnically and geographically divided—a cartography of culture zones. Liberal aesthetics and the security mindset are mutually reinforcing. And the jettisoning of each, I suggest, is necessary for the development of happiness in post-war Sri Lanka (and in the United States and Europe). It is not the threat of violence that causes the problem the security state responds to, it is the security state that produces the violence it subsequently uses to justify its existence. Coming out of a long war, Sri Lanka is hopefully winding down this process—there are fewer checkpoints and more outdoor concerts. Writing from a United States that appears driven by demagoguery, rogue policemen, and ever-spreading guns and fear, this winding down does not seem to be happening there anytime soon.

In this book, I have argued that musical giving has the power to undermine the security state. And one way to do so, I suggested, is by telling Sri Lankan cultural history as a story of giving between communities rather than the mere production of identities and differences. I wish to conclude by saying that an aim for a post-war Sri Lanka built on histories of giving should be to treat cultural traditions and peoples as variations of the same thing—not the same people, but people whose cultures historically relate, and who are relatable to each other in a non-hierarchical way. Such a public performance of *that*, if it were possible, would generate more than a little happiness. As Hattutowa says at the end of his article (quoting Pharrell), "Clap along if you feel like that's what you wanna do!"

REFERENCES

Abeysinghe, W. A. 1991. *Kaviya, Gītaya hā Samājaya* (Poetry, Song, and Society). Colombo: S. Godage and Brothers.
Ahubudu, Ariesen. 1960. "Dēshiya Sangīta Kramayak Ōna" (We Need a National Music Style). *Dinamina* (January 11): 4.
Alawathukotuwa, Manoj. 2013. *Evolution of Sound Recording Techniques and Their Impact on the Growth of Music in Sri Lanka*. PhD dissertation, University of Delhi.
Allen, Matthew. 1997. "Rewriting the Script for South Indian Dance." *TDR (The Drama Review*, 41(3): 63–100.
Amarasekara, Thilekedhasa. 2002. *Daha Ata Sanniya Yāga Vimarsanaya* (An Analysis of the 18 Sanniya Yāga Systems). Colombo, self-published.
Amarasuriya, Harini and Jonathan Spencer. 2015. "'With That, Discipline Will Also Come to Them': The Politics of the Urban Poor in Postwar Colombo." *Current Anthropology* 56 (S11): S66–S75.
Ambalavanar, Devadarshan. 2006. *Arumuga Navalar and the Construction of a Caiva Public in Colonial Jaffna*. PhD dissertation, Harvard University.
Ambos, Eva. 2012. "From Multiculturalism to Transculturality: The Politics of Heritage in Sri Lanka." *The Network Newsletter*, no. 61: 46.
Appadurai, Arjun. 1981. *Worship and Conflict under Colonial Rule*. Cambridge: Cambridge University Press.
Appadurai, Arjun, ed. 1986. *Social Life of Things: Commodities in Cultural Perspective*. Cambridge: Cambridge University Press.
Aravinda, Jayantha. 2000. "Characteristic Features of Sinhala Folk Song." *Journal of the Royal Asiatic Society of Sri Lanka* 45: 129–134.
Ariyapala, M. B. 1956. *Society in Mediaeval Ceylon*. Colombo: K. V. G. De Silva.
Ariyaratne, Sunil. 1983. *Hindustani Anukaranaya saha Sinhala Gītaya* (Sinhala Songs and Hindi Tune Imitation). *Sanskruta*, no. 1–2, (March 17): 56–59.
Ariyaratne, Sunil. 1985. *An Enquiry into Baila and Kaffrinna*. Maradana: S Hepakapuge.
Ariyaratne, Sunil. 1986. *Gramophone Gī Yugaya* (The Gramophone Era in Sinhala Music). Colombo: S. Godage and Brothers.
Ariyaratne, Sunil. 1989. *Sindu Vistaraya: An Investigation into the Word "Sindu" in Sinhala Literature and Music*. Colombo: Dayawansa Jayakody & Co.
Asad, Talal. 1993. *Genealogies of Religion: Discipline and Reasons of Power in Christianity and Islam*. Baltimore, MD: Johns Hopkins University Press.
Attali, Jacques. 1985 (1977). *Noise: The Political Economy of Music*. Minneapolis: University of Minnesota Press.
Austin, J. L. 1975 [1962]. *How to Do Things with Words*. Cambridge, MA: Harvard University Press.
Babb, Lawrence. 1996. *Absent Lord: Ascetics and Kings in a Jain Ritual Culture*. Berkeley: University of California Press, 1996.

Balasugumar. 2009. "The Traditional Music and Dance [of] Eelam Tamils." http://eelamtamilsdanceandmusic.blogspot.com/2009/11/traditional-music-dance.html
Bandara, Karunaratna. 2000. *Udarata Bera Vādana Kalāva* (The Art of the Up Country Drumming). Maharagama: Taranji Prints.
Bandara, Karunaratna. 2004. *Pahatarata Bera Vādana Sampradāya* (The Low Country Drumming Tradition). Colombo: S. Godage and Sahodarayo.
Barker, Adele. 2011. *Not Quite Paradise*. Beacon Press.
Bartholomeusz, Tessa J. 2002. *In Defense of Dharma: Just-War Ideology in Buddhist Sri Lanka*. London: Routledge Curzon.
Bass, Daniel. 2012. *Everyday Ethnicity in Sri Lanka: Up-Country Tamil Identity Politics*. New York: Routledge.
Bastin, Rohan. 2002. *The Domain of Constant Excess: Plural Worship at the Munnesvaram Temples in Sri Lanka*. New York & Oxford: Berghahn Books.
Bataille, George. 1988. *Accursed Share, Volume 1: Consumption*. Cambridge, MA: Zone Books.
Bate, Bernard. 2005. "Arumuga Navalar, Saivite Sermons, and the Delimitation of Religion, c. 1850." *IESHR* 42(4): 467–482.
Baym, Nancy. 2011. "The Swedish Model: Balancing Markets and Gifts in the Music Industry." *Popular Communication* 9(1): 22–38.
Beaster-Jones, Jayson. 2014. "Beyond Musical Exceptionalism: Music, Value, and Ethnomusicology." *Ethnomusicology* 58(2): 334–340.
Beaster-Jones, Jayson. 2016. *Music Commodities, Markets, and Values: Music as Merchandise*. New York: Routledge.
Becker, Judith. n.d. "Drumming in the Sri Lankan Tovil Healing Ceremonies." Unpublished manuscript.
Belkind, Nili. 2014. *Music in Conflict: Palestine, Israel, and the Politics of Aesthetic Production*. PhD dissertation Columbia University.
Bennett, Jane. 2001. *The Enchantment of Modern Life: Attachments, Crossings, and Ethics*. Princeton, NJ: Princeton University Press.
Bennett, Tony and Patrick Joyce, eds. 2010. *Material Powers: Cultural Studies, History and the Material Turn*. New York: Routledge.
Benton, Lauren. 2010. *A Search for Sovereignty: Law and Geography in European Empires, 1400–1900*. Cambridge, UK: Cambridge University Press.
Berkwitz, Stephen. 2007. *The History of the Buddha's Relic Shrine*. New York: Oxford University Press.
Berkwitz, Stephen. 2016. "Reimagining Buddhist Kingship in a Sinhala Prasasti." *The Journal of the American Oriental Society* 136 (2): 325–341.
Berlant, Lauren. 2011. *Cruel Optimism*. Durham: Duke University Press.
Bernstein, Anya. 2013. *Religious Bodies Politic: Rituals of Sovereignty in Buryat Buddhism*. Chicago: University of Chicago Press.
Bessire, Lucas and David Bond. 2014. "Ontological Anthropology and the Deferral of Critique." *American Ethnologist* 41(3): 440–456.
Birla, Ritu. 2009. *Stages of Capital: Law, Culture and Market Governance in Late Colonial India*. Durham: Duke University Press.
Blackburn, Anne. 2001. *Buddhist Learning and Textual Practice in Eighteenth-Century Lankan Monastic Culture*. Princeton, NJ: Princeton University Press.
Blackburn, Anne. 2010. *Locations of Buddhism: Colonialism and Modernity in Sri Lanka*. Chicago: University of Chicago Press.
Blacking, John. 2000 [1973]. *How Musical Is Man?* Seattle, WA: University of Washington Press.
Bohlman, Philip V. 1988. "Traditional Music and Cultural Identity: Persistent Paradigm in the History of Ethnomusicology." *Yearbook for Traditional Music* 20: 26–42.
Bohlman, Philip V. 1999. "Ontologies of Music." In *Rethinking Music*, edited by Nicholas Cook and Mark Everist. New York: Oxford University Press: 17–24.
Bohlman, Philip V. 2002. *World Music: A Very Short Introduction*. New York: Oxford University Press.
Borges, Jorge Luis. 1998 (1944). "The Library of Babel." *Collected Fictions*. Translated by Andrew Hurley. New York: Penguin Books.

Born, Georgina. 2005. "On Musical Mediation: Ontology, Technology and Creativity." *Twentieth-Century Music* 2(1): 7–36.

Born, Georgina. 2010. "For a Relational Musicology: Music and Interdisciplinarity, Beyond the Practice Turn." *Journal of the Royal Musical Association* 135(2).

Bourdieu, Pierre. 1972. *Outline of a Theory of Practice*. Cambridge: Cambridge University Press.

Bradshaw, Alan. 2015. "Marxist Music Studies." *Folcaal* blog. http://www.focaalblog.com/2015/04/14/alan-bradshaw-marxist-music-studies/

Brathwaite, Kamau. 1983. "Caribbean Culture: Two Paradigms." In *Missile and Capsule*, edited by Jurgen Martini. Bremen: Universitat Bremen: 9–54.

Brinner, Benjamin. 2009. *Playing Across a Divide: Israeli-Palestinian Musical Encounters*. New York: Oxford University Press.

Brow, James. 1996. *Demons and Development: The Struggle for Community in a Sri Lankan Village*. Tucson: University of Arizona Press.

Bryant, Levi. 2011. *The Democracy of Objects*. Open Humanities Press.

Bryant, Levi, Graham Harman, and Nick Srnicek. 2011. *The Speculative Turn: Continental Materialism and Realism*. Melbourne, Australia: re.press.

Bullis, Douglas, ed. 2000. *The Mahavamsa: The Great Chronicle of Sri Lanka*. Originally written by Thera Mahanama-stavira, fifth century CE.

Chakrabarty, Dipesh. 2000. *Provincializing Europe: Postcolonial Thought and Historical Difference*. Princeton, NJ: Princeton University Press.

Chakrabarty, Dipesh. 2009. "The Climate of History: Four Theses." *Critical Inquiry* 35(2): 197–222.

Chandraprema, C. A. 1991. *Sri Lanka: The Years of Terror: The JVP Insurrection 1987–1989*. Colombo: Lake House.

Chatterjee, Partha. 1986. *Nationalist Thought and the Colonial World: A Derivative Discourse?* Minneapolis: University of Minnesota Press.

Cheah, Pheng. 2003. *Spectral Nationality*. New York: Columbia University Press.

Cheng, William. 2016. *Just Vibrations*. Ann Arbor, MI: University of Michigan Press.

Choi, Vivian. 2012. *After Disasters: The Persistence of Insecurity in Sri Lanka*. PhD dissertation, University of California, Davis.

Cimini, Amy and Jairo Moreno. 2016. "Inexhaustible Sound and Fiduciary Aurality." *Boundary 2* 43(1): 5–41.

Clastres, Pierre. 2010. *Archeology of Violence*. Translated by Jeanine Herman. Los Angeles: Semiotext(e).

Claus-Bachmann, Martina, ed. 2004. "Women and Music in Sri Lanka." Special Issue, *The World of Music 46, 2003–2004*.

Cohen, Cynthia. 2003. "Engaging with the Arts to Promote Reconciliation." In *Imagine Coexistence: Restoring Humanity After Violent Ethnic Conflict*, edited by Antonia Chayes and Martha Minow. Jossey-Bass: 267–294.

Cohen, Matthew Isaac. 2006. *The Komedie Stamboel. Popular Theater in Colonial Indonesia, 1891–1903*. Athens, OH: Ohio University Press.

Collins, Steven. 1982. *Selfless Persons*. Cambridge: Cambridge University Press.

Copeman, Jacob. 2011. "The Gift and Its Forms of Life in Contemporary India." *Modern Asian Studies* 45(5): 1051–1094.

Corbin, Alan. 1998. *Village Bells: The Culture of the Senses in the Nineteenth-Century French Countryside*. New York: Columbia University Press.

Cumaratunga, Munidasa. 1938 [2000]. *Virit Väkiya* (Treatise on Sinhala Meters). Colombo: S. Godage and Brothers.

Daly, Erin and Jeremy Sarkin. 2007. *Reconciliation in Divided Societies: Finding Common Ground*. Philadelphia, PA: University of Pennsylvania Press.

Daniel, Valentine. 1984. *Fluid Signs: Being a Person the Tamil Way*. Berkeley: University of California Press.

Daniel, Valentine. 1996. *Charred Lullabies: Chapters in an Anthropography of Violence*. Princeton: Princeton University Press.

Daughtry, Martin. 2015. *Listening to War: Sound, Music, Trauma, and Survival in Wartime Iraq*. New York: Oxford University Press.

Davies, James. 2006. "Julia's Gift: The Social Life of Scores, c. 1830." *Journal of the Royal Musical Association* 131(2): 287–309.
Day, Matthew. 2010. "How to Keep It Real." *Method and Theory in the Study of Religion* 22: 272–282.
De Mel, Vasana. 2006. *Music as Symbol, Music as Emissary: A Study of the Kalypso and the Baila of Sri Lanka*. PhD dissertation, UCLA.
De Queiroz, Fernão. 1992 [1930]. *The Temporal and Spiritual Conquest of Ceylon*. New Delhi: Vedam Books.
De Silva Jayasuriya, Shihan and Jean-Pierre Angenot. 2008. *Uncovering the History of Africans in Asia*. Leiden; Boston: Brill.
De Silva, Premakumara. 2000. *Globalization and the Transformation of Planetary Rituals in Southern Sri Lanka*. Colombo: International Centre for Ethnic Studies.
De Silva, Premakumara. 2011. "Struggle for Survival: Case of the Veddas' Culture in Sri Lanka." *SAARC Culture: Diminishing Cultures in South Asia* 2, 127–174.
DeLoughrey, Elizabeth. 2011. "Island Writing, Creole Cultures." *Cambridge History of Postcolonial Literature*. Edited by Ato Quayson. Cambridge: Cambridge University Press.
Derrida, Jacques. 1992. *Given Time I: Counterfeit Money*. Chicago: University of Chicago Press.
Derrida, Jacques. 1996. *Archive Fever: A Freudian Impression*. Chicago: University of Chicago Press.
Derrida, Jacques. 2009. *The Beast and the Sovereign, Volume I*. Chicago: University of Chicago Press.
Dewaraja, L. S. 1994. *The Muslims of Sri Lanka: One Thousand Years of Ethnic Harmony 900–1915 AD*. Colombo: Lanka Islamic Foundation.
Dillon, Emma. 2012. *The Sense of Sound: Musical Meaning in France, 1260–1330*. New York: Oxford University Press.
Dissanayake, Wimal. 2006. *Enabling Traditions: Four Sinhala Cultural Intellectuals*. Trentham Books.
Durges, Jane. 2013. *Ritual and Recovery in Post-Conflict Sri Lanka*. New York: Routledge.
Dyer, Jeffrey. 2017. "Nationalist Transformations: Music, Ritual, and the Work of Memory in Cambodia and Thailand." *Yale Journal of Music & Religion* 3(2): 26–42.
Egge, James R. 2013. *Religious Giving and the Invention of Karma in Theravāda Buddhism*. New York: Routledge.
Eisenlohr, Patrick. 2007. *Little India: Diaspora, Time, and Ethnolinguistic Belonging in Hindu Maritius*. Berkeley: University of California Press.
Engelhardt, Jeffers. 2014. *Singing the Right Way: Orthodox Christians and Secular Enchantment in Estonia*. New York: Oxford University Press.
Feld, Steven. 2012 [1982]. *Sound and Sentiment: Birds, Weeping, Poetics, and Song in Kaluli Expression*. Durham: Duke University Press.
Feld, Steven. 1996. "Pygmy POP. A Genealogy of Schizophonic Mimesis." *Yearbook for Traditional Music* 28, 1–35.
Ferguson, James. 2006. *Global Shadows: Africa in the Neoliberal World Order*. Durham: Duke University Press.
Fernando, K. S. 1987. *Sanni yakuma hevat daha ata sanniya*. Colombo: Rajaye Mudrana Departmentuva.
Field, Garrett. 2013. "'Handa Eliya' (The Moonlight): Mahagama Sekera's Experimental Prose." *Sagar: A South Asia Research Journal* 21, 16–27.
Field, Garrett. 2013. *Music for the Majority: Sinhala Song and the 1956 Cultural Revolution of Sri Lanka*. PhD dissertation, Wesleyan University.
Field, Garrett. 2014. "Music for Inner Domains: Sinhala Song and the Arya and Hela Schools of Cultural Nationalism in Colonial Sri Lanka." *The Journal of Asian Studies* 73(4): 1043–1058.
Field, Garrett. 2017. *Modernizing Composition: Sinhala Song, Poetry, and Politics in Twentieth-Century Sri Lanka*. Stanford: University of California Press.
Finch, Martha. 2012. "Rehabilitating Materiality: Bodies, Gods, and Religion. *Religion* 42(4): 625–631.
Fisher, Alexander J. 2014. *Music, Piety, and Propaganda: The Soundscapes of Counter-Reformation Bavaria*. New York: Oxford University Press.
Fox, Aaron. 2014. "Repatriation as Reanimation through Reciprocity." In *The Cambridge History of World Music*, edited by Philip V. Bohlman. Cambridge: Cambridge University Press: 522–554.

Frasca, Richard Armando. 1990. *Theatre of the Mahabharata: Terukkuttu Performances in South India*. University of Hawaii Press.
Fukushima, Kiko. 2011. "Peace and Culture: Fostering Peace through Cultural Contributions." In *Conflict and Culture: Fostering Peace through Cultural Initiatives*, edited by Joint Research Institute for International Peace and Culture, Aoyama Gakuin University. New York: The Japan Foundation: 5–14.
Gaasbeek, Timmo. 2010. *Bridging Troubled Waters? Everyday Inter-Ethnic Interaction in a Context of Violent Conflict in Kottiyar Pattu, Trincomalee, Sri Lanka*. PhD dissertation, Wageningen University.
Gaasbeek, Timmo. 2013. "Flying Below the Radar: Inter-Ethnic Marriages in Sri Lanka's War Zone." In *Disaster, Conflict and Society in Crises: Everyday Politics of Crisis Response*, edited by Dorothea Hilhorst. New York: Routledge: 167–184.
Gamburd, Michele. 2013. *The Golden Wave: Culture and Politics after Sri Lanka's Tsunami Disaster*. Indiana University Press.
Gell, Alfred. 1998. *Art and Agency*. New York: Oxford University Press.
Godelier, Maurice. 1999. *The Enigma of the Gift*. Translated by Nora Scott. Chicago, IL: University of Chicago Press.
Goehr, Lydia. 1992. *The Imaginary Museum of Musical Works*. New York: Clarendon Press.
Gombrich, Richard. 2012 [1971]. *Precept & Practice: Traditional Buddhism and the Rural Highlands of Ceylon*. New York: Routledge.
Gombrich, Richard and Gananath Obeyesekere. 1988. *Buddhism Transformed*. Princeton: Princeton University Press.
Goodhand, Jonathan. 2012. "Securing the State, Enforcing the 'Peace.'" *Asian Survey* 53(1): 64–72.
Goodhand, Jonathan, Jonathan Spencer and Benedikt Korf. 2011. *Conflict and Peacebuilding in Sri Lanka: Caught in the Peace Trap?* New York: Routledge.
Goonasekera, Sunil. 2007. *Walking to Kataragama*. Colombo: International Centre for Ethnic Studies.
Graeber, David. 2001. *Toward an Anthropological Theory of Value*. Palgrave MacMillan.
Greene, Paul. 2004. "The *Dhamma* as Sonic Praxis: *Paritta* Chant in Burmese Theravada Buddhism." *Asian Music* 35(2): 43–78.
Gunawardena, Charles A. 2005. *Encyclopedia of Sri Lanka*. New York: Sterling Publishers.
Guruge, Ananda, ed. 1965. *Return to Righteousness: A Collection of Speeches, Essays and Letters of the Anagarika Dharmapala*. Colombo: Department of Government Printing.
Hallisey, Charles. 2003. "Works and Persons in Sinhala Literary Culture." In *Literary Cultures in History: Reconstructions from South Asia*, edited by Sheldon Pollock. Berkeley: University of California Press: 689–746.
Halverson, John. 1971. "Dynamics of Sanni Exorcism: The Sinhalsese Sanni Yakuma." *History of Religions* 10, 334–359.
Haniffa, Farzana. 2007. "Muslims in Sri Lanka's Ethinc Conflict." *ISIM Review* 19: 52–53.
Hansen, Thomas Blom. 2012. *Melancholia of Freedom: Social Life in an Indian Township in South Africa*. Princeton: Princeton University Press.
Harrison, Frances. 2013. *Still Counting the Dead: Survivors of Sri Lanka's Hidden War*. Portobello Books.
Harvey, David. 2010. *A Companion to Marx's* Capital. London: Verso.
Heim, Maria. 2004. *Theories of the Gift in South Asia: Hindu, Buddhist, and Jain Reflections on Dana*. New York: Routledge.
Heras, Henry. 1933. *Studies in Pallava History*. Madras: B. G. Paul & Co.
Herder, Johann Gottfried and Philip V. Bohlman. 2017. *Song Loves the Masses: Herder on Music and Nationalism*. University of California Press.
Hibbets, Maria. 1999. "Saving Them From Yourself: An Inquiry into the South Asian Gift of Fearlessness." *Journal of Religious Ethics* 27(3): 437–462.
Hiltebeitel, Alf. 1988. *The Cult of Draupadi, Vol. 1*. Chicago: University of Chicago Press.
Holbraad, Martin and Morton Axel Pederson, eds. 2017. *The Ontological Turn: An Anthropological Exposition*. Cambridge: Cambridge University Press.

Holt, John Clifford. 1991. *Buddha in the Crown*. New York: Oxford University Press.
Holt, John Clifford. 1996. *The Religious World of Kirti Sri: Buddhism, Art and Politics in Late Medieval Sri Lanka*. New York: Oxford University Press.
Holt, John Clifford. 2004. *The Buddhist Vishnu: Religious Transformations, Politics and Culture*. New York: Columbia University Press.
Holt, John Clifford. 2016. *Buddhist Extremists and Muslim Minorities: Religious Conflict in Contemporary Sri Lanka*. New York: Oxford University Press.
Hyde, Lewis. 2007 [1983]. *The Gift: Creativity and the Artist in the Modern World*. Vintage Books.
Ilangasinha, H. B. M. 1992. *Buddhism in Medieval Sri Lanka*. New Delhi: Sri Satguru Publications.
Indrapala, K. 2005. *The Evolution of an Ethnic Identity: The Tamils in Sri Lanka c. 300 BCE to c. 1200 CE*. Colombo: Vijitha Yapa Publications.
Irving, David. 2010. *Colonial Counterpoint: Music in Early Modern Manila*. New York: Oxford University Press.
Jankowsky, Richard C. 2007. "Music, Spirit Possession and the In-Between: Ethnomusicological Inquiry and the Challenge of Trance." *Ethnomusicology Forum* 16(2): 2007.
Jankowsky, Richard C. 2010. *Stambeli: Music, Trance, and Alterity in Tunisia*. Chicago: University of Chicago Press.
Jayawardena, Kumari. 2007. *Erasure of the Euro-Asian: Recovering Early Radicalism and Feminism in South Asia*. Colombo: Social Scientists' Association.
Jazeel, Tariq. 2013. *Sacred Modernity: Nature, Environment and the Postcolonial Geographies of Sri Lankan Nationhood*. Liverpool: Liverpool University Press.
Jeganathan, Pradeep. 2004. "Checkpoint: Anthropology, Identity and the State." In *Anthropology in the Margins of the State*, edited by Veena Das and Deborah Poole. Santa Fe: SAR Press: 35–67.
Kapferer, Bruce. 1983. *A Celebration of Demons: Exorcism and the Aesthetics of Healing in Sri Lanka*. Washington, DC: Smithsonian Books.
Kapferer, Bruce. 1997. *The Feast of the Sorcerer: Practices of Consciousness and Power*. Chicago: University of Chicago Press.
Kapferer, Bruce. 2011. *Legends of People, Myths of State: Violence, Intolerance, and Political Culture in Sri Lanka and Australia*. New York: Berghahn Books.
Kariyawasam, Tissa. 1995. *Buddhist Ceremonies and Rituals of Sri Lanka*. Kandy, Sri Lanka: Buddhist Publication Society.
Kartomi, Margaret. 1990. *On Concepts and Classifications of Musical Instruments*. Chicago: University of Chicago Press: 67–68.
Kemper, Steven. 1991. *The Presence of the Past*: Chronicles, Politics, and Culture in Sinhala Life. Ithaca: Cornell University Press.
Kemper, Steven. 2015. *Rescued from the Nation: Anagarika Dharmapala and the Buddhist World*. Chicago: University of Chicago Press.
Kersenboom, Sasakiya C. 2016 (1987). *Nityasumangali: Devadasi Tradition in South India*. Delhi: Motilal Banarsidass.
Klima, Alan. 2002. *The Funeral Casino: Meditation, Massacre, and Exchange with the Dead in Thailand*. Princeton: Princeton University Press.
Korf, Benedikt. 2009. "Cartographic Violence: Engaging a Sinhala Kind of Geography." In *Spatializing Politics: Culture and Geography in Postcolonial Sri Lanka*, edited by Catherine Brun and Tariq Jazeel. Sage Publications: 100–121.
Kottegoda, Jayasena. 2003. *Pahataraṭa Śāntikarma Sāhitya* (History of Low-Country Rituals). Self-published.
Kottegoda, Jayasena. 2004. *Bharatiya ha deshiya tala paddati piliganda sasandanatmaka aDyayanayak*. Boralesgamuwa: Jayasena Kottegoda.
Kulatillake, C. de S. 1974. *Lankava sangita sambhavaya*. Colombo: Lake House Publications.
Kulatillake, C. de S. 1976a. *A Background to Sinhala Traditional Music of Sri Lanka*. Colombo: Department of Cultural Affairs.
Kulatillake, C. de S. 1976b. *Metre, Melody, and Rhythm in Sinhala Music*. Colombo: Sinhala Music Research Unit, Sri Lanka Broadcasting Corp.

Kulatillake, C. de S. 1991. *Ethnomusicology. Its Content and Growth; and Ethnomusicological Aspects of Sri Lanka*. Colombo: S. Godage and Brothers.

Kumarathunge, K. M. Saman. 2004. "Sabaragamu Davula Saha Elu Vādana Kalāva Visēsata" (the Davula of Sabaragamu and the Specialties of Its Art). *Sanka* special edition published for the National Drumming Festival: 108–128.

Lacan, Jacques. 1977. *The Four Fundamental Concepts of Psychoanalysis*. London: Hogarth Press.

Ladzekpo, CK. "Gahu Dance-Drumming." Unpublished manuscript.

Laidlaw, James. 2000. "A Free Gift Makes No Friends." *The Journal of the Royal Anthropological Institute* 6(4): 617– 634.

Latour, Bruno. 2005. *Reassembling the Social: An Introduction to Actor-Network-Theory*. New York: Oxford University Press.

Latour, Bruno. 2011. *On the Modern Cult of the Factish Gods*. Durham: Duke University Press.

Lawrence, Patricia. *Work of Oracles, Silence of Terror: Notes on the Injury of War in Eastern Sri Lanka*. PhD dissertation, University of Colorado, Boulder, 1997.

Lederach, John. 2005. *The Moral Imagination: The Art and Soul of Building Peace*. New York: Oxford University Press.

Ledford, Julian. 2015. "Review: Ana Maria Ochoa Gautier, *Aurality*." *Ameriquests* 12(1). http://www.ameriquests.org/index.php/ameriquests/article/view/4111

Levertove, Denise. 2002. *The Collected Poems of Denise Levertov*. New York: New Directions.

Lévi-Strauss, Claude. 1969 (1949). *The Elementary Structures of Kinship*. Boston: Beacon Press.

Llored, Patrick. 2014. "Zoopolitics." *SubStance* 43(2): 115–123.

Louis, Prakash and E. Deenadayalan. 2011. *Post-War Sri Lanka*. Bangalore: Other Media Communications.

Lubkemann 2005. "Migratory Coping in Wartime Mozambique: An Anthropology of Violence and Displacement in 'Fragmented Wars.'" *Journal of Peace Research* 42(4): 493–508.

Mabbett, Ian W. 1993. "Buddhism and Music." *Asian Music* 25(1–2): 9–28.

Mahmood, Saba. 2015. *Religious Difference in a Secular Age: A Minority Report*. Princeton, NJ: Princeton University Press.

Makulloluwa, W. B. 2000. *Hela Gī Maga*. Battaramulla: Samskrtika Katayutu Depārtamēntuva.

Malalgoda, Sugathadhasa. 1998. *Yak Beraya*. Colombo: S. Godage and Brothers.

Manuel, Peter. 2015. *Tales, Tunes, and Tassa Drums: Retention and Invention in Indo-Caribbean Music*. Champaign, IL: University of Illinois Press.

Marx, Karl. 1981. *Das Kapital*. Synergy International of the Americas, Ltd.

Maunaguru, Sinniah. 1992. *Paḷaiyatum putiyatum, nāṭakam, araṅkiyal*. Batticaloa: Vipulam Publication.

Maunaguru, Sinniah. 1993. *Īḻattu Tamiḻ nāṭaka araṅku*. Yālppāṇam: Yālppāṇap Palkalaik Kaḻakam.

Maunaguru, Sinniah. 1998. *Maṭṭakkaḷappu marapuvaḻi nāṭakaṅkaḷ* (Traditional Folk-Dramas of Batticaloa). Chennai: Parkar.

Maunaguru, Sinniah. n.d. *Kooththu*. Unpublished manusacript, Trikone Centre for the Arts.

Mauss, Marcel. 2010 (1925). *The Gift: Forms and Function of Exchange in Archaic Societies*. New York: W. W. Norton.

Mazzarella, William. 2013. *Censorium: Cinema and the Open Edge of Mass Publicity*. Durham: Duke University Press.

McDaniel, Justin. 2011. *The Lovelorn Ghost and the Magical Monk: Practicing Buddhism in Modern Thailand*. New York: Columbia University Press.

McDowell, Chris. 1996. *A Tamil Asylum Diaspora: Sri Lankan Migration, Settlement and Politics in Switzerland*. Berghahn Books.

McGilvray, Dennis. 1983. "Paraiyar Drummers of Sri Lanka: Consensus and Constraint in an Untouchable Caste," *American Ethnologist* 10: 1: 97–115.

McGilvray, Dennis. 1998. *Symbolic Heat: Gender, Health, and Worship among the Tamils of South India and Sri Lanka*. Middletown, NJ: Grantha.

McGilvray, Dennis. 2004. "Jailani: A Sufi Shrine in Sri Lanka." In Ahmad, Imtiaz and Helmut Reifeld, eds., *Lived Islam in South Asia: Adaptation, Accommodation & Conflict*. Delhi: Social Science Press: 273–289.

McGilvray, Dennis. 2008. *Crucible of Conflict: Tamil and Muslim Society on the East Coast of Sri Lanka*. Durham: Duke University Press.

McGilvray, Dennis. 2014. "A Matrilineal Sufi Shaykh in Sri Lanka." *South Asia History and Culture*. 5(2): 246–261.

McIntosh, Janet. 2009. *The Edge of Islam: Power, Personhood, and Ethnoreligious Boundaries on the Kenya Coast*. Durham: Duke University Press.

Mbembe, Achille. 2000. *De la postcolonie: Essai sur l'imagination politique dans l'Afrique contemporaine*. Paris: Karthala.

Meegama, Sujatha. 2010. "South Indian or Sri Lankan? The Hindu Temples of Polonnaruva, Sri Lanka." *Artibus Asiae* 70(1): 25–45.

Meegama, Sujatha. 2011. *From Kôvils to Devâles: Patronage and "Influence" at Buddhist and Hindu Temples in Sri Lanka*. PhD dissertation, University of California, Berkeley.

Mintz, Sidney and Richard Price. 1992 [1976]. *The Birth of African-American Culture: An Anthropological Perspective*. Beacon Press.

Mitchell, Lisa. 2009. *Language, Emotion, and Politics in South India: The Making of a Mother Tongue*. Bloomington: University of Indiana Press.

Mohan, Rohini. 2015. *The Seasons of Trouble: Life Amid the Ruins of Sri Lanka's War*. Verso.

Morcom, Anna. 2015. "Music and Capitalism: An Introduction." Focaal Blog. http://www.focaalblog.com/2015/04/01/anna-morcom-music-and-capitalism-an-introduction/

Morris, Rosalind. 2000. *In the Place of Origins: Modernity and its Mediums in Northern Thailand*. Durham: Duke University Press.

Morton, Timothy. 2010. *The Ecological Thought*. Cambridge, MA: Harvard University Press.

Muller, Carol. 1999. *Rituals of Fertility and the Sacrifice of Desire: Nazarite Women's Performance in South Africa*. University of Chicago Press.

Nettl, Bruno. 1989. *Blackfoot Musical Thought: Comparative Perspectives*. Ohio: The Kent State University Press.

Nichols, Robert. 2014. *The World of Freedom. Heidegger, Foucault, and the Politics of Historical Ontology*. Stanford: Stanford University Press.

Niyamatolika. 1971. *The Word of the Buddha*. Kandy: The Buddhist Publication Society.

Novak, David. 2013. *Japanoise: Music at the Edge of Circulation*. Durham: Duke University Press.

Nurnberger, Marianne. 1998a. *Dance is the Language of the Gods: The Chitrasena School and the Traditional Roots of Sri Lankan Stage-Dance*. Amsterdam: VU University Press.

Obeyesekere, Gananath. 1958. "The Structure of a Sinhalese Ritual." *Ceylon Journal of Historical and Social Studies* 1(2): 192–202.

Obeyesekere, Gananath. 1963. "The Great and the Little in the Perspective of Sinhalese Buddhism." *Journal of Asian Studies* 22(2): 139–153.

Obeyesekere, Gananath. 1966. "The Buddhist Pantheon in Ceylon and Its Extensions." In *Anthropological Studies in Theravada Buddhism*, edited by Manning Nash. Southeast Asia Studies 13, 1–26.

Obeyesekere, Gananath. 1968. "Theodicy, Salvation and Rebirth in a Sociology of Buddhism." In *Dialectic in Practical Religion*, edited by Edmund Leach. Cambridge: Cambridge University Press: 7–40.

Obeyesekere, Gananath. 1969. "The Sanni Demons: Collective Representations of Disease in Ceylon." *Comparative Studies in History and Society* II: 2: 174–216.

Obeyesekere, Gananath. 1981. *Medusa's Hair: An Essay on Personal Symbols and Religious Experience*. Chicago: University of Chicago Press.

Obeyesekere, Gananath. 1984. *The Cult of the Goddess Pattini*. Chicago: University of Chicago Press.

Obeyesekere, Gananath. 1990. *The Work of Culture: Symbolic Transformation in Psychoanalysis and Anthropology*. Chicago: University of Chicago Press.

Obeyesekere, Gananath. 2002a. *Imagining Karma: Ethical Transformation in Amerindian, Buddhist, and Greek Rebirth*. Stanford: University of California Press.

Obeyesekere, Gananath. 2002b. "Where Have All the Vaddas Gone? Buddhism and Aboriginality in Sri Lanka." In Neluka Silva, *The Hybrid Island: Culture Crossings and the Invention of Identity in Sri Lanka*. Chicago: University of Chicago Press.

_____. n.d. "Colonial Histories and Vädda Primitivism." http://vedda.org/obeyesekere5.htm.
Ochoa Gautier, Ana María. 2013. "Disencounters between Music's Allure and the Expediency of Culture in Colombia." *Latin American Research Review* 8, 12–29.
Ochoa Gautier, Ana María. 2014. *Aurality: Listening and Aurality in Nineteenth-Century Colombia*. Durham: Duke University Press.
Ochoa Gautier, Ana María. 2016. "Acoustic Multinaturalism, the Value of Nature, and the Nature of Music in Ecomusicology." *Boundary 2* (43:1): 12–29.
O'Connell, John Morgan and Salwa El-Shawan Castelo-Branco, eds. 2010. *Music and Conflict*. Urbana, IL: University of Illinois Press.
Ohnuma, Reiko. 2017. *Unfortunate Destiny: Animals in the Indian Buddhist Imagination*. New York: Oxford University Press.
Paige, Aaron. 2008. "Acoustic Entanglements: Negotiating Folk Music in Naiyanti Melam Performance." *Indian Folklore Research Journal* 9: 45–66.
Paige, Aaron. 2010. "Fashioning a Filmi Folk: Dravidianism, Democracy, and Musical Stereotype in Early Tamil Cinema." Society for Ethnomusicology annual meeting, Los Angeles, CA, November.
Pathmanathan, S. 1978. *The Kingdom of Jaffna*. Colombo: Arul M. Rajendran.
Payutto, P. A. 1997. *A Constitution for Living*. Bangkok, Thailand: Buddhadhamma Foundation.
Peebles, Gustav. 2010. "The Anthropology of Credit and Debt." *Annual Review of Anthropology* 39: 225–240.
Peebles, Patrick. 2001. *The Plantation Tamils of Ceylon*. Leicester University Press.
Peebles, Patrick. 2006. *The History of Sri Lanka*. Greenwood Press.
Pettan, Svanibor, ed. 1998. *Music, Politics, and War: Views from Croatia*. Zagreb: Institute of Ethnology and Folklore Research.
Piekut, Jonathan. 2014. "Actor-Networks in Music History: Clarifications and Critiques." *Twentieth-Century Music* 11(2): 191–215.
Pieslak, Jonathan. 2009. *Sound Targets: American Soldiers and Music in the Iraq War*. Bloomington and Indianapolis: Indiana University Press.
Pilzer, Josh. 2010. *Hearts of Pine: Songs in the Lives of Three Korean Survivors of the Japanese "Comfort Women."* New York: Oxford University Press.
Pollock, Sheldon. 2006. *The Language of the Gods in the World of Men: Sanskrit, Culture, and Power in Premodern India*. Berkeley: University of California Press.
Pollock, Sheldon, ed. 2011. *Forms of Knowledge in Early Modern South Asia*. Durham: Duke University Press.
Poovey, Mary. 2008. *Genres of the Credit Economy: Mediating Value in Eighteenth- and Nineteenth-Century Britain*. Chicago: University of Chicago Press.
Povinelli, Elizabeth. 2011. *Economies of Abandonment*. Durham: Duke University Press.
Povinelli, Elizabeth. 2014. "Geontologies of the Otherwise." *Theorizing the Contemporary*, https://culanth.org/fieldsights/465-geontologies-of-the-otherwise, January 13.
Qureshi, Regula. 2002. *Music and Marx: Ideas, Practice, Politics*. New York: Routledge.
Qureshi, Regula. 2006. *Sufi Music of India and Pakistan: Sound, Context, and Meaning*. Oxford University Press.
Radano, Ronald. 2003. *Lying up a Nation: Race and Black Music*. Chicago: University of Chicago Press.
Radano, Ron, and Philip V. Bohlman. 2000. *Music and the Racial Imagination*. Chicago: University of Chicago Press.
Raghavan, M. D. 1967. *Sinhala natum*. Colombo: M. D. Gunasena.
Raghavan, V. 1949. "Nagasvara." *Journal of Music Academy* 20: 155–159.
Raheja, Gloria. 1988. *The Poison in the Gift*. Chicago: University of Chicago Press.
Rajapakse, Waidyawathie. 2002. *Daladhā Māligāva Saha Tūrya Vādanaya* (The Temple of the Tooth and Its Percussion Music). Colombo: S. Godage and Brothers.
Rajasingham-Senanayake, Darini. 2002. "Identity on the Borderline: Modernity, New Ethnicities, and the Unmaking of Multiculturalism in Sri Lanka." In *The Hybrid Island*, edited by N. Silva. Colombo: Social Scientists' Association: 41–70.

Ramanayake, U. B. 1986. "Sinhalese Traditional Art of Drums." *Vidyodaya Journal of Arts Sciences, and Letters* 14(1): 1–24.
Ranasinha, Ravindra. n.d. "Making a Culture-Oriented Drama Therapy." Unpublished Manuscript.
Rancière, Jacques. 1991. *The Ignorant Schoolmaster*. Stanford, CA: Stanford University Press.
Rancière, Jacques. 2009. *Aesthetics and Its Discontents*. Polity.
Rasaratnam, Madurika. 2016. *Tamils and the Nation: India and Sri Lanka Compared*. London: Hurst.
Rawski, Evelyn and Jessica Rawlins, eds. 2005. *China: The Three Emperors, 1662–1795*. London: Royal Academy of Arts.
Reed, Susan A.. 2010. *Dance and the Nation: Performance, Ritual, and Politics in Sri Lanka*. Madison: University of Wisconsin Press.
Richardson 2005. *Paradise Poisoned: Learning about Conflict, Terrorism, and Development from Sri Lanka's Civil Wars*. International Centre for Ethnic Studies.
Ritter, Jonathan, and Martin Daughtry. 2007. *Music in the Post-9/11 World*. New York: Routledge.
Roberts, Michael. 1990. "Noise as Cultural Struggle: Tom-Tom Beating, the British, and Communal Disturbances in Sri Lanka, 1880s–1930s." In *Mirrors of Violence: Communities, Riots and Survivors in South Asia*, edited by Veena Das. Delhi: Oxford University Press: 240–285.
Roberts, Michael. 1995. *Exploring Confrontation: Sri Lanka: Politics, Culture, and History*. Chur, Switzerland: Harwood Academic Publishers.
Roberts, Michael. 2004. *Sinhala Consciousness in the Kandyan Period*. Colombo: Vijitha Yapa Publications.
Roda, Allen. 2014. "Tabla Tuning on the Workshop Stage: Toward a Materialist Musical Ethnography." *Ethnomusicology Forum* 23(3): 360–382.
Rogers, John. 1990. "Historical Images in the British period." In *Sri Lanka: History and the Roots of Conflict*, edited by Jonathan Spencer. London: Routledge: 87–106.
Rogers, John D. 1994. "Post-Orientalism and the Interpretation of Premodern and Modern Political Identities: The Case of Sri Lanka." *The Journal of Asian Studies* 53(1): 10–23.
Rommen, Tim. 2015. "*Creolité*, (Im)Mobility, and Music in Dominica." *The Journal of Musicology* 32(4): 558–591.
Ross Carter, John. 1993. "Music in the Theravada Buddhist Heritage: In Chant, in Song, in Sri Lanka." In *On Understanding Buddhists: Essays on the Theravada Tradition in Sri Lanka*. Albany: SUNY Press: 133–152.
Saddharmālaṃkāraya. 1971 (14th century). Colombo: MD Gunasena.
Sahlins, Marshall. 1972. *Stone Age Economics*. Routledge.
Sahlins, Marshall. 2017. "The Original Political Society." *Hau: Journal of Ethnographic Theory* 7(2): 91–128.
Sakakibara, Chie. 2009. "'No Whale, No Music': Iñupiaq Drumming and Global Warming." *Polar Record* 45 (235): 289–303.
Samaranayake, Nilanthi. 2011. "Are Sri Lanka's Relations with China Deepening? An Analysis of Economic, Military, and Diplomatic Data." *Asian Security* 7(2): 119–146.
Samaranayake, Premaratne. 2013. "Siṃhala Gītayē Dakshina Bhāratīya Balapäm" [South Indian Influences in Sinhala Song]. *Haṅda* 9(3): 17–24.
Sambamoorthy, Pichu. 2010. *Dictionary of South Indian Music and Musicians* 5, edited by M. B. Vedavalli. Chennai: The Indian Music Publishing House.
Sarachchandra, Ediriweera. 1952. *The Folk Drama of Ceylon*. Colombo: Department of Cultural Affairs.
Saramago, Jose. 2003. *The Cave*. Mariner Books.
Sartori, Andrew. 2008. *Bengal in Global Concept History: Culturalism in the Age of Capital*. Chicago: University of Chicago Press.
Sartori, Andrew. 2014. *Liberalism in Empire*. University of California Press.
Satkunaratnam, Ahalya. 2009. *Moving Bodies, Navigating Conflict: Practicing Bharata Natyam in Colombo, Sri Lanka*. PhD dissertation, University of California, Riverside.
Schalk, Peter, ed. 2002. *Buddhism Among Tamils in Pre-Colonial Tamilakam and Ilam*. Uppsala Universitet.
Schalk, Peter. 2011. "Canon Rejected: The Case of Pauttam among Tamils in Pre-Colonial Tamilakam and Ilam." In *Kanonisierung und Kanonbildung in der asiatischen Religionsgeschichte*, edited by Max Deeg et al. Wien: Österreichische Akademie der Wissenschaften: 233–258.

Schalk, Peter, ed. 2013. *Buddhism Among Tamils in Pre-Colonial Tamilakam and Ilam, Part 3*. Uppsala Universitet.
Schaefer, Donovan. 2015. *Religious Affects: Animality, Evolution, and Power*. Durham: Duke University Press.
Schofield, Katherine. 2014. "The New Cultural Histories of Music/of India." *Cultural Musicology*. https://culturalmusicology.org/katherine-butler-schofield-the-new-cultural-histories/
Schultz, Anna. 2013. *Singing a Hindu Nation: Marathi Devotional Performance and Nationalism*. New York: Oxford University Press.
Schweitzer, Kenneth. 2013. *The Artistry of Afro-Cuban Batá Drumming: Aesthetics, Transmission, Bonding, and Creativity*. University Press of Mississippi.
Scott, David. 1994. *Formations of Ritual: Colonial and Anthropological Discourses on the Sinhala Yak Tovil*. Minneapolis: University of Minnesota Press.
Scott, David. 1999. *Refashioning Futures*. Princeton: Princeton University Press.
Scott, James C. 1998. *Seeing Like a State: How Certain Schemes to Improve the Human Condition Failed*. New Haven, CT: Yale University Press.
Scott, James C. 2010. *The Art of Not Being Governed: An Anarchist History of Upland Southeast Asia*. New Haven: Yale University Press.
Sedaraman, J.E. 1966. *Uda rata tāla shastraya*. Colombo: M.D. Gunasena.
Sedaraman, J. E. 1997 (1968). *Uda rata Naetum kalava*. Colombo: M.D. Gunasena.
Seeger, Anthony. 2004 [1988]. *Why Suya Sing*. Champaign, IL: University of Illinois Press.
Seizer, Susan. 2005. *Stigmas of the Tamil Stage*. Durham: Duke University Press.
Seligmann, C. G. and B. Z. Seligmann. 2010 [1911]. *The Veddas*. Cambridge: Cambridge University Press.
Seneviratna, Anuradha. 1975. "Musical Rituals of the Dalada Maligawa Pertaining to the Temple of the Sacred Tooth." *Sangeet Natak* 36: 21–42.
Seneviratna, Anuradha. 1979. "Pancaturya Nada and the Hewisi Puja." *Ethnomusicology* 23(1): 49–56.
Seneviratne, H. L. 1978. *Rituals of the Kandyan State*. Cambridge: Cambridge University Press.
Seneviratne, H. L. 2000. *The Work of Kings: The New Buddhism in Sri Lanka*. Chicago: University of Chicago Press.
Shanmugalingam, Kulanthai M. 2012. "Drama and Theatre Arts among the Tamils of Sri Lanka." https://activetheatremovement.wordpress.com/2012/03/29/drama-and-theatre-arts-among-the-tamils-of-sri-lanka/
Sheeran, Anne. 1997. *White Noise: European Modernity, Sinhala Musical Nationalism, and the Practice of a Creole Popular Music in Modern Sri Lanka*. PhD dissertation, University of Washington.
Sheeran, Anne. 1998. "Sri Lanka." In *Garland Encyclopedia of World Music*, edited by Anne Arnold. New York: Routledge: 954–972.
Sheeran, Anne. 2002. "Baila Music: European Modernity and Afro-Iberian Popular Music in Sri Lanka." In *The Hybrid Island: Culture Crossings and the Invention of Identity in Sri Lanka*, edited by Neluka Silva. Chicago: University of Chicago Press.
Shell, Marc. 2014. *Islandology: Geography, Rhetoric, Politics*. Stanford University Press.
Sherinian, Zoe. 2013. *Tamil Folk Music as Dalit Liberation Theology*. Bloomington: Indiana University Press.
Shulman, David. 2016. *Tamil: A Biography*. Cambridge, MA: Harvard University Press.
Silva, Neluka, ed. 2002. *The Hybrid Island*. Colombo: Social Scientists' Association.
Simpson, R. 1984. *Ritual Tradition and Performance: The Beravā Caste of Southern Sri Lanka*. PhD dissertation, University of Durham.
Simpson, R. 1997. "Possession, Dispossession and the Social Distribution of Knowledge Among Sri Lankan Ritual Specialists." *Journal of the Royal Anthropological Institute* (N.S.) 3, 43–59.
Sivasundaram, Sujit. 2007. "Buddhist Kingship, British Archaeology and Historical Narratives in Sri Lanka, c. 1750–1850." *Past and Present* 197, 111–142.
Sivasundaram, Sujit. 2013. *Islanded: Britain, Sri Lanka and the Bounds of an Indian Ocean Colony*. University of Chicago Press.

Sivathamby, Kartigesu. 2005. *Being Tamil and Sri Lankan*. Colombo: Aivakam.

Skilling, Peter, and Jason Carbine, Claudio Cicuzza, and Santi Pakdeekham, eds. 2012. *How Theravada is Theravada? Exploring Buddhist Identities*. Seattle: University of Washington Press.

Slomanson, Peter. 2013. "Sri Lankan Malay." In *The Survey of Pidgin and Creole Languages*, Volume III, edited by Susanne Maria Michaelis, Philippe Maurer, Martin Haspelmath, and Magnus Huber. New York: Oxford University Press: 77–85.

Soneji, Davesh. 2012. *Unfinished Gestures: Devadāsīs, Memory, and Modernity in South India*. Chicago: University of Chicago Press.

Spencer, Jonathan. 2014. "Anthropology, Politics, and Place in Sri Lanka: South Asian Reflections from an Island Adrift." *South Asia Multidisciplinary Academic Journal* 10: 2–13.

Spencer, Jonathan, Jonathan Goodhand, Shahul Hasbullah, Bart Klem, Benedikt Korf, and Kalinga Tudor Silva. 2015. *Checkpoint, Temple, Church and Mosque: A Collaborative Ethnography of War and Peace*. Chicago: University of Chicago Press.

Steingo, Gavin. 2016. *Kwaito's Promise: Music and the Aesthetics of Freedom in South Africa*. Chicago: University of Chicago Press.

Sterne, Jonathan. 2003. *The Audible Past: Cultural Origins of Sound Reproduction*. Durham: Duke University Press.

Sterne, Jonathan, ed. 2012. *The Sound Studies Reader*. Routledge.

Stewart, James. 2017. "Dharma Dogs: Can Animals Understand the Dharma? Textual and Ethnographic Considerations." *Journal of Buddhist Ethics* 24: 39–62.

Stewart, Kathleen. 2007. *Ordinary Affects*. Durham: Duke University Press.

Stirr, Anna. 2017. *Singing Across Divides: Music and Intimate Politics in Nepal*. New York: Oxford University Press.

Stirrat, Jock. 2006. "Competitive Humanitarianism: Relief and the Tsunami in Sri Lanka." *Anthropology Today* 22(5): 11–16.

Stirrat, R. L. and Heiko Henkel. 1997. "The Development Gift: The Problem of Reciprocity in the NGO World." *The Annals of the American Academy of Political and Social Science* 554: 66–80.

Stokes, Martin. 2010. *The Republic of Love: Cultural Intimacy in Turkish Popular Music*. Chicago: University of Chicago Press.

Strathern, Alan. 2007. *Kingship and Conversion in Sixteenth-Century Sri Lanka*. Cambridge: Cambridge University Press.

Strathern, Marilyn. 1988. *The Gender of the Gift*. Berkeley: University of California Press.

Subrahmanyam, Sanjay. 1997. "Connected Histories: Notes Towards a Reconfiguration of Early Modern Eurasia." *Modern Asian Studies* 31 (3): 735–762.

Subramaniam, Samanth. 2015. *This Divided Island: Life, Death, and the Sri Lankan War*. Thomas Dunne Books.

Suraweera, Sumuditha. 2009. *Sri Lankan, Low-Country, Ritual Drumming: The Raigama Tradition*. PhD dissertation, University of Canterbury.

Surya Sena, Devar. 1978. *Of Sri Lanka I Sing: The Life and Times of Devar Surya Sena*.

Surya Sena, Devar . 2008. *Music of Sri Lanka*. Colombo: Vijitha Yapa Publications.

Swearer, Donald. 1995. *The Buddhist World of Southeast Asia*. Albany: State University of New York Press.

Sykes, Jim. 2011. *The Musical Gift: Sound, Sovereignty, and Multicultural History in Sri Lanka*. PhD dissertation, University of Chicago.

Sykes, Jim. 2013. "Culture as Freedom: Musical 'Liberation' in Batticaloa, Sri Lanka." *Ethnomusicology* 57(3): 485–517.

Sykes, Jim. 2015. "Sound Studies, Religion, and Public Space: Tamil Music and the Ethical Life in Singapore." *Ethnomusicology Forum* 24(3): 380–413.

Sykes, Jim. 2018a. "South Asian Drumming Beyond Tala: The Problem with 'Meter' in Buddhist Sri Lanka." *Analytical Approaches to World Music*.

Sykes, Jim. 2018b. "On the Sonic Materialization of Buddhist History: Drum Speech in Southern Sri Lanka." *Analytical Approaches to World Music*.

Tagliacozzo, Eric. 2009. "Navigating Communities: Distance, Place, and Race in Maritime Southeast Asia." *Asian Ethnicity* 10 (2): 97–120.

Tambiah. Stanley. 1968. "The Magical Power of Words." *Man* 3(2): 175–208.
Tambiah. Stanley. 1976. *World Conqueror and World Renouncer: A Study of Buddhism and Polity in Thailand against a Historical Background*. Cambridge: Cambridge University Press.
Tan Sooi Beng. 1993. *Bangsawan: A Social and Stylistic History of Popular Malay Opera*. New York: Oxford University Press.
Tanaka, M. 1997. *Patrons, Devotees, and Goddesses: Ritual, and Power among the Tamil Fishermen of Sri Lanka*. New Delhi: Manohar Publishers.
Taylor, Tim. 2012. *The Sounds of Capitalism: Advertising, Music, and the Conquest of Culture*. Chicago: University of Chicago Press.
Terada, Yoshitaka. 2008. "Temple Music Traditions in Hindu South India: Periya Melam and Its Performance Practice." *Asian Music* 39(2): 108–151.
Thiranagama, Sharika. 2011. *In My Mother's House: Civil War in Sri Lanka*. Philadelphia: University of Pennsylvania Press.
Thompson, James. 2005. *Digging Up Stories*. Oxford: Manchester University Press.
Thongchai, Winichakul. 1997. *Siam Mapped: A History of the Geo-Body of a Nation*. Honolulu, HI: University of Hawaii Press.
Tomlinson, Gary. 1993. *Music in Renaissance Magic: Toward a Historiography of Others*. Chicago: University of Chicago Press.
Tomlinson, Gary. 2007. *The Singing of the New World: Indigenous Voice in the Era of European Contact*. Cambridge: Cambridge University Press.
Trainor, Kevin. 2007. *Relics, Ritual, and Representation in Buddhism: Rematerializing the Sri Lankan Theravada Tradition*. Cambridge: Cambridge University Press.
Trouillot, Michel-Rolph. 1998. "Culture on the Edges: Creolization in the Plantation Context." *Plantation Society in the Americas: An Interdisciplinary Journal of Tropical and Subtropical History and Culture Plantation Society in the Americas* 5(1): 8–28.
Vaidik, Aparna. 2010. *Imperial Andamans: Colonial Encounter and Island History*. Palgrave Macmillan.
Vaughan, Genevieve. 2004. "Language as Gift and Community." http://www.gift-economy.com/articlesAndEssays/languageAsGift.pdf.
Verdeja, Ernesto. 2009. *Unchopping a Tree: Reconciliation in the Aftermath of Political Violence*. Philadelphia: Temple University Press.
Vimalarajah, Luxshi and R. Cheran 2010. "Empowering Diasporas: The Dynamics of Post-War Transnational Tamil Politics." *Berghof Occasional Paper No. 31*. Berlin: Berghof Conflict Research.
Viveiros de Castro, Eduardo. 1992. *From the Enemy's Point of View: Humanity and Divinity in an Amazonian Society*. Chicago: University of Chicago Press.
Viveiros de Castro, Eduardo. 2004. "Exchanging Perspectives: The Transformation of Objects into Subjects in Amerindian Ontologies." *Common Knowledge* 1(3): 463–484.
Viveiros de Castro, Eduardo. 2016. *The Relative Native: Essays on Indigenous Conceptual Worlds*. Hau Books.
Vogt, Beatrice. 1998. *Skill and Trust: The Tovil Healing Ritual of Sri Lanka as Culture-Specific Psychotherapy*. Amsterdam: VU University Press.
Walcott, Ronald. 1978. *Kohomba Kankariya: An Ethnomusicological Study*. PhD dissertation, University of Sri Lanka, Vidyodaya Campus.
Walker, Rebecca. 2013. *Enduring Violence: Everyday Life and Conflict in Eastern Sri Lanka*. Manchester University Press.
Wedeen, Lisa. 2008. *Peripheral Visions: Publics, Power, and Performance in Yemen*. Chicago: University of Chicago Press.
Weerakkody, D. P. M. 2011. "Sri Lankan: Musical Heritage." *The Oxford Encyclopedia of the Music of India*, edited by Pandith Nikil Ghosh. New Delhi: Oxford University Press: 1000–1006.
Wegman, Rob. 2005. "Musical Offerings in the Renaissance." *Early Music* 33(3): 425–437.
Weidman, Amanda. 2006. *Singing the Classical, Voicing the Modern: The Postcolonial Politics of Music in South India*. Durham: Duke University Press.
Weiner, Annette. 1992. *Inalienable Possessions: The Paradox of Keeping-While Giving*. Berkeley: University of California Press.

Whitaker, Mark. 1999. *Amiable Incoherence: Manipulating Histories and Modernities in a Batticaloa Hindu Temple*. Amsterdam: VU University Press.
White, Shane and Graham White. 2006. *The Sounds of Slavery: Discovering African American History through Songs, Sermons, and Speech*. Boston, MA: Beacon Press.
Wickramasinghe, Nira. 2002. "From Hybridity to Authenticity: The Biography of a Few Kandyan Things." In *The Hybrid Island: Culture Crossings and the Invention of Identity in Sri Lanka*, edited by Neluka Silva. Chicago: University of Chicago Press: 71–92.
Wickramasinghe, Nira. 2006. *Sri Lanka in the Modern Age: A History of Contested Identities*. Honolulu: University of Hawaii Press.
Wickremasinghe, Nira. 2014. *Metallic Modern: Everyday Machines in Colonial Sri Lanka*. Berghahn Books.
Willford, Andrew. 2006. *Cage of Freedom: Tamil Identity and the Ethnic Fetish in Malaysia*. University of Michigan Press.
Wilson, Jayaratnam. 2000. *Sri Lankan Tamil Nationalism: Its Origins and Development in the Nineteenth and Twentieth Centuries*. London: Penguin.
Winslow, Deborah. 1984. "A Political Geography of Deities: Space and the Pantheon in Sinhalese Buddhism." *Journal of Asian Studies*, 43(2): 273–291.
Winslow, Deborah and Michael Woost. 2004. *Economy, Culture and Civil War in Sri Lanka*. Bloomington: University of Indiana Press.
Wirz, Paul. 1954. *Exorcism and the Art of Healing in Ceylon*. Leiden: E. J. Brill.
Wolf, Richard K. 2000. "Tamil Nadu." In *The Garland Encyclopedia of World Music*, Vol V, South Asia: The Indian Subcontinent, edited by Alison Arnold. New York: Garland Publishing Inc: 903–921.
Wong, Deborah. 2001. *Sounding the Center: History and Aesthetics in Thai Buddhist Performance*. Chicago: University of Chicago Press.
Wong, Deborah. 2014. "Sound, Silence, Music: Power." *Ethnomusicology* 58(2): 347–353.
Yalman, Nur. 1967. *Under the Bo Tree: Studies in Caste, Kinship, and Marriage in the Interior of Ceylon*. Berkeley, University of California Press.
Zizek, Slavoj. 2002. *Welcome to the Desert of the Real*. New York: Verso Books.

INDEX

Abdullah, M.S.M., 121
Actor Network Theory, 4, 48
agency, 12, 16, 19
Akkaraipattu, 100, 131, 168
Akmeemana, Gamini, 201–203
Aluthgama, 19, 33
Amarasekera, Colonel A.S., 217–218
Ambalangoda, 165–166
Ambos, Eva, 158–159
Ampara (region), 34, 106–109, 119, 234
Anuradhapura
   Kingdom, 74–75, 140–141, 151, 202
   town, 109, 126, 221, 229, 234
Ariyapala, M.B., 149–152
art, 12, 14, 17, 40, 47, 187
   object, 12, 17, 55
   reconciliation through, 204, 233–235
   in relation to Buddhism, 27
Arunasalam, Kannan, 125
Aru Sri Art Theatre group, 180–181
Aryacakravarti Dynasty, 97
Äsala Perahera, 24, 90–92, 146–147. *See also under peraheras*
Attali, Jacques, 57–58
Ayurvedic medicine, 20, 66, 77–78

Baig, Mohideen, 198–201, 204
Baila (genre), 124–126, 179, 200, 205–207, 213, 223
Balasugumar (musicologist), 104, 111
bali ritual, 21, 73, 79, 94
Bandaranaike, S.W.R.D., 30
Bandaranayake, Dharmasiri, 229–235
bandaras, 93
Bass, Daniel, 112
Bataille, Georges, 172
Batticaloa, 30–39, 99–102, 105–120, 124–126, 132–137, 142–149, 181–185
Becker, Judith, 78
Bengali music, 192–193, 222

Bennett, Jane, 58
Bentara Korale. *See under* Korales
Bera Pōya Hēvisi, 21–23, 48, 70, 79, 82–83, 85–88, 132, 152, 216.
   See also under musical giving
Beravā, 24–29, 66–96, 131–138, 158–159, 216, 224
   caste, 12, 19–23, 47–51, 55–57, 201
   drumming, 12, 22, 28, 35, 154–156
   rituals, 21, 36, 39–43, 57, 142–143, 205, 219
Bernstein, Anya, 7
bhutas, 93
Birla, Ritu, 18, 57
Bodu Bala Sena (Buddhist Defense Force), 33, 189, 207
Borges, Jorge Luis, 87
Britain, 224–225
   independence from, 14, 23
British
   colonialism, 17, 24, 29–30, 75, 111, 210–212
   colonial liberalism, 12
Bryant, Levi, 160
Buddhism
   Buryat, 7–8
   doctrinal, 8, 27
   musicology of, 26–27
   Sinhala, 5–6, 12–13, 19–20, 22–30, 42–43, 65, 218
   Sinhala, cosmology, 65, 91–94
   Theravāda, 8, 20, 26–27, 82, 92–93
   Tibetan, 7
Buddhist chant. *See pirit*
Buddhist Defense Force. *See* Bodu Bala Sena
Burghers, 121, 123–127, 220
Buryat Republic, 7

care. *See* technologies of care
Carnatic music, 24, 37, 41–42, 98–102, 106, 133, 135, 139, 157, 172–176, 180
Cassiere, Marhoum Saudara, 196–198, 204–207

caste, 15, 32, 55, 67–69, 101, 113
  activism against, 102–104
  Karaiyar, 111
  lower, 23, 67–68, 91, 138
  Mukkuvar, 101–102, 106
  oppression, 117
  Paraiyar, 39–40, 101–104, 112, 131, 145–146
  upper, 23–25, 67, 89, 101
  Vanniyar, 44, 97
  Vēḷāḷar, 106
Ceylon. *See* Sri Lanka
Chakrabarty, Dipesh, 9
Chelliah, Kathiramalai, 116
Cheng, William, 55–56
Chennai, 174–176
Chola kings, 74, 148
Christian, 33, 38, 57, 100, 110–111, 121–123, 129, 131, 183, 202, 207
  Judeo-Christian ontologies of sound, 5–9
  Protestant missionization, 98
  Sinhala, 36–37, 121–122, 199, 223
  Tamil, 36, 121, 123, 126, 205–206
Cilappatikāram, 98, 107, 137
Cohen, Cynthia, 184–186
Colombo, 64–65, 74–75, 116, 176, 212–213
  Bharata Natyam in, 138
  during the war, 14, 32–34
  Kaffirs in, 124–125
  kooththu in, 112, 117–118, 235
  nurthi style in, 202
  University for the Visual and Performing Arts, 24
  Wellawatte neighborhood, 100, 103, 109
Coomaraswamy, Arjun, 174
Copeman, Jacob, 41–42
culture zones, 99, 119, 126–129, 132–134, 149, 185, 239

Dalada Maligawa. *See* Temple of the Tooth
dāna, 20, 93–94
dance, 23, 95, 159, 220, 235
  Bērava, 21, 29, 41, 132, 156, 201, 224
  Bharata Natyam, 24, 41, 106, 116–117, 137–139, 175–176, 180
  education, 23, 88, 137
  in institutions, 24, 175
  Kaffir, 124–125
  Kandyan, 25, 89–92, 96, 136–139, 153, 216
  speech, 132–135
  Sri Lankan Tamil, 104–118, 132
  women and, 24, 41, 68, 140, 150
davula. *See under* drum
Dayasheela, Herbert, 19, 65–68, 89
deities
  Four Warrant Gods, 90, 92–93, 195
  Gods of the Four Quarters, 92, 216
  Kali, 106, 171
  Kataragama, 92–94, 106

  Murugan, 104, 106–107, 109
  Natha, 92, 94
  Pattini, 21, 76, 84, 92, 94, 107, 132, 136
  Pulastya, 22, 216
  Ravana, 14, 22, 100, 118, 137, 210, 214, 216–219
  Sakka, 22, 81–82, 91–92, 148, 151
  Valli, 93, 106
  Vishnu, 22, 92, 94, 101, 215
demons. *See yakku*
Derrida, Jacques, 219
De Silva, John, 220, 223
devadasis, 24, 41
devatava, 93
deva tovils, 21, 25, 66–67, 71, 76, 78–79, 82, 94, 136
Devol Deviyo, 76, 94
Devol Maduva, 21, 76, 132
Dewaraja, L., 131
Dhamma, 93
Dhammadipa, 41
Dharmapala, Anagarika, 219, 221
dhol. *See under* drum
dholki. *See under* drum
displacement, 33, 97, 110, 119, 141, 170
dosas, 77
drama. *See* theater
drum
  davula, 20, 22, 69–70, 73, 102, 137, 142–145, 157, 159, 180–181
  dhol, 102, 146
  dholki, 124–125
  gäta beraya, 20, 22, 25, 28, 69–72, 87, 90, 133–134, 137, 139, 140, 142–143, 150–151, 153, 157, 180–181, 188
  low-country, 20, 71, 139
  maddalam (Kerala drum), 134, 136
  maththalam (Tamil drum), 37, 105–106, 113–114, 132–138, 140–142, 150, 157, 182
  mridangam, 121, 133–134, 136, 150, 157, 168–169, 180
  parai, 40, 101–104, 106–107, 109, 112, 134, 143–147, 170, 176–177
  rabāna, 125
  speech, 20, 22, 27, 48, 86, 157 (see also *padas*)
  tabla, 5, 88, 106, 112–113, 121, 123, 160, 181–182
  thavil, 41, 95–96, 101–110, 129, 170, 175–176
  urumi, 101
  uṭukkai.i, 106
Dutch colonialism, 24, 75, 136, 211
Dutugämunu, King, 151–152

ecomusicology, 4
economy, 14, 17, 66
  capitalist, 52, 95
  gift, 7, 52, 95
  monetary, 12, 17

as part of public sphere, 19
sonic gift, 7, 69, 95
Eelam
    cultural region, 98
    independent Tamil country, 30, 32, 100
    music, 104–105
efficacy
    performative, 52
    ritual, 23, 41, 66, 69, 80, 89
    sonic, 5–6, 12, 14, 20, 42, 46–48, 55–58, 155
Ekanayaka, Tanya, 182–185, 187
equality, 12, 104, 185
ethnonationalism. *See under* nationalism
exchange, 13–14, 47, 50–52
    economic, 3, 17–18, 55, 57
    musical, 11, 40–41, 57, 94, 185
    sonic, 12–13, 48–49, 69

Fernando, K.S., 83–84
Foucault, Michel
    care of the self, 11, 52
    episteme, 3

Gam Maduva, 76, 84, 132
gaman matra, 87, 205
gäta beraya. See under *drum*
ghosts, 14, 26, 63–68, 93
Ghouse, Mohammed, 199
gī, 20, 153
gift
    as anarchism, 47–50, 59
    in anthropology, 12, 16, 47–58
    in Buddhism, 20, 42–43, 94
    from the gods, 6, 20, 48
    to the gods, 5–6, 20, 22, 41–42, 49, 96
    in Hinduism, 42, 57
    in precolonial Sinhala society, 41, 95
    See also exchange; economy; musical giving
Gonsalves, Jacome, 122
guru musti, 87–89
gurunnänse, 19, 21–23, 28, 65, 75–77, 82–88, 156, 216

harambes, 87
harps, 98–100, 134, 146–149
Herder, Johann Gottfried, 3
hēvisi ensemble, 22, 40, 70, 73, 104, 129, 132, 143–144, 146, 158–159
Hindu
    deities, 28, 49, 92, 132, 136, 150, 218
    epics, 14, 22, 37, 109, 111
    festivals, 107, 129, 171, 173
    identity, 28, 35, 42, 44, 98, 121, 148, 157, 224
    rituals, 5, 9, 40, 106, 174
    Sri Lankan Tamils, 5, 29, 39, 49, 100, 105, 171
Hinduism, 28, 42, 98, 157
Hindustani music, 173, 221–223
horanäva, 22, 70, 73, 146, 151, 157

Howell, Gillian, 177
human–animal relations, 7, 10, 40, 82–83
human–demon relations, 10, 81–82, 93
human–divine relations, 5–6, 10, 13, 23, 43, 49, 93, 171
human–nonhuman relations, 5–6, 9, 16, 40, 48–49
hybridization, 10, 40, 43–44, 58, 126–127, 129, 142, 152, 196, 202, 223
Hyde, Lewis, 47, 49, 52

identity
    caste, 67
    communal, 13, 160, 186
    development of, 53
    episteme, 4–14, 43–46, 53–54, 57, 95, 125, 153, 170, 186, 194, 235
    ethnic, 13–14, 19, 23, 26, 32, 35, 41, 45–46, 96, 138
    familial, 171
    in music studies, 4–12, 26, 29, 36–37, 43, 53–54, 58, 95–96, 98, 104, 125, 158, 167, 170, 186, 210
    national, 116, 129, 166, 180, 186, 213, 217
Ilangasinha, H., 150
Inbam (musician), 103–104
India
    music and dance in, 24, 28, 41–42, 83, 91, 101–104, 106, 112, 116–117, 133–139, 143–149, 150–151, 219–222
    origins in, 13–14, 28, 38, 127, 149
    relations with, 28–30, 38, 44, 98, 157–158, 172–176
    Sri Lanka as separate from, 13, 207, 210–219, 222–224
Indian Ocean Region, 13, 28, 125, 225
indigenous
    aesthetic systems, 10, 59
    knowledge systems, 7, 10
    relations, 18–19, 22, 40, 69, 216–217
    traditions, 27, 106, 116, 131, 138, 160, 166
    See also Väddas
Indo–Sri Lankan Accord, 30
inoculation, 8–10

Jaffna
    Battle for, 31–32
    city, 30–39, 100, 103, 147, 170, 181–184, 229
    kingdom, 74, 97
    music festival, 117, 176, 180, 186
    Peninsula, 103, 110
    Tamils in, 95, 98, 99, 126, 131, 137
    Tamil musical revival in, 35, 101, 108–116, 133–137, 149, 168–169, 174–176
Janata Vimukti Peramuna, 30, 32
Jathika Hela Urumaya, 31
Jayakody, Friar Marceline, 122
Jayasinghe, Kishani, 202–205

Jesuits, 36, 38
Jeyaraj, D.B.S., 95, 190–192

Kaffirs, 123–126, 143
Kalakshetra Institute, 138
Kalalaya School of Music and Dance, 138
Kalinga Magha, King, 74, 97
kamma. See karma
Kandy. *See* up country
Kandy, Lake, 188, 195
Kandyan
   dance, 25, 89–92, 95–96, 136–139, 153, 188, 216, 223
   Kingdom, 24–25, 37, 41, 44, 75, 91–92, 136, 138, 155, 195, 220
Kapferer, Bruce, 42–43, 78–79, 84, 94
Karainagar, 110
karma, 8, 20, 27, 40, 59, 74, 77, 92–93
Karuna, Colonel. *See* Vinayagamoorthy Muralitharan
Karunadasa, O.P., 90
Kataragama. *See under* deities
Kataragama pilgrimage site, 106, 120, 131, 172, 207
Kattankudy, 30, 34, 119, 121, 126, 174
Kerala, 29, 90, 134–137, 139–140, 149–151
Kersenboom, Saskia, 41
Kilinochchi, 100, 174, 180, 229
Kohomba Kankariya, 25, 88–92, 112, 136, 138–139, 160, 216
kooththu, 36–40, 107–108, 113, 122, 229, 235
   Batticaloa, 113–118, 132–134
   history of, 136, 158
   as musical gift, 101–108, 112
   similarities with Beravā drumming, 132–134
   tenmodi style, 111, 113–115
   relation to *terukkuttu*, 36, 107, 134–136
   vadamodi style, 111, 118
Korales
   Bentara, 19, 67, 75–76, 86
   as colonial administrative division, 75
   Raigam Korale, 67, 75–76
   as regional styles, 74–75
Kotte Kingdom, 74, 139, 147, 149–150, 157
Krishna, T.M., 174–175
kudi kinship system, 97–98
Kulatillake, C. de S., 28, 139–140, 143, 145, 147–148, 151–155

Lawrence, Patricia, 171
Lederach, John, 193–194
liberal aesthetics, 14, 17, 40, 42, 57, 127, 185, 239
liberalism, 12, 14, 17–19
Liberation Tigers of Tamil Eelam (LTTE), 30–32, 63–64, 100, 102–103, 107
   119, 168–171, 180, 191, 229
   defeat of, 31–32, 188
   relationship with arts, 39, 103, 113, 116–117, 169, 198, 206–207, 233–235

low country
   drumming, 19–20, 25, 28, 69, 71, 76, 79, 87, 139, 143, 149, 152, 171
   rituals, 25, 35, 76, 95, 153, 159
LTTE. *See* Liberation Tigers of Tamil Eelam

maddalam. See under drum
magic, 19–20, 26, 55, 57–58, 65–66, 68, 78, 84, 107
magul bera, 70, 79, 87
Mahabharata, 37, 109, 116
Mahavamsa, 41, 215, 217–218
Mahmood, Saba, 46
Malaiyaha Tamils, 102, 111–112
Malayali, 135–136, 199
Malay
   cultural influence, 139–140, 220
   singers, 14, 50, 195–198
Mandothari (wife of Ravana), 118
Manoharan, A.E., 200
maththalam. See under drum
mātras, 20, 132, 152–155
Maunaguru, Sinniah, 116–118, 132, 135, 182, 218, 229, 235
Mauss, Marcel, 47–48
McDaniel, Justin, 26
McGilvray, Dennis, 29, 102, 120–121, 131, 144–147
migration
   cultural, 128–129, 210
   musical, 198, 218
   of people, 45, 97, 107, 110, 213, 217, 224–225
mridangam. See under drum
Mullaitivu, 14, 34, 64, 100, 103–105, 110–111, 132, 134, 144, 168–170
Murugan. *See under* deities
   musical giving, 6, 14–17, 19–20, 26, 41, 47–52, 63–64, 67–68, 131, 160, 168, 172–173, 187, 193–194, 198
   Bera Pōya Hēvisi as an example of, 22, 48
   contrasted with music as commodity, 208–209
   failure of, 178–179
   as framework for reconciliation, 194
   hoarding of musical gifts, 69, 87, 89
   kooththu as an example of, 36
   musicological potlatch, 160–161
   ontology of music as gift, 17, 51–54
   postwar, 180–188
   as technology of care, 165
   theft of musical gifts, 23
Musicmatters, 181–182, 185
Muslims, 10, 100, 131, 174
   ethnic and religious group, 30–34, 43, 119–121, 127, 129
   influential musicians, 36, 198–204
   music of, 36, 120–121, 125, 195–198
   Rohingya, 11–12
   Sufi devotionalism, 119–121
   violence against, 30–31, 33–34, 107, 119, 189
Myanmar, 11, 45, 148

nadagam, 37–39, 110–113, 115–117, 122, 153, 229, 235
nadaswaram, 95–96, 101–103, 106–107, 109–110, 150–151, 169–170, 175–176
Narendrasinghe, King, 90, 155
nationalism, 10–11, 43, 45, 69
   ethnonationalism, 12, 14, 41, 45, 59, 158, 178, 217, 219, 225, 235
   Sinhala Buddhist, 29, 38, 42–43, 71, 222
   Tamil, 33 (*see also* Eelam)
Natya Shastra, 42, 137–139
Nayakkar court culture, 44, 91–92, 138
NGOs (non-government organizations), 13, 31, 64, 168, 176–179, 231
nibbana, 20, 27, 92–94
Nichols, Robert, 11
nirvana. See *nibbana*
North Indian music. *See* Hindustani music

Obeyesekere, Gananath, 84, 136, 214–216, 218
Ochoa Gautier, Ana Maria, 9, 52

padas, 22, 69, 78–79, 82, 84, 86–89, 94, 132–135, 153–155
pahata rata. See low country
Pali, 20, 147–148, 151–154
Panchadcharam, Premalatha, 145
pan system, 98, 134–135
Paraiyar
   caste, 39–40, 101–104, 112, 131, 145–146
   drumming, 39–40, 112, 131–132, 143–146, 158
Pararajasingham, Joseph, 32
Pararajasingham, S.K., 173
Pathmanathan, Subashini, 137–139, 169
Pattini. *See under* deities
peace
   through musical giving, 20, 47–48, 158, 180–184, 187–190, 193–194, 231–235
   in Sri Lanka, 14, 31, 33, 68, 177, 187–190, 193–194, 235, 237–238
Peiris, Eshantha, 166–167, 181–182, 204
peraheras, 24–25, 41, 70–71, 73, 90–92, 94, 207
   Äsala Perahera, 24, 90–92, 131, 146, 153
personhood, 5, 9–11, 95
Pillai, Yazhpanam Thedchanamoorthy, 175
pinkama, 93
pirit, 14, 20, 64, 70–71, 81–82, 93–94, 152, 155
Point Pedro, 14, 30, 63–64
Polonnaruwa, 44, 74, 97, 149, 156–157
Portuguese
   colonialism, 24, 28, 74–75, 100–101, 123–124
   influence, 124–126, 200
   Passion Plays, 36
Povinelli, Elizabeth, 18–19
pretayo, 65, 93
Pujavaliya, 150–151
Purandara Dāsa, 98

rabāna. See under drum
Radio Ceylon, 28, 190, 199, 221–223
rāga, 134–135, 156
rāgam-taṉam-pāllavi, 135
Raghavan, M.D., 127
Raigam Korale. *See under* Korales
Rajadhi Rajasinghe, King, 90
Rajan (musician), 169–170
Rajapaksa, Mahinda, 33–34, 95, 158–160, 189–191, 193, 201
Rajarata (region), 74, 97
Rajasinha II (king), 215
Ramanathan Academy of Fine Arts, 175
Ramayana, 14, 22, 37, 109, 118, 218
Ras Ceylon, 188–190
Ratana Sutta, 81–82
Ravana. *See under* deities
reconciliation
   postwar, 13, 29, 33, 177–179, 180, 190–194
   use of arts in, 13, 40, 47, 58, 177–179, 180, 185–187, 190–194, 204, 231–235
Reed, Susan, 23, 25, 136
reincarnation, 7–9, 59
relational musicology, 4
Roberts, Michael, 44–45, 154–155, 223
Rogers, John, 44
Ruhuna (region), 74, 92

Sabaragamuwa (region), 20, 25, 69, 75–76, 126, 142, 159, 215–216
sabda pujāva, 22, 73–74
Saddharmālamkāraya, 150
Sahlins, Marshall, 47–50
Saiva, 92, 97, 138, 148
Saiva Mangaiyar Kalaham, 138
Sakka. *See under* deities
Samantapasadika, 147, 152
samsara, 92–93
Sangam
   literature 98, 147
   period, 107, 145, 147–148
Sanni Yakuma, 65–66, 68, 76–82, 88–89
Sarachchandra, Ediriweera, 38–39, 90, 115–117, 235
Satkunaratnam, Ahalya, 138
Schaefer, Donovan, 50
Scott, James C., 10, 59
secularism, 5–9, 22–23, 36–37, 46–47
self, the, 6, 47, 50, 159
   art as expression of, 11, 14, 17, 56, 79
   bounded notion of, 8–9, 11, 14, 95
   in Buddhist doctrine, 8, 94
   care of, 11, 52
   not-selves, 8, 59, 94
Seligmann, Brenda and C.G., 141–142, 215
Sena, Devar Surya, 122–123, 152, 202, 221
Shanmugalingam, 105–111
Sherinian, Zoe, 104

Simpson, Bob, 67
Singho, Phillippo, 37
Sinhala
    ethnic identity, 13, 23, 26, 45, 49, 91–92, 100–102, 121, 148, 150, 158, 171, 204, 207, 214, 219
    nationalist movement, 25, 29–30, 38, 42–43, 71, 91, 95, 222
    "Sinhala Only" language law, 30, 190
    See also Buddhism; Christians; nationalism
Sinhala music
    connection to North Indian music, 13–14, 155, 219–223
    as distinct tradition, 28–29, 137, 152, 155, 160, 201–202, 218–219, 222–224
    drumming, 29, 133, 135, 216
    history, 118, 137, 157, 202
    indigenizing of, 91, 137, 152, 157, 160, 210–214
    medieval music, 28, 149–157
    meter, 152–155
    oral modes of communication, 44
    organology, 72–73, 102
    relational development of, 10, 36, 127, 200–222, 223–225
    sung poetry, 19, 21, 78, 152–153, 155–157
Sirambiyadi, 124–126
Sirisena, Maithripala, 33–34, 192–193, 201, 203
Sivagnanam, Jeyasankar, 102–103
Sivathamby, Kartigesu, 113–114, 172–174
sivpada, 20, 122, 153–155
sonic efficacy. *See under* efficacy
sonic exchange. *See under* exchange
sonic generosity, 11–12, 15–16, 20, 26, 41, 43, 47, 53–54, 96, 180, 185, 192, 208. *See also* musical giving
sonic protection, 15, 19–20, 22–23, 26, 41–42, 49, 63–65, 93, 96, 168, 209, 235. See also *pirit*
soul, 7–8, 15, 48, 56
sound studies, 4
Southeast Asian influence, 139–140, 195–198, 220
Spencer, Jonathan, 212, 225
Sri Lanka
    islanding of, 13, 210–214, 222–225
    popular music in, 14, 28, 36, 127, 198–207, 222
    recent political history of, 29–36
    tsunami (2004), 13, 23, 31, 100, 103, 119, 165–170
Sri Lanka Broadcasting Corporation, 173
Sri Lankan civil war, 13–14, 23, 29–36, 39–40, 47, 63–65, 100, 103–104, 168, 188, 220
    music during the, 113–114, 117–118, 170–173, 176, 188–189
    pre-war, 40, 102–103, 126
    war mentality, 238–239
    See also reconciliation
Sri Lankan Tamil music. See *kooththu*

Steingo, Gavin, 12
Stewart, Kathleen, 50
Subrahmanyam, Sanjay, 225
sung poetry, 19, 21, 78, 152–153, 155–157
Suniyama (ritual), 76, 83–84
Surasena, Peter, 90–91
Swami Vipulananda Institute of Aesthetic Studies, 177, 181

tabla. *See under* drum
Tagore, Rabindranath, 193, 221
tālam, 83, 86, 135
    South Indian, 133–134
    in Sri Lankan Beravā drumming and *kooththu*, 132–133
talampota, 73, 112, 123, 139, 153
Tambiah, Stanley, 56–57
Tamil
    connection with South India, 29, 36–38, 74, 90–92, 98, 111–112, 120–123, 133–139, 212
    ethnic identity, 35, 43–44, 112, 125–127, 134–135, 138, 157–158, 212
    language, 150, 190–191, 200, 219
    violence against, 30–33, 173
    See also Eelam; nationalism; Liberation Tigers of Tamil Eelam
Tamil Makhal Viduthalai Pulikal, 31
Tamil music. See *kooththu*
Tamil Nadu, 29, 111–112, 134–139, 148–149, 198–200
Tanaka, M., 129
technologies of care, 11, 15, 18–19, 43, 54–56, 165–166
Temple of the Tooth, 24, 28, 31, 70, 90–91
Tennent, James Emerson, 100
tevāva, 22, 73
thammättama, 22, 70, 72, 103, 144–145, 151, 157, 159, 180–181, 206
thavil. *See under* drum
theater
    isai nadagam, 112–113
    Japanese Noh, 38
    nadagam, 37–38, 110–111, 115–117, 122, 153, 229, 235
    See also *kooththu*
Thiranagama, 32–33
Thirukkural, 147
Thompson, James, 113–114
Thupavamsa, 150–151
Tony (Malay singer), 195–198
Trainor, Kevin, 73
Trincomalee, 34, 99
Trojan Kanthavo, 231–235

United National Party, 30, 232
up country, 23–25, 69–71, 75, 87–92, 102, 126, 147, 182, 195–196

drum language, 71–88
drumming, 20, 69, 134, 149
 ritual, 88–90, 136–137, 158–159, 216
 Tamils, 102, 111–112
 See also Kohomba Kankariya;
  Malaiyaha Tamils
urumi. *See under* drum
uṭukkai. *See under* drum

Väddas
 indigenous people of Sri Lanka, 22, 69, 82, 126, 137, 140–143, 205, 210, 213–216
 music and culture, 107, 126–128, 140–143, 207, 213–216
Vaisnava, 92, 97
Vannams, 25, 89–91, 122, 153, 155
Vanni (region), 31, 37, 111, 126, 178
Vaughan, Genevieve, 53
Vijaya, Prince, 13, 214–216
Vinayagamoorthy Muralitharan (Col. Karuna), 31
Vipulanandar, Swami, 99, 103–104, 224
Vishnu. *See under* deities

Vithiananthan, Suppirananiam, 115–118, 235
voice, 9

Walcott, Ronald, 87–88
Weber, Max, 26
Weiner, Annette, 50–51, 53
Wellawatte (neighborhood), 32, 34, 100, 103, 199
Wijegoonawardene, Pabalu, 218–219
Williams, Pharrell, 236–237, 239
 "Happy", 236–238
Winichakul, Thongchai, 129
Wirz, Paul, 82–83, 132

yak beraya, 19–22, 25, 43, 69–72, 76, 79, 86–89, 133–134, 139–143, 150–157, 180–181
yakku, 20–21, 42, 78–81, 93, 142, 154–155
yak tovils, 21, 25, 42–43, 65–68, 76–79, 82, 94, 166, 170–171
yazh. *See harps*
Yazh Nool, 99, 104

zoopolitics, 40

www.ingramcontent.com/pod-product-compliance
Ingram Content Group UK Ltd.
Pitfield, Milton Keynes, MK11 3LW, UK
UKHW041959230426
12048UKWH00008B/431